APT

D0687997

DISCARDED

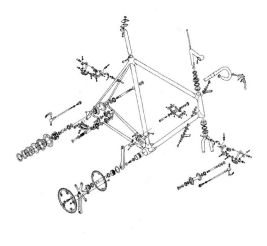

BICYCLE TECHNOLOGY

UNDERSTANDING THE MODERN BICYCLE AND ITS COMPONENTS

2ND EDITION, REVISED,
UPDATED, AND EXPANDED

ROB VAN DER PLAS
AND
STUART BAIRD

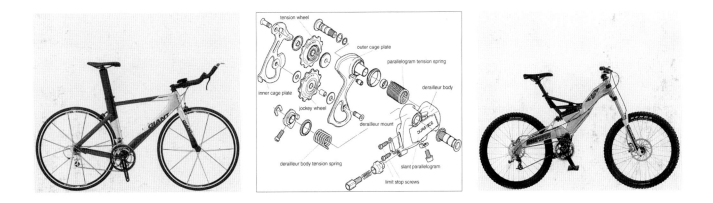

CYCLE PUBLISHING / VAN DER PLAS PUBLICATIONS, SAN FRANCISCO

Copyright © 2010 Rob van der Plas & Stuart Baird. All rights reserved
Printed in Hong Kong

Publisher's information:
Cycle Publishing / Van der Plas Publications
1282 7th Avenue
San Francisco, CA 94122
USA
http://www.cyclepublishing.com
E-mail: con.tact@cyclepublishing.com

Distributed or represented to the book trade by:
USA: Midpoint Trade Books, Kansas City, KS
UK: Chris Lloyd Sales and Marketing Services / Orca Book Services, Poole, Dorset
Australia: Woodslane Pty Ltd, Warriewood, NSW

Cover design:
Cycle Design, San Francisco

Publisher's Cataloging in Publication Data:
Van der Plas, Rob and Stuart Baird. Bicycle Technology: Understanding the Modern Bicycle and its Components
1. Bicycles and bicycling—handbooks and manuals.
28 cm. Bibliography: p. Includes index
I. Title: Understanding the Modern Bicycle and its Components
II. Authorship: Baird, Stuart, coauthor
Library of Congress Control Number: 2010905463
ISBN 978-1-892495-66-2

ABOUT THE AUTHORS

Rob van der Plas is a mechanical engineer with a lifelong passion for the bicycle. Having grown up in the Netherlands, and having honed his cycling and mechanical skills in England, he has lived in California since 1968. During the years since then, he has always maintained his interest in the bicycle and cycling as an activity.

Since 1974, he has been writing articles explaining technical and safety aspects of the bicycle in a variety of American, British, German, and Dutch cycling magazines, addressing both the bike trade and the general consumer markets. These articles have covered everything from riding in traffic and safe handling techniques off-road to frame construction materials and the workings of gearing, brakes, and lighting systems.

His first book appeared in 1978, and he has been writing bicycle-related books ever since, many of which were translated into other languages. His previous English-language books include *The Penguin Bicycle Handbook* (1983), *The Mountain Bike Book* (1984), *The Bicycle Repair Book* (1985), *Mountain Bike Maintenance* (1994, 2008), *Road Bike Maintenance* (1997), *Simple Bicycle Repair* (2005), and *Bicycle Repair* (2007).

Since 1993, he has been actively involved in the annual International Conference of Cycling History (yes, there really is such a thing). Not only has he attended each session, he has also been responsible for editing and publishing the conference proceedings.

In addition to his writing and publishing activities, he is still a regular cyclist himself, using his bike for everyday transportation, as well as for fitness and for touring. Of course, he maintains his own bicycles.

Contributing author **Stuart Baird** took up cycling in the early 80s and soon "went off the deep end," acquiring a couple of custom bikes, leading hundreds of rides, editing a club newsletter for almost two decades, and writing and publishing a well-received book of cycling routes.

In addition to logging a few thousand miles of recreational riding each year, Mr. Baird is relatively unusual among cyclists in that he has competed in time trials, and (at the opposite end of the cycling spectrum) does regular long-distance self-contained tours. That may be the result of the liberal arts philosophy instilled in him at Lawrence University in Appleton, Wisconsin, where he earned a degree in mathematics and was elected to Phi Beta Kappa.

Computer simulations were often his focus at the University of Illinois, the U.S. Air Force, and in industry, and resulted in his book *Performance Cycling* (2000), parts of which have been included in this book. He is also an amateur musician who has performed in dozens of Gilbert and Sullivan productions. Formerly employed in the aerospace and avionics industries, he is now retired and able to indulge his love of cycling any day of the week.

Authorship Note: On most issues covered in the book, the authors voice their shared opinions or experiences. Whenever "I," "me," or "my" are used, it refers to Rob van der Plas.

TABLE OF CONTENTS

INTRODUCTION

Our aim in writing this book is to provide the interested reader with a thorough insight in the workings of the bicycle and its many components. It is neither a bicycle buyer's guide nor a repair manual, of which there are plenty on the market, nor does it contain riding or training guidelines. However, it provides the insights in the technical aspect of the bike that will help you handle the bike more effectively, as well as select a bike and its components in an informed way.

Although the subject is technical in nature, we have tried to keep the text comprehensible to "ordinary" cyclists, without diluting the contents to the point of superficiality. It will help you to become a truly discerning cyclist, one who doesn't buy into every bit of hype used to sell cyclists on bikes and components that aren't really any better than simpler or older items that they may already have.

Throughout the book, we have also provided a historical perspective. Though that may at first seem to be out of place in a book with "modern bicycle" in its subtitle, it serves a very practical purpose: many ideas have been around before, and if they didn't work then, you'll need some good reasons as to why

they're now being presented as "new." There's a wonderful Chinese proverb that, transliterated, reads "On Ko Chi Shin," meaning "to understand the future, you must study the past." The historical references and illustrations given throughout the book give you an opportunity to do just that.

A Word About Units

The modern bicycle is what you might call a "metric machine": Things are measured in mm (millimeters) and weighed in g (grams), distances are measured in km (kilometers), and speeds in either km/h (kilometers per hour) or m/s (meters per second).

If you grew up with pounds and ounces, inches and feet, try to get over it: the metric system is easy enough to understand. In fact, it works just like dollars, dimes, and cents: all units are divisible by 10, 100, 1,000, etc. Once you get an idea of the size of one cm (about 3/8 in.) or the mass of one kg (about 2.2 lbs), it will be easy to move between all those other units and their

mutual relationship. And fortunately, some units, like the second and the hour, are also valid in the metric system.

Technology Defined

There's a tendency, especially amongst U.S. cyclists, to assume that only the lightest road racing bikes and the "coolest" mountain bikes and their respective components are technologically interesting. However, there's much more to it than that. There is as much technological finesse in a 14-speed hub gear or a hub-generator-based lighting system as there is in the cleverest mountain bike suspension or the lightest carbon-fiber frame or wheelset.

And it is not only the latest products that are of technological interest. Most of those products have gone through a gradual development process that has its roots in the industry going back several decennia, and sometimes more than a century. In this book, we will do justice both to the new and the old, covering all types of bicycles and their components. Of course, if you're interested only in the aspects related to high-end modern road or mountain bikes, you will find plenty of information to satisfy your curiosity in this arena as well.

INTRODUCTION

1

HISTORY AND DEVELOPMENT OF THE BICYCLE

THIS CHAPTER will give some insight into the way the bicycle was developed from its primitive origins of the early 19th century to its current state. This is not going to be a comprehensive bicycle history, but it will provide some context for the chapters that follow.

BICYCLE CHARACTERISTICS

Two aspects were fundamental to the development of the modern bicycle:

❑ The ability to balance a single-track vehicle, i.e., with its two wheels in line;

❑ A method of transferring power generated by the rider to a driven wheel.

BALANCE:

The first recognizable ancestor of the bicycle was developed by Carl Friedrich Drais zu Sauerbronn, also known as Carl Von Drais. Drais saw it as a substitute for the horse (which was in short supply at the time, due to a very harsh winter), allowing travel over significant distances at more than twice the speed of walking, he named it *"Laufmaschine,"* or "running machine." In later years

LEONARDO DIDN'T DO IT

One of the most persistent myths in cycling history is that Leonardo da Vinci "invented" a bicycle. No, he didn't. The sketch of a bicycle that was allegedly discovered in 1974 turned out to be a hoax, drawn in by a prankster during the manuscript restoration. It was based on two circles drawn on the other side of the page, and then pencilled in to turn it into what looked like an elementary bicycle.

For a fuller account of the Leonardo controversy and its unmasking, see Hans-Erhard Lessing, "The Evidence Against 'Leonardo's Bicycle'" in *Proceedings of the 8th International Cycling History Conference.*

it began to be referred to as "Draisine" after its inventor.

The rider sat on a padded beam, balancing himself above and between two wheels behind each other, and propelled himself by pushing off alternating with the left and the right foot, while rolling along. The important principle was that this single-track vehicle could be balanced with the steerable front wheel: when the machine starts to lean one way or the other, turn the steering wheel in that same direction, and the machine would right itself.

PROPULSION

Even before Drais had developed his machine, others had developed methods of driving

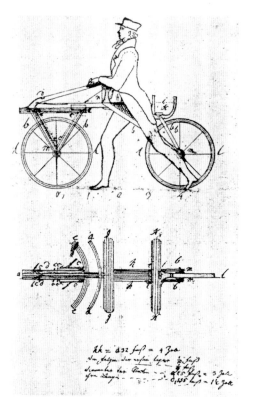

wheeled vehicles by manpower. Most of these were four-wheeled carriages of some sort, and though some were very elaborate, a few were more practical, such as the hand-cranked three-wheeler made by the paraplegic clocksmith Stephan Farfler for his own use.

BICYCLE DEVELOPMENT

Nearly two centuries have passed since the first bicycles emerged. In the following sections, we'll describe briefly what technical developments have taken place since.

Left and above: Figs. 1.1 and 1.2. Draisines old and new. A modern reconstruction of Drais' presumed patent drawing, (the patent itself has not been preserved) left, and a modern children's version, which provides a child a wonderful way to learn to balance on two wheels before he or she is ready to ride a regular pedal-driven bicycle.

TINKERING WITH THE DRAISINE

Drais' machine, though protected by a patent, was soon copied in many places by different people. Some built them under license from Drais, others simply pirated the design, either for their own use or to sell to whomever was willing to buy them. Most notable amongst the former was the English coach maker Denis Johnson, whose "pedestrian curricle" was available in several versions, including a ladies' model. However, interest soon diminished, and by 1830, they were all but forgotten relics of a short-lived craze.

Meanwhile, though, some handymen had been tinkering

DE SIVRAC WAS A FAKE

In 1891, the otherwise respected French author Louis Baudry de Saunier published the first edition of his book *Histoire Générale de la Vélocipède*, and in that he claimed that a hundred years earlier a certain Count de Sivrac would have invented, and ridden, an unsteered, two-wheeled cycle called Célérifère. And in book after book, that piece of "information" has been copied blindly. Well, it turned out none of it was true, there was no Count de Sivrac, and the Clélérifère was in fact a light horse-drawn carriage imported from England.

with the propulsion aspect, applied both to two-wheelers and, more typically, to three- and four-wheeled vehicles.

In England, Louis Gompertz had devised a hand-operated ratchet-drive to one of Johnson's machines. Even before Gompertz, back in Germany in 1817, Johann Carl Siegismund Bauer had designed (but probably never built) a treadle mechanism to drive the rear wheel of a Draisine. Neither of these devices led to any further development.

Three- and four-wheelers, meanwhile, fared somewhat better. In England, *Mechanics Magazine* reported throughout the 1820s, 30s and 40s of inventions relating to this kind of machine, most of which were foot-propelled by means of a treadle mechanism.

It was not until the 1850s that commercial production of such machines was begun. It was Willard Sawyer, of Dover, who put the new kind of "velocipedes," or "cycles," in the public eye. Both these terms would later be

used for bicycles, thus leading to some confusion as to how many wheels a particular machine may have had. Also in Scotland such machines were built during the second quarter of the 19th century.

By that time, though, draisines had practically disappeared, and even tricycles and other human-powered machines remained rare during this entire period. The vast majority of the people in Europe, let alone America, had never seen, nor even heard of, either a draisine or a tricycle.

WHAT ABOUT MACMILLAN?

Here's a case of mistaken identity—both of the machine and possibly the man. The much-depicted machine described as a replica of Kirkpatrick MacMillan's machine was built much later than the claimed 1842 date, and there's a photo of MacMillan riding...a tricycle.

And as for the oft-quoted report of a "gentleman" who knocked over a child in Glasgow's Gorbals district, it is obvious that a blacksmith, as MacMillan was, would not have been referred to as a "gentleman" at the time. Besides, the machine in question is described as being cranked by hand, and that is not exactly what the various presumed MacMillan replicas are.

For more information on this subject, see Nicholas Oddy, "Kirkpatrick MacMillan, the Inventor of the Bicycle or the Invention of Cycling History," in *Proceedings of the 1st International Cycling History Conference*, Glasgow, 1990.

Fig. 1.3. Here we have MacMillan himself, riding... that's right: a *tricycle*. The word cycle in the 1840s invariably meant *tricycle*, and there is no evidence to support the claim that he invented—or ever rode—a *bicycle*. Also note the hand-levers, which appear to be used for steering.

THE VELOCIPEDE

At some time, probably in the late 1850s, a workman's tricycle had been converted to be driven by means of cranks installed on

Above: Fig. 1.4. Typical velocipede. This is Michaux' second model, built between 1867 and 1871, with what was referred to as a "diagonal" frame, a design that provided improved frame stiffness over the earlier "serpentine" frame.

the front wheel. It is likely that Ernest Michaux, elder son of coach builder Pierre Michaux, applied this type of crank-driven front wheel to an old draisine, thus creating the first pedal-driven velocipede, which would become known as the "bone-shaker" in Britain.

Michaux eventually set up manufacturing such velocipedes starting in 1867. The venture was encouraged and financed by the wealthy Olivier brothers from Lyons. The Oliviers and their friend Cadot introduced a number of improvements, such as a hand-operated brake and an improved frame design, which were patented in 1869 under the Michaux company name (but *not* by either Michaux personally).

The basic principle of the pedal-driven front wheel, however, was not protected by any patent—until Pierre Lallement (who may or may not have been the one who first had the idea of the crank-driven front wheel) emigrated to the U.S. and was granted a patent there. This patent would later end up in the hands of "Colonel" Albert E. Pope, who used it to extract usury license fees from anyone building, making, or selling any kind of bicycles in America.

THE HIGH-WHEEL

On the velocipede, the speed was limited by the size of the front wheel and the rider's pedaling speed. Thus, making the driven wheel bigger could enable higher speeds. But to make

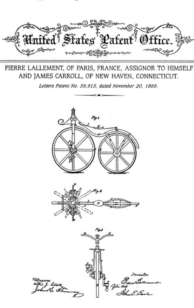

really big wheels, a different way of wheel-building was required. Whereas the velocipede ran on what were essentially wagon wheels, it was the invention of the wire-spoked wheel that enabled the introduction of wheels big enough to attain speeds of 30 km/h (19 mph) and more.

The wire-spoked wheel was first used on a machine made by Eugène Meyer in France. However, it was the English manufacturers, who quickly eclipsed the French velocipede makers starting in 1870, who integrated this development in large-scale manufacturing.

With its ever bigger front wheel, a new design soon emerged. Referred to as the high-wheel, this type still had a directly-driven front wheel, but the rider was placed directly over the front wheel, allowing maximum force to be applied to the pedals. The rear wheel was much smaller, which led to the term "penny-farthing" (for the

Above: Fig. 1.5. Pierre Lallement's velocipede patent of 1866.

Left: Left: Fig. 1.6. Eugène Meyer's 1869 machine with tension-wire-spoked wheel. More about this in Chapter 9.

Right: Fig. 1.7. Typical early high-wheel, or "penny-farthing," This one built by Rudge in 1872. Once safety bicycles were introduced, starting in 1885, high-wheels would often be referred to as "ordinary" bicycles.

two English coins that were very large and very small respectively) to describe these machines.

The high-wheel bicycle went through a development period during which increasingly lighter and faster (and more dangerous) machines were introduced. The problem with the high-wheeler was that it had a tendency to topple over forward, jettisoning the rider head-first over the handlebars, which was referred to as a "header." It remained a toy for athletic and daring young men.

During this same period, though, tricycles were also being made, and the latter were mainly popular with women and the less daring. Both high-wheel bicycles and tricycles remained quite expensive throughout this period, and thus they remained in use mainly by the privileged classes.

THE SAFETY BICYCLE

During the 1880s, many manufacturers, eager to expand their market share, introduced designs that offered more safety than the high-wheel. Some used gearing to

allow the use of a smaller front wheel, others, notably in the U.S., put the large driven wheel in the back and used a tiny front wheel, yet others used an indirectly-driven rear wheel, placing the rider between the wheels.

Eventually, the design that won out was the one with a chain-driven rear wheel. Though both Meyer-Guilmet and Lawson had tried to introduce such designs around 1879, it was not until John Kemp Starley introduced the 1885 model of his Rover safety bicycle that this design took off, especially when it was combined with the pneumatic tire, several years later. Within a few years, the high-wheel was all but dead, overtaken as it was both literally and figuratively by the safety bicycle.

The tricycle, meanwhile also seemed to be dying a slow death, although a few manufacturers continued to offer three-wheeled machines for both single riders and couples. However, these were now invariably based on the features of the safety bicycle, with chain-driven rear wheels and pneumatic tires.

20TH CENTURY DEVELOPMENTS

During much of the 20th century, bicycle developments were confined to "tweaking" of details, rather than overall redesign of the machine as a whole. Although some original, and different, designs were introduced at times (such as the small-wheeled

Left, right, and above: Figs 1.8–1.10. Safety bicycles in different flavors: Meyer-Guilmet's first chain-drive bicycle of 1879 (left); a Humber Kangaroo "dwarf safety" of 1885 (above); and John Kemp Starley's first, second, and third Rover designs of 1884 and 1885 (right), showing remarkable development within a single year's production.

folding bicycles of the 1960s), none of them had enough impact to change the overall look of the bicycle in general.

Perhaps the most important development during this time has been the introduction, and perfection, of gearing systems. This subject will be covered quite thoroughly in Chapters 11–13, but if you're really interested in these developments, we'd like to refer you to another book: *The Dancing Chain,* by Frank Berto (see Bibliography for details).

THE 21ST CENTURY

It is a little early to look at the most recent development in a historical perspective, but perhaps it is safe to expect more minor refinements rather than revolutionary change. Probably high-end bikes will continue to be made lighter—for those willing to pay the price. Electronic

gear changing, and perhaps electronic brake controls, are likely to be perfected. Electric-assist bikes may become more common, due to the development of lighter and more efficient

Above: Fig. 1.11. The most significant development of the 20th century was derailleur gearing, and no one has contributed more than Paul de Vivie, whose pen name was Vélocio. He is shown here with a bichain, or double-chain bicycle.

Left and bottom right: Figs. 1.12 and 1.13. A hundred years separate these two bicycles. The 1908 Tour de France bike (left) looks very similar to the 2010 Raleigh (or any other make) road bike (right), but the latter weighs a lot less, has effective brakes, 20-speed gearing, and tires that are inflated to twice the pressure and weigh about half of those on the 1908 machine. Consequently, it is probably also faster and more responsive, but perhaps less comfortable to ride.

batteries. However, overall, the majority of bicycles in use 100 years from now will probably look much like what most people ride today.

For those who predict a future dominated by streamlined fully enclosed pedal-driven machines zipping along at high speed on elevated super bikeways, don't hold your breath. The practical advantages of the basic bicycle far outweigh the presumed benefits of those dream machines. Anybody who doesn't believe that is reminded that these ideas have been around since the 1930s, and essentially, they have come to

Above: Fig. 1.14. Almost a mountain bike: This French PRF touring bike, introduced in 1928, had balloon tires, derailleur gearing, and most of the other features of a mountain bike.

nought in the past, and that is unlikely to be any different in the future.

THE MODERN BICYCLE IN PERSPECTIVE

In large outlines it may seem the bicycle has not changed much since the pneumatic-tired safety bicycle was first introduced in the late 1880s. For over a hundred and twenty years now, almost all bicycles made share the characteristics of the bicycle. Nevertheless, technical development has not stood still, and this design has gone through quite a number of refinements over the years.

Probably the most obvious change has been the introduction of gearing, both by means of hub gearing and by means of derailleurs. The former were mainly developed in England and Germany, the latter in France and Italy.

But also other details of the bicycle have gone through significant developments. Today's

bikes are available with remarkably efficient brakes—ranging from lightweight rim brakes to hub brakes and disk brakes, some cable-operated, others hydraulically operated. And especially during the last 20 years, the introduction of suspension systems has changed the experience of cycling.

One thing to keep in mind, though, is that there has never been such thing as a "standard" bicycle. At a time when most bikes on the road are mountain bikes (or at least look like mountain bikes), there are various other kinds of machines available as well, and different models may be popular in different countries or regions.

This was no different in the past: at the time of the high-wheel, there were also tricycles, while some velocipedes were still around; and when the safety bicycle was introduced, the old high-wheels did not disappear

overnight. There were numerous different styles of safeties available as well.

At the same time, throughout all phases of its history, technical improvements were constantly being made. To the casual observer, today's bicycle may look like last year's model, but there are subtle developments going on all the time.

It was no different in the past: Although to today's cyclist, one high-wheel bike may look like any other, in the days of the high-wheel also refinements were constantly being introduced. Even in the days of the boneshaker, the introduction of ball bearings and other developments, such as improved materials and design details, made for constant change and evolution. Then as now, some changes were not necessarily improvements, but were meant only to boost sales or reduce manufacturing costs rather than benefit the rider.

Left: Fig. 1.15. With the new millennium, we seem to have entered the "carbon age," with that material finding ever-increasing use on high-end bicycles and components.

Right: Fig. 1.16. The other most prominent recent development is suspension, though the idea is not new, it has certainly taken off in the last two decades.

ANATOMY OF THE BICYCLE

T HERE ARE quite a number of different types of bicycle on the market, now as in the past. The first section of this chapter is an overview of the various models out there, while the latter part is a brief summary of the various components found on every bike.

BICYCLE TYPES

Today's categorization of bicycle types runs something like this:

- ❏ Road Bikes

- ❏ Mountain Bikes

- ❏ Hybrids, City Bikes, and Comfort Bikes

- ❏ Single-speed and fixed-gear bikes

- ❏ Touring and trekking bikes

- ❏ Tandems

- ❏ Folding bikes

- ❏ Cargo bikes

- ❏ Recumbents

- ❏ Tricycles

- ❏ HPVs

- ❏ Electric-assist bikes

In the following sections, we'll take a very cursory look at each of these categories, pointing out their main characteristics and uses.

Left: Fig. 2.1. Typical modern road bike with 20-speed derailleur gearing. In this, and many other photos in the book, pedals are not shown installed on the bike.

ROAD BIKES

Originally intended for racing, road bikes are also popular for casual riding and exercise on smooth pavement. They are light in weight, typically less than 11 kg (24 lbs), run on narrow high-pressure tires, and have drop handlebars.

Though most modern road bikes have derailleur gearing, with a tendency to add more and more gears, a recent trend has been fixed-gear bikes, or "fixies." Their simplicity is enticing, with no gears to shift and only one brake, on the front wheel. In fact, these machines are essentially track racing bikes made "street legal" by adding that front brake. More practical is the single-speed, which at least uses a freewheel, though no multi-speed gears, and has brakes both front and rear. Most bikes in this category can be used either one way or the other: They have two brakes and a reversible rear wheel, with a freewheel on one side and a fixed cog on the other.

MOUNTAIN BIKES

First developed, as the name implies, for riding up and down mountainous terrain, they have

Above: Fig. 2.2. A modern but more traditional road bike from Bianchi. It has a steel frame and weighs just 500 g (18 oz.) more than it would with a carbon frame—at less than half the price.

Right: Fig. 2.3. Santa Cruz full-suspension mountain bike with hydraulic disk brakes.

Above: Fig. 2.6. Gary Fisher Paragon "hardtail" mountain bike, i.e. without rear suspension. The original mountain bikes made do without any suspension, relying on the high-volume tires for shock absorption.

Left: Fig. 2.4. Breezer Greenway fully equipped urban commuter bike.

Right: Fig. 2.5. Modern 3-speed roadster from Raleigh U.K.

proven useful for riding under less strenuous conditions as well. They have fat tires, flat handlebars, and lots of gears. In addition, most modern mountain bikes have suspension, either just in the front or both front and rear.

HYBRIDS, CITY BIKES, AND COMFORT BIKES

All of these are close relatives of the mountain bike, although their tires are not quite as fat. They usually afford a more upright rider position and are equipped with luggage racks, chain guard, fenders, and lighting. Many are available with a step-through frame for easy mounting and dismounting, as favored by many women and older riders. Many of these machines also have front suspension, and in some countries, notably Germany, they often have rear suspension as well.

TOURING, TREKKING, AND RANDONNEUR BIKES

Touring bikes are designed with long-term comfort and load-carrying in mind. They usually look like road bikes, but with more voluminous tires and a sturdier overall construction. They have low gears for grinding up long climbs, and they should accommodate fenders and lights (though in America, few come equipped that way from the manufacturer, so you'd have to install your own).

Trekking bikes are harder to define, and I've never really understood why the term is used at all, except that it was somehow imported from Germany. They're flat-handlebar bikes meant for dirt road touring, so most of them finish up looking much like hybrids with luggage racks.

Randonneur bikes are intended for randonneur events—long-distance non-racing events such as Boston–Montreal–Boston or Paris–Brest–Paris which must be completed within a specified time. The randonneur rules require a minimum complement of lighting and tools. Similar to touring bikes in overall appearance,

Above: Fig. 2.7. Modern touring bicycle from Raleigh USA.

Above: Fig. 2.8. Tandem based on a custom-built frame by Bernie Mikkelson.

Bottom left: Fig. 2.9. Modern custom-built randonneur bike from Terrafirma.

Right: Fig. 2.10. Folding bike with front and rear suspension from a company modestly called Downtube.

they tend to be built of lighter materials and they lack the luggage carrying features of loaded-touring bikes. Since comfort is an important criterion for these machines, they usually have somewhat shallow frame angles, a longish wheelbase, and relatively fat tires.

FOLDING BIKES

These machines have a frame that can be folded or separated for easy storage, with some of them actually designed to fit in a standard-size suitcase. Most have small wheels, and they come in a wide range of models. To compensate for the inherent discomfort of small wheels (at least on

less-than-perfect road surfaces), some models have suspension.

TANDEMS

The tandem is a bicycle built for two (or sometimes more), with in-line wheels further apart than a single bike, and with multiple seats. They come in many different styles, with characteristics that range from those of the road bike and mountain bikes to those of folding bike and recumbents.

CARGO BIKES

Though not everyday bike-shop fare, this kind of bicycle is coming more and more into its own as it has been discovered that many items can be quickly and economically transported by bike. Most of these have a smaller front wheel with a large platform or container above it. Other types are available as well, including three-wheelers for both cargo and people transport.

Top left: Fig. 2.11. The Hiker-Trike, a tricycle with hand- and foot-drive.

Bottom left. Fig. 2.12. Cargobike, this one built by the Dutch Azor company.

Right: Fig. 2.13. Tom Ritchey's coffee bike design for Project Ruanda.

Interestingly, as China and India are motorizing their infrastructure to the point of moving everything that was once transported by bicycle, many western countries are rediscovering the bicycle for practical use. Pioneering countries are Denmark and Holland, with a lively cargo bike industry. In the United States, Eugene, Oregon is home to several innovative bike builders who offer cargo bikes.

Tom Ritchey, one of the California mountain bike pioneers, designed a number of special-purpose cargo bikes for Project Ruanda, a charity in which he is active. A good example of these is the bike he designed for Ruandan coffee farmers, allowing small farmers to transport their wares to market without being forced to sign the fruits of their labor over to a large plantation-based operator.

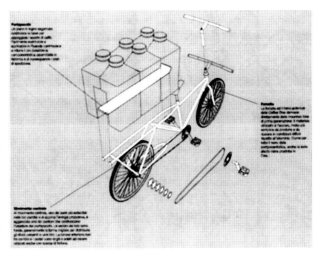

RECUMBENTS

Bicycles that place the rider low to the ground between the wheels in a reclining positions are still around (as they have been for about 100 years). They have a small but devoted following who appreciate their aerodynamic advantages as well as their comfort and safety benefits. Most have small wheels, and some run on three wheels.

TRICYCLES

Traditional road-type trikes, with two wheels in the rear and one in front, are still available today, though quite rare. However, in recent years, a plethora of original designs with three (and sometimes 4) wheels have been introduced in recent decades. Three wheelers too come in a wide variety, ranging from the heavy machines popular in Florida retirement communities to lightweight racers, recumbents, and cargo haulers.

HPVs

Those letters stand for Human-Powered Vehicle. With an aerodynamic enclosure, these machines are meant to go fast. They are mainly used in special land-speed competitions, and have formed the basis for the development of human-powered aircraft. To date, their oft-touted suitability for commuting and intra-urban use have not materialized.

ELECTRIC-ASSIST BIKES

Attach a motor to a bicycle, and *voilá*, a new mode of transport is born. In this department, history has repeated itself numerous times, with little motors being added to bicycles, mutating to machines with only token pedals, and finally no pedals at all. The latest development is by means of a small electric motor and a lightweight battery.

Referred to variously as E-bike or "pedelec," the current incarnation holds at least some promise, because they are designed to require the rider to provide at least part of the propulsive power: when you stop pedaling, the motor also stops. They have a limited range, which makes them suitable for most commuting and urban utility cycling, but not for longer tours.

Top left: Fig. 2.14. HP Velotechnik short-wheelbase recumbent, made in Germany, which seems to be a hotbed of recumbent innovation.

Bottom left: Fig. 2.15. The Go-Go is a fully faired three-wheeler. This too is a German design, from the same studio as the Smart Car. Unlike most other fully faired bikes and trikes, this is a stable product—but at a price. But in all fairness, it is in the same price range as some of those "high-tech" featherweight road bikes, and a lot more practical.

Right: Fig. 2.16. And to round out this page of German products, here is a Kalkhoff E-bike from the same country. The motor and battery hail from Japan, though, where E-bikes are a dime a dozen these days.

PARTS OF THE BICYCLE

Fig. 2.17 shows a typical bicycle with the names of the various components. Most of the same components can be found on any bike—though sometimes in a different form or mounted in a different location. To ease the process of describing these many parts, we will treat them in "functional groups" as follows:

❏ frame

❏ wheels

❏ brakes

❏ gearing system

❏ drivetrain

❏ steering system

❏ saddle and seatpost

❏ suspension

❏ accessories (including lights and luggage-carriers)

In the chapters that follow, the workings of the various parts will be discussed, arranged roughly on the basis of these same functional groups.

COMPONENT GRUPPOS

The Italian word *gruppo*, which of course stands for "group," and is referred to as group-set in Britain, refers to a component package from a single manufacturer. Until around 1960, even the fanciest bikes would be equipped with components from different manufacturers.

A typical road bike of the 1960s may have had Campagnolo hubs, crankset, derailleurs, and headset. The brakes might be from Mafac, the pedals from Lyotard, the seatpost from Simplex, and the rims from Fiame. But when Campagnolo gradually expanded its offerings

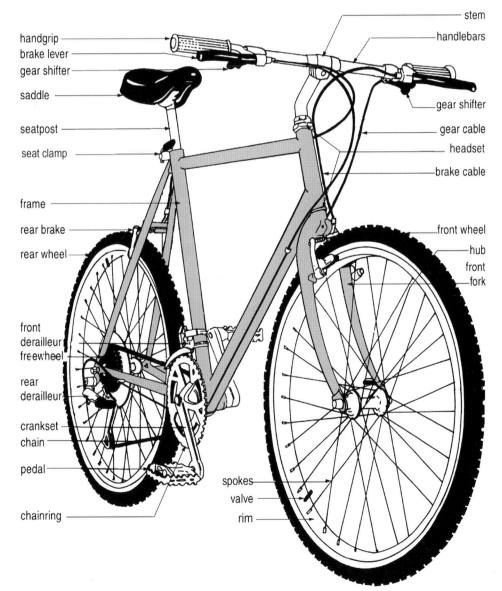

handgrip
brake lever
gear shifter
saddle
seatpost
seat clamp
frame
rear brake
rear wheel
front derailleur
freewheel
rear derailleur
crankset
chain
pedal
chainring
spokes
valve
rim
stem
handlebars
gear shifter
gear cable
headset
brake cable
front wheel
hub
front
fork

Left: Fig. 2.17. Part designation, shown on the basis of a generic hybrid bicycle without suspension. All parts shown here are also found on other bikes, though specific models may have some parts that are not shown here, and no accessories are included in this illustration.

to include pedals, brakes, and seatposts as well, the gruppo concept was born.

Soon other manufacturers caught on to the idea, sometimes combining forces to be able to offer a gruppo under one name, although the components may have been made by several different companies. Eventually, bikes would be unofficially designated by the component gruppo they were equipped with: You might have a "Campagnolo Record bike," or a "Shimano Dura-Ace bike," etc.

In the 1980s it came to a point where Shimano would not supply bike makers with individual components of their choice, insisting that they purchase the whole gruppo. In the U.S. and Europe, anti-trust litigation brought by bike manufacturers and other component makers eventually broke up this strong-arm practice.

Today, even though most of the components may come from one manufacturer's certain gruppo, you may find that some of the components are either from the same manufacturer's higher or lower price gruppo or

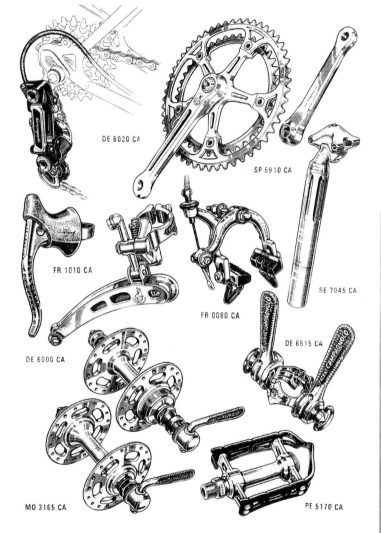

Above: Fig. 2.18. Drawing by the French illustrator Daniel Rebour of a 1984 component gruppo. This is a Campagnolo Nuovo Record gruppo as it was built throughout the 1970s and 1980s.

Right: Fig. 2.19. Partial modern Shimano Dura-Ace road gruppo. The full gruppo also includes hubs, brakes, chain, pedals, and seatpost.

from another manufacturer altogether.

Of course, for some components the gruppo concept has its advantages. Gears and brakes, for instance, can be ideally matched to their controls and to the chain, chainrings, and sprockets if they are pre-selected by the component manufacturer in the form of a gruppo. For other items, it is perhaps merely a matter of aesthetics, with the bike's various components sharing a common appearance.

For the discerning cyclist, it may instead be advantageous to select components from various makes and models to suit his or her specific needs. Unfortunately, that may get more expensive than buying an "off-the-peg" bike with the gruppo selected by its manufacturer: It will be impossible to beat the prices that component makers charge the bike manufacturers for their complete gruppos.

FUNCTIONAL GROUPS

The following sections provide brief introductions to the various components of the bicycle. More detailed descriptions can be found in chapters 8 through 21.

THE FRAME

Together with the front fork, the frame forms the frameset. Together, they can be considered the bike's backbone—the structure to which all the other components are attached, either directly or indirectly. Although different materials (which in turn allow for frames of different shapes) may be used on some bikes, most frames still comprise a tubular metal structure as shown in Fig. 2.18.

The front part, called main frame, consists of top tube, seat tube, downtube, and head tube. The rear part, referred to as rear

triangle, comprises thinner tubes, called seatstays and chainstays.

Smaller parts are attached to the various tubes to hold other components of the bicycle: dropouts, or forkends, to hold the wheels; brake bosses to hold the brakes; seat clamp to hold the saddle; and the bottom bracket shell to hold the bearings for the cranks. The bearings for the steering system are installed in the head tube.

THE WHEELS

After the frame, the wheels are the most critical part of the bicycle. Each wheel, shown in Fig. 2.19, consists of a hub and a network of spokes connecting it to the rim, on which the tire and the inner tube are mounted. The hub runs on ball bearings, and the ends of its axle are held in at the forkends at the front fork or the dropouts at the frame's rear triangle.

Left: Fig. 2.20. A modern road bike frame. Although steel frames are still made, many of today's road bikes have carbon-fiber composite frames and forks, like this one from Kona.

Right: Fig. 2.21. A conventional bicycle wheel as used on a mountain bike. These days many manufacturers also offer wheels with special hubs and special spoking configurations.

The tire is inflated by means of a valve that protrudes inward through the rim. On high-end bikes, most wheels are held in by means of a quick-release mechanism, whereas they may be held in with hexagonal axle nuts on many simpler bikes.

THE DRIVETRAIN

Also known as the transmission, this is the group of components that transfer the rider's input to the driven wheel (usually the rear wheel). In addition to the gearing system (covered separately below) the drivetrain includes the cranks, held at the frame's lowest point by means of the bearings of the bottom bracket, the pedals, the chain, the chainrings (the large gear wheels attached to the right-side crank), and the cogs, or sprockets (the smaller gear wheels attached to the rear wheel hub), as well as the freewheel mechanism built into or attached to the rear wheel hub.

THE GEARING SYSTEM

The vast majority of bicycles sold in the U.S. these days are equipped with derailleur gearing, while in recent years there has been a bit of a comeback of hub gears for use on some city and commuter bikes. The derailleur system achieves changes of gear ratio, needed to adapt the rider's effort and pedaling speed to differences in terrain conditions, by moving the chain from one combination of front chainring and rear cog to another.

Selecting a bigger chainring in the front or a smaller cog in the back results in a higher gear, e.g. for fast riding on a level road; selecting a smaller chainring or a larger cog provides a lower gear, e.g. for riding uphill. The number of available gears is calculated by multiplying the number of chainrings on the front by the number of cogs in the back—for example, 3 x 9 = 27 for mountain bikes and 2 x 10 = 20 for road bikes.

These "chain-derailing" operations are carried out by means of the front and rear derailleurs

respectively (the one on the front is more commonly called changer in the U.K., where the rear derailleur may be referred to as "mech," short for mechanism).

The derailleurs are operated by means of shifters, which are usually installed on the handlebars, although on older road bikes, they may be found on the frame's downtube (and in fact, some of us still prefer this method even for new bikes). On modern road bikes, these shifters are generally integrated with the brake levers, making for convenient shifting—but expensive repair or replacement if there is a problem. In all cases, the front derailleur is controlled from the left-side shifter, while the rear derailleur is controlled from the shifter on the right. The shifters are connected with the derailleur mechanisms by means of flexible cables.

In the case of hub gearing, shown in Fig. 2.23, gear changes are achieved by means of a kind of gear box integrated in the rear wheel hub, although there is also a version that is connected with the front chainring and the cranks—mainly used on

Left: Fig. 2.22. Typical derailleur gear train as used on a mountain bike.

Right: Fig. 2.23. The alternative to derailleur gearing is hub gearing, such as this modern 9-speed hub from SRAM.

recumbent bicycles and on some downhill mountain bikes to replace the front derailleur. Most hub gear systems are operated by means of a single shifter, installed on the handlebars, via a flexible cable.

Whereas derailleur gearing usually has a large number of (slightly) different gear ratios, hub gears are generally limited to a maximum of 7 or 8 speeds, although (more expensive) 14-speed hub gears are also available. Two- and three-speed models are still available, and may be quite adequate for many people's everyday bicycle use.

Despite the smaller number of gears, these devices usually have a range that may be quite adequate for most riding conditions short of loaded touring, road racing, and out-and-out mountain bike riding.

THE BRAKES

Most bicycles are equipped with one form of hand-operated brake or another. All these stop the bike by pushing a pair of brake pads against the sides of the wheel rim or another part that rotates with the wheel.

The brakes themselves are attached to the fork and the frame's rear triangle. Each brake is controlled by means of a lever mounted on the handlebars—one on the right, usually for the rear brake, and one on the left, usually for the front brake. A flexible cable connects the lever with the brake itself. Fig. 2.27 shows a typical rim brake with

matching brake lever and control cable, as used on a mountain bike.

Some bikes use brakes that act on the hub instead of on the rim. These include disk brakes, mainly found on mountain bikes; drum brakes, found on some city bikes and (as an auxiliary brake) on some tandems; and the coaster brakes (called

Above: Fig. 2.27. Parts of the steering system on a flat-handlebar bike.

Above: Fig. 2.24. Typical road bike brake of the dual-pivot design.

Left: Fig. 2.25. Brake and controls on a mountain bike with direct-pull brakes.

Bottom right: Fig. 2.26. A cable-operated disk brake as installed on a mountain bike. This type of brake may also be hydraulically operated.

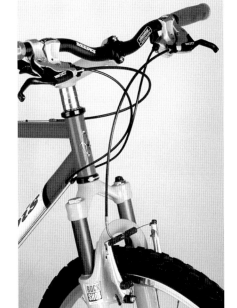

backpedaling brake in Britain), found on simple utility bikes and cruisers. The latter are installed only on the rear wheel and are operated by means of the chain when the rider pedals backward.

Disk brakes are either operated by cables, just like rim brakes, or by means of a hydraulic system, as on cars and motorcycles. Drum brakes are generally operated via cables. Alternately, on traditional heavy-duty roadsters—rarely seen in the U.S. and Britain these days—the brakes may be operated via rigid rods with pivoted connections.

THE STEERING SYSTEM

The steering system is quite critical, not only for riding in curves, but also for balancing the bike even when riding a straight course. It comprises the front fork, which holds the front wheel; the handlebars; the stem, which connects these two parts; and the headset, which allows the entire system to pivot in the frame's head tube.

SADDLE AND SEATPOST

Although perhaps the least glamorous part of the bicycle, the saddle, or seat, is not only important for comfort, but also for control of the bike. It is normally held in place in the frame's seat tube by means of a seatpost, which is clamped in by means of a binder bolt. Of course, on tricycles and

recumbents, different kinds of seats and their supports are used that are specifically designed for those machines.

SUSPENSION

Many modern bikes come with some form of suspension. That may range from a simple suspension seatpost and/or a flexible handlebar stem to a complex system with telescoping front forks and a multi-linkage rear suspension.

Suspension, too, is nothing new, dating back to the early days of cycling, but it has become much more common (and sophisticated) in recent years. Modern suspension systems were first widely applied to mountain bikes, but they are now also getting more common on hybrid and city bikes, and even folding bikes.

Above: Fig. 2.28. Seat, seatpost, and seat clamp.

Left: Fig. 2.29. Typical front suspension fork as used on most mountain bikes.

Right: Fig. 2.30. One of many possible rear suspension configurations, this one from Specialized.

ACCESSORIES

Chapters 19, 20, and 21 will deal with luggage carrying equipment, lighting, and other accessories respectively.

Ranging from front and rear racks to trailers, load carrying equipment deserves to be taken seriously. Though in the U.S. most people are still used to thinking of the bicycle only as sports equipment, it is also a very practical means of transport, and it is entirely possible to use it as such with the right equipment.

Of all the accessories for bicycle use, lighting systems are probably the most critical for safety when riding at night. Over the last two decades, there has been a rash of technical development of lighting systems, both battery- and generator-powered.

There is also a wide range of other accessories available for the bicycle. They range from simple to high-tech, and from very important to trivial—which in turn depends on the circumstances of the bike's use.

Left: Fig. 2.31. Modern lighting system from Cygolite, using ultra-bright LEDs and a rechargeable battery pack.

Right: Fig. 2.32. A bike with bells and whistles. This Breezer town bike comes with lights, fenders, racks, panniers, chain guard, lock, kickstand, and a bell.

3

THE BICYCLE IN MOTION

THE BICYCLE may be the most energy-efficient vehicle on the road (or off-road for that matter). The reason for this efficiency is basic to all bicycle designs, both past and present, and nothing is likely to change that in the future.

BICYCLE EFFICIENCY

Von Drais hit on it as early as 1817, when he introduced his *Laufmaschine,* or Draisine. It is the energy saved by rolling along without having to lift your body by a couple of inches with every step, as is done when walking.

Yet not all bikes are equally efficient, and certainly today's bike is a lot more efficient than Von Drais' machine and the early boneshakers. Here's an overview of the factors that determine the bicycle's efficiency and how they have improved to achieve the present level of efficiency.

Any wheeled vehicle is moved forward on level ground by a propulsive force great enough to overcome the following forms of resistance:

❑ Rolling resistance of the wheels on the road surface;

❑ Air resistance, or aerodynamic drag;

❑ Friction resistance of internal moving parts;

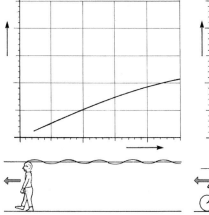
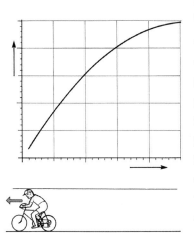

Left: Fig. 3.1. Walking and cycling compared. The graph shows the potential energy that is "wasted" in walking by lifting the body with each step. This energy is "saved" when cycling.

Going uphill, another resistance has to be overcome as well:

❑ Gravitational resistance;

And, finally, when accelerating (and in the opposite direction, when braking):

❑ Inertia.

In the following sections, we'll take a closer look at each of these factors and explain how they can be minimized.

ROLLING RESISTANCE

The major factors contributing to rolling resistance are the following:

❑ Load of bike, rider and luggage;

❑ Deformation of the tires as they compress under the rider's weight, causing the rubber and air molecules within them to collide with each other;

❑ Sag, or the amount by which the tire is deformed under load as compared to its perfectly circular diameter;

❑ Length of contact patch between the tire and the road;

❑ Tire pressure, which largely determines the two preceding factors on any given tire;

❑ Wheel diameter;

❑ Accuracy of the complete wheel's circularity and straightness;

❑ Road surface, specifically concerning its smoothness and hardness.

If you take a large-diameter, perfectly round hoop and give it a push, it will roll along on a smooth, level plane quite nicely for some time, but it will slow down gradually and eventually fall over when it has slowed down too much. Most of what causes it to slow down is rolling resistance, and at low speeds, rolling resistance is also the major force that must be overcome on a bicycle.

The first bicycles had heavy, not precisely round, wooden wheels with a steel band around the circumference, and they were ridden on dirt roads or cobble-stone streets. All these factors resulted in high rolling resistance, and subsequent developments to reduce rolling resistance have included the following:

❑ Near-perfectly round wheels, avoiding energy loss due to the wheel, and with it the bike, being forced up-and-down as it rotates, as well as sideways wobbling;

❑ Flexible pneumatic tires that deform around any minor unevenness of the road surface rather than bouncing up and down;

❑ Lightweight tires that can be inflated to a high pressure;

❑ Hard, smooth road surfaces, which allow for the use of those high-pressure tires.

Right: Fig. 3.2. For any given tire and inflation pressure, the power to overcome rolling resistance is roughly proportional to the road speed..

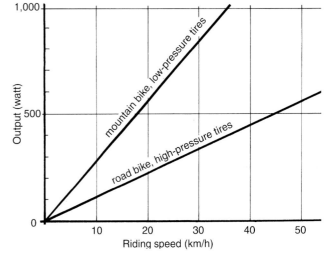

Rolling resistance is proportional to weight and speed. However, at higher speeds it becomes less and less significant relative to air drag, which increases disproportionally more at higher speeds.

AERODYNAMIC DRAG

If you've ever ridden into a headwind, you know how much the effect of air resistance can impede the cyclist's progress. Aerodynamic drag (or aerodynamic resistance) is also a factor if there is no headwind. However, the headwind example makes it easier to demonstrate that it is very much speed-dependent. Cycling at 20 km/h (12.5 mph) on a day without wind, air resistance doesn't hold you back significantly. But against a headwind of 20 km/h,

your speed relative to the air is doubled. However, the aerodynamic drag (a resistive force) will be 4 times as much.

Aerodynamic drag is the component of aerodynamic force opposite to the direction of motion. It is due to a number of related factors, primarily:

❏ Reaction force caused by reduced air pressure behind (i.e. on the "downwind" side) of bike and rider;

❏ Turbulence of air caused by the movement of the air relative to bike and rider;

❏ Friction of air against the surface of bike and rider.

All these resisting forces are highly speed-dependent, being proportional to the square of the

relative speed between the biker and the air (regardless whether caused by forward movement alone or in combination with a full or partial headwind). In other words, twice as fast means four times as much drag, and even a 10% increase in riding speed results in 21% increase in drag.

There are two aspects of aerodynamic drag. One is form drag, resulting from the shape of the object and the turbulence it produces. The reduced air pressure in the turbulence behind a moving object actually creates a suction that tugs backward on the object. Some shapes are obviously more "aerodynamic" (streamlined) than others and reduce this turbulence. An aircraft fuselage and the profile of a sports-racing car approach the ideally streamlined shape that minimizes form drag. A racing bicyclist on a standard road bike falls considerably short of that ideal, however, and an upright recreational rider or mountain biker is worse yet.

The other aspect of aerodynamic drag is skin friction, resulting from the friction of the air against the surface of the moving object. For simplicity, however, we characterize both aspects with one number, the coefficient of aerodynamic drag or C_D, a quantification of how "slippery" the moving object is. This number is considered constant, even though in reality it varies slightly with wind speed and direction.

NEWTON'S LAWS

The basis for the discussion of what makes a bicycle go, and what slows it down, are explained simply by Newton's laws, which—in case you don't remember—are stated as follows:

1. If a balanced force system acts on a particle at rest, it will remain at rest. If a balanced force system acts on a particle in motion, it will remain in motion in a straight line without acceleration.

2. If an unbalanced force system acts on a particle, it will accelerate in proportion to the magnitude and in the direction of the resultant force.

3. When two particles exert forces on each other, these forces are equal in magnitude, opposite in direction, and co-linear.

Aerodynamic drag is proportional to C_D.

Yes, this is the same C_D that automobile advertisements love to brag about. However, aerodynamic drag is also proportional to frontal area (imagine the vehicle coming toward you silhouetted against the sky.) It does little good to have a low C_D if the frontal area is large—as it is for most cars. For bicycling, both the C_D and the frontal area must include the rider in addition to the bicycle itself.

Aerodynamic drag is also proportional to the density of the air. Although the density of air seldom changes significantly during the course of an event, for completeness we can look at the factors that influence air density.

❏ Temperature: Air is less dense at higher temperatures. Density (and therefore aerodynamic drag) drops about 0.35% for every gain of 1 degree Celsius (1.8 degrees Fahrenheit).

❏ Barometric pressure: For example, density at a pressure of 29 inches of mercury (737 mm Hg) is 3% less than at a pressure of 30 inches (762 mm). Altitude (elevation, or height above sea level) has a significant effect. Barometric pressure drops about 1% for every 80 meters (262 feet) gain in altitude. In Colorado Springs, with an altitude of 5,900 feet, aerodynamic drag is typically only 80% of what it is in Wilmington, Delaware, at about 80 feet above sea level.

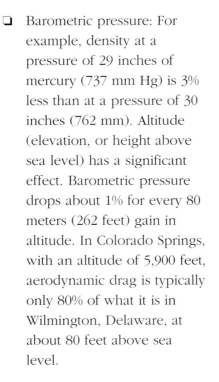

❏ Humidity: Perhaps surprisingly, at 20° C (68° F), air is 1% less dense when the relative humidity is 100% than when it is perfectly dry.

Putting these all together, for a record attempt you'd ideally pick a hot, humid day, possibly with rain threatening (for low barometric pressure), in a place like La Paz, Bolivia (altitude 3,570 m, or 11,909 ft.). Most of cycling's world records were indeed set at high altitude velodromes.

However, not only are some of these low-density-producing conditions unlikely to occur simultaneously, but some may reduce the amount of power a cyclist is able to develop. Perhaps for such reasons, the increases in speed at high altitude are not as great as one might expect.

Even more important to aerodynamic drag is speed, because drag is proportional to the square of the airspeed. The airspeed in turn depends on the bicycle's (ground) speed, the wind speed, and the relative direction of the

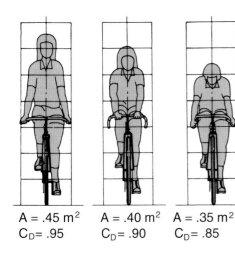

A = .45 m²   A = .40 m²   A = .35 m²
C_D= .95 C_D= .90 C_D= .85

Left, above, and right: Air resistance and what you can do about it.
Left: Fig. 3.3. The frontal area of bike and rider is the main factor in a bicycle's air resistance, and can be reduced by riding in a "racing" rather than an upright "touring" position
Above: Fig. 3.4. A crouched body position combined with a small fairing improves the Drag coefficient, C_D, of bike and rider.
Right: Fig. 3.5. A full-body fairing mounted on a recumbent bicycle offers both lower frontal area and improved drag coefficient, C_D.

wind. In some cases, the wind may be blowing in the same direction as the bicycle is moving—a tailwind—and be strong enough to move the bicycle sufficiently fast all by itself. A large pack of riders may also move the air along fast enough that riders within the pack can coast. Aerodynamic drag then proves to be an asset.

Usually, however, drag acts against the cyclist, because the bicycle's own speed makes almost any wind conditions seem like a headwind. As with rolling resistance, aerodynamic drag is always viewed as a force opposite to the direction of motion, even if it occasionally has a negative value that makes the term "drag" seem a misnomer.

GRAVITATIONAL RESISTANCE

Gravity resistance is the effect of the bicycle's weight, and in case of its moving parts, their weight in particular. Weight is itself the product of two factors: the mass of the object, measured in kg,

and the acceleration due to gravity, referred to as g.

Mass is a property of an object that depends on its size and composition. The mass of an object is the same no matter whether the object is on the surface of the earth, on the moon, or out in space.

At any given spot on the earth, the acceleration due to gravity is constant, but its precise value varies slightly from place to place depending on latitude, altitude, and elevation. The variation is a consequence of the universal law of gravitation between any two objects. The most massive object in our vicinity is the earth. As we climb higher or move toward its bulging equator, we move farther from its center, weakening the gravitational attraction.

The International Committee on Weights and Measures has adopted 9.80665 m/s^2 (meters per second per second), or 32.174 ft/s^2, as the standard

value of g, used for defining weights in terms of mass. That standard value is what the actual value would be at sea level at 45 degrees, 32 minutes, and 33 seconds of latitude. Since most of the landmass of the United States lies to the South of this line, the actual value is slightly less in most areas, whereas in Canada and Britain the actual value is close to or higher than the standard. In San Francisco, it is 9.79965.

While mass affects weight, which affects rolling resistance, more important to the cyclist is the direct effect of gravity on rider and bicycle when the terrain is not flat.

Gravity opposes the cyclist's efforts on uphills and assists on downhills, again in proportion to weight. Unlike, say, a tennis ball tossed before a serve, the bicycle never moves absolutely vertically. The portion of gravity that most interests us is just the vector component in line with the

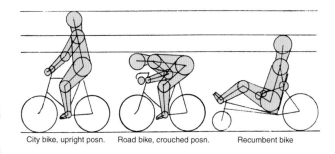

City bike, upright posn.   Road bike, crouched posn.   Recumbent bike

Above: Fig. 3.6. Not all recumbents necessarily have a smaller frontal area than a road bike, depending on the rider's position.

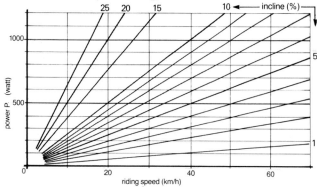

Left: Fig. 3.7. Riding uphill at various speeds and gradients, with an example of the resulting reaction forces that must be overcome by the rider.

motion of the bicycle. Only a fraction of the full acceleration due to gravity affects that motion, and that fraction is proportional to the steepness of the grade the bicycle is climbing or descending.

FRICTION RESISTANCE

Friction has many sources. The chain rubs against the gear teeth, and its individual links and bushings rub against each other and against the chain lubricant. In the pedals, bottom bracket, hubs, headset, and freewheel, bearings rub against each other, their lubricant, and the bearing races that confine them.

Even the wheels, frame, axles, crankarms, and other parts deform, causing their molecules to collide, creating heat, just as rubbing two sticks together does. While the heat produced is not enough to start a fire, it is nonetheless energy that is not being used for moving the bicycle forward. This is what we have labeled "friction resistance" in the following discussion.

On a well-lubricated, well-adjusted quality bicycle, friction resistance is almost insignificant compared to aerodynamic drag and tire rolling resistance. Yet, if you've ever ridden an old American cruiser after some years of neglect, you'll know that it can be quite significant. Here

are the factors that keep it to a minimum.

❏ Selecting high-quality components for all moving parts, especially hubs, pedals, crankset, chain, and internal gear hub (where used): Especially in these parts, it matters whether your bike is equipped with high-quality moving parts or with cheap knockoffs.

❏ Regular cleaning, adjustment, and lubrication of all moving parts.

For purposes of this discussion, we will express friction resistance as a simple multiplier called "friction factor." For a theoretical bicycle without any friction losses, the friction factor would be 1 (or 100%), and for a poorly maintained low-quality bike it may be as low as 0.7 (or 70%). For a well-maintained, but not brand new, quality bike it is probably around 0.92, or 92%.

Above and right: Figs. 3.8 and 3.9. Things like a dirty, tight chain and worn bearing races can significantly increase a bicycle's overall friction resistance.

INERTIA

The discussion so far has dealt only with the forces needed to achieve a given speed. But bringing the bicycle up to speed, or changing its speed, is another issue altogether. Newton's second law states that acceleration is in proportion to, and in the direction of, the force applied. Most important in any discussion of acceleration (or for that matter deceleration, which is the same as negative acceleration) is that the force needed to accelerate is proportional to the mass of the object—bike and rider in our case. A 70 kg rider on a 20 kg bike (90 kg total) needs 12.5% more force to accelerate than the same rider on a 10 kg bike (80 kg total).

However, some parts of the bicycle don't only have to be moved in the direction of travel, but around as well. In particular the wheels, which form a significant "rotating mass," greatly affect how easy it is to accelerate the bike up to speed. In addition to accelerating the bike forward, you also have to

accelerate the wheels (and other rotating parts) in their respective circles of rotation. The energy needed to make those wheels rotate does not come free of charge.

The "moment of inertia" is a measure of its resistance to a change in angular velocity. It depends not only on the object's mass, but also on the distribution of that mass relative to the axis of rotation. If the rotating object is comprised of individual parts, the moment of inertia of the total object is the sum of the moments of the individual parts. For each part, the moment of inertia is the product of its mass and the square of the radius of gyration, that is, its distance from the axis of the whole object.

The bicycle wheel consists of several parts that rotate about a stationary axle: hub shell, freewheel (on the rear wheel), spokes and nipples, rim, tire and inner tube with valve, and probably a protective rim strip. The rim may have a mass of 0.45 kg and be situated 0.308 m from the center of the axle; its contribution to the moment of inertia would therefore be 0.45 x 0.308 x 0.308 = 0.0427 kg-m². All the spokes of one wheel together may have a mass of 0.23 kg, roughly half the rim's mass, but the center of each spoke is only about half the rim's distance from the axis, say 0.152 m. The contribution of the spokes to the moment of inertia is therefore only about 0.0053 kg-m², roughly

one-eighth that of the rim. The moments for the remaining parts are calculated the same way, and summed to obtain the moment of inertia of the entire wheel.

FORCE EQUATIONS

Transforming the above verbiage into mathematics, the following are the equations for the forces acting on the bicycle, other than the rider's pedaling. For rolling resistance, it is:

$$F_R = g\ m\ C_R\ C_F$$

And for gravity:

$$F_G = g\ m\ \%G/100$$

where:

F_R The force of rolling resistance

F_G The force of gravity (the force in line with the bicycle's motion; not the force pressing it onto the ground)

g   The acceleration due to gravity

m   The mass of the rider and bicycle

C_R The coefficient of tire rolling resistance

C_F The coefficient of friction, or "efficiency" of the bicycle

%G The grade (or gradient) of the slope, expressed in percent, which is why it must be divided by 100.

For aerodynamic drag, the formula is:

$$F_D = 0.5 * C_D * \rho * v_a^2 * A$$

where:

F_D The drag force, in N

C_D The coefficient of aerodynamic drag

ρ This is the Greek letter rho, which stands for the air density, in kg/m³

V_a The airspeed, in m/s

A   The frontal area, in m²

Because the terms in these equations are expressed in mks units, the forces all come out in N (newtons). To express it in non-metric units, the equations also need some conversion factors.

Let's take some examples. For a recreational rider on a paved surface, the coefficient of tire rolling resistance may be about 0.005, and the coefficient of friction 0.9. Suppose the rider weighs 175 pounds and his bike weighs 25 pounds. First, express the quantities in mks: total mass, (175 + 25) * 0.454 kg per pound = 90.8 kg (see the Glossary for this and other unit conversion factors). Rolling resistance is therefore 9.8 m/s² * 90.8 kg * 0.0045 = 4.0 kg-m/s² or N. At one newton per 0.2249 pounds, or about 0.90 pounds of force pushing backward on the bicycle.

On level ground, computing the force due to gravity is trivial: it is zero, because the grade is zero. Up (or down) a 2% grade, one that rises (or drops) 2 feet vertically for every 100 horizontally, the force of gravity is 9.8 * 90.8 * 2/100 or 17.8 N (about 4 lbs) pushing backward (or forward in the case of a downslope). It is no surprise that even on a fairly easy grade, this force is a lot greater than rolling resistance. Suppose this rider has his hands atop the bars and his arms are straight, not bent at the elbows. His frontal area is then about 0.40 m² (4.3 square feet), his drag coefficient about 1.0. Typical air density is 1.2 kg/m³. Suppose the bicycle is moving at 15 miles per hour into still air, that is 6.71 m/s (meter per second). Aerodynamic drag is therefore 0.5 * 1.0 * 1.2 * 6.71 * 6.71 * 0.40 = 10.8 N, or about 2.4 pounds.

The total forces acting on the bicycle, i.e., the forces that the

TORQUE

Torque is the product of two factors: a tangential force that produces rotation, and the distance between the point at which that force is applied and the axis of rotation. In the mks system, torque is measured in mN (meter-newton).

Just as in the linear world force is the product of mass and acceleration, in the rotational world the analogous torque is the product of moment of inertia and angular acceleration. If an object with a moment of inertia of 0.8 kg-m² is accelerated 9 radians per second per second, the torque producing that angular acceleration must be 0.72 kg-m²/s², or (because a newton is a kg-m/s²) 0.72 meter-newton.

Under any normal conditions, a bicycle wheel is firmly in contact with the ground. Its angular acceleration is precisely determined by the linear acceleration of the entire bicycle, and vice versa. An angular acceleration of 2 π radians per second per second is the same as 1 revolution per second squared. One revolution in linear terms is the circumference of the circle, or 2 π times the radius. So for a bicycle wheel, linear acceleration equals angular acceleration times the radius of the wheel, or angular acceleration equals linear acceleration divided by the radius of the wheel.

Because bicycles occasionally have wheels of different sizes and often have wheels with different moments of inertia, we had better use a subscript to distinguish between the two wheels of a bike. Let the subscript i stand for either f (for the front wheel) or r (for the rear wheel). If L_i is the torque on wheel i, I_i is wheel i's moment of inertia, r_i is wheel i's radius, and a is the linear acceleration:

$$L_i = I_i \, a/r_i$$

Thus, because torque is force times radius:

$$F_i \, r_i = I_i \, a/r_i$$

$$F_i = I_i \, a/r_i^2$$

Call F (with no subscript) the total force acting on the bike, not only from the forces due to acceleration of its two wheels, but from aerodynamic drag, rolling resistance, gravity, braking, and pedaling. Then if m is the mass of the bike and rider:

$$F = m \, a + (I_f \, a/r_f^2) + (I_r \, a/r_r^2)$$

$$F = (m + I_f \, / \, r_f^2 + I_r \, / \, r_r^2) \, a$$

With the above equation, you can calculate the effect that the moments of inertia and radii of the wheels have upon the bicycle's acceleration. (This formula ignores the forces due to angular acceleration of the feet, pedals, crankset, chain, and jockey wheels, which are small to negligible.)

rider's pedaling has to counter, are therefore 4.0 + 0 + 10.8 = 14.8 N on level ground; 4.0 + 17.8 + 10.8 = 32.6 N up the 2% grade; and 4.0 − 17.8 + 10.8 = −3.0 N down the 2% grade. The last one has a negative sign: gravity offsets the drag forces and would move the bike forward even if the rider doesn't pedal.

POWER

Although the forces on the bicycle and rider are important, power is even more so. You can change the amount of force you apply to the pedals whenever you like, just by changing gears. At any speed, the force can be tailored to suit your preferences and riding style. But you have much less freedom regarding the power that is needed to move

the bike along. As long as conditions stay the same—the same total force from rolling resistance, gravity, and aerodynamic drag—the same power output is needed in order to maintain the same speed.

As mentioned before, power is the rate of doing work. An equivalent definition is that power is the product of the force applied to a body and the velocity of that body:

power = force * velocity

If the force is expressed in N and the velocity in m/s, the power will be expressed in W (watt). Working with non-metric units again requires multiplying by some conversion factor.

Both force and velocity imply a direction: they are vector quantities. If we are talking about the

power needed to keep a bicycle moving, the direction is of course the direction along the bicycle's path of motion, which is also the way we have already defined the forces on the bicycle.

A certain fraction of the power the rider applies to the bicycle at a particular speed goes toward offsetting each of the various forces. To counter rolling resistance, for example, the power needed is the force of rolling resistance times the speed of the bicycle. To counter an uphill slope, if any, the power needed is the force of gravity in line with the bicycle's motion times the speed of the bicycle. A downhill slope is almost as easy to understand. Power is again involved, and it is still force times velocity, but this time the amount is negative, because the force of gravity on a downhill is negative. So on

MOMENT OF INERTIA

The moment of inertia of a rotating object is a measure of its resistance to a change in its angular velocity. It depends not only on the object's mass, but on the distribution of that mass relative to the axis of rotation. If the rotating object is comprised of individual parts, the moment of inertia of the total object is the sum of the moments of the individual parts. For each part, the moment of inertia is the product of its mass and the square of the radius of gyration,

that is, its distance from the axis of the whole object.

For example, a bicycle wheel consists of several parts that rotate about a stationary axle: the hub shell, the freewheel (if it is a rear wheel on a derailleur bicycle), spokes and nipples or possibly a solid disc, a rim, a tire, and (if it is a clincher wheel) a tube and probably a protective rim strip. The rim may have a mass of 0.45 kg and be situated 0.308 m from the center of the axle; its contribution to the moment of inertia would therefore be 0.45 x 0.308

x 0.308 or 0.0427 kg-m². All the spokes of one wheel together may have a mass of 0.23 kg, roughly half the rim's mass, but the center of each spoke is only about half the rim's distance from the axis, say 0.152 m. The contribution of the spokes to the moment of inertia is therefore only about 0.0053 kg-m², roughly one-eighth that of the rim. The moments for the remaining parts are calculated in the same way and summed to obtain the moment of inertia of the entire wheel.

a downhill, the rider in effect gets a credit, an amount that can be subtracted from the total power required. Finally, aerodynamic drag can also be positive or negative, but here the velocity that matters is not the speed of the bicycle relative to the ground but the speed relative to the air. The power needed to offset motion through the air is the force of aerodynamic drag times relative air speed.

Add those three quantities—the power needed to offset rolling resistance, the power needed to offset gravity, and the power needed to offset aerodynamic drag—and you have the total power you need to apply in order to maintain your speed under constant conditions. If conditions change—your tire loses air, the slope gets steeper, you change to a tucked position, the headwind picks up, or you decide to go faster or slower—then the power output will also change. But when conditions are stable, speed and power are locked together with an equation:

$$P = (F_R + F_G) * v_g + F_D * v_a$$

In this equation, P is power; the forces F_R, F_G, and F_D are rolling resistance, the force of gravity, and aerodynamic drag respectively, just as we defined them earlier; and v_g and v_a are ground speed and airspeed respectively.

Let's use the same examples we did above. The rolling resistance was 4.0 N. On level ground, the force of gravity was 0; on the 2% slope it was 17.8 N or –17.8 N depending on whether the bike was going up or down the slope. Aerodynamic drag was 10.8 N. The bike was moving 15 mph into still air, so both ground speed and airspeed were 6.71 m/s. Total power needed to maintain that speed on level ground is (4.0 + 0) * 6.71 + 10.8 * 6.71 = 99 W. Up and down the slope the corresponding power levels needed are 219 W and –20 W respectively. Except perhaps with a track bike, it is difficult to apply a negative 20 W pedaling; it looks like either speed will be increasing, or an additional force—braking—will have to be applied to maintain a constant speed.

It is important for the cyclist to remember that it is *power* that is locked together with speed, not merely *force*. Many cyclists seem to think that to achieve a higher speed, they must push harder on the pedals. Increased force certainly does increase power, as long as the cadence doesn't drop; but it is equally effective, and easier on the knees, to increase power by adopting a faster cadence with no increase in force. Most effective of all is to be able to apply a high force at a high cadence: that is how high power is developed.

ACCELERATION

The elapsed time, distance covered, and speed attained by an accelerating bike involve more complicated calculations than merely applying "F = m * a"; the reason is a physical property known as moment of inertia, which is explained in the sidebar on page 38. In addition, air resistance is always a major factor for a bicycle, and it varies a great deal as speed changes.

Right: Fig. 3.10. Energy consumption diagram, comparing cycling with walking and running (from Wilson, *Bicycling Science*).

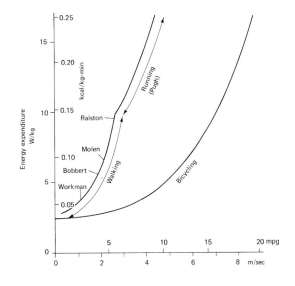

ENERGY

Once you know how much power is being applied, it is easy to calculate energy expended (or work done):

$$E = P * t$$

Where:

E = energy, or work;

P = power;

t = elapsed time.

This is another equation that will be used often, but one so easy that you won't need a computer program. In the way the equation is used here, P will be constant throughout the time interval, but the equation is equally valid if power varies and P is the average value of power during the time interval t. If P is in watts and t in seconds, E will be in joules. Like power, energy is a scalar, not a vector.

BICYCLE WEIGHT

The first question many cyclists ask about any bicycle is "how heavy?" Yes, the effect of the bicycle's weight is significant enough to be noticed. There are similar looking bikes that vary in weight between 8 kg (17.6 lbs) and 14 kg (30.8 lbs), and there are even ridden bikes out there that weigh more than 20 kg (44 lbs). You may wonder how they can make one bike so much lighter than another?

The use of aluminum versus steel for the frame doesn't even get close to explaining the difference. A quality steel frame weighs around 1,400 g (about 3 lbs.), while a similarly dimensioned, equally strong and stiff aluminum frame will be a mere 200 g lighter than that, and even the use of magnesium, titanium, and carbon-fiber as frame materials don't achieve more than minor weight savings beyond that.

The best answer is probably "a little bit here and a little bit there," while a bit of cheating also helps. First the latter point: don't believe everything you

read. Claimed weights are not always for complete bikes (almost always, they forget to include things like the pedals and the saddle). In addition, the low weight is likely to apply only to the smallest size available.

As for honest weight savings, little bits here and there can add up to significant weight savings. 300 g on the frame, another 300 g on the wheels, 200 g on the tires, and 200 g on the crankset, and presto, you've reduced the bike's weight by one kg (2.2 lbs.). A typical bicycle consists of over 1,000 bits and pieces, and saving just a few grams on each of those, can add up to much less overall weight.

There are, however, two downsides to many of these weight savings: strength and cost. Often, the lighter weight is achieved by making parts less substantial, and consequently weaker. And as for cost…, once you get below about 10 kg (22 lbs.), additional weight savings can increase the price of the bike exponentially. It takes an estimated $1,500 for the first kg in reduction, $3,000 for the next kg, and even more beyond that.

Left: Fig. 3.11. Weight matters: Like most other major bicycle brands these days, Trek offers a sub-9 kg bike. This is their Madone 6.9, equipped with almost every weight-saving component available.

4 THE CYCLIST IN MOTION

WE'VE SEEN in the preceding chapter why the combination of bike and rider is such an energy-efficient mode of transport. That chapter dealt primarily with the mechanical aspects of the bicycle, whereas in this chapter we'll take a closer look at the human side of the equation. Simply put, what it takes to ride a bicycle.

POWER GENERATION

The human body is constantly producing energy. Even at rest, enough energy is being produced to keep the body at a temperature of about 36.8 degrees C, and to keep the heart pumping blood, the lungs pumping air, and the brain active to control what's going on. Any physical movement requires increased energy output, whether it is walking, talking, or cycling.

In effect, the body is a kind of fuel cell, producing energy out of the nutrients, the air, and the sunlight it takes in. There are actually three distinct mechanisms of producing energy:

❏ The ATP-CP system, which produces very high power, but only for a maximum of about 10 seconds duration.

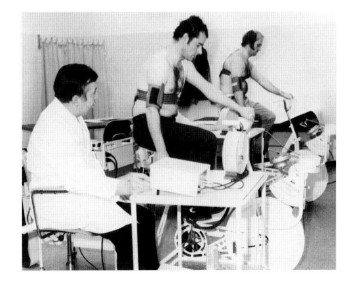

Right: Fig. 4.1. Tour de France riders being subjected to ergometer testing in a sports physiology laboratory.

❑ The lactic-acid cycle, or anaerobic metabolism, which can produce relatively high power output for a duration of 30 to 120 seconds.

❑ The oxygen cycle, or aerobic system, which can produce steady long-duration power output.

In practice, the first two are usually grouped together and

Above: Fig. 4.2. Special devices like this Victor Pedal Power Meter can be used to measure the force on the pedal, and by extension, taking into account the pedaling rate, the rider's output.

Below: Fig. 4.3. Another such device is the Cyclops Powertap, which measures the load on the rear hub.

referred to as anaerobic, while the third system is referred to as aerobic metabolism.

Aerobic is the metabolism that sustains the body at rest and when modest physical output is required. It is sustained entirely by the oxygen that is released through breathing and the energy stored in the blood in the form of glycogen. This energy-generating system can be maintained almost indefinitely, but it is modest in output: for most people it can provide no more than about 100 W (watts), or about 0.13 hp (horsepower). Racing cyclists typically have

"STANDARD" BIKE AND RIDER

People of course vary in size and riding styles, and bikes vary somewhat, too. For our discussion, it makes sense to pick one standard to use in all examples. Somewhat arbitrarily, our standard rider will be a male of average size, dressed in usual racing style clothing, in a full racing crouch upon a more-or-less standard road bike.

For the record, these conditions mean that the coefficient of tire rolling resistance 0.0033, coefficient of friction 0.92, and coefficient of aerodynamic drag 0.88 respectively, that the frontal area is 0.36 square meters, and that he and the bike together have a mass of 90 kg (that is, they weigh about 198 pounds).

raised that to twice that figure through training and conditioning.

The anaerobic metabolism allows for short-duration high-power-output. It is much less efficient than the anaerobic system, but it is what you use in a quick sprint to win a race, or perhaps to get out of the way of an accident about to happen.

How much power can be generated anaerobically varies widely for individual cyclists, largely determined by muscle fiber type and training.

Although the aerobic metabolism can be maintained for a

This may be a little higher than the mass of a world-class athlete on a state-of-the-art bike, but probably more representative of typical American male performance-oriented cyclists. Of course the data will differ for a different sort of rider, but adopting this standard rider will usually not alter the general conclusions. We will try to point out the exceptions when it does, and you may of course redo the calculations with data more closely representing yourself.

The air our rider passes through is also reasonably standard: dry, 20° C (68° F), at sea level: density 1.20 kg/m^3, and we assume the local acceleration due to gravity is more typical of the United States at 9.80 m/s^2.

long time, it is not infinite either, because it is limited to the amount of glycogen that can be stored in the blood. For most riders, it is depleted after about 200 km, or 125 miles of riding.

When all the glycogen is gone, the body turns to FFAs, or free fatty acids, using the energy stored in the form of body fat. It is possible through appropriate

training (and perhaps with the help of caffeine) to condition the body to call on FFAs earlier, so that the total duration over which energy is available can be extended beyond that 200 km point. It is also the only form of exercise that can be used for weight control, because it actually consumes some body fat.

Riders in stage races, such as the Tour de France, expend more energy each day than the number of calories they can consume, so they rely on the FFA process to some extent. As a

Right: Fig. 4.5. Early attempts at scientific evaluation of cyclists' performance and physical characteristics often included chest X-rays, which at the time (1909) were presumed to be harmless.

result, they often lose significant weight during those three weeks in the saddle.

OXYGEN AND POWER OUTPUT

The human fuel cell has an efficiency of about 25%, which is similar to that of other common types of engines. The amount of energy produced beyond the basic minimum to keep the body functioning can be correlated to the amount of oxygen

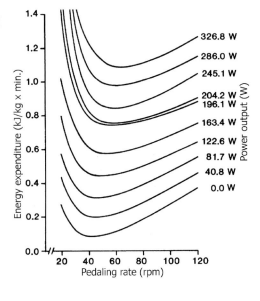

Above: Fig. 4.4. 1980s tests conducted at the Japan Bicycle Research Center were amongst the first to corroborate performance with power output, as measured by the rider's Oxygen consumption, or $\dot{V}O_2$.

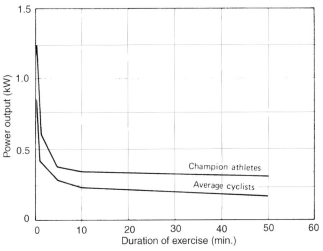

Left: Fig. 4.6. Overall possible output level depends on the duration of the exercise, and varies greatly by rider fitness.

Right: Fig. 4.7. Pedaling rate and output level. The highest outputs are achieved at high pedaling rates.

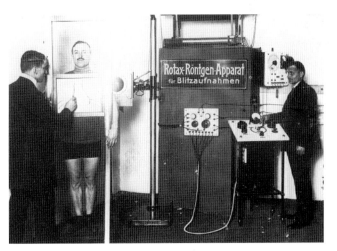

EFFICIENCY OF THE HUMAN BODY

Human efficiency can be defined as the amount of energy the human body consumes compared to the amount of useful work it performs. It is well known that the bodies of athletes operate at a higher efficiency than those of non-athletes. As used in nutrition, a Calorie (properly called a kilocalorie) is a unit of energy equal to 4,186.8 joules. If the human body were 100% efficient, a person could eat a particle of food with a nutritional value of one Calorie and subsequently burn it up doing 4,186.8 joules of work. For example, a typical male does that much work pedaling at 32 km/h (20 mph) on a level windless road (which requires a power level of 160 watts) for a little over 26 seconds.

Alas, the human body is nowhere near 100% efficient. The average fit person may have a body that operates at 24% efficiency, which means he would need to consume a little over 4 Calories to perform the above task. Touring cyclists tested at power outputs in the 75– 220 watt range routinely show efficiencies of about 27%. An athlete at the apex of conditioning may increase his body's efficiency to 30%; a couch potato could well operate at under 10%, if he operates at all.

Just as a body has a particular mass, a body is only so efficient, and there is little or nothing one can do to improve that efficiency in the short term. However, that a body is capable of, say, 24% efficiency does not imply that it is actually operating at that level. For example, if you are thrashing about, attempting to pedal at 200 rpm in a very low gear, you are consuming a lot of energy compared to the effect it has on your progress. Likewise, if you are in a high gear attempting to climb a steep hill, your cadence will falter and efficiency will plummet. Somewhere in between there is a range of cadences at which efficiency is about as high as it can be; above or below that range, efficiency drops off as some of the pedaling force is wasted.

You cannot necessarily develop the same amount of power throughout that maximum-efficiency range. Your power at 120 rpm may be just as high as at 80 rpm, but your efficiency may be below par, or your power at 50 rpm may be 10% down but your efficiency may still be just as high. We know that for most cyclists, the cadence range allowing peak (or near-peak) efficiency is fairly wide, and that training can usually extend that range to higher cadences. It is obviously difficult to measure the efficiency of a particular cyclist's body at a particular cadence, though it has

been done. In one such study the cadence at which racing cyclists were most efficient was reported to be 60 to 70 rpm, though possibly to the detriment of their knee joints, leg muscles, and endurance.

Many cyclists feel they obtain a better workout by pedaling slowly with a relatively high pedaling force than they do by spinning the pedals against little resistance. Is that true? It depends on what "better" means, of course. If the idea is merely to expend more energy, then efficiency is hardly a consideration. Expending more energy does not seem to be what they have in mind; it is more likely they are trying to find a shortcut, to obtain some benefit without expending more effort than necessary.

It may be better to ask what the goal of the workout is. Is it to build power, to be able to go faster? (It usually is.) If so, then does a lower cadence increase the cyclist's speed, or equivalently, does shifting to a lower gear and faster cadence slow the cyclist down? No, it probably doesn't—try it yourself. Therefore the energy being expended is practically the same either way, and neither cadence is preferable to the other from the standpoint of a total body workout. The sure way to expend more energy and obtain a better workout is obvious: speed up.

consumed. One liter of oxygen requires 5 liters of air, because air contains only about 20% oxygen. One liter of oxygen must be absorbed per minute to produce about 280 W of energy. But because the human fuel cell has a 25% efficiency, that one liter per minute only provides 70 W of external energy.

This knowledge makes it possible to measure the human output by the amount of oxygen consumed by the cyclist. The energy expended by the cyclist can be measured based on the amount of oxygen consumed, or burned, during a set period of time, and can be converted to a standard unit of energy measurement, such as kJ/kg * min. by dividing the measured value by the subject's body mass in kg.

Clearly, the human body's ability to generate power is limited by its capacity to absorb oxygen, and one objective of training is to increase that ability, measured as lung capacity. Oxygen absorption decreases with age, typically down to about half of what it was at age 20 by the time age 80 is reached. However, continued training can prevent much of this decrease.

POWER, SPEED, AND EFFICIENCY

Back in the 1950s, a couple of German sports physiologists got the idea to establish what would be the most efficient pedaling rate. They put some subjects (who were not trained racing cyclists) on cycling ergometers (home trainers equipped with

EFFICIENCY OF THE HUMAN BODY (CONTINUED)

It is possible to distribute the effort of a workout unevenly among different muscle groups, which may be what some cyclists are thinking when they feel that low cadences give their legs a better workout, compared to… compared to what? The sets of muscles used in pedaling at different cadences are the same, unless the cyclist radically alters his position or the adjustment of the bicycle. The perceived effect is quite different, of course. It may help to remember a trick some time-trialists use to determine what would be a proper cadence. If the cadence is too high, the lungs will start to hurt before the legs do; if the cadence is too low, the legs begin to hurt first. This gives only a rough guide, because at the power required to be competitive in a time trial, both the lungs and legs will simultaneously be screaming for relief, even for some time after the rider stops pedaling. In any case, there is no evidence to suggest that low cadences provide a better workout, either for the body as a whole or for the muscles used in pedaling. Even if the cyclist is one of those whose efficiency is somewhat higher at relatively low cadences, there is no reason to suppose that a workout will be "better" at those cadences as well.

Other factors may also affect efficiency. For example, if it is especially cold or hot, more than usual of the body's energy will probably be diverted to maintaining the normal body temperature, leaving less for output. A cyclist who has not yet warmed up his muscles prior to intensive activity is undoubtedly sub-par in efficiency.

Similarly, a cyclist whose bike does not fit perfectly may waste energy sitting up, stretching, and stopping, may be distracted by discomfort, or may simply be unable to apply power well. Perhaps one who is comfortable expending 100 watt of power may operate more efficiently at that output than when forced to crank out 300 watt; but perhaps more likely, the higher output level may be inherently more efficient if the body spends relatively little energy on non-productive efforts, such as digestion and circulation, and more on propelling the bike.

calibrated measuring equipment) and told them to pedal away at different rates, each time measuring the volume of oxygen they consumed per minute, and translating that figure into energy input, which they compared with the measured energy output on the ergometer.

They concluded that the highest energy efficiency was reached at a pedaling rate of around 35–45 RPM. They published their results, and with great enthusiasm declared that racing cyclists should use much higher gears and pedal much more slowly than was (and still is) the practice. Similar tests were conducted in Japan during the

1970s, and with similar, though slightly higher results (40–50 RPM).

What's wrong with that picture? Simply put, you don't win bicycle races with efficiency but with speed. Nobody expects to win a Formula One race in a car with a gas-saver engine. And at higher speeds, the low pedaling rates translated into such high forces (due to the high gears required), that the cyclists would not be able to deliver.

Meanwhile, there is enough evidence to suggest that most riders can perform at a higher speed for a longer time at pedaling rates in the range of 80–120 RPM. One of the objectives of training is to raise the pedaling rate a rider can sustain. Although at the same time the muscles should also be developed to deliver more force, the higher pedaling rates turn out to be key to high performance.

In fact, even if speed is not the only objective, higher pedaling rates turn out to be

favorable. Touring cyclists find that "spinning" at a higher cadence in a lowish gear can be maintained over a longer period, and distance, than when maintaining a low cadence to maximize presumed efficiency. After all, it is not only lung capacity that limits a cyclist's output. The muscle force that can be delivered has its limits as well.

One of the first research projects that has looked at pedaling rate in conjunction with output was published in 1977 and it is still valid today (see Fig. 4.7). Although again the highest overall efficiency was reached at 40-60 RPM, depending on output level, the overall output increased beyond that point, reaching a maximum at 120 RPM, which was the maximum pedaling rate that could be maintained by the test subjects (trained bicycle racers, this time).

Above: Fig. 4.8. Don't be fooled by the somewhat archaic looking bike in this picture from Nijmegen University, in the Netherlands. Taking the tests out of the laboratory this way allows for more realistic measuring of critical factors like oxygen consumption.

Right: Fig. 4.9. Power output and how long it can be maintained. These are typical sample curves with a simple message: if you start out too fast, you won't be able to continue.

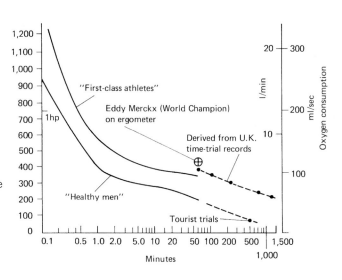

5
MATERIALS FOR BICYCLE CONSTRUCTION

BICYCLES AND THEIR COMPONENTS have been made from a wide variety of materials. Today steel and aluminum alloys may be the materials which first come to mind, but titanium, carbon-fiber, various plastics, rubber, leather, and occasionally other materials are also used.

MATERIALS OVERVIEW

When discussing the choice of materials, it is important to distinguish between the bicycle's frame and its various other components. The first bicycles—the draisines and hobby horses of the early 19th century—were made largely of wood, both for the frame and other parts. But gradually more and more parts were replaced by iron and other metals. By the early 1870s, the high-wheel was almost entirely made of steel.

Above and right: Figs. 5.1 and 5.2. Modern bicycles and components use materials ranging from steel tubing (right) to carbon-fiber (above), and beyond. The right choice of materials can reduce the bicycle's weight without compromising its strength.

METALS AND THEIR ALLOYS

Iron, aluminum, copper, and titanium are all metals, and they vary much in their properties, making the one more suitable for certain components than others. However, none of these metals in their pure state exhibits all the qualities the engineer needs. For

that reason, these pure metals are mixed with other components, usually other metals or minerals. When any metal is thus combined with one or more other element, the resulting material is referred to as an alloy.

Thus, steel is an alloy of iron and a small percentage of carbon and possibly other elements. Compared with pure iron, steels with these additional ingredients are much stronger, but may also have other properties—for example, greater or lesser resilience, brittleness, and susceptibility to rust—which may or may not be desirable in a particular application.

There is some confusion about the use of the term *alloy*, most people, including many in the bike trade, thinking all alloys are made with aluminum. In reality, essentially all metals used in bicycle construction are some form of alloy, be it simple steel (iron with a little carbon), chrome-moly steel (iron with a little carbon, chromium, and molybdenum), aluminum alloy, or what-have-you. The same goes for what's referred to as titanium, which in practice is invariably a titanium alloy.

The terminology used by manufacturers is often less than accurate. One major bicycle manufacturer claims to have "Scandium" tubes. Well, scandium is a rather rare metal that is used in a tiny fraction of a percentage point to minimize the loss of strength and resilience of aluminum when welded. Those tubes aren't made of scandium, but of an aluminum alloy with just a tiny bit of scandium.

OTHER MATERIALS

The other material frequently used for bicycle frame construction is carbon, or more accurately carbon-fiber composite. For other components, other materials are also used, ranging from leather and natural rubber to various plastics and composites, and even wood and bamboo sometimes find application on certain parts.

MATERIALS PROPERTIES

In this context, the word "quality" should be understood to mean "characteristics," rather than referring to relative superiority. The most important materials qualities to be discussed here are the following:

❏ *density* (how heavy?)

❏ *tensile strength* (how strong?)

❏ *elasticity* (how stiff?)

❏ *hardness* (as the name implies)

❏ *fatigue strength* (how resistant to load variations)

TABLE 3.1. SUMMARY OF MATERIALS PROPERTIES

Material	Specific Density (g/cm³)	Tensile Yield Strength (N/mm²	Strength to Weight Ratio ([N/mm²] / [g/cm³])	Modulus of Elasticity (N/mm²)	Brinell hardness
Carbon steel	7.8	250–360	47	200,000	100
Chrome-moly steel	7.8	1,200–3,000	158–395	200,000	200–580
Aluminum (pure)	2.7	40	15	70,000	23
Aluminum alloy	2.7	200–600	74–222	70,000	50–105
Titanium (pure)	4.7	280	60	120,000	N/A
Titanium alloy	4.7	400–1,100	85–234	120,000	N/A
Magnesium alloy	1.7	100–350	59–206	47,500	47–78
Carbon-fiber	1.5–2.0	150–1,300	100–867	50,000–200,000	N/A

WEIGHT AND DENSITY

Specific density is a measure of how much mass a standard size piece of a material has, or, more popularly expressed, how heavy it is. It is expressed in g/cm^3. Water is the standard, at $1 \ g/cm^3$. Wood and bamboo have densities of around $1 \ g/cm^3$, aluminum and its alloys weigh in at $2.7 \ g/cm^3$, while steel has a density of around $7.6 \ g/cm^3$—regardless whether it is simple carbon steel or some expensive alloy.

So, does that mean that a steel bike frame weighs 3 times as much as one made of aluminum alloy, or 7 times as much as one made of wood? No, of course not, because steel is so much stronger than those other materials that it was actually introduced to save weight on the earliest (wooden) draisines and velocipedes. The same goes for aluminum: although the material has a lower density than steel, it is also less strong, so an aluminum bicycle frame is not necessarily lighter than one made of steel.

Titanium is about 35% lighter than steel, and, depending on its specific alloy and temper, nearly as strong. Thus, it is possible to make titanium frames and other parts that are as strong as those made of steel—but at a lower weight.

Most commonly used on quality bikes these days is aluminum, both for frames and components. Aluminum's density is approx one third of that of steel, but its strength, again depending on alloy and handling factors, is also only about a third of that of steel. That it is possible to make

CONVERTING UNITS OF DENSITY, STRENGTH, AND STIFFNESS

In this discussion we use metric units, not only for lengths and forces (and weights), but also for compound units such as those for density, strength, and stiffness.

The unit for *density* ("specific weight" in somewhat inaccurate popular parlance) is gram per cubic centimeter, or g/cm^3.

To convert to or from $lbs./in.^3$, multiply the metric figure by 1.42.

The unit for *strength* is newtons per square millimeter, or N/mm^2. To convert to psi ($lbs./in.^2$), multiply the metric figure by 145.

The unit for *modulus of elasticity* is Nm/mm^3, which can also be expressed in N/mm^2. To convert to psi (lbs. per square inch), again multiply the metric figure by 145.

STRENGTH AND HARDNESS

As mentioned elsewhere, for any given material, there is a correlation between hardness and strength. Thus, hardness can be used for a quick estimate of a material's strength.

That only goes for the same material under various conditions, such as e.g. a particular alloy before and after welding, stress-relieving, tempering, or cold-working. You can't use it to compare different alloys.

There is more to this subject matter, because for some purposes, local hardness is important in its own right. Thus, any part subjected to friction, such as ball bearings, sprockets, and chains, should be as hard as possible to minimize wear and friction losses. Unfortunately, very hard often also means very brittle, and you don't want the part to break up. For that reason, it is often better to make the surface harder than the interior of the part through some form of surface treatment process.

For steel parts, this can be done by what's referred to as nitriding, whereas for aluminum and titanium parts, the technique used is hard-anodizing. The depth to which these processes are carried out is important, to make sure the hard layer does not wear off too soon on the one hand, or the entire part does not become too brittle on the other.

an aluminum frame lighter than a steel one is owed to certain dimensioning and forming tricks that will be described below.

Although aluminum is light, there are lighter metals, some of which have also been used for bicycle frames. Magnesium and beryllium both have a density of approx. 1.8. And here too, you won't find either of these metals used any other way than alloyed with other metals.

Carbon-fiber is even lighter than magnesium, and about as strong as titanium alloy. Since carbon is highly resistant to fatigue loading, being able to withstand many more cycles of load

variations, it lends itself for making lightweight components suitable for applications that are subject to vibrations. Unfortunately, the material does have other disadvantages, mainly its limited impact resistance.

STRENGTH

Enter the characteristic called tensile strength. It is a measure of how much force can be applied to a standard piece of material before it breaks. It's established by loading a rod with a 1 mm square section until it breaks, and it is measured in

N/mm^2, where the N stands for newtons. You only need to know that the higher the number, the greater the strength of the material in question.

By the time the ultimate tensile strength is reached, the material is seriously deformed. Therefore, more important than this ultimate tensile strength is what is referred to as (tensile) yield strength: to stress beyond which the material gets permanently deformed. Designing to the limit of a material's ultimate yield strength instead of its yield strength would mean the bicycle may get badly bent out of shape, though it may not break.

STRENGTH-TO-WEIGHT RATIO

As mentioned before, a lighter material does not necessarily translate into a similarly lighter bike. What matters is how much weight of the material is needed for the same required strength.

The fourth column in Table 3.1 provides some insight into this issue. Thus, though aluminum weighs about a third of what steel weighs, its strength is also only about a third, so most types of aluminum alloys finish up with about the same strength-to-weight ratio as steel alloys: to make an equally strong aluminum part, you end up with about the same weight as its steel equivalent.

More promising in this respect, as can be learned from the table, are titanium and carbon, both of which have higher strength-to-weight ratios than either steel or aluminum.

There is another factor, though, stiffness-to-strength ratio, which will be covered in more detail in a sidebar on page

51. The illustration below, from a Reynolds Tubing catalogue, demonstrates that it is actually possible to make an equally strong and stiff frame using (special) steel tubing than any aluminum, magnesium, or even titanium tubing. (Carbon is not included in this comparison, but it, too, has its limitations.)

Fig. 5.3. Strength-to-weight and stiffness-to-weight ratios for various frame materials as offered by Reynolds Tubing.

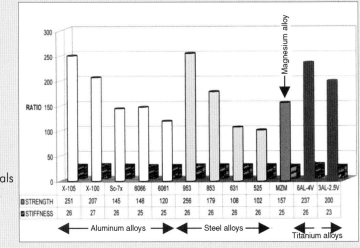

	X-105	X-100	Sc-7x	6066	6061	953	853	631	525	MZM	6AL-4V	3AL-2.5V
STRENGTH	251	207	145	148	120	256	179	108	102	157	237	200
STIFFNESS	26	27	26	25	25	26	26	26	26	25	26	23

Aluminum alloys ← → ← Steel alloys → ← Titanium alloys

Pure iron has a tensile yield strength of around 100 N/mm^2, but adding carbon to turn it into steel can bring that figure up to 360 N/mm^2. Beyond that, fancier steel alloys can reach yield strengths of around 3,000 N/mm^2.

Plain aluminum comes in at only about 40 N/mm^2, but its alloys can reach 600 N/mm^2, depending on what percentages of what materials are added.

It is interesting to note that while alloying can add a lot of strength, it does not make much difference to the density of a material. That's simply because we're talking only tiny percentages of the other materials added to the base material.

In addition to alloying, many materials can be made stronger by means of work-hardening and/or heat treatment and/or age-hardening. Thus, the strongest steel and aluminum bicycle tubing types may owe their exceptional strength to a combination of all three factors. Keep in mind though, that the welding and brazing processes used to join tubes together in frame building can have the opposite effect, weakening the material locally in the area referred to as "heat affected zone," the area about 1–2 cm from the weld seam. Especially aluminum alloys are susceptible to loss of strength close to the welds and should be stress-relieved afterward to retain their strength.

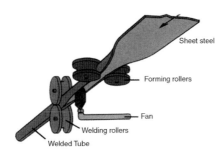

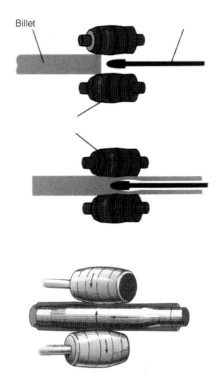

Above and right: Figs. 5.4–5.6. Steel tube making procedures. Above: welded tubing fabrication. Top right: seamless tube manufacture. Bottom right: manufacture of butted tubing.

STIFFNESS-TO-STRENGTH RATIO

Especially for lighter-weight materials (or more correctly, lower-density materials), the relationship between strength and stiffness is equally important as the strength-to-weight ratio. Stiffness is expressed as modulus of elasticity, measured in N/mm^2.

Here too, Table 3.1 helps provide some insight. Thus for steel, it doesn't much matter how strong the particular alloy, the modulus of elasticity is all the same. If, for instance, you make a frame tube out of a stronger type of steel alloy, you could theoretically make it either with a smaller diameter or a smaller wall thickness. Or you could make an equally strong crank arm out of a stronger aluminum alloy and much more slender. However, because the modulus of elasticity is the same, the thinner part would bend much more, and you might finish up with a "wobbly" frame or a crankarm that bends when you put any force on it.

This is not to say there's no use for stronger materials. But it does mean that the designers of bicycles and components have to work on the relative dimensions and the shape of parts so as to compensate for this. Both "oversize" aluminum and titanium frame tubes and hollow cranks and spindles were developed with an eye on maintaining both strength and stiffness using light materials.

TUBE DIAMETER, STRENGTH, AND STIFFNESS

Traditionally—ever since the mid-1920s—most bicycle frames have been made with main tubes that have the following outside diameters.

- Top tube: 25.4 mm (1 in.)

- Down tube: 28.6 mm (1⅛ in.)

- Seat tube 28.6 mm (1⅛ in.)

- Head tube : 31.7 mm (1¼ in)

French manufacturers use slightly different true metric dimensions. There has always been more variation in the chainstays and seatstays, some of which were also made non-round and/or tapered.

For tandems, carrier bikes, and more recently mountain bikes, larger-diameter tubes have been in use to accommodate the higher forces to which those frames are subjected. Such larger-diameter tubes are referred to as "oversize" tubes.

With the proliferation of aluminum frames along came a trend to use quite dramatically oversized tubes. Although that technique had already been used by small French builders before World War II, it was popularized in the 1980s by the American manufacturers Klein and Cannondale, and it is now pretty much standard on all aluminum bikes. Here's why:

The three main objectives in frame optimization are:

- strong enough for the load;

- as light as possible;

- stiff enough for steering stability.

To achieve enough strength, all that counts is how many square mm of a material are in the tube. In fact, it doesn't even have to be a tube but could be a solid rod. So for a given material—let's say high-carbon steel with a tensile strength of 360 N/mm^2—you could either use a 12 mm diameter solid rod, a 25.4 mm diameter tube with 1.4 mm wall thickness, or a 32 mm diameter tube with 1.0 mm wall thickness. They all have 100 mm^2 of cross-section, so they can all handle a load of 36,000 N, and they all weigh exactly the same, namely 780 g/m (gram per linear meter).

But how about that third criterion, stiffness? That all comes down to how much resistance the thing has against bending, and there the diameter plays a major role. If you clamp in a 1 m long length of each of these shapes and apply a standard force at the other end, the distance over which they deform, or bend, differs quite dramatically:

- The 32 mm diameter tube with 1.0 mm wall thickness bends by 10 mm.

- The 25 mm diameter tube with 1.4 mm wall thickness bends by 18 mm.

- The solid rod of 12 mm diameter not only bends "off the map," it actually permanently deforms and does not recover its shape when the load is released.

So it is clear we can't use the solid rod for bicycle frame construction; and indeed, their use was abandoned about 150 years ago. In fact, to prevent collapse under compressive and/or bending stresses, the rod would have to be much greater in diameter than needed for tensile loading.

Of the two other tubes, it is obvious that the 32 mm tube with 1.0 mm wall thickness deformed less than the 25.4 mm tube with 1.4 mm wall thickness. Both will do the job, but under a heavier load, the larger-diameter tube holds up better than the one with the smaller-diameter.

This was all based on the use of steel tubing. Things get even more interesting with the switch to aluminum tubing. As explained elsewhere in this Chapter, bending is dependent on the material's modulus of elasticity, and for aluminum that is only about one third of what it is for steel (any aluminum, any steel, regardless of tensile strength).

SAFETY FACTOR

An important aspect in determining the strength of an item is what's called a safety factor. What it comes down to is that it is not enough to make something that carries a certain load just strong enough to withstand that load.

To make sure the product withstands the load even with some variations in load, sudden applications of a load, inaccuracy of calculation, additional loads, and after years of wear and tear,

engineers apply a safety factor. The factor is basically a multiplier: A safety factor of 2 means the theoretical strength of the design is twice as strong as the expected load, etc.

STIFFNESS

Modulus of elasticity is the name for measuring stiffness (or its opposite, flexibility). It is the force needed to bend a standard piece of the material over a set distance within its "plastic range,"

i.e. it will spring back to its original shape and size afterward. Regardless of alloying and other strength-enhancing techniques, all steel alloys essentially have the same modulus of elasticity (which, by the way, is the same as that of unalloyed iron), namely $20 * 10^6$ Nm/mm³, or 200,000 N/mm², but for aluminum and its alloys the figure is about 70,000 N/mm².

A lot of noise has been made about bicycle frame stiffness, some of it justified, but much more just irrelevant. True, you

TUBE DIAMETER, STRENGTH, AND STIFFNESS (CONTINUED)

If you compare a steel tube with an aluminum one of the same diameter and wall thickness, you'll find that the aluminum one deforms 3 times as much as the steel one (81 mm versus 27 mm).

Because aluminum is both lighter than steel and has less tensile strength, you could increase the wall thickness threefold, to 3 mm. This would result in the same strength and the same weight as the steel tube. Two problems with that:

1. It still bends more than the steel tube;

2. You haven't saved any weight over the steel tube, even though it is a chunk more expensive.

The answer to this dilemma lies in the informed choice of tube diameter and wall thickness. If you choose a 35 mm tube and 1.0 mm wall thickness, the thing doesn't deform any more than the steel tube, and you've got a tube that weighs only 40% of the 25 mm steel tube. And that in short is why you'll find all those oversized aluminum frame tubes.

However, this too is not the end of the story, because your aluminum tube still is not as strong as the steel tube. If a manufacturer thinks it is strong enough, he could achieve the same strength with a steel tube with an even smaller wall thickness. So it turns out that, at the end of the day, a steel frame can be made almost as light, and at least as strong and stiff, as one made with oversized aluminum tubing.

Another constraint to consider is a tube's resistance to denting and buckling. When the ratio of diameter to wall thickness reaches 30, the tube's structural integrity is compromised to the point where it is easily dented or even crushed, beer-can-style.

And we haven't even mentioned aesthetics yet, nor any environmental concern (making aluminum requires very large amounts of energy compared to the production of even the highest grade steel). Aesthetically, many cyclist much prefer the elegant look of a traditional steel frame, and are pleased to note that steel frames are making a bit of a comeback in the "connoisseur" market for "fixies" and high-end road bikes.

don't want your frame to be so flexible that the steering becomes unpredictable or permanent deformation takes place. However, the claim that "energy gets lost" in frame flex is a bit exaggerated: Given an adequate overall frame design, within the limits of measurability, essentially all energy you put into pushing the pedals comes out at the rear wheel. Flexing losses are negligible in comparison to all other losses.

For a strong and heavy rider, a certain frame may feel too flexible, whereas the same frame may feel too stiff for a light rider. However, you won't go any faster on a stiff frame than on a more flexible one. The bigger

STEEL ALLOY DESIGNATIONS

There are at least three standardized material designations for steel alloys. The first one lists the alloying materials used, the second and third are material specification numbers (each referenced to a table in which the materials' components and characteristics are defined).

Here is an explanation of the first method, based on an example of a material designated "25 CrMo4":

❑ The first 2 digits (25) stand for the carbon content in hundredth of a percentage point, in this case 0.25%.

❑ The sets of 2-letter digits following (Cr, Mo) list the other major alloying elements in decreasing order, in this case first chromium and then molybdenum.

❑ The concluding number represents the percentage of the highest alloying component multiplied by 4/100, in this case, 4 x 0.25% = 1% chromium.

This same material can be found in the materials number tables as DIN 1.7218 or as SAE/ANSI 4130. It is a low-alloy steel commonly used for both frame tubing and other components and accessories, with a tensile strength of 850 N/mm².

Only the first three alloying elements are listed (carbon, chromium, and molybdenum), but some other components may be present (in smaller percentages) as well. Therefore not all materials specified as e.g. "4130" are fully identical.

Individual manufacturers often have their own designations, most famously Reynolds 531, which is (or rather was, because you don't see it much anymore these days) an alloy with about 0.25% carbon, 0.8% chromium, 0.6% manganese, 0.2% molybdenum (with some nickle, silica, and some other minor elements

Fig. 5.7. Probably the most famous, and most imitated manufacturer's bicycle tubing label, showing that all frame tubes, stays, and forks are made of Reynolds 531 (a manganese-molybdenum steel) tubing, and that the frame tubes are butted.

thrown in for good measure). Technically, it could be designated 25 CrMn3, but the manufacturer refers to it as a "manganese-molybdenum steel."

More recently, Reynolds (and other tubing makers) have introduced even stronger, work-and/or air-hardening steel alloys, and a slew of new labels has cropped up. (As an aside, it should be mentioned here that the original Reynolds tubing company, based in England, has nothing to do with the American Reynolds company, a manufacturer of carbon composites, including sophisticated bicycle wheel sets, to whom they had sold merely the rights to use the name.)

problem with frame flex is that it may cause the chainwheel to rub on the front derailleur cage when exerting maximum, i.e. accelerating, force on the pedals. The biggest difference is likely to be in your head: with all the hype about frame "rigidity," you will think you're faster on that stiffer bike, and thus perhaps you will.

HARDNESS

For some parts, it does matter just how hard the material is. Ball bearing parts and drivetrain parts, including sprockets and chains, would wear out too fast if their surfaces were not hard enough. It even matters on tire covers, which, though flexible, should be hard enough at the surface to resist puncturing and minimize wear.

Hardness is measured by means of a testing machine that pushes a very hard ball into the surface of the material. The size of the impression left is related to a somewhat arbitrary scale, the most common of which is called "Brinell hardness number." The higher the number, the harder the material. For plain steel the number is about 100, and depending on the alloy, method of manufacture, and heat treatment, values as high as 580

ALUMINUM ALLOY DESIGNATIONS

As for steel alloys, so for aluminum (and other) alloys too, there are a number of designations to distinguish them. The international designation, derived from the German DIN standard, identifies the material and its alloying components similarly to the method described for steel alloys, except that the base material is listed first. Thus, "AlZnMgCu1.5" stands for an aluminum (Al) alloy with zinc (Zn), magnesium (Mg), and copper (Cu).

More common for bicycle construction is the (American) SAE/ANSI standard: a 4-digit number. The alloys commonly used for bicycle frame tubes fall into the 6xxx and 7xxx series. In 6xxx series alloys, magnesium and silica are the main alloying elements, whereas 7xxx series

alloys it is zinc. 6xxx alloys are not quite as strong but lend themselves better to hydro-forming, allowing optimized tube shapes.

Two examples that are commonly used are 6060 or 7075. These numbers are referenced in a table in which the alloying formula and materials properties are listed. For example, 7075 is the same AlZnMgCu1.5 mentioned above.

Some of these materials are more suitable for welding (e.g. frame tubes), others for machining (e.g. chainrings), forging (e.g. cranks), or cold-forming (e.g. handlebars). For frame tubes, 7075 is most suitable due to its high tensile strength and good weldability. Even stronger will be the same material with minor additions of titanium, scandium, or zirconium, because the weld zone will be stronger after heat treatment and/or

precipitation hardening (also known as age hardening).

In addition to these standardized material designations, many manufacturers may quote their proprietary trade names. Examples of such designations are Dural, Ergal, Titanal, while other manufacturers refer to their materials by one of the obscure alloying elements. An example of this is the term "Zirconium": while only a tiny trace of it will be present, the name used may suggest you're buying a bike made entirely of this rare earth metal.

Fig. 5.8.
Materials label for a heat treatable 6061 aluminum alloy made by Reynolds.

can be achieved. For aluminum and its alloys, the Brinell number falls somewhere between 23 and 105.

Hardness of most metals can also be affected by material composition, temperature treatment, and work hardening. It is important to note that the surface hardness need not be identical to the hardness of the material deeper inside the part.

There tends to be a relationship between tensile yield strength and hardness. This allows for a quick and dirty test for strength without requiring full-blown tensile testing machinery. Just subject the piece to a Brinell hardness test and figure out what tensile yield stress this corresponds to.

CYCLIC LOADING AND SHOCK LOADS

When you take a paperclip and bend it straight, and then bend it back, and so on, at some point it will suddenly fail, i.e. break. The same can happen to any other

metal object (as well as those made of most other materials). This phenomenon is called (metal) fatigue failure, and is due to repeated cycles of load changes that may be caused by bending, vibrations, or any other repeated varying applications of force. You may have heard the term applied to aircraft failures, where it is obviously more critical than in paperclip design.

Metal fatigue also matters in bicycle design, both as applied to the frame and to other parts. Whereas the paperclip failed after only a few cycles of load change, aircraft and bicycles go through many cycles. In the case of the bicycle, they may be due to the pedaling motion, wheel rotation, and vibrations from the road surface.

For steel, regardless which alloy and how strong, it is possible to predict whether a particular component will stand up to a lifetime of load variations or not: If it does not fail within 7 million load variations, it will also

Left and above: Figs. 5.9 and 5.10. Aluminum frame tubes, straight (left) and hydroformed (above).

withstand an infinite number. So manufacturers "only" have to fatigue test frames and other components for that number of load cycles to be assured the product will never fail.

Unfortunately, aluminum is not so predictable, and in fact, just because one aluminum test specimen withstands 7 million cycles, it does not follow that the next one won't fail much sooner. For that reason, it is necessary to design aluminum frames and components with a more generous safety factor. Heavily loaded points of aluminum structures should be reinforced to prevent failure.

Closely related is the effect of sudden, or shock, loads, as for example may be applied to the bike or one of its components in a crash. But there are more mundane situations, such as when the rider mounts by jumping on, rather than by gently sitting down on the seat and gradually increasing pedaling load. Whatever the normal capacity of the bike, the seat, the pedal, and the crank, these parts must all be designed to handle such situation as well.

CONCLUSIONS

The various materials properties all effect the strength and design of a bicycle or any of its components. Let's consider a part made of carbon steel that weighs 100 g. If you made the same part

of magnesium, it would weigh only 24 g. However, because magnesium has a much lower tensile yield strength than carbon steel, you'd have to beef it up threefold, and then it would weigh 72 g. Lighter, but not much, and it may look very bulky and would certainly be a lot more expensive.

If, on the other hand, you were to choose a stronger steel alloy, say one that has twice the tensile yield strength, you could safely make the same part half as heavy, at 50 g. It would cost more, but not as much as magnesium, and it will look a lot nicer.

This is only one example of the interaction of different materials properties. Another important one is the relationship between tensile yield strength on the one hand and modulus of elasticity on the other. This is a relationship that affects mainly the relative merits of small-diameter tubing (and other hollow structures) and larger-diameter ones, each time considering the

material used as well as the wall thickness. This issue will be discussed in some detail in the next chapter, which is devoted to design criteria for the bicycle and its parts.

MATERIAL SPECIFICS

In this section, we'll take a closer look at the various materials that were mentioned previously. We'll also discuss the material qualities

Left and right: Figs. 5.11 and 5.12. Aluminum bikes are nothing new. The 1936 Monark Hawthorn Silver King (left) as well as this 1948 BMW (right) are early versions built for the American and German markets respectively.

TITANIUM ALLOY DESIGNATIONS

The international designation for titanium alloys is similar to that for aluminum (and other non-ferric metals). It consists of the letter code Ti (titanium), followed by the letter codes for the alloying elements in order of prevalence. An example would be Ti6Al4V, for a titanium alloy with 6% aluminum and 4% vanadium.

The SAE/ANSI designation refers to titanium alloys by a "Grade" designation. Under this system, grades 1 through 4 are "commercially pure" titanium of increasing tensile strength, and the other grades refer to various alloys. The most common one is Grade 5, and corresponds to the above-mentioned Ti6Al4V. Another common alloy is Grade 9 (Ti3Al2.5Va), which is easier to weld at about the same high strength.

Again, both tubing and bike manufacturers often coin their own designations for such alloys. Reynolds (U.K.) at least

bases their code on the international designation for a Grade 5 titanium alloy: their 6-4Ti stands for Ti6Al4V.

Fig. 5.13. Materials label for one of the strongest titanium alloys on the market, a Group 5 Titanium alloy made by Reynolds.

and how they are optimized in each case.

STEEL AND ITS ALLOYS

The simplest steel alloy is iron with carbon; within limits, its strength increases with carbon content. The relatively strong high-carbon steel is also referred to as high-tensile steel. For quality bicycles, stronger, and more expensive, steel alloys are typically used. Distinction is made between three groups of steel alloys:

❑ Unalloyed steel: Less than 1.5% alloying materials.

❑ Low-alloy steel: No more than 5% alloying materials.

❑ High-alloy steel: More than 5% alloying materials.

Both low- and high-alloy steels contain small percentages of two or more of the following materials:

❑ Carbon (C): Raises the strength from 100 N/mm² for pure iron to anything up to 250 N/mm², depending on carbon content.

❑ Manganese (Mn): Increases tensile strength by about 100 N/mm² for each 1 percent of manganese, while also improving weldability.

❑ Chromium (Cr): Improves tensile strength and some other material qualities.

❑ Molybdenum (Mo): Increases tensile strength and fatigue strength, also allowing the material to be heat treated for greater strength.

❑ Nickel (Ni): Increases tensile strength, while improving weldability and impact strength.

❑ Vanadium (Va): Prevents brittleness and improves weldability.

❑ Silica (Si): Increases tensile strength and improves some other material qualities.

❑ Aluminum (Al): Improves the material's crystalline structure and reduces gas formation when it is heated.

In all cases, these benefits only apply under limited conditions and in specific (small) percentages. And of course, they won't be all combined in a single alloy. On the other hand, several of the resulting alloys may gain in more ways than just tensile strength. Specifically, the possibility to increase the materials strength further with certain subsequent procedures are significant for some alloys.

Whereas most alloys lose some of their strength in the

THE COST OF TITANIUM

Titanium is an excellent material for both frames and other components. But why is it so expensive? It's not inherent in the material cost, which, though significantly higher than it is for steel or aluminum, does not justify the hefty premiums that are often charged.

It's also not due to significantly greater difficulty in welding or machining. These are

both quite similar to the level of difficulty of the same process for high-grade steel and aluminum alloys.

Our best guess is that in many cases it is "what the market will bear," i.e. riders are quite willing to pay more for items made of titanium than they for similar items made of other materials, because they've been made to believe they're more "high-tech."

Right: Fig. 5.14. Carbon repair job. There are specialists who do this kind of work.

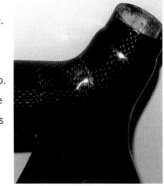

heat-affected zone (the area close to the welded or brazed joint), some either regain their strength or even become stronger if subjected to the correct temperature sequence afterward, in the form of heat-treating and/or tempering. Other alloys can be significantly improved with "cold working," e.g. when the tubes are drawn or otherwise formed.

Iron itself keeps quite well when exposed to the elements, but as soon as carbon is added to make steel, it becomes very susceptible to corrosion, or rust. For this reason it always needs to be protected with paint or some other surface coating. Only certain types of high alloys, such as stainless steel, do not require such surface protection.

ALUMINUM AND ITS ALLOYS

Aluminum has one third the weight, but only 40% of the strength of steel: Specific density 2.7; tensile strength 40 N/mm². That would suggest the material may be unsuitable for bicycle use due to its low strength. However, it turns out aluminum can

Left: Fig. 5.15. Not all that looks like it actually *is* carbon. This brake lever received a "carbon-look" paint job.

be alloyed to great advantage, increasing its strength without significantly affecting its density.

In fact, aluminum alloys are widely used for bicycle frames, components, and accessories. Some of these alloys (with suitable post-weld heat-treating or age hardening) can reach tensile strengths of 800 N/mm². Typical alloying elements to improve the material qualities of aluminum alloys are the following:

❏ Silica (Si): Lowers the melting point, making the material more suitable for some shaping processes, and improves work hardening properties of AlMn alloys.

❏ Copper (Cu): Forms Al₂Cu with aluminum, increases work-hardening properties, but also makes the alloy less corrosion resistant.

❏ Magnesium (Mg): Improves crystal structure and corrosion resistance.

❏ Manganese (Mn): Forms Al₆Mn, greatly increasing tensile strength of non-work-hardening alloys.

❏ In addition, one or more of the following minor elements

may be added:

Zinc (Zn): Forms MgZn₂ in conjunction with magnesium, significantly increases the alloy's work-hardening susceptibility, for improved tensile strength.

Titanium (Ti): For decreased grain size and improved malleability weld-zone properties and air-hardening.

Zirconium (Zi): Pretty much like titanium, but a lot more expensive.

Scandium (Sc): Pretty much like titanium, but a lot more expensive.

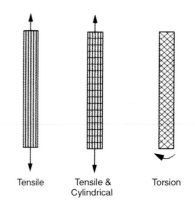

Tensile   Tensile &   Torsion
    Cylindrical

Above: Fig. 5.16. Carbon-fiber orientation and stress orientation.

Below: Fig. 5.17. A short-lived idea: Reynolds CFS tubing, carbon tubes with TIG-weldable end pieces.

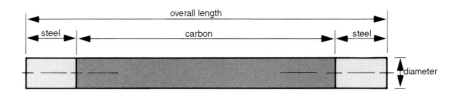

Unlike most other metals, aluminum lends it self to a forming process called extrusion. This technique is used for making continuous, more or less complex profiles, such as for tubes (relatively simple) and bicycle rims (more complex). In this process the aluminum is heated close to its melting temperature and pushed through a shaped die.

Aluminum, much like e.g. "stainless" steel, forms a hard oxide surface film when exposed. This surface film protects the material from further oxidation, making it unnecessary to paint the product. However exposure to salt would penetrate this protective layer, so it doesn't quite work in an environment near the sea or where salt is used to remove snow in winter.

TITANIUM AND ITS ALLOYS

Although pure titanium is a fine material, and has been used for bicycle components, its

mechanical qualities can be vastly improved by alloying. The most common alloying elements are aluminum, vanadium, and manganese. With a density of 4.6, the basic material is about 40% lighter than steel but about 70% heavier than aluminum.

The tensile strength of commercially pure titanium is about 280 N/mm², but with the addition of oxygen and/or alloying with aluminum, vanadium, and/or manganese, the tensile strength can be increased to 800–1,100 N/m—on a par with high steel alloys. Unfortunately, this goes at the expense of the material's ductility and weldability, for which reason compromises are made.

Another potential problem is that titanium tends to form what is known as "twin-crystalline" grain structure, which leads to

reduced fatigue strength. Consequently, items that are subjected to cyclical loading (i.e. just about every part of a bicycle) should be made a bit beefier than required on account of tensile strength only.

Titanium forms a thin, hard oxide surface film, which protects the underlying material from further oxidation. Consequently, it is not necessary to paint items made of titanium. This surface layer also is a bit of an impediment to welding, but this problem is overcome by means of modern welding techniques (specifically TIG-welding).

MAGNESIUM ALLOYS

With a density of only 1.74, magnesium is the lightest metal suitable for bicycle component manufacture. Due to its corrosiveness (in small particles, it is even flammable), pure magnesium is not weldable. It is usually alloyed with aluminum, zinc, manganese, silicon, copper, and (in trace quantities) zirconium. Although frames have been made, either cast in one piece or using tubes (either TIG-welded or lugged "screwed-and-glued"), magnesium alloy is now mainly used for castings such as those for suspension forks.

A finished frame can weigh about the same as one made of carbon composite, but is much more robust and pretty much

Left and above: Figs. 5.18 and 5.19. Essentially the same product—a short-cage rear derailleur—in carbon (left) and in aluminum (above). The weight difference is 49 g.

immune to the kind of catastrophic failure associated with carbon. It also absorbs shocks better than most of the other materials in use, and it is considerably cheaper than other materials for high-end frames (it's in plentiful supply: the oceans are full of it). The problem of galvanic corrosion (electro-chemical interaction between magnesium components and those made of other materials) can be avoided with proper surface treatment, such as anodizing or painting.

CARBON, ETC.

The term "carbon" is used as a shorthand for carbon-fiber composite—any of the modern materials made up of a high-strength fiber embedded in epoxy. These materials have become increasingly popular for the manufacture of lightweight bicycle frames and other components. Though natural carbon-fibers are the most commonly used, other fibers, both natural and man-made, are suited to this application as well. In all of these compounds, the fibers contribute the tensile strength, and the epoxy is the bonding material that keeps the fibers in place.

Carbon-fibers are incredibly strong under tensile loading, but that does not mean the finished frame tubes are equally strong—they have about the same strength as titanium alloy. However, being much lighter even than aluminum, carbon provides the highest strength-to-weight ratio of all commonly used frame materials.

Whereas in metals the crystalline structure makes the material equally strong in all directions, fibers are strong only in one direction: under tensile (i.e. pulling) loading along their length. Thus, to make an item resist the actual forces that will be applied to it in use, the fibers must be oriented in various directions and embedded together in epoxy. This is usually done by layering differently oriented fiber mats before they are epoxy-bonded together. All manufacturers do this, but some have coined fancy acronyms for this process. Strength and consistency are maximized when the material is compacted in such a way that

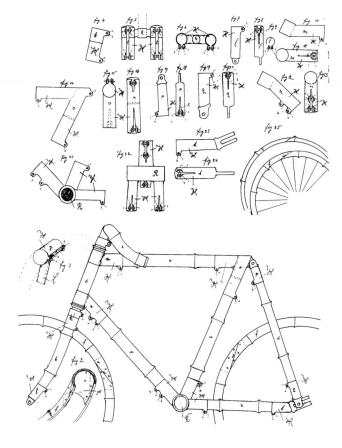

Left and right: Figs. 5.20–5.22. Bamboo old and new. 1895 patent drawing for bamboo bicycle by Grunder & Lemisch, of Austria (left) and one of their 1897 bikes (upper right); and a 2009 bamboo bike built with hemp composite lugs by Calfee, of California (bottom right).

voids are minimized. This may be achieved with a combination of heat and pressure, as done in Trek's patented OCLV-process.

Many minor parts and accessories are made with short-fiber-reinforced plastics. Although carbon-fibers are often used for this purpose, this material is not to be confused with the material described above. In the former, random short carbon-fibers strands are mixed in the epoxy before the material is cast into a mold. The material is relatively light and stable in form—as long as it does not get very hot: Bikes in bike shop windows supported by kickstands made of this material have been reported falling over because the stands collapsed in the heat of the sun through the windows.

Around 2000, Reynolds introduced an interesting alternative type of tubing called CFS, or

Above: Fig. 5.23. Catastrophic frame failure on a carbon-frame bike. Though strong in tension, carbon-fiber composites are easily damaged, and when they fail, they do so in a big way.

Right: Fig. 5.24. Carbon frame tubes integrated with aluminum lugs.

Carbon Fibre Steel. It consisted of carbon tubes with TIG-weldable steel end pieces. The product did not find many takers amongst frame builders, and was soon withdrawn. In practice, whenever carbon-fiber is used, they are either made of tubular members with the joints built up with carbon-fiber, or the entire frame is made in one piece.

And then there is fake carbon. Many carbon-fiber composites have a distinct exterior appearance, reminiscent of braided matting. That has led some manufacturers of cheap products to paint items to look like that. Usually these items are made of aluminum or short-fiber-embedded plastics. Beware, if the label doesn't say it is carbon, it probably isn't.

And More...

In a way, carbon-fiber can be compared to wood, or more specifically bamboo, and it is interesting to note that that material has also been used for the construction of bicycle frames. The

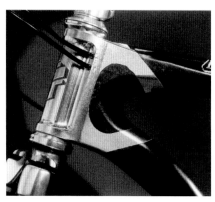

advantage of carbon-fiber over bamboo is that it is not restricted to the tubular shape, so the frame, or whatever other part, can be made as a single integral structure, without the need for joints. Also, of course, being a natural material, bamboo cannot be counted on as being dimensionally as accurate as metal and carbon-fiber parts.

Another innovative material is a magnesium composite. This involves a base made of e.g. carbon-fibers already in the shape of the finished product, that is then impregnated with molten magnesium. To date, it has only been used experimentally, but it may well hold promise for the manufacture of strong, lightweight, and resilient components.

As mentioned before, other fibers can be used the same way as carbon, including both synthetic and natural ones. The most common alternative to natural carbon is polyacrylonitrile (PAN) and para-aramid (such as Kevlar). Amongst the natural fibers tested, there are some that show unexpected potential. Flax, for instance, has been used experimentally, and was found to give the composite material a damping effect without loss of torsional stiffness. The result is that it transmits less shock load to the rider than identical frames made with carbon-fiber or other common materials. Though flax is not as strong as carbon, it is also considerably lighter, resulting in just about the same strength-to-weight ratio.

The other rather common material used on bicycles is rubber—for tires, brake pads, handgrips, etc. Natural rubber, called latex, is very flexible, but also very soft, making it unsuitable for the casings of bicycle tires. For this reason, rubber is usually vulcanized, which is a process of integrating sulphur, and depending on the degree of vulcanization, various characteristics can be improved. Latex is used, however, for inner tubes, where flexibility is the main criteria.

Finally, butyl, nylon, various other kinds of plastics, and leather are also in use for certain bicycle components. They all should be selected and treated with their specific characteristics in mind. Thus, for example, nylon should not be exposed to the sun, and leather must be protected from moisture.

FRAME TUBE DETAILS

Regardless whether they're made of steel, aluminum, titanium, or magnesium, metal tubes used in bicycle frame construction fall into several categories:

❏ welded tubes (usually steel)

❏ seamless welded tubes (usually steel)

❏ cold-drawn tubes (high-strength steel or any other alloy—aluminum, titanium, even magnesium)

Within each of these categories, the tubes can be either:

❏ plain gauge

❏ single-butted

❏ double-butted

❏ multiple-wall-thickness

Carbon-fiber tubes fall into their own category, which will be described separately elsewhere in this chapter.

Welded tubes are the cheapest to make, and they are mainly used for low- to mid-range bikes. The tubes are formed by bending a sheet of metal (typically carbon steel) and welding it together from the inside to form a cylindrical shape. These tubes are then pulled through a die to make sure they are perfectly round and dimensioned on the outside. The weld seam is only visible, and can be felt, on the inside. There's nothing really wrong with this construction method, but the tubes tend to be on the heavy side. Though not generally known, even this method lends itself to making butted or even multiple wall-thickness tubes, using sheets of metal that are formed between special rollers that are shaped appropriately. Because this method for making butted tubes is best suited to short sections and significant differences in wall

Left: Fig. 5.25. Calfee, of Santa Cruz, California is one of the pioneers of carbon frame construction. This is their Dragonfly road bike model.

Right: Fig. 5.26. Littoria laminated wood bicycles (not just the frame), made in Italy 1939 in response to the designation of steel tubing as a military good.

thickness, it is most appropriate for welded (lugless) frame construction.

Seamless welded tubes are made the same way as welded tubes, but they are subsequently pulled over an internal die as well as through an external one. The result is that the seam disappears. This too is a perfectly fine method of making tubes, and because it is usually applied with higher-grade steel alloys, these tubes are often lighter that regular welded tubes, and they can be found on high-grade bicycle frames. In this case butting, if required, has to be done after the seem has been eliminated, making this a more expensive process, and is more appropriate for lugged or lugless brazed construction.

Cold-drawn tubes are typically made of the highest grade materials. The process starts out with a solid billet, that is hollowed out and then pulled through and over dies in a number of steps until the desired diameter and wall thickness are achieved. Don't take the word "cold" too literally, though: for steel, cold working only means it

is done at temperatures below 1,000 degrees C, which is about twice as hot as the inside of a pizza oven. However, some processes can be performed at significantly lower temperatures. The process is used with high-strength alloys, and therefore results in the lightest steel tubes, used for high-quality frames.

SURFACE TREATMENT

All metals oxidize when exposed to the elements, some more, some less. The way to prevent corrosion is to form a protective impermeable layer of some sort over the entire surface of the material. Depending on the material in question and its specific application, there are a number of different processes in use to achieve that effect.

The surfaces of bicycle frames—whether of steel or aluminum—as well as many other

steel parts have traditionally been protected against corrosion by means of painting. Minor steel parts are often chrome-plated. In the early days of the bicycle, nickel-plating was often used for both high-end frames and components.

Steel corrodes quickly, and the problem is that the corrosion, or "rust" just keeps going deeper and deeper into the material. On the other hand, aluminum, magnesium, and titanium all corrode quickly when exposed to the air. However, they all "self-protect" by forming a surface layer of an oxide compound, which protects the material underneath. Therefore it is not as essential for these materials to be painted or otherwise coated as it is for steel.

To keep them shiny, unpainted aluminum components are usually treated in an electrolytic process called anodizing, which converts the outer layer into a much harder, pretty impenetrable form of aluminum oxide that protects the underlying material against the elements.

An interesting aspect of anodizing is that it can be used to harden the surface of the material to a sufficient depth to make the item much more wear resistant. This is referred to as deep-anodizing, which is simply achieved by maintaining the process over a longer period of time. Especially parts of the transmission, such as chainrings, benefit from deep-anodizing, because the hardness not

Left and right: Figs. 5.27 and 5.28. Exogrid is a process that combines cut-out titanium tubes with carbon-fiber liners for an improved combination of strength and torsional stiffness at a low weight.

only minimizes wear, but also reduces friction.

For painted parts, i.e. mainly frames, there are a number of different ways to go about it. The quality varies from cheap and nasty to expensive and durable, but the difference is not so much in the paint used as in the preparation and the number of layers of paint applied.

A popular finish for low-end components is referred to as powder-coating. This process uses a dry electrostatically charged spray of fine plastic particles, after which the component is heated in an oven so the plastic particles melt and form a tough, relatively thick but not very smooth impermeable layer. The result is not as pretty as finely polished and anodized aluminum, but it is a lot cheaper and quite durable.

So much for permanent corrosion protection. However, there are other parts on the bicycle that need protection too, parts that cannot be projected effectively in the same way because they are not fixed and stationary.

For screw-threaded and clamped components, grease is most suitable. For just about everything else, wax is best. In fact, wax is also useful for as an extra protection of painted surfaces.

Right: Fig. 5.29. Use a was-based product to protect both painted and unpainted exposed parts of the bike (except the rims on a bike with rim

LUBRICANTS

Closely related to the use of grease and wax for surface protection is the subject of lubrication. This applies to all bearings—whether ball bearings or so-called journal bearings, mainly the bushes, pins, and rollers of the chain.

Ball bearings, and the very similar roller- and pin-bearings are found in the hubs, the pedals, the bottom bracket, the headset, and the freewheel mechanism. The most effective form of lubrication for these is by means of mineral oil. However, because oil runs rather thin, it is hard to keep the lubricant in place, and for that reason it is often replaced by grease.

The most important criterion for effective lubrication in most cases is what's called "film strength." Synthetic oils and other synthetic lubricants tend to have the highest film strengths. These are all readily available in automotive supply stores. For general bicycle use, a relatively high-viscosity (i.e. thick-flowing)

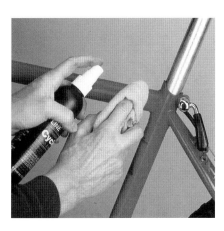

oil, such as SAE 60, will be most appropriate.

There are other practical aspects to consider in selecting lubricants. Thus, although oil is more effective than grease for most bearing applications, it is awfully runny, and you probably don't want your bicycle to leave a puddle behind wherever it has been parked for a while. For that reason, bearings usually get packed with grease instead of oil.

Bicycle-use-specific lubricants are also available. Though they tend to be just more expensively packaged versions of the same lubricants that can be bought in bulk. That packaging does have its advantage, because kept in a little tube dispenser, the product is better protected against contamination than when it gets scooped out of a big can.

Various special chain lubricants have been developed specifically for motorcycle and bicycle chain lubrication. These contain small particles of either graphite or e.g. Teflon. At least as important as lubricating the chain is cleaning it.

Purpose-specific lubricants are also used for other components, such as hydraulic brakes and hydraulic suspension systems. These are readily available as automatic transmission fluid, or ATF, in any automotive supply store. Just make sure you choose one with the right DOT-specification per the manufacturer's instructions.

6

THE BASICS OF BICYCLE DESIGN

A FRAME, TWO WHEELS, and a bunch of other parts to make it work, that is how any bicycle is designed and built. This chapter gives an overview of the considerations that go into designing the overall assembly.

DESIGN CONSIDERATIONS

Here is a summary of the primary considerations that come into play:

❏ size;

❏ strength;

❏ durability;

❏ stability;

❏ efficiency;

❏ aerodynamics;

❏ comfort;

❏ weight; and…

❏ cost.

Important to note, though, is that not all these considerations are equally important for all types of bicycles and all types of riders. For example, if a bike is designed for time-trialing or the cycling portion of a triathlon event,

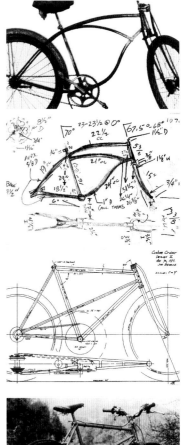

Right: Fig. 6.1. Birth of a bicycle design. These are some of the crucial stages that went into Joe Breeze's development for what was probably the first custom-built modern mountain bike, back in 1978.

size and efficiency may matter more than any of those other criteria, especially to those for whom cost is no object.

Now for a few words about each of the constraints that effect each of these qualities:

SIZE

The bike must fit the rider comfortably, both while riding and while mounting and dismounting, and even when stopped. It affects frame design, limiting how high the top tube can be, how far the handlebars can be from the seat, how high the bottom bracket, and how big the wheels can be.

But other factors also effect the size of both the frame and other components. For instance, the length of the cranks: they should allow efficient rotation of the legs within the range of flexibility and power of the rider's knee joints. And they should be close enough together laterally so they don't knock against the rider's ankles. Or take the handlebars: how wide, how high, how far forward, how large their diameter, and how they are bent are all important sizing considerations.

The size of the wheels is also significant—not only their diameter, but also their width, both at the tires, at the rims, and at the hubs. Wheel size mattered even more for early boneshakers and high-wheel bicycles with their directly driven front wheel. To make them go faster, they had to be big in diameter, and that put other constraints on the machine's overall design.

But even today, despite indirectly driven rear wheels, there are clear limits to wheel size. For a bike to fit a small rider, the wheel size may have to be smaller than for a larger rider, but that also affects many other aspects of overall design, including the frame angles and steering geometry.

STRENGTH

You don't want the bicycle to collapse under the rider's weight, and you may also want it to survive an accidental impact. But that does not mean the designer should just beef up every part to make sure it is very, very strong. Because there's a downside to beefing things up: the resulting bikes and parts may become too heavy, bulky, and/or expensive. One of the most basic tenets of

Lower limb (a)	Seat tube	Upper chest (b + c)	Top tube
80	51	100	53
81	51.7	101	53.4
82	52.4	102	53.8
83	43.1	103	54.1
84	53.7	104	54.4
85	54.3	105	54.7
86	54.9	106	55
87	55.5	107	55.3
88	56.1	108	55.6
89	65.7	109	55.9
90	57.5	110	56.2
91	57.9	111	56.5
92	58.5	112	56.8
93	59	113	57.1
94	59.5	114	57.4
95	60	115	57.7
96	60.5	116	58
97	60.9	117	58.3
98	61.3	118	58.6
99	61.7	119	58.8
100	62.1	120	59
		121	59.2
		122	59.4
		123	59.6
		124	59.8
		125	60

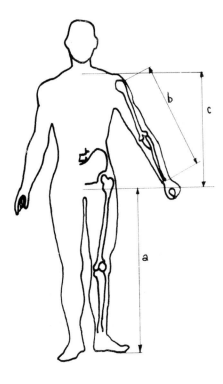

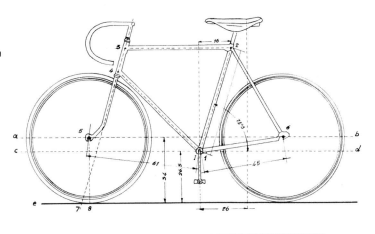

Left, right, and above: Figs. 6.2–6.4. The Italian Cycling Federation bike fit system. It still works well, providing you're a male of average proportions (see Chapter 22 if you're not).

SELECTING A FRAME THAT FITS THE RIDER

The objectives of correct sizing are threefold:

❏ Allow a position that is comfortable for the rider;

❏ Allow a position that allows efficient operation of the bike;

❏ Allow a position that provides safe and effective balance on the bike.

All published recommendations given for bicycle sizing are mere "rules of thumb," and not scientifically established. Quite sophisticated fitting systems are available in high-end bike shops, and although they use more accurate tools and methods, they are not necessarily based on more science either. With these caveats in mind, here are some fitting guidelines:

The three most relevant measurements on the rider are the following, measured as shown in Fig. 6.2 on page 67.:

A. Leg length;

B. Torso length;

C. Arm length.

For a male person of average proportions, it is usually adequate to combine leg length and torso length by measuring from the floor to the clavicle, shown as dimension D. (See chapter 22 for specific recommendations for women and anyone with "non-average" proportions.)

Transferred to the bicycle, these determine nominal frame size (measured as seat tube length) and top tube length. Other sections of this chapter go into some detail about the various other frame tube lengths.

Until the 1980s, most bicycles, regardless of size, had the same predetermined top tube length, and all that was changed to accommodate a shorter or taller rider was the seat tube length. Because the top tube was usually kept horizontal, the head tube length as well.

These days, most manufacturers offer "proportional sizing," meaning that also the top tube length will be longer for a larger frame size than it is for a smaller one. Actually, on most of today's bike designs, it is not so much the seat tube length that's a critical factor as the top tube length.

Just the same, as a first step in choosing a frame size, straddle height is a good starting point: The rider should be able to straddle the top tube with enough clearance to get both feet on the ground. That does not necessarily translate into a certain seat tube length, because it also depends on the bottom bracket height, which can vary by as much as 4 cm (1⅝ in.) from one bike design to another.

A frame with a low bottom bracket (and therefore a relatively long seat tube for any given straddle height) is favored for touring and randonneur bikes, while a high bottom bracket (and thus a short seat tube length for a given straddle height) works better for mountain bikes as well as road bikes. All other bike types fall somewhere in between.

For the top tube length, there is a practical restriction in that the distance between the bottom bracket and the front wheel axle must be enough for the rider's foot to clear the front wheel. For a small rider, that can be achieved by using a shallower head tube angle and more fork rake (see Chapter 10).

The angle of the seat tube, though usually the same as that of the head tube, can be steeper than the head tube angle for a short top tube, or shallower for a long top tube.

The chainstay length, finally, is determined by the desired weight distribution between front and rear wheel, and should be longer for touring bikes, mountain bikes, and city bikes than it is for road bikes, and tends to be shortest of all on singlespeeds and track bikes.

All other adjustments are a matter of rider comfort and are affected by means of adjusting the seat position and the handlebar height and position (the latter nowadays variable only by choosing a handlebar stem with more or less rise and/or reach (see Chapter 10).

engineering design is deciding just how strong to make structures, and in which places.

Factors to consider, of course, are the rider's weight and that of any load he or she may be carrying on the bike. But other things come into play too, such as any shocks from the road, which in turn depends on the particular machine's intended use: more severe for off-road riding than for road use.

And then the bike has to withstand unplanned forces, such as when the bike is involved in a crash. This too depends on the bike's intended use. If it is a bike for a professional road racing team, there will be mechanics and spare bikes on hand to replace anything that fails in such cases, but that same design may not be suitable if it is a bike for an individual rider, and even less if it is intended for everyday use. On the other hand, many cyclists seem to believe that they are better served with a bike that is "just like the pros ride," and most manufacturers are only to happy to oblige, and the result is a lot of people riding bikes that are not as suitable for their purpose as they could be.

DURABILITY

Just because a bike is strong (or heavy) does not necessarily make it more durable. Durability has to do with the quality of frame and components and how

well they are protected. To give an example, a Dutch city bike is not a particularly high-quality machine. Its frame is only made of welded carbon steel tubing. Nevertheless, it will probably last a lifetime, because of some unusual design features, such as the following:

❑ High-quality baked enamel paint finish on frame and accessories;

❑ Stainless steel and/or high-quality chrome-plated steel components;

❑ Anodized aluminum components;

❑ Fully enclosed chaincase, protecting the entire drivetrain and keeping it lubricated;

❑ Integrated accessories, such as lock, lighting, and luggage rack.

Of course, for some bikes all those features are either not appropriate or not necessary. However, one way or the other, the bike's designer has to consider

Right: Fig. 6.5. Smart designs, but no production. Dutch industrial designer Frans de la Haye's structurally sound 1982 design turned out to be too expensive for series production.

Left: Fig. 6.6. Designer gone crazy. The German industrial designer Colani thought he'd reinvent the wheel so to speak, with his superlight design. Unfortunately, it was neither ridable nor structurally sound.

how much durability is needed for a particular bicycle type.

STABILITY

In the context of general bicycle design, stability refers to the bicycle's predictable behavior in balancing, steering, braking, and accelerating. Stability requires such things as a perfectly aligned frame and fork, so both wheels

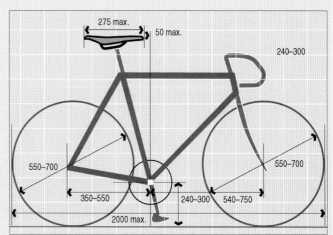

run along the same path, and accurately adjusted ball bearings in wheels, pedals, crankset, and headset, so wobbles, vibrations, and oscillations are kept to a predictable minimum. Of course, the accuracy of the components installed on the bike will be equally important as that of the frame itself.

Stability also means that the frame and the other components are all strong and stiff enough to stay true to the original design

Left: Fig. 6.7. Greame Obree, of Scotland, not only designed and built this one-sided monecoque bike himself, he also developed the rider position that goes with it. After the fact, the UCI decided they didn't like either Obree, his bike, or his position, and changed the rules to disqualify his one-hour record.

conditions. But, contrary to what many cyclists believe, stability also requires a bit of flexibility in the frame, the wheels, and some other parts. That is because this flexibility acts to absorb shocks and dampen vibrations. More about this characteristic under *Comfort*, below.

EFFICIENCY

Low resistance and minimized wasted effort translates into high efficiency, which is probably more important in the design of bicycles than it is for any other vehicle on earth. In this respect, bicycle design has come a long way since the days of the wooden-wheeled boneshaker. But even today, it can't be taken for granted that every bicycle is adequately efficient.

UCI DESIGN LIMITATIONS

The governing body of bicycle racing, the UCI, or Union Cycliste Internationale, keeps redefining the limitations of design criteria for the machine that may be used in sanctioned competitions and record attempts.

Historically, they have several times changed those criteria to invalidate legitimate records after the fact, most notably those set by Greame Obrey of Scotland, who used a very unconventional riding position

when breaking the long-standing one-hour record. Currently, the limitations are as presented in the accompanying illustration.

But don't be surprised if they get changed the next time someone sets a new record…

Fig. 6.8. UCI regulation bicycle dimensions, as of March 2010.

275 max.

50 max.

240–300

550–700

550–700

350–550

240–300   540–750

2000 max.

Numerous factors come into play in minimizing resistance and wasted energy. Some of these are within the manufacturer's domain, others are up to the rider. The manufacturer can strive to design the bike so that the rider's position on it allow him or her to ride in the most efficient position, and select the components to provide both high efficiency and adequate ease of maintenance consistent with the bike's intended primary use.

Of course, a lot of factors that effect efficiency are left to the mercy of the rider, and beyond the manufacturer's control. Take the wheels, for instance: if they are not kept perfectly round and straight, they will make the bike go up and down, losing energy (and how perfect is "perfect," anyway?). Or the tires: if they're not inflated just right for the surface, they either cause losses due to rolling friction (if under-inflated) or road shock (if overinflated). And the drivetrain: a clean, well-lubricated chain runs smoothly, whereas a little dirt or rust can decrease its efficiency significantly.

AERODYNAMICS

For any bicycle intended to be ridden at speed, aerodynamic drag becomes an issue. This applies to both the bike and the rider (in the form of rider position). Although the UCI has ruled against validating records set in certain rider positions and frame configurations, that ruling should not matter to most cyclists.

Designing the bike so that it allows a riding position that is compact and aerodynamically favorable should be one of the considerations when designing a bike. In addition, the use of ovalized frame tubing, bladed spokes, and components shaped for favorable aerodynamics can have a measurable effect on speed (or on endurance at a given speed).

Reducing the aerodynamic drag by 10% during a brisk ride under typical conditions would result in a speed that is about 3% higher. Of course, a 10% reduction in the bike's drag may lower the total drag on bike and rider by only about 3%, so the effect of a streamlined bike is more

likely to be an increase in speed of 1% or less.

Round items, such as frame tubes and the rider's legs, are particularly aerodynamically unfavorable. If they could have an "aero" shape with a length 4 times their thickness, they'd generate only about 10% as much drag (at least in theory). This kind of proportions cannot be achieved by using tubular structures, whereas it is possible to design a monocoque frame this way.

In aerodynamics, the sum of the parts is not necessarily the same. This is largely due to something called aerodynamic interference: the airstream around one part being diverted and causing turbulence at another part nearby. To take an example, the brake cables, though

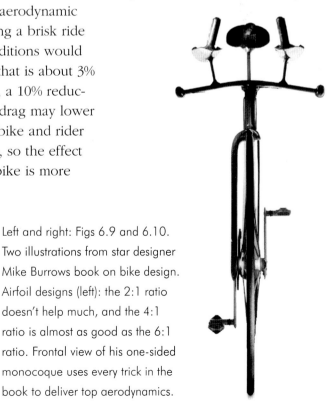

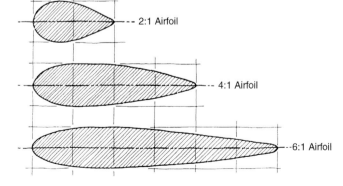

Left and right: Figs 6.9 and 6.10. Two illustrations from star designer Mike Burrows book on bike design. Airfoil designs (left): the 2:1 ratio doesn't help much, and the 4:1 ratio is almost as good as the 6:1 ratio. Frontal view of his one-sided monocoque uses every trick in the book to deliver top aerodynamics.

2:1 Airfoil

4:1 Airfoil

6:1 Airfoil

tiny in diameter, add significantly more to the drag when they are some small distance away from frame tubes or handlebars.

The downside of some aerodynamic features is that they make the bike more susceptible to the effect of side wind. Drag-reducing things like disk wheels (and then most seriously in the front), or even high-profile "aero" rims can seriously effect the steering and actually *increase* aerodynamic drag whenever the wind direction is more to the side than frontal.

COMFORT

If the bike is not comfortable, it doesn't matter how fast, light, or strong it is, it won't be much fun to ride. Unfortunately, too many cyclists, magazine writers, and manufacturers seem to overlook this important aspect of bicycle design. Too often, we'll read how light, how fast, or how "rigid" a bike is, while little attention is then paid to whether it is comfortable enough to ride for any length of time.

Of course, comfort may depend on a number of other characteristics, including weight, size and efficiency. But one of the primary fallacies that we would like to expose here is the idea that bikes should be "rigid." In the first place, that is an incorrect term, because that would mean something like infinitely stiff, and short of a block of granite, nothing really is. What's meant is stiff—relative to other bikes.

When a bike is ridden only on a perfectly smooth surface, such as a racing track, that may be OK, because there are no shocks or vibrations to deal with. But on any normal road surface, even tarmac, the stiffest bikes transmit shocks to the rider which adversely effect both comfort and efficiency, and actually handling as well.

Randonneurs, who tend to ride long distances at a good clip

Above: Fig. 6.11. Wind tunnel testing of the combination bike and rider.

Left: Fig. 6.12. Many manufacturers have done all they can to optimize aerodynamics. It would be nice if they paid equal attention to reliability, practicality, and serviceability.

on regular roads, have known this for a long time. They don't go for the narrowest tires, and the stiffest frames. In a test carried out for *Bicycle Quarterly*, this idea was put to the test by two strong, experienced riders, and the results were pretty conclusive: comfort is really, really important if you want to maintain a high speed for a long distance on real roads.

Some of the things that can be done to make a bike comfortable include the following, dependent on the specific preferences of the rider and what kind of use the bike will be subjected to:

❏ Frame tubes that are not too large in diameter and wall thickness;

❏ Seat and steerer tube angles that are not too steep, and a fork that is appropriately raked;

❏ Small-diameter seatstays and fork blades;

❏ Tires that are not too narrow and don't carry too much pressure;

❏ A saddle that is somewhat flexible;

❏ Rear suspension or suspension seatpost;

❏ Front suspension or sprung handlebar stem;

❏ Padded handlebar tape or handgrips;

❏ Adjustable handlebar stem, making it possible to adapt the rider's position to suit the circumstances.

Of course, not every bike needs to have all, or even most of, these features, but they are all items that can be considered. You may find that the super-high-efficiency road bike that has none of these features and costs as much as a small car is not necessarily the best—nor even the fastest—bike for real use.

On the other hand, there's also some "voodoo" in bicycle design, related to the rider's feelings about the bike. Anyone who switches from a "clunker" to a lightweight road bike, will be most impressed by its low weight

and the rolling ease of its high-pressure tires.

It will be this feeling that makes one believe that this bike is more responsive and efficient. That in itself may well be what makes one ride faster, and triggers enthusiasm to ride faster and farther.

WEIGHT

Weight matters, even though it is largely an issue of this same "voodoo" effect that we mentioned above. Complete bicycles range in weight from 7 kg (16 lbs) to 20 kg (44 lbs). That may look like a wide range, but for any given bicycle type the range is much narrower, like 8 to 11 kg for a road bike and 12 to 15 kg for a full-suspension mountain bike. And compared to the 70–100 kg of body weight the typical American male brings to the equation, those weight differences can't be terribly significant.

If we put a hypothetical 70 kg rider on a 15 kg bike, that

adds up to a total weight (or, expressed more accurately, mass) of 85 kg. Switching to a 7 kg bike represents a reduction of 7/85 * 100 = 8%, and that is probably just enough to notice in the bike's responsiveness in terms of acceleration, hill climbing, and braking. So going from a heavy mountain bike to a light road bike will give noticeable relief. But the difference between a 10 kg road bike and one weighing 8 kg is only about 3%, and you're not likely to notice a measurable difference in performance based on weight only.

A lot of U.S. cyclists regularly load their bicycles into or onto automobiles in order to go somewhere else to ride, and they regularly sense how light (or heavy) their bikes are, especially if they occasionally handle someone else's bike. While it is true that they get a warped idea of how weight affects the riding qualities of the bike, how easy the bike is to load is a legitimate concern, especially for slightly-built female or elderly cyclists.

Above and right: Figs. 6.13 and 6.14. Getting inspiration: Japanese manufacturers examining the products of mountain bike pioneers like Charlie Cunningham and Tom Ritchey in 1981.

What you notice is the fact that a lighter bike feels nicer when you pick it up, when you wheel it around, when you play with it, and when you load or unload it. And that may be what puts you in a frame of mind that allows you to perform better. It's not so much the bike's qualities and the effect it has on the rider's disposition.

Given similar materials, a lighter bike is also somewhat more pleasant to ride for another reason: the weight savings are due to the use of thinner-wall tubing, lighter wheels, etc. All this gives better shock absorption, which adds to the ride's comfort—the most overlooked characteristic of bicycle design. That also helps make it feel more enjoyable to ride, and therefore seemingly faster.

Note, though, that this mainly applies to bikes made of standard dimensions. It works for going from 1 mm wall-thickness regular steel tubing to 0.6 mm high-strength steel tubing (needed to achieve the same strength). It doesn't necessarily work when going from regular size steel tubing to significantly oversize aluminum tubing.

Cost

Yes, cost is a major concern in bicycle design. It is quite possible to make a bike that matches the rider perfectly and is both light, strong, and comfortable. But it won't be cheap, and there won't be many customers who can afford the product. If the manufacturer intends to sell in volume, he'll need to keep the price down to something more people can afford.

Whereas it is quite possible to overcome all sort of technical hurdles, the one hurdle that defies such challenging approaches is cost. It really should not be necessary to pay as much for a bicycle as for a small car.

The major way to keep costs down is by selecting standard components. Companies like Shimano, SRAM, and Campagnolo make most of the moving parts

Above and right top and bottom: Figs. 6.15–6.17. Testing, testing: New bicycles and component designs are (or at least should be) extensively tested for possible failures. Although modern computer techniques, such as Finite Element Analysis, do a good job at predicting stresses, some destructive testing is still required to prevent e.g. fatigue failure.

in a wide range of prices and qualities, weights, and sizes. Staying within those standard ranges can keep the price down. That's not to say they don't make some parts that are hideously expensive, but that is different from buying or making special items, such as those Alex Moulton had to make for my friend's bike.

Of course, higher quality and precision components are more expensive than those of lower quality and accuracy. But you may wonder just how good is good enough. If a $20 tire weighs 400 g, should you pay three times as much for one that weighs 350 g? If one derailleur costs $25, do you really want to specify a top-of-the-line model that more than four times as much, and is a little nicer, more polished, and a few grams lighter?

In general, things get more expensive when you are trying to save weight. Although it is not so hard to make a 10 kg road bike (there are some nice bikes like that to be had for around $1,000), bringing the weight down another one or two kg raises the price almost astronomically.

THE UCI AND BICYCLE DESIGN

It has been claimed that the world cycle racing federation, the UCI (*Union Cycliste Internationale*), has played a major

role in defining how bicycles are designed (see *UCI Design Limitations* below). Clearly, the overwhelming majority of bicycles are neither intended nor used for bicycle racing, and the UCI regulations do not apply to those machines.

Many cyclists naively think that if the winner of the Tour de France rides a certain make and model, that particular make and model must be the best, and that's the bike they want to ride. Never mind they don't have the champion's body, nor his support. The effect, however is, that these people will want to buy bikes that are built to UCI regulations even if they aren't so suitable for their particular use.

Yes, in countries like the USA, many cyclist choose to ride what are essentially road racing bicycles. However, it cannot be denied that entirely different categories of bicycles have also evolved, ranging from mountain bikes to folders and from comfort bikes to recumbents. Interestingly, the UCI design limitations have not prevented

any manufacturer or designer from offering machines that do not adhere to those limitations.

SUMMARY

In short, bicycle design, like any other form of engineering design, is a balancing act. First the designer must identify the kind of use and user for which the machine is intended. Then the most important objective has to be defined: Should the bike above all be fast, light, comfortable, durable, compact, foldable, beautiful, cheap, or what-have-you? Then the other criteria have to be weighed and compared: given that for durability additional mass is necessary, how heavy a bike will buyers accept? If to keep the price down the bike must become less comfortable, how long will buyers' rides be, and how little comfort will they tolerate?. How much heavier is OK in the quest for durability, or how much less comfortable to keep the price down?

Right: Fig. 6.18. Not all bikes look the same. This Dursley-Pedersen, which gained some popularity during the early 20th century, shows that it can be done differently. However, elegant though it was, it had some disadvantages in everyday use.

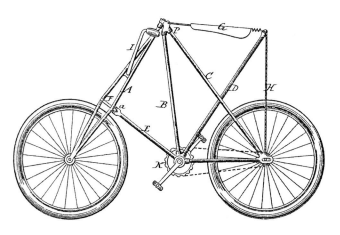

In practice, most bikes are designed to meet a certain price point. To make a $1,000 road bike, you can figure out which component gruppo to choose, or what replacements to make to a given gruppo. Then it is possible to figure out how much money is left for the frame, and that will tell whether it is going to be carbon steel, chrome-moly steel, aluminum, titanium, or carbon.

Of course, there are situations where cost is no object, and those are the bikes that finish up in the hands of professional bike racing teams. Even those bikes won't necessarily be the best of everything.

A pro racing bike need not have the quality finish that most high-end customers expect for their money. And it is also important to distinguish between durability, reliability, and serviceability. A pro's bike does need to be reliable for at least the duration of a race, for there's a significant time penalty if it breaks down. It need not be durable, that is, need not last more than one season or perhaps even one race. Aside from the ability to change wheels rapidly, it need not permit service in the field: what pro even fits a frame pump?

Many consumers in the U.S., ironically, may have similar needs: they neglect their bike's maintenance, can't fix a flat, carry only one tool (their cell phone), and plan to "upgrade" their bike every year or two anyway.

In contrast, more technically savvy riders may tolerate minor reliability issues if they can be corrected out on the road or in the home workshop. They will expect a good bike to last many years (preferably forever), and may need pump pegs, straightforward cable routing, chainring bolts that are not hidden behind a crankarm, chains that can be repaired with an ordinary tool, stems that can be adjusted throughout a useful height range, wheels that can be trued in the boondocks if a spoke breaks, hub quick-releases that actually release the wheel quickly, and other service-friendly features.

Left and right: Figs. 6.19 and 6.20. Two of the criteria for a practical bicycle are mass-manufacturing and serviceability. However interesting and useful a design may be, it not much use if it can't be made economically or can't be maintained and repaired by the rider.

7

COMMON BICYCLE DETAILS

IN THIS CHAPTER, we will explain the workings of a few basic details found on many bicycle parts. Though most of these items are also found on all sorts of other devices—from cars to kitchen appliances—their use on bicycles and their components is somewhat specialized.

Covering them together here has the advantage that their workings do not need to be explained again in the individual chapters that cover components where they are used. Even though this is not meant to be a repair manual, we thought it would be beneficial to also include brief instructions on handling them. The following items will be covered here:

❏ Screw-threaded connections;

❏ Ball bearings;

❏ Quick-release mechanisms;

❏ Cable controls;

❏ Wedged connections.

SCREW-THREADED CONNECTIONS

Most of the parts on your bicycle are held in place by means of screwed connections. This applies not only to common nuts and bolts, but also to more intricate components. A discussion of

Right: Fig. 7.1. Details of screw-threaded connections.

screw-thread connections, simple though they may seem, may be useful. Three functions are involved: tightening, loosening, and adjusting.

All screw-threaded connections consist of two parts: a cylindrical part (also-called the male part, or given a specific name such as a bolt or an axle) with a helical groove cut around the circumference; and a hollow part (also-called the female part, for example a nut) with a matching groove cut around the inside of the circular hole.

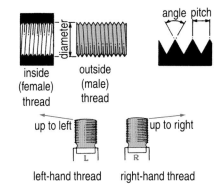

When turning the male part relative to the female one (or vice versa, which has the same effect), the male part enters the female one further or less far, depending on which direction it is turned. If it enters further when turning clockwise, the system has right-hand thread, which is common for all regular nuts and bolts; if it enters further when turning counterclockwise, it has left-hand thread, which is used in a few places, e.g. on the left-side pedal.

Usually, there is a washer (a metal ring) between the female part and any other part that is clamped or screwed in underneath. This is to reduce friction, making it easier to tighten and loosen the connection (thus indirectly increasing the effectiveness of the connection). A larger (both in diameter and thickness) washer may also serve to distribute the force over a larger contact area. Sometimes the washer takes the form of a spring washer (e.g. on connections that might otherwise come loose under vibration). In other cases the washer is "keyed," which means it can only be inserted in a specific orientation (especially between screwed parts of adjustable ball bearings, to allow tightening the one part without affecting the adjustment of the other part). See Fig. 7.4 for examples of these and some other auxiliary items.

To tighten a screw-threaded connection, turn one of the parts clockwise relative to the other (assuming it has right-hand screw thread; counterclockwise in the case of left-hand screw thread) until it butts up against the component that is to be secured. If all is well, the resistance when turning the parts relative to each other is quite low up to this point and will suddenly increase. At this stage, the two helical grooves are being pushed relative to each other and the end surfaces of the components rub against each other, until the force between them is so great that the connection becomes firm.

The main characteristic by which screw-threaded components are identified is the outside diameter of the male part,

measured in mm for metric components. Even though the diameter of two threaded connections may be the same, there are other aspects in which they can differ. In addition to the question of right- or left-handed thread, there may be a difference in pitch (measured as the distance between consecutive grooves on the male part, either in mm or as "threads per inch"), and there may be a difference in the angle of the groove. The latter is not an issue for most minor items, but can matter when matching more delicate items such as crankset and headset bearing parts.

When replacing bolts and nuts on a modern bicycle, be careful to use only metric ones. In some sizes, it is hard to tell metric and non-metric nuts and bolts apart (e.g. in the 5 mm size, which is deceptively similar to $3/16$ inch) and would ruin the components due to the difference in thread pattern. The way to check if they're not marked accordingly (e.g. on the head of a bolt) is by means of a thread gauge, lining it up with the

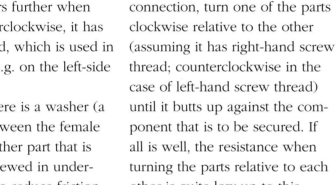

Left: Fig. 7.2. Not just nuts and bolts, but many other components on the bicycle too make use of screw-threaded connections, like here on a bottom bracket bearing unit.

Right: Fig. 7.3. Many screw-threaded connections have to be tightened, loosened, or adjusted using two wrenches, one on either part.

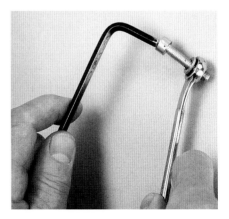

thread with the "saw-tooth" pattern of the gauge.

To loosen the connection, turn the part in the opposite direction, which at first requires force to overcome the resistance of the end surfaces, until the resistance to turning becomes much less when merely adjusting the position of the two parts relative to each other.

What holds the connection in place when fastened is the force between the helical grooves when tightened, and any other forces should be minimized to reach this force. A connection will not hold as reliably if you feel great resistance all the way due to dirt, damage, or corrosion of threads or other surfaces. Therefore, it is easiest to tighten or loosen a connection with clean and corrosion-free screw threads and end surfaces, slight lubrication, and the use of a smooth, hard-surfaced washer between the end surfaces.

To tighten or loosen a screwed connection, one part has to be turned in the appropriate direction with a precisely fitting tool with enough leverage, such as a screwdriver, a wrench or a hexagon key (referred to as Allen wrench), while the other part must be held steady. In the case of a nut-and-bolt connection, you'll need to hold the nut with a matching tool, while in the case of something screwed directly into the bicycle frame, you can hold the frame by hand or clamped in a work stand.

If you have difficulty loosening a connection that has been in place for a long time, spray some penetrating oil (e.g. WD-40) at the point where the male part engages the female, and wait 2–3 minutes before trying again.

When reinstalling a screwed connections, make sure the parts are clean, undamaged, and not corroded—and clean, lubricate, and/or replace them with new parts if they are not. Always use a smooth washer under the head of any bolt or nut.

Bolt heads come in a variety of shapes. The hexagon-recess, or Allen head screw has become quite prevalent on bicycles, and it is indeed the most elegant and effective design. It is less prone to damage than the older flat screw cut, cross-head, and hexagonal head designs. There's also the so-called grub screw (worm screw in Britain), which doesn't have a head at all—it can disappear completely into the female part. Nowadays, these usually have a (small) hexagonal recess in the end so they can be adjusted with a tiny Allen wrench, whereas older ones are adjusted with a small screwdriver.

To prevent accidental loosening of screwed connections, there are a number of different solutions. On many parts a double set of nuts is used, a thin so-called locknut and a regular nut, which are tightened against each other for a more effective hold. In fact, even a single nut may serve that same purpose if

the bolt is screwed into a threaded hole of the part and then a nut is screwed on from the other side to lock it in place. In such cases (e.g. the pivot bolts on a dual-pivot brake), it should be disassembled by first removing the nut, then the bolt. It is assembled by first screwing in the bolt until the pivot feels just right, then screwing on the nut while holding the bolt.

Nuts used on screws and bolts for accessories are often equipped with a spring washer, or lock washer, between the accessory and the nut to take up vibrating motions without loosening. More effective than the lock washer is the locking insert nut, in which a little nylon insert gets deformed around the screw thread and pushes in firmly enough to stop the nut from coming loose. Accessories should always be held with a minimum of two screws or bolts in order to minimize the effect of the unsupported mass that would cause parts to vibrate loose if held in only one spot.

When tightening threaded connections, do not apply more

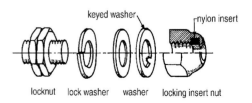

Above: Fig. 7.4. Some of the methods used to prevent screw-threaded connections from coming undone.

torque than required—to avoid damaging the head of the bolt or some other part. For this reason, choose tools of a length that is commensurate with the part in question. A 5 mm bolt or nut should not be handled with a 10-inch long adjustable wrench but with a small one (and preferably with a fixed rather than an adjustable wrench), which will have an appropriate length to prevent overtightening. Ideal would be to use a torque wrench on all connections, but for most components it is not so easy to find out just how much torque is appropriate. Choosing moderate size tools is usually quite adequate.

Large aluminum screw-threaded components, such as bottom bracket and headset parts, should be handled with great care to avoid damage to the screw thread. For this reason, use only the specific tools made for these components.

When screw-threaded connections are used for adjustment, there may be one male and two female components, and the latter two are tightened against each other once the correct adjustment has been established.

Since this is most commonly done in the case of adjustable ball bearings on the bike, this will be described in detail under *Ball Bearings* on page 84.

QUICK-RELEASE MECHANISMS

These devices are most frequently used on the wheels to allow easy removal and installation of the wheels. The same principle of operation is also found on many brakes, in order to open them up far enough for easy wheel removal, and sometimes on the clamp that holds the seatpost to facilitate easy seat height adjustment. They all work on the same principle, which involves a cam-shaped device connected to a lever that can be twisted to tighten or loosen a connection. In most cases, the cam is hidden inside some other part, so it is hard to figure out how it works without a drawing.

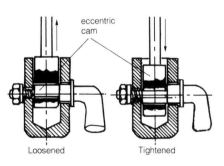

Above: Fig. 7.5. Principle of quick-release operation.

Left: Fig. 7.6. Quick-release operating detail.

When the lever is in the "open" position, the small end of the cam is engaged, leaving the connection loose. When the lever is placed in the "closed" position, the long end of the cam is pushed just past the engagement point (the tension being at its highest when the high point of the cam was engaged), which ensures that the tension is high enough but enough force would have to be applied to move it back to the "open" position to prevent accidental opening.

If the lever is not marked with the words "open" and "close," you can still tell which is which by observing what happens when you move the lever from one position to the other. Most modern levers are shaped with a convex (bulged) surface that faces out when closed and a concave (cupped) surface showing when open.

When closed, properly-adjusted quick-releases should be sufficient for operating the bike safely; when open, it should be sufficient for removing the freed part, without the necessity of adjusting anything else. Unfortunately, the current trend to equip the tips of front forks of bicycles with ridges (known as "lawyer's lips") makes it impossible to use the quick-release mechanism of the hub the way it was intended. You can, of course, still loosen and tighten the mechanism properly just using the lever, but the ridges on the ends of the fork blades require loosening the thumb nut at the other side to

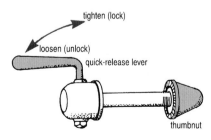

provide enough clearance to slip over these ridges to remove or install the wheel.

These ridges are being provided to prevent accidental wheel disengagement due to liability problems (hence the name "lawyer's lips"). However, when handled properly, there is no risk of accidental wheel disengagement even on forks without these ridges.

Initial adjustment of the quick-release mechanism is done when the bike is assembled in the factory or the bike shop, but you will probably have to do it again at some point later on after wear and tear or other factors have affected the adjustment. Proceed as follows:

QUICK-RELEASE HANDLING PROCEDURE:

1. Set the lever in the "open" position.

2. Place the device (wheel or seatpost) in position. If it can't be done, loosen the

thumb nut at the other end far enough until things fit.

3. Place the item to be held in the exact position and orientation it should be.

4. Screw in the thumb nut until all slack is taken up, but don't forcibly tighten it.

5. Flip the lever over into the "closed" position, if possible—if it cannot be moved fully into the "closed" position, unscrew the locknut in half-turn increments until the lever can be closed with firm hand force.

6. If the lever can be closed without applying a firm force to overcome its resistance somewhere between the opened and closed positions,

it is not tight enough. In that case, loosen it and turn the thumb nut in further until it can only be closed with significant hand force.

7. Check once more whether the device is aligned properly and loosen, then re-tighten it if necessary.

A partially-closed quick-release is unsafe: A wheel is in danger of coming loose if the quick-release is not fully closed and clamping tightly; and a brake quick-release should not be used in between the fully closed and fully opened positions (it should not be used it half open, instead of properly

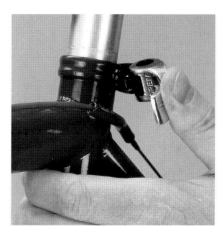

Left and above: Figs. 7.7 and 7.8. Wheel quick-release open and closed.

Right: Figs. 7.9 and 7.10. Brake and seat clamp quick releases.

adjusting the brake), or the brake may open at the worst possible time.

CABLE CONTROLS

Flexible cable controls are commonly used on the bicycle to operate hand brakes and gear shifting devices. They're often referred to as "Bowden cables" after their inventor.

The cable control combines a flexible, but non-stretching, stranded inner cable, or wire, to take up tension forces, with a flexible but non-compressible wound spiral outer cover, or sleeve, to take up compression forces. The ends of the outer cover are restrained in fixed cup-shaped attachments, while the inner wire has a soldered or crimped-on nipple at one end and is clamped to a moving part of the derailleur or the brake at the other end.

In some cases, the cables are sold only as matched sets in a

CABLE ROUTING NOTES

All current cable-operated brake-shifting systems from SRAM, Campagnolo, and Shimano run the shifter cables under the handlebar tape. The first 250—300mm of shifter housing is a combination of extreme bends that if not set up properly can result in much greater friction and decreased life of the shifter housing and cables. Greater care needs to be taken to make sure that the shifting is smooth and precise. Here are some tips to make sure that your shifting is smooth, fast and precise:

1. The shifters from all three companies offer alternate routing of cables as they exit the shifter. One option routes the cable housing in front of the bar and the other routes the cables straight out of the back of the shifter and toward the back of the bar. In all cases, the straight shot out the back of the shifter to the rear of the bar will be result in the least kinks and the smoothest shifting possible. Unfortunately, most bikes come assembled in the front location because it looks "tidier" under the bar tape.

2. Next, as the housing exits from under the handlebar to be routed to the downtube, the traditional method has been to route the right side shifter housing to the right side of the down tube. This produces a sharp bend to the housing as it exits from under the bar tape, decreased turning radius before the cables bind, and creates housing rub against the side of the head tube. Route the right side shifter housing to the left side of the downtube (It will follow the same path as the rear brake cable) and then route the left side shifter housing to the right side of the down tube. The shifter cables will need to cross each other mid way down the downtube in an X pattern in order to reach their proper location on either side of the bottom bracket. This routing will result in much smoother arcs to the housing, less friction, and no rubbing or slapping of the shifter housing on the sides of the head tube.

3. Lubrication: Even though shifter housings may be Teflon-lined, and most high-end cables have some sort of friction reducing finish, it still does not match the shifting performance that can be achieved with lubrication. One type of lubricant that works well is Buzz's Slick Honey.

One reason why down-tube shifters—old-fashioned thought they may seem—work so well is that they don't need outer cables. Except at the guides at the bottom bracket, they don't even need lubrication.

length that is specific to a particular make and model, e.g. in the case of many modern gear-change mechanisms. Otherwise, you can just buy the outer sleeve by the foot or the meter and buy the inner cable in sections long enough to match any application (just make sure the nipple has the right shape and the cable has the same diameter as the original cable used).

To prevent corrosion, apply some lubricant between the inner cable and the outer sleeve. When installing a cable, run the inner cable through a wax-soaked cloth. Later, you can apply just a little oil from a spray can of lubricant at the points where the inner wire disappears into the outer sleeve whenever you do regular maintenance.

The tension of any control cable is adjusted by means of a barrel adjuster, which works in conjunction with the clamping attachment for the inner cable. Although you can usually adjust the system adequately just using this device, you may at times have to undo the clamping nut or screw and clamp the cable in at a slightly different point.

CABLE ADJUSTING PROCEDURE:

1. Check to make sure any quick-release device that may be provided in the system is tensioned, and if not, tension it.

2. Verify whether it is still "out of adjustment" once the quick-release is set properly. If not, proceed to Step 3.

3. Loosen the locknut by several turns, which can usually be done by hand, without the need for a tool.

4. Turn the adjusting barrel out relative to the part into which it is screwed (to increase) or in (to reduce) the tension on the cable. Loosening will open up the brake or make the derailleur shift later; tightening will do the opposite.

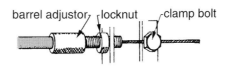

Above: Fig. 7.11. Basic cable adjusting mechanism.

Left: Fig. 7.12. Cable details, showing inner cable, outer cable, or housing, and several nipple types.

Right: Fig. 7.13. Modern cable adjuster on a rear derailleur.

5. Holding the adjusting barrel with one hand, tighten the locknut again.

6. Check to make sure the mechanism is adjusted as intended. If not, repeat until it is.

NOTE:

On most modern road bikes, there is an adjuster without a locknut installed on the brake levers and the derailleurs. In that case, instead of following Steps 3 through 5, merely turn the adjuster out or in to achieve tightening or loosening respectively. In case of the brakes, this only works properly if you first undo the brake quick-release—and don't forget to tension it again afterward.

CABLE FRICTION

Cable friction can significantly diminish the effectiveness of a cable control system. It can be minimized (improving operation

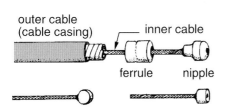

outer cable
(cable casing)   inner cable

ferrule   nipple

barrel adjustor

of the brakes or the gears) by keeping the outer sleeve as short as possible, providing the radius of any curves in the cable is at least 10 times the diameter of the outer cable. Thus, given that most cables measure about 6 mm (¼ inch) in diameter, they can be routed with a curve radius as tight as 6 cm (2.25 in.). However, you may find routing them just a little less tightly "looks" better and that is OK too—within reason.

The cable friction increases drastically with any broken or kinked strands of the inner cable or pinched outer cable. Replace any inner or outer cable that has any of these signs of damage.

The most common way to prevent fraying of the inner cable is by installing a little cap over the end, which then gets crimped on. Remove it by pulling it off with pliers. To install a new cap, you must be careful the cable does not fray as you're trying to push it on. Then use pliers to crimp it on.

A better way to prevent frayed cables is to solder the strands of the cable together before you cut the cable, right at the spot to cut. Unfortunately, it is hard to impossible to solder most modern stainless steel cables.

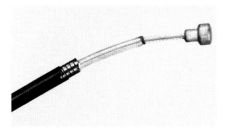

BALL BEARINGS

One of the reasons the bicycle is such an efficient vehicle is the widespread use of ball bearings. They're everywhere on the bike: wheels, pedals, cranks, headset, and freewheel mechanism. This section deals with their function and maintenance.

Ball bearings have to take up different kinds of rotating loads depending on their use on the bicycle. The two main categories are axial and radial loads. On wheel bearings, for example, almost the entire load is perpendicular to the wheel axle, and this is referred to as radial loading. The required basic configuration of a radially loaded bearing is as shown in Fig. 7.21 (top right), with the bearing balls rolling between an inner and an outer bearing race.

The headset bearing, on the other hand, takes mainly a load that is "straight up-and-down," in line with the axis of the steerer tube. This is referred to as axial loading, and the optimum configuration for an axially loaded bearing is with the balls arranged between two same-size bearing races arranged one above the other and axially aligned.

Of course, not all loads fall precisely into one of these two basic categories. The headset

Left: Fig. 7.14. Typical modern cable with low-friction sleeve, or liner, between inner and outer cable.

bearings not only take those axial loads from the road, but they also have to allow the steerer tube to rotate relative to the rest of the bike. And the wheel bearings not only take axial loads, as they do rolling straight ahead, but also some radial loads when cornering. Especially the pedals and the crankset must be designed for offset loads, because the rider pushes hard on one end at a time. Thus, the best way to design the bearings depends on their exact application on the bike, as summarized in Fig. 7.21.

OTHER BEARINGS

Ball bearings are not the only type of bearing in use. Two other varieties are pin (or roller) bearings and journal bearings. The former type uses cylindrical rollers instead of balls between the inner and outer bearing races, while the latter are just plain bushings without any intermediary parts, relying on the lubricant's film strength to minimize friction.

Both of these types are suitable for large radial loads. Roller bearings are sometimes used in the bottom bracket and the pedals. It is even possible to design a variant that will take up a combined radial and axial load, as encountered on the headset. This type of loading calls for tapered rollers running on slanted bearing race surfaces.

Journal bearings are most suitable for high loads at low rotating speeds. The chain consists of what is essentially a multitude of little journal bearings held together by the chain links. Also the derailleur's tension and jockey pulleys usually run on journal bearings. Keeping journal bearings clean and well lubricated is even more critical than it is for other bearing types.

There are also some pedals with journal bearings, but that brings up an interesting problem. Whereas the thrust on the spindle works opposite to the direction of rotation when ball bearings are used, it works in the direction of rotation in the case of journal bearings, as illustrated in Fig. 7.18.

All pedals and cranks are designed with right-hand screw thread for the right pedal and left-hand screw thread for the left pedal. This works to tighten the pedals under the effect of pedaling forward—providing the pedal runs on ball bearings (or roller bearings). However, with journal bearings, the effect is that the pedaling torque tends to loosen the screw-threaded connection between the pedal and the crank. That means that these pedals have to be tightened much more forcefully than other pedals to prevent them from coming loose unintentionally.

BALL BEARING TYPES

Two different types of ball bearings are in use on the bicycle: adjustable and non-adjustable ones. The latter usually referred to as sealed bearings. Actually, those "sealed" bearings are not really fully sealed either, and a more accurate description would be either machine bearings or cartridge bearings, the latter being the term used elsewhere in this book.

The conventional adjustable bearing, also-called cup-and-cone bearing, consists of a cup-shaped bearing race and a cone-shaped one, between which the bearing balls are contained—either loosely or held in a retainer ring—embedded in lubricant. One of the two parts (cone or cup) is adjustable by means of a screw-threaded connection, and is locked in position once it is properly adjusted by means of a lockring screwed up tightly against the screwed bearing part with an intermediate keyed washer (stopped against rotation by means of a lip or flat section that engages a groove or flat section in the male part).

The advantages of the cup-and-cone bearing are threefold:

❑ They are easy to design for a combination of axial and radial loads;

❑ They can be made very light in weight;

❑ They allow adjustment to compensate for wear.

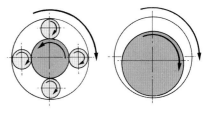

Above: Fig. 7.18. Direction of rotation forces of ball bearing and journal bearing compared.

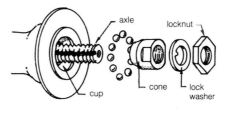

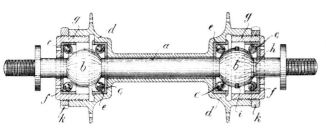

Left, above, and right: Figs. 7.15–7.17. Patent drawing for the 1894 adjustable bearing by Sachs (left); Adjustable cup-and cone bearing (above); cartridge bearing (right).

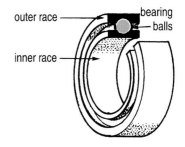

To achieve adjustment on a cup-and-cone bearing, the cup and the cone are screwed closer together or further apart, which reduces or increases the space for the bearing balls. The disadvantage is that it is hard to seal such a bearing against the intrusion of dirt and water, possibly leading to wear and deterioration. For the manufacturer, the disadvantage is the fact that there are many loose parts, making installation more difficult and costly.

The cartridge bearing has been the industry's answer to reduce assembly cost, but has been cleverly disguised as being more "high-tech" (which it isn't). It consists of pre-assembled non-adjustable components: an outer bearing race, an inner bearing race, a bunch of bearing balls held together in a retainer ring, and a set of usually neoprene (artificial rubber) seals.

Their biggest disadvantage is that they are not adjustable and hard to lubricate, although that

may well be offset by less need for lubrication due to better protection against the intrusion of water and dust. When the bearing does get worn or damaged, the entire bearing assembly—the cartridge—has to be pulled off and replaced, requiring special matching tools.

To adjust the conventional adjustable bearing proceed as follows.

CUP-AND-CONE BEARING ADJUSTING PROCEDURE:

1. Loosen the locknut at the end of the bearing assembly.

Above: Fig. 7.19. Close-up of cartridge bearing as used on a wheel hub.

Left: Fig. 7.20. Close-up of adjustable bearing with the dust cap removed.

Right: Fig. 7.21. Different types of loading on ball bearings.

2. Lift the keyed washer clear off the cone.

3. Turn the screwed component (usually the cone, but it may be a cup-shaped part, such as on the headset) in (to tighten) or out (to loosen).

4. Tighten the locknut again while holding the cone or the bearing race with another tool.

When you tighten the two screw-threaded parts against each other, the effect tends to be a slight tightening of the bearing; for that reason, the bearing should feel just a tiny bit loose before you do that. Even so, check to make sure the bearing is adjusted to run smoothly without noticeable play—and if not, tighten or loosen the parts a little and repeat the operation until it is.

Lubrication, though most efficient by means of a thick mineral oil, is usually—and less messily—done with bearing grease, which gets inserted between the bearing surfaces and in which the bearing balls are embedded. Before lubricating a bearing, though, it must be

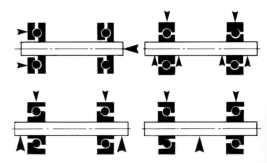

thoroughly cleaned out with solvent and a clean cloth. Whatever you do, don't spray thin lubricant at ball bearings, because that is likely to introduce surface dirt as well as wash out any lubricant inside.

When inspecting a ball bearing, watch out for pitted or corroded surfaces—of the bearing balls or either of the bearing races (cup and cone). Replace any parts that are damaged this way, because they will soon ruin the bearing races and remaining balls.

WEDGED CONNECTIONS

Some items on the bicycle are connected by means of slanted planes, or wedges. Examples of such items are found in the conventional handlebar (i.e. the type used with a threaded headset) and square-tapered cotterless cranksets, as well as the cotter pins on cottered cranks.

The principle of the wedged connection is that a given force results in a much higher perpendicular force if transmitted via

two matching slanted planes. The smaller the angle of the slanted plane relative to the longitudinal plan, the higher the resulting force is (see Fig. 7.23).

If a wedged connection comes loose, it is usually because one of the surfaces is deformed. But keeping the connecting bolt tightened is essential as well. The surfaces must be perfectly smooth and clean, although a lubricant, sparingly applied to one of the surfaces helps tightening the connection as well.

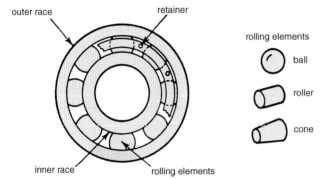

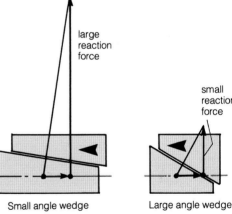

Above: Fig. 7.22. The most common types of rolling-element bearings. A needle bearing (not shown) is a roller bearing with more smaller-diameter rollers. A journal bearing (not shown) does not have rolling elements but relies on a thin layer of lubricant between the inner and outer races, and therefore is technically also referred to as a "fluid-film bearing."

Right: Fig. 7.23. Wedge connection and resulting perpendicular force compared for different slant angles.

8

THE FRAME

TRADITIONALLY, most bicycle frames are constructed of metal tubing, welded together into a roughly diamond-shaped structure. The front fork is held in the frame's head tube by means of the headset. At the lowest point of the frame is another short tubular piece that contains the crankset bearings.

Often frame and fork are combined and sold as a single unit. Together, they are referred to as a frameset.

WHAT'S NEW IN FRAMES

Worldwide, the vast majority of bicycle frames are still

Fig. 8.1. Modern frame made as an integral whole built up out of layers of oriented carbon-fiber embedded in epoxy instead of using separate tubes connected at the joints. It's light and stiff, but also fragile and expensive.

built this same way, using steel tubing. However, over the last two decades, high-end frame construction and design have changed quite a bit, mainly due to the use of different materials and the proliferation of suspension systems, especially on mountain bikes. As for materials, most frames sold in the u.s. are now made of aluminum alloy, while also titanium, carbon-fiber, and even magnesium are in use. However, high-strength steel alloy seems to be making a comeback on the new breed of "fixies," or lightweight single-speed bikes, and are still widely used in cyclo-cross racing.

The problem with many of the "new" materials is that frames and forks made with them are more fragile on impact and less repairable than steel frames and forks are. Some of them, such as carbon-fiber, can fail catastrophically in case of an impact that would have led to no more than a bent tube on a steel frame, which is much less likely to lead to serious injury, and is much less expensive to fix.

Even amongst metal frames, there has been a shift, away from conventional straight tubing toward specially formed tubular frame members that have varying diameters, wall thicknesses and even overall shapes along their length.

FRAME SIZE

Frame size is usually defined as the length of the seat tube, measured along the tube axis in one of two ways:

❏ From the center of the bottom bracket to the top of the seat lug (referred to as C–T, and usually quoted in inches);

❏ From the center of the bottom bracket to the center of the top tube (referred to as C–C, and usually quoted in cm).

The first measure is the conventional method used in the English-speaking world. In most cases, the same frame will be quoted approximately 15 mm, or $^5/8$ in. less when measured center-to-center than when measured from the center of the bracket to the top of the seat lug.

Since many modern frames don't have a horizontal top tube, the second way of measuring can

Above: Fig. 8.2. A conventionally constructed lugged steel frame.

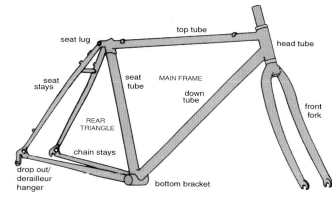

Left: Fig. 8.3. Nomenclature of frame parts.

FRAME ECONOMICS

In a typical bicycle, the frame represents about 40% of the complete bike's total value. A stock, off-the-shelf bike is sold as a complete unit comprising the frame and a set of other components selected by the manufacturer for that particular model. However, it is also possible to buy (usually for more money) a custom bicycle, equipping a bare frame with components of the customer's choice: all readily available, along with advice, from the bike shop. A

further step up in customization (and usually price) is a bike based on a real custom-built frame, made to measure for a particular cyclist by a specialist frame builder.

When choosing a custom bike or frame, it is also customary to select frame and components of similar quality, and therefore similar price categories, so the ratio of 40% frame, 60% other parts usually applies here too.

If you are on a tight budget, it may be smart to select the highest quality frame you can

afford, and save on components of a lower price category. There are two reasons for this. In the first place, the frame can last a lifetime, while the other parts will probably have to be replaced sooner or later, which will be a good time to upgrade them if desired. In the second place, the difference between components may lie more in their finish than in their inherent quality, and it makes no sense to pay extra for a shiny finish when you are on a tight budget.

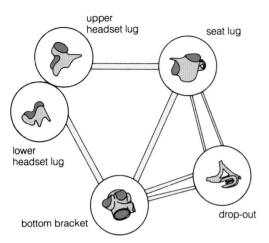

upper headset lug

seat lug

lower headset lug

bottom bracket

drop-out

be rather hard to define. What many manufacturers do to get around this, they measure from the center of the bottom bracket to an imaginary point along the seat tube where a horizontal top tube would be if it did exist, running horizontal from a point just

Left: Fig. 8.4. Traditionally, steel frames are built with external lugs, and this illustration identifies their designations.

below the headset. Still, it is rather vague and open to individual interpretation.

It would probably be best to give several sizes: straddle height (distance between the ground and the top of the top tube), minimum and maximum distance between saddle and bottom bracket, and minimum and maximum handlebar height. In addition, the top tube length, measured horizontally between

TUBE STRENGTH, WEIGHT, AND STIFFNESS

This is perhaps a good place to clear up some confusion about weight and strength. Within any metal—whether steel, aluminum, or titanium—all alloys have practically the same density (as described in Chapter 5). The difference in weight comes only from differences in wall thickness and tube diameter. If two tubes have the same diameter but the one has a smaller wall thickness, it will be correspondingly lighter.

If a relatively weak alloy is used, as on most welded tubes, adequate tube strength can only be achieved by using a relatively greater wall thickness. When a stronger high alloy is used, the same overall tube strength can be achieved with less wall thickness.

To give an example, let's compare a tube of the same diameter made of plain welded

carbon steel with one of the same diameter made of cold drawn chrome-molybdenum steel. The former has a tensile strength of 541 N/mm^2. A 1 in. (25.4 mm) diameter tube with 1.4 mm wall thickness using this material can handle a tensile load of 57,000 N. The high-strength alloy tube has a tensile strength of 1,050 N/mm^2. If this stronger material is used instead, the same 57,000 N load can be handled by a tube of the same diameter with a 0.7 mm wall thickness, and it should be clear that it will be about half as heavy.

As the wall thickness is reduced, the tube will become less stiff, regardless how strong the material. So, given identical frames, the one made of high-quality steel will feel more flexible as well as lighter. What governs stiffness is the modulus of elasticity (see Chapter 5). Since that is less for aluminum than for steel, a frame made of

aluminum tubes of the same dimensions would be even more flexible. Even if the wall thickness is increased to make it equally strong, it would become so flexible that a phenomenon called "plastic deformation" might set in, that is, the frame might permanently bend under a load which wouldn't trouble the steel frame.

To get around this issue, most builders choose to make aluminum frames with "oversize" tubing, i.e. the tubes have a greater outside diameter. For strength, they still need the same total amount of material, but it is spread over a larger diameter, and therefore the wall thickness can be kept smaller. There is a limit to how large and thin tubes can be made, because if it exceeds a certain ratio, of perhaps 1:50, the tubes might buckle like a beverage can being crushed.

the seat tube and the top of the head tube, should be quoted.

FRAME CONSTRUCTION

Fig. 8.3 shows the way a typical conventional "diamond-shaped" frame is built up. The four relatively large-diameter main frame tubes are arranged in the form of a trapezoid (though because one tube is short, this part of the frame is often called the "main triangle"), to which is attached a rear triangle made up of pairs of smaller-diameter tubes.

The main frame tubes are called top tube, head tube, down tube, and seat tube. The rear triangle's members are referred to

as seatstays and chainstays. The pairs of chainstays and seatstays are connected by means of short "bridges," usually made of tubing, but sometimes flat plates (on low-end bikes) or pre-formed parts similar to lugs (on high-end bikes).

The main frame and the rear triangle are joined at the top and bottom of the seat tube. At the lowest point of the frame, where down tube, seat tube, and chainstays meet, is a short tubular member that runs perpendicular to the other tubes and is referred to as the bottom bracket shell. At

Right: Fig. 8.5. Custom frames are built by framebuilders using a jig like this one to position the tubes to the desired angles and positions.

BUTTED TUBES AND MORE

The difference between plain gauge tubing and butted tubing is that the former has the same wall thickness along its entire length, and the latter is thinner in the middle than at one or both ends. On single butted tubes only one end is thicker, and on double-butted tubing both ends are thicker. Butting is done for one or both of two reasons: to allow welding or high-temperature brazing at the ends of otherwise thin-walled tubes, and/or to add strength where needed.

The highest strength steel alloy butted tubes have a wall

thickness of only 0.5 mm in the middle and have butts that go up to about 1 mm. For materials that are not as strong, or for frames that are designed for high forces, a wall thickness of 0.7 mm is more typical, and the ends will be up to 1.2 mm. Titanium tubes usually have dimensions close to those for steel tubes.

For aluminum tubes butting is not quite as important, because the material is so much weaker than steel or titanium that it requires more wall thickness for adequate strength. But with the use of oversize tubing, the wall thickness can be kept to a minimum,

making butting advantageous for aluminum tubing as well.

So what about the "triple butted," "quadruple butted," etc. that is claimed for some bike frames? An odd choice of words: "Butt" means end, and we've never seen a tube with more (or less) than two ends. What those advertising copy-writing types mean is tubing with multiple wall thicknesses. Multiple thicknesses can be achieved with modern manufacturing techniques, and are not a bad idea for some tubes, such as the down tube of a bike with rear suspension, which may have loads applied at certain locations that are not at one end or the other.

the ends, where seat and chain-stays meet, they are attached to flat parts referred to as dropouts, in which the rear wheel is installed.

Assuming derailleur gearing is used on the bike, the

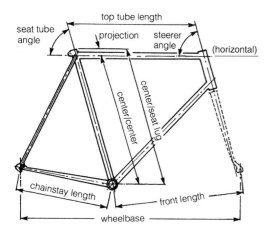

right-hand dropout is usually equipped with an attachment lug for the derailleur. Finally, there are often a number of small parts, referred to as braze-ons, which allow the installation of various components and accessories, and to provide stops or guides for gear and brake cables.

Usually the top of the seat tube is split in the back and equipped with a clamp to hold the seatpost. The clamp may be either integral with the lug, referred to as seat cluster, or a

separate clamp around the top of the seat tube. The connections between the frame tubes can be made with or without lugs (reinforcement members into, or sometimes over, which the tubes are attached). Although most of today's frames are welded, there are also other processes in use: brazing, used for high-strength thin-wall steel tubing as well as for all lugged steel frames, and bonding, using an epoxy to hold carbon (and sometimes aluminum) tubes and lugs together.

WELDING AND BRAZING OF STEEL

The difference between brazing and welding (not only TIG welding, but other types of welding as well) is that the material used for welding is a rod of the same base material as that of the tubes—steel for steel tubes, aluminum for aluminum tubes, and titanium for titanum tubes. This requires a much higher temperature than brazing.

Brazing materials for use with steel tubes fall into two main categories, referred to as "bronze" and "silver" brazing. They have more in common than the names imply. Both are alloys consisting of mainly copper and nickel. The "silver" alloy also contains about 50% silver,

and its effect is that the material flows thin at a lower temperature (about 600 degrees C) than regular bronze brazing alloy (about 800 degrees C). This makes the silver brazing process more suitable for really thin-wall tubing, because heating that too much would weaken the metal.

Now for welding: for steel, that takes place at temperatures above 2,000 degrees C, so the trick is to do it very quickly. For that reason the process is carried out using a machine that feeds the welding wire and blows an inert gas around the heated work piece.

In welding, the weld rod material fully flows together with the material of the tubes and becomes indistinguishable from it. But even in brazing, there is a

certain degree of alloying between the brazing material and the tube material, though only at the boundaries.

All these processes actually harden (and thus strengthen) the material immediately at the joint. However, the heating and subsequent cooling of the tube a short distance away from the actual joint creates a weakened area, referred to as the "heat-effected zone." Weakening in this area is quite significant in the case of aluminum, and for that reason it is often recommended to reinforce particularly sensitive areas, like the bottom of the down tube, just below the down tube to head tube joint, by welding on a reinforcing gusset.

LUGGED STEEL FRAME CONSTRUCTION

The use of external lugs to connect steel frame tubes dates back to the early days of the bicycle, when the connecting lugs were made of cast iron. Significant weight savings were made with the introduction of pressed steel lugs, first used in the U.S. by Pope's Columbia. This method was soon copied by Raleigh in the U.K., who could advertise their product as "the all-steel bicycle." The hydraulic presses used for making the steel lugs had actually been developed by German metal toy manufacturers.

The use of heavy cast iron lugs has long since been abandoned world-wide, and pressed steel is still the most common material for bicycle frame lugs. Another process for making lugs is "investment," or "lost wax" steel casting. This process leads to precisely dimensioned lugs. Using investment cast lugs, the gap between the outside of the tube and the inside of the lug can be minimal and consistent.

When brazing a lugged frame, the lugs and the ends of the tubes are heated, and a brazing material is melted to penetrate the gap. When cooled off,

Right: Fig. 8.7. Tom Ritchey, one of the fathers of the mountain bike, at work brazing a steel frame.

WELDING OF ALUMINUM

It is trickier to weld aluminum than steel because of surface oxidation. Upon contact with air, or any other source of oxygen, a thin, extremely hard surface layer of aluminum-oxide is formed. The aluminum-oxide has a much higher melting point than the aluminum itself, thus preventing the melted aluminum of the two parts from bonding properly.

The solution is to weld with an alternating current source, which can break up the aluminum-oxide layer. However, the root of the weld (the opposite side, away from the welding surface) often still does not bond properly due to remnants of the oxide layer.

Consequently It is critical to weld aluminum only in an inert gas atmosphere, using either TIG (tungsten inert gas) or a MIG (machine inert gas) process. The latter process creates a rather crude looking heavy weld "slug" and is mainly found on low-end bike frames, whereas the TIG process is purely applied by hand and requires significant skill.

Due to its high coefficient of thermal expansion, aluminum welding tends to lead to deformation of the work piece (e.g. the bike frame being welded). This effect can be minimized by preheating the material and by

securely holding the individual parts together in place by means of a welding jig.

Finally, due to weakening of the weld zone, the material loses much of its strength. This is subsequently recovered by means of a heat treatment process, applied either to the entire work piece or selectively to the area of the weld.

Fig. 8.8. TIG-welder at work on an aluminum frame.

the brazing material forms a strong solid bond between the tube and the lug. Withing limits, the smaller the gap, the stronger the bond, and that is the reason

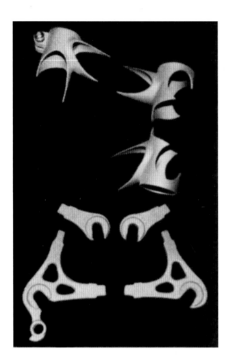

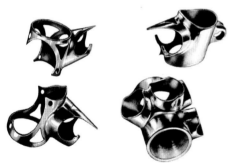

why investment cast lugs are so suitable for the purpose. In fact, on a good brazed joint, some local alloying takes place, with the molecules of the brazing material and those of the tubes and the lug mingling.

However, pressed steel lugs also have their advantages. When heated, they can be bent slightly without damage, so they can be adapted to minor differences in frame angles. Investment cast lugs cannot be bent, and thus are

Above and top left: Fig. 8.9 and 8.10. Henry James investment-cast steel lugs and bottom bracket shell.

Lower left: Figs. 8.11. Haden pressed steel lugs and bottom bracket shell.

Right: Fig. 8.12. Seat lug on a lugged Rivendell frame with investment cast lugs before painting.

suitable only for the specific frame angles for which they are designed.

LUGLESS FRAME CONSTRUCTION

Today it is more common even for steel frames to be built without the use of lugs, just as is done for most aluminum and other metals. To achieve that, the tubes have to be very accurately cut and mitered at the ends, so that they fit around each other perfectly, leaving only the tiniest gap. The ends are then heated, while the tubes are held together in a jig, after which the brazing material is inserted and allowed to penetrate and build up slightly around the joint areas. This

HYDROFORMING

Whereas conventional frame tubes have a regular, usually cylindrical shape, many aluminum frames have tubes that vary in diameter and shape along their length. Beyond that, some aluminum frames are built up as a single unit (at least for the main

frame, which then is usually no longer built up like the conventional trapezoid but as a monocoque structure.

The technique used to achieve all these different shapes is referred to as hydroforming. In this process, the material is placed in a die inside an enclosed pressure vessel, and

hydraulic liquid is injected at very high pressure to deform the metal as desired. Since this process takes place at room temperature, the material strength and weldability are not reduced. In fact, the process actually enhances the material's molecular structure, giving it greater strength and hardness.

process is referred to either as "lugless" or "fillet" brazing, and can be recognized by its smooth, slightly rounded joint contours. The main advantage of this technique is that it offers great flexibility in the choice of frame angles and tube diameters. The resulting frames weigh about the same as similarly dimensioned lugged frames, because the extra brazing material just about offsets the weight savings achieved by not using lugs.

Most frames today, however, are TIG-welded. The term stands for Tungsten Inert Gas welding. TIG-welded joints can be recognized by rather abrupt, though not rough, contours at the joints. The process is used for steel, aluminum, magnesium, and titanium frames alike, though for each of these materials, specific welding wires are used and the process is carried out at material-specific temperatures. As with lugless brazing, the entire frame is held in a jig while it is being built.

A cheaper welding process is called MIG-welding, where the M stands for "machine-fed wire." Whereas TIG-welding is done by hand with careful application of the weld rod, MIG-welding is done by machine. It results in a rather crude looking weld bead, and is used mainly on low-end aluminum bike frames.

JOINT FINISH

To achieve an attractive appearance, the joints can be filed smooth, regardless whether they are brazed or welded. Although claims are made for and against this practice by various builders, to date there is no evidence of either method is superior, as long

Right: Fig. 8.13. Detail of TIG-welded joint on a Titus titanium frame.

DIFFERENT TUBES

Main frame tubes used to be perfectly cylindrical from beginning to end, while only fork blades and chainstays were tapered. That's still true for many frames, but in recent years the trend has been toward main frame tubes that vary in diameter and shape.

A departure from cylindrical tubes may better accommodate the forces that are applied to the different locations along the length of the tubes. What really matters for strength is not so much the force applied as the resulting stress, which is the force per square mm of the material. Using a technique called finite element analysis, it is possible to define the stresses at any point along the frame tubes. In a conventionally built frame, those stresses are higher in certain locations than in others.

Where they are higher, the material may be overstressed, and where they are lower, there is more material, and consequently more weight than necessary. To try to equalize the stresses, it's often more effective to vary the diameter and/or shape of the tube than simply to vary the wall thickness, as in butting.

Modern manufacturing techniques, such as hydroforming, make it possible for manufacturers to shape aluminum and some other materials accordingly.

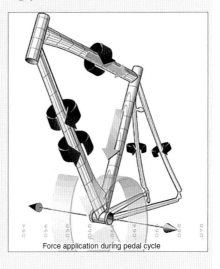

Fig. 8.14. One manufacturer's (Litespeed) representation of rationale for forming tubes, generally by hydroforming to best accommodate the stresses to which the frame is subjected.

as the filing does not cut into the base metal and retains the weld's smooth contours.

CARBON FRAME CONSTRUCTION

Carbon frames can be made in one of two ways:

❑ using carbon tubes bonded together at the joints;

❑ using monocoque construction as an integral

Left: Fig. 8.15. Superlight carbon road bike frame and fork.

Above and right: Figs. 8.16 and 8.17. Carbon is a fine material, but it's sensitive to abuse and can fail catastrophically upon impact.

unit built up in two halves that are joined together.

In the former, the tubes are held in a jig when the joints are wrapped with overlapping differently oriented mats of impregnated carbon-fiber cloth.

AND FINALLY

In recent years some manufacturers have adopted a combination

CARBON-FIBER FRAME CONSTRUCTION METHODS

Carbon frames are constructed either of two methods: "bladder molded" or "tube-to-tube."

For a bladder-molded frame (the most common form), carbon mats that have been pre-impregnated with resin are hand-laid in specific patterns and thicknesses over a nylon or latex bladder. The "pre-preg" carbon is then inserted in a mold that is heated up to high temperatures to melt the resin, while the bladder is inflated to a high pressure to drive out any air in the material and push the carbon to its final

shape. After cooling, the seatstays and chainstays are bonded to the front triangle.

Tube-to-tube construction is very different from Monocoque. It allows much more flexible manufacturing and very low frame weights. In this method, each tube is made individually to exacting standards. The tubes are then mitered like you would miter an alloy tube for a bicycle. Glue is applied to the ends of the mitered tubes and then the frame is pre-assembled in its final

Fig. 8.18. Overlapping of oriented carbon-fiber mats in the construction of a Trek bike frame.

geometry. The frame is then reinforced by wrapping carbon around all the joints. After the finished frame is cured the result is a very light, sub-900 gram, frame (at least in the smallest size).

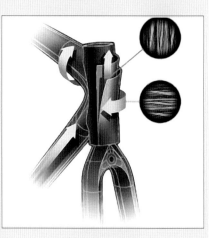

---

of materials for their top-end frame tubes. Typically this technique combines cut-out titanium tubes, compressed around a thin carbon composite tube. The result is an exceptionally high strength-to-weight ratio, increased shock damping (compared to single-material tubes of the same diameter)—all at an astronomic price, of course Figs. 5.26 and 5.27, on page 64, show examples of this technique, referred to as Exogrid.

FRAME DESIGN

There are a number of factors that determine the overall design of a bicycle frame. These include the size of the frame, as well as what is generally referred to as frame geometry: the length and angles of the individual tubes and their relationship.

FRAME ANGLES

The frame angles are those of the head tube and the seat tube, measured with respect to the ground. On most modern road bikes, both the head tube angle (also-called steerer angle) and

CARBON-FIBER FRAMES

Even before carbon-fiber frames hit the market, some manufacturers were making bikes by bonding metal tubes into lugs made of short-fiber-reinforced epoxy. It was not until 1987 that the first experiments with all-carbon made it to ridable bicycles. And even at that early stage, these two approaches emerged.

The pioneers in carbon monocoque construction are Kestrel in the U.S. and Look in France. Both claim to have been first off the block with series-production frames, although several custom frame builders had also worked with the same materials and techniques.

Monocoque frames can be made in parts that are later joined together or they can be made in a process called "bladder molding," as described in the sidebar on page 96.

All-carbon bikes made with tubes are made with lugs that are built up of layered carbon-fiber matting embedded in epoxy wound around the areas where the tubes join. A pioneer in this method is Calfee, of Santa Cruz, which also goes as far back as 1987. By now, this same company has expanded its range with some models that use bamboo for the frame tubes and hemp fiber instead of carbon for the joints, resulting in a bike with the absolute minimum "carbon footprint." Although none of the major manufacturers use bamboo and hemp yet, the same techniques used are now common with most carbon-fiber frame builders.

With either method, it is important to keep in mind which parts of the frame will be stressed in which direction. To accommodate stresses, the fibers are oriented in a crossing and overlapping pattern, and the more heavily loaded areas are reinforced with more layers.

Left: Fig. 8.19. Early example of carbon frame tubes epoxied (bonded) around aluminum lugs. Note the bulged shape of the frame tubes where they fit over the lug.

Right: Fig. 8.20. Detail on an early Kestrel bladder-built carbon frame.

the seat tube angle are at about 73 degrees. However, they don't have to be the same. A numerically larger angle is called "steeper' (i.e. more nearly vertical); a smaller angle, "shallower" (i.e. closer to horizontal).

Making the seat angle shallower places the rider further back on the bike, so the chainstays also have to be made longer to keep a reasonable ballance. It is often done for utility bikes to allow the rider to reach the ground without compromising the distance between the seat and the pedals. This is most extreme on recumbent bikes.

Making the seat angle steeper allows for the construction of a shorter frame and places the rider further forward. This is often done for time trial bikes to achieve a more forward-posed "aero" rider position, but it can also be done to accommodate short riders, so you'll often find it on a manufacturer's smallest frame sizes.

The head tube, or steerer, angle must be considered in conjunction with the fork, and this issue will be covered in detail in Chapter 10, which deals with the steering system. Simply put, a shallower angle (requiring more fork rake) makes for more comfort but generally a less agile bike, whereas a steeper angle results in a harsher but more responsive bike. For riding on a track or perfectly smooth asphalt, the steep frame angle is fine, but it is not good for a bike ridden in the real world of potholed roads or even moderately pitted and grooved asphalt.

OTHER FRAME VARIANTS

Other frame designs, using the same basic construction method but with different tube configurations, have been more or less popular at times, especially for women's bikes and special-purpose machines. In addition, quite

different frame designs, often based on specific manufacturing techniques, have been making some inroads in recent years. Fig. 8.23 shows some of the different designs based on conventional manufacturing techniques. Some of the more revolutionary designs based on differing techniques will be covered separately.

To determine which of the shapes shown in Fig. 8.23 is suitable, the purpose must be kept in mind. If the lightest, strongest and stiffest frame possible is desired, then this is the wrong place to look. If, on the other hand, the most important criterion for a particular rider is to obtain a low straddling point, then this may go at the expense of some other factors. To get the same strength or stiffness, increased weight due to the selection of thicker walled tubing may be accepted.

From a technical standpoint, the important thing is to form a strong and direct connection between the tie points. A frame structure should resist both the vertical forces applied by the rider's weight, and the various lateral and torsional forces that are exerted due to asymmetrical

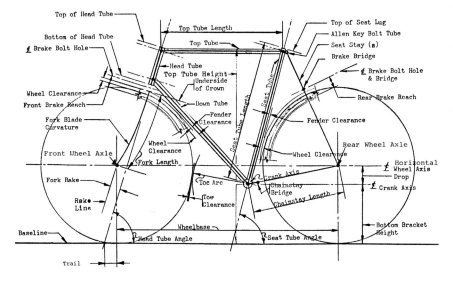

Left: Fig. 8.21. Fully worked-out design drawing for a touring bike. This illustration is from Richard Talbot's 1979 publication *Designing and Building Your Own Frameset*, and it is as valid today as it was at the time.

loading under movement. Braking, steering and vibrations also cause variable forces that must be absorbed.

All these criteria can be easily met if weight is not an object. But in bicycle design it is always a goal to minimize frame weight. A prospective designer or interested tinkerer might wish to compare the effect of forces on various frame designs by making models of thin metal or wood rods, pinned together at the joints, freely pivoted. Only the designs that do not collapse are structurally sound, and the various women's models shown do not pass this simple test.

Fig. 8.22 shows the distribution of forces on the conventional bicycle frame resulting from vertical, static loading. As you can see, the various tubes are arranged in such a way that the forces are always applied in line with the tube's linear axis, either in tension or in

compression. This design was developed in the late eighteen-eighties and has essentially formed the basis for all bicycle frames since that time. These findings cannot only be confirmed in layman's fashion with the modeling technique mentioned above, but also in engineering terms by means of a relatively easily accessible technique known as finite element analysis.

It took a little longer before bicycle designers realized that the asymmetrical and variable forces applied during motion must also be considered. These did not pose such a problem on early bicycle frames, due to the use of very thick-walled tubing or even solid members of significant diameter, which are adequately stiff. In recent times, more attention has been paid to this factor due to the inherent lack of stiffness of very thin-walled tubing. Ideally, the frame

should have some vertical flexibility, because this provides shock damping, while retaining maximum lateral stiffness to prevent instability. Of all the designs used to date, the conventional diamond-shaped frame remains the most satisfactory, especially if

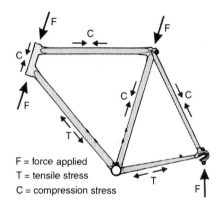

F = force applied
T = tensile stress
C = compression stress

Above: Fig. 8.22. Forces and stresses to which a statically loaded bike frame is subjected. It gets more complicated once you start pedaling.

Left: Fig. 8.23. Some of the alternate frame configurations that are still in use on some bikes. Except the one top left, all of the designs shown here aim at providing a lowered top tube. Except for the one top right, all these options result in decreased stability.

Below: Fig. 8.24. Dynamic (pedaling) forces cause torsional loading.

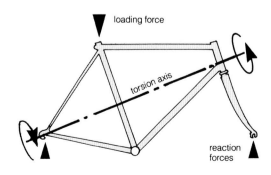

large diameter, thin-walled tubing is used.

Some different design details have been introduced at times, especially in conjunction with the use of other materials than steel, not all of which offer real advantages. The once popular raised-chainstay mountain bike frame design shown in Fig. 8.26 loses its triangulated integrity, in order to achieve a greater amount of chain clearance. It weighs considerably more than a frame with straight chainstays.

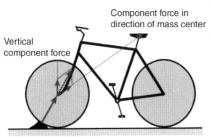

Reaction force due to obstacle

Reaction force due to pothole

Reaction force due to horizontal impact

DESIGN CONSTRAINTS

Of course, the first constraint to consider is the rider. Whatever else also matters, the bike must fit the rider comfortably. The discussion in Chapter 7 described the most important dimensions that should be considered as they apply to a conventional frame. Just where the rider's hands, feet, and seat must be placed on a bicycle for best control over the machine is a matter of basic ergonomics and has essentially remained unchanged since the turn of the 20th century. The use of "Tri-bar" handlebars, allowing a lower and more stretched-out posture, only works if speed alone matters, rather than control over the bike.

A shorter tube is stiffer and provides less shock absorption than a longer one. Consequently, a small frame is both relatively light and relatively stiff, and as these attributes are considered desirable, there has been a trend to reduce both the height and length of the bicycle frame

Left: Fig. 8.25. The effects of external impacts on the combination of frame and fork. Depending on the bicycle's intended use, these must also be considered in the frame design.

Right: Fig. 8.26. Raised-chainstay frame design, which was sometimes used to increase chain clearance above the ground for mountain bikes before suspension became almost universal on mountain bikes.

intended for a rider of a given size. To achieve the reduced dimensions, clearances between the wheels and the frame are minimized.

On the other hand, it makes no sense to make the frame so small that seat and handlebars have to be raised and extended by means of an overly long seatpost and handlebar stem, because these extensions are themselves less stiff, giving the bike not more, but less stability overall.

Another factor that greatly influences overall frame stiffness is the length (and the diameter) of the head tube: frame designs that maximize head tube length, within the given sizing constraints, achieve greater steering stability by holding the front fork more securely. As for the diameter of the head tube, the introduction of integrated headsets, fully embedded in a head tube of greater diameters does contribute to overall frame stiffness and steering predictability.

Most common designs work fine for the majority of male riders. If you're anywhere from 160 cm (5 ft. 3 in.) to 188 cm (6 ft. 2 in.), and your limbs are not unusually long or short in

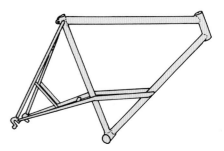

proportion, you probably won't have any difficulty finding a standard frame to fit you. For women, as well as men whose physique differs from that norm, more specific information can be found in Chapter 22.

The other major considerations in determining the dimensions and angles of a bicycle frame are the following:

❑ Wheel size (small: fit smaller riders, low mass for quick acceleration; large: less shock from road or trail);

❑ Tire width (narrow: low mass, low rolling resistance for efficiency esp. racing; wide: support heavier loads, ride on rough or broken surfaces);

❑ Bottom bracket height (low: stability; high: clearance over rocks and logs, pedal clearance when cornering);

❑ Bottom bracket to front wheel (short: quick handling; long: relaxed handling, less road shock);

❑ Chainstay length (short: reduced mass, quick handling; long: relaxed handling, less road shock, heel clearance for panniers);

❑ Head tube length (short: fit smaller riders; long: fit taller riders, allow greater handlebar height range, but reduces directional stability);

❑ Seat tube length (short: fit smaller riders, stiffer frame, reduced mass; long: fit taller riders);

❑ Top tube length (short: fit smaller riders or riders with shorter torso, e.g. women; long: fit taller riders, riders with longer torso);

❑ Steerer tube angle (shallow: less road shock; steep: quick handling);

❑ Seat tube angle (shallow: less road shock; steep: reduced mass, quick handling);

❑ Chainstay and seatstay bridge clearance (short: reduced mass, stiffer frame, allow short-reach brakes; long: allow larger tires for rough surfaces or greater reliability, allow fenders);

❑ Rear dropout spacing (fit standard rear axle widths).

The following sections describe how these various dimensions and angles are related to the overall design of the bicycle frame.

Wheel Size

Most adult bikes today roll on wheels that have an outside diameter of 650 to 700 mm. However, folding bikes, BMX bikes, children's bikes, and recumbents are typically designed around smaller diameter wheels (recuments sometimes for different diameters front and rear). For large-size mountain bikes, 29-in.

Left: Fig. 8.27. Frame geometries of road bike and touring bike compared. In addition to the different geometry, the touring bike must be built with stiffer tubing (either larger diameter, greater wall thickness, or both) to withstand the (greater) forces over the increased tube lengths.

Right: Fig. 8.28. This Joe Breeze prototype had a cross frame with tension ties. Elegant, but the torsional stiffness of this design may be questionable.

wheels, with an outside diameter of about 735 mm, have gained some popularity in recent years.

Bottom Bracket Height

For comfort, It's nice to have the bottom bracket as close to the ground as practical. However, it must be high enough so the pedal does not scrape on the ground (and possibly lead to a fall) when cornering. The Germans—world champions in issuing regulations and specifying standards as they are—even have a national DIN standard that specifies how the pedal must clear when the bike leans over by 23 degrees with the crank in bottom position. And that, in turn, depends on the crank length and the pedal width.

The following dimensions have been found to work well for different bicycle types:

Road bikes: 28 cm (11 in.);

Mountain bikes: 30–35 cm (12–14 in.);

Touring and randonneur bikes: 30 cm (12 in.);

City bikes: 46 cm (12 in.);

Track bikes: 27 cm (10.5 in.).

These figures are all based on the use of 170 mm cranks and 700C or 26-inch wheels, which are the most common on adult bikes. Shorter and longer cranks require correspondingly less or more bottom bracket height (the range of crank sizes is 165 mm to 180 mm for most adult machines).

There is another way of measuring bottom bracket height that is referred to as "drop" and measures how much lower the bottom bracket is than the wheel axles. To convert from bottom bracket drop to bottom bracket height, use the following formula:

$$BBH = 0.5\ Dw - BBD$$

where

BBH = bottom bracket height

BBD = Bottom bracket drop

Dw = actual, measured, wheel diameter.

Front Length

The main concern about the distance between the bottom bracket and the front wheel is that there should preferably be no overlap between the front wheel and the rider's toe with the crank pointing forward, which might otherwise lead to a fall when steering. Although skilled road racers can handle overlap, for most of us mere mortals, it is a lot safer to be able to steer clear of your forward foot. Here too, the crank length plays a significant role, but so does the size of the rider's foot and the diameter of the front wheel.

Although the toe clearance requirement may be waived on road racing bikes (because high-speed cycling never requires large steering movements), it is quite critical for mountain, touring, and city bikes, and the use of fenders requires even more clearance. As a guideline, the distance between bottom bracket and front wheel axle is usually about 55 cm (22 in.) on a road bike, about 58 cm (23 in.) on a recreational bike,

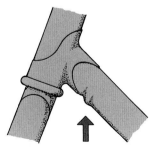

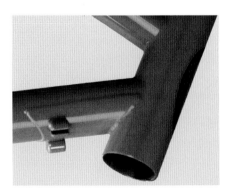

Left: Fig. 8.29. Upon frontal impact, this point may get damaged: the bottom of the downtube, just behind the head tube joint.

Right: Fig. 8.30. Reinforcing gusset at the frame's most sensitive point.

and should be at least 60 cm (24 in.) if fenders will be installed.

Chain Stay Length

Chain stay length is the distance between the bottom bracket and the rear wheel axle. It should be enough to provide clearance between the seat tube and the tire. And for bikes designed for use with fenders (touring and city bikes, a minimum of 40 mm additional fender clearance is needed.

The seat tube angle also plays a role in this equation, because the shallower that angle, the further the rear wheel will have to be brought back for adequate clearance. More about this subject under *Seat Tube Angle*, below.

Touring and city bikes, as well as carrier bikes, need quite long chainstays for another reason as well. To safely carry luggage over the rear wheel, as much as possible of the load should be carried in front of the rear wheel axle, while any panniers there should not interfere with the back of the rider's foot when pedaling.

The resulting longer chainstays (and also the seatstays) have to be beefed up a little to make them strong enough over that greater length. That's one of the reasons this kind of bike frame cannot be made as light as a road bike frame. Here is a summary of typical seatstay

lengths for frames of different categories.

Road bikes and track bikes: 40 cm (16 in.)

Mountain bikes: 43 cm (17 in.)

Touring bikes and city bikes: 45 cm (18 in.)

Head Tube Length

The head tube length defines the distance between the upper and lower headset bearings. It has been established that a longer head tube results in more steering stability. On bikes for smaller riders, this dimension will tend to get rather small, and for that reason a smaller than usual front wheel will be advantageous.

To keep the head tube long enough on small bikes, some manufacturers provide a top tube that slopes downward from the head tube to the seat tube. This allows a low seat position and step-over clearance. Though not pretty, this solution can work, as long as the rider accepts a more upright posture than the typical racing posture with the

Right: Fig. 8.31. Simple frame stiffness test for torsional forces applied to the bottom bracket. One of the surprising facts learned from this test was that, all else being equal, lateral stiffness increases with the length and diameter of the head tube.

handlebars level with, or lower than, the seat.

On bikes with front suspension, the head tube length is also compromised—by the amount of fork travel (see Chapter 18 for an explanation). And of course, providing adequate clearance for fenders on a touring or city bike also works to limit the head tube length.

Seat Tube Length

The distance between the bottom bracket and the top of the seat tube, measured along the seat tube axis, is the frame's nominal size. There are two ways of measuring this, as described in Fig. 8.6 on page 92.

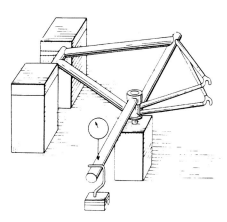

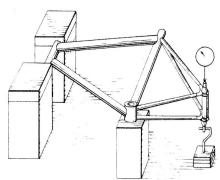

Top Tube Length

This is the distance between the center of the top of the head tube (just below the upper headset bearing) and the center of the seat tube, measured horizontally. It should depend on the rider's arm and torso length, and is affected by both the seat tube angle and the head tube angle. Although the use of a different handlebar stem can compensate for a top tube length discrepancy, that in turn may affect steering and handling.

Steerer Tube Angle

The angle of the head tube (and consequently also of the fork's steerer tube) relative to the ground. A steeper angle calls for less fork rake (as explained in Chapter 10) and vice-versa for a shallower angle. The shallower angle also either increases the wheelbase or reduces the top tube length.

Seat Tube Angle

This is the angle of the seat tube relative to the ground. A shallower angle places the rider further back, increasing load on the

rear wheel versus the front wheel. It may also allow the rider to reach the ground without getting off the seat.

Chainstay and Seatstay Bridge Clearance

This is the amount of space between the outside diameter of the rear wheel with tire mounted and the cross pieces that connect the pairs of seatstays, near the top, and chainstays, behind the bottom bracket. The seatstay bridge location limits the tire size (plus clearance for fenders if applicable) on the one hand, and is limited by the size of the brake arms on the other. The chainstay bridge position must allow the rear wheel with inflated tire to be removed and installed. In either case, the use of fenders requires at least 20 mm (¾ in.) extra clearance.

Another concern is the available width between the seatstays and chainstays (as well as between the fork blades). The bridge pieces should be long enough to provide clearance on either side of the tire to allow for slight wheel variations, and

Left: Fig. 8.32. Area around the bottom bracket with specially shaped tubes from Columbus.

Right: Figs. 8.33–8.36. Different types of dropouts: top left: horizontal; top right: vertical; bottom left: track; bottom right: 2-piece (used on most high-quality aluminum frames).

especially on utility bikes and mountain bikes to allow for some buildup of mud on the tire without rubbing against the stays.

Dropout Spacing

The insides of the rear dropouts should be spaced consistent with the over-locknut dimension of the hub to be installed. It is less for single-speeds and fixed-wheel bicycles than for derailleur bicycles, and more for modern derailleur bikes with 9, 10, or 11-speed cassettes than for older (up to about 1980) derailleur bikes with 5- or 6-speed freewheels.

SUSPENSION BIKE FRAMES

For full-suspension bikes, the entire world of bicycle design seems to be turned upside-down so to speak. Pivot points have to be created and attached, with the areas where they are attached

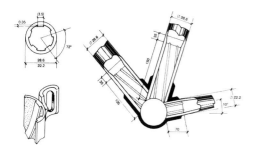

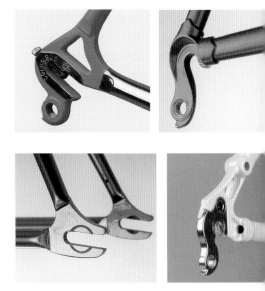

reinforced. Clearances have to be calculated differently, and a number of other factors must be considered. However, by and large, the same considerations still have to be accounted for as described for conventional frame designs.

The design of frames for hardtail mountain bikes, i.e. those with front suspension only, is similarly to those for conventional bikes, although different clearances below the head tube must be available, consistent with the amount of suspension travel (a measure of how far the fork can move up or down).

It is also possible to increase a frame's flexibility without the use of separate spring elements. One such method is to use more flexible tube configurations for the rear stays. They can be made with a smaller than usual diameter and/or they may be curved. It is also possible to place a simple elastomer pad in the connection between the top of the seatstays and the seat tube. Although the chainstays are not hinged, they will offer enough flex to provide a minor amount of shock absorption. This method results in enough shock absorption to make a ride over rough ground not only more comfortable, but actually allow higher riding speeds.

Some manufacturers (notably Specialized) integrate some proprietary insert in an opening in the seatstays and fork blades, claiming shock absorption on their account. However, at least one technical reviewer found

removing these inserts made no difference, so what helps seems to be the cutout, not the insert.

FRAME DETAILS

In this section, we'll take a look at some of the smaller parts of the frame: lugs, bottom bracket shell, dropouts, and other attachments and reinforcements.

LUGS

Although most frames are made without lugs these days, lugged frames are still around, and apparently there is even a resurgence of them. Most lugged frames are made of steel, and the lugs themselves vary from accurately fitting investment cast to simple pressed steel, to very ornate variants of either type.

It's not impossible to make a lugged aluminum frame, where the tubes are either screwed and glued, or otherwise fitted into or around aluminum lugs. The first aluminum frames to gain popularity in the late 1970s were built this way, and some of them are now considered collector's items (and remarkably comfortable to ride). Even today, internal lugs

Right: Fig. 8.37. Frames for downhill bikes defy most conventional wisdom regarding frame design. They are more akin to motorcycle frames than to conventional bicycle frames.

may be used inside welded aluminum frame, as is indeed done by Cannondale on some models.

With brazed steel bikes, the highest quality joint at the lowest weight can be achieved when the frame tubes extend all the way and are mitered to match each other's shape inside relatively short external lugs. If the lugs are longer, it may be for style or it may be because the tubes are not mitered but cut off straight, at some sacrifice in strength.

On the finest brazed steel bikes, the lugs are intricately worked. The purpose of that is to assure perfect penetration of the brazing material and to allow checking that it is indeed so. On some frames, the ends of the lugs are filed down to a smooth tapered shape, which is done to minimize stress-raisers, sudden changes in overall material thickness that are potential failure spots. Other frame builders hold that removing any material will weaken a structure. However, we've never seen a frame failure one way or the other.

BOTTOM BRACKET SHELL

On a brazed frame, as well as on most welded ones, the bottom bracket is essentially a lug. Most of what was said above for (external) lugs also applies to the bottom bracket. In addition, it is important that the screw thread on both sides for the actual bottom bracket bearing installation be perfectly aligned and the ends, called "faces" perfectly flat and perpendicular to the bearing axle.

On series bikes, this work is the manufacturer's responsibility, whereas many custom-frame builders leave it to the bike shop who installs the bottom bracket. Even on a non-custom bike frame, facing may be required to remove a thick and uneven layer of paint, to allow proper installation of the bottom bracket.

DROPOUTS

In this section, we'll address only rear dropouts, whereas the fork-ends, sometimes referred to as front dropouts, are covered under *The Front Fork* in Chapter 10.

For non-derailleur bikes, the rear dropouts are horizontal and

open rearward. These are called "track dropouts" from their use on track bikes. The rear dropouts of derailleur bikes either open downwards ("vertical dropouts," logically enough) or open forward, slanted at an angle of about 30 degrees; somewhat confusingly, the latter are called "horizontal" dropouts.

Track dropouts are designed that way so that the rear wheel does not slip out under the high pedaling forces that are often applied to them. Sometimes they are used with a wheel axle positioning device to adjust and fix the wheel axle in place. Vertical dropouts allow for easy wheel removal and installation on a bike with minimal tire clearance. They require an accurately built frame because they don't allow minor wheel adjustments.

Horizontal dropouts are more suitable for mass-manufactured bicycles, although they are by no means inferior per se. They allow some wheel axle adjustment, but they do require more radial tire clearance in the frame's rear triangle to install and remove the wheel.

The right-hand dropout on a derailleur bike has an extension with a threaded hole to install the rear derailleur. On most quality aluminum and carbon frames,

Left: Fig. 8.38. Something special: these Speedhound dropouts (with specially designed frame to take them) are bolted to the seatstays and chainstays. This frame will accommodate a belt drive.

they consist of two parts, a short and thick aluminum extension of the dropout itself, and a bolted-on stainless steel part with a threaded hole for derailleur installation. This method provides more shear strength than aluminum or carbon can provide at this sensitive location to prevent irreparable damage and allow replacement if needed.

BRIDGE PIECES

These are used to connect the seatstay and chainstay pairs. The one connecting the seatstays usually has a hole for the installation of a caliper brake. They range from simple flat plates on simple utility bikes to elegantly contoured investment castings on high-end bikes. The latter are not only much prettier, but also better at keeping the stays aligned.

FRONT DERAILLEUR LUG

Most high-end bikes are equipped with a front derailleur that is not attached by means of a clamp around the seat tube, but bolted on to a lug that forms an integral part with the frame.

BRAKE BOSSES

Bikes designed for the use of cantilever or direct-pull brakes have threaded brake bosses installed on the seatstays (on some older bikes they may be under the chainstays, for use with the no longer fashionable roller cam or U-brake).

If the frame is designed for use of disk brakes, it will have standard brake caliper mounting hardware attached to the seat-stays or chainstays. A simpler flat plate with a slot may be present on frames designed for use with internal hub brakes, such as drum brake, roller brake, or coaster brake.

BRAZE-ONS

There's a whole slew of other minor parts that are attached to frames. They include brake mounts on frame and fork for cantilever or direct-pull brakes, as well as internally threaded bosses for the installation of wa-ter bottle cages, luggage racks, etc. Although still referred to as braze-ons, they may be welded on (on welded frames) or bonded (on carbon-fiber frames).

Any of these threaded bosses should be protected by keeping a matching bolt screwed in when they are not in use for mounting the matching component or ac-cessory. If the frame does not have such braze-ons, it is still possible to mount accessories by means of clips clamped around the frame tubes. Indeed, some frame builders prefer not to in-stall braze-ons, in the belief that they weaken the frame. Since there have been no reports of

such failures, this fear is proba-bly unjustified.

REINFORCING GUSSETS

Heavily-loaded parts of the bike can be reinforced or stiffened by means of flat or contoured plates welded or brazed on. One typi-cal location is under the down-tube (which allows a frame to survive an accidental frontal im-pact, as may occur in mountain biking).

Another sensitive area—on bikes with disk brakes or other hub brakes—is the left-hand seatstay. Significant force is ap-plied there during braking. To prevent bending there, a gusset can be installed connecting the chainstay to the seatstay.

FRAME FINISH

The subject of finishing pro-cesses, as covered in Chapter 5, applies largely to the frame. Vir-tually all steel frames and most welded aluminum frames are painted or lacquered. Titanium frames can be left bare, due to the self-protection provided by the material's natural corrosion. Carbon-fiber frames can be either left as is or painted.

Right: Fig. 8.39. Even carbon monocoque frames are not exactly new: This Vitus frame dates to 1989.

Magnesium, though also self-protected by a corrosion layer, needs to be protected inside and out with paint to prevent damage due to electro-galvanic corrosion where it comes in contact with other metals (e.g. the seatpost and even the headset and bottom bracket bearings).

Chrome plating can be used to advantage on particularly scratch-sensitive locations on steel frames, such as the right-hand chainstays, the seat lug and the dropouts.

What is not painted or other-wise coated on an aluminum frame should preferably be anod-ized, although a really good natural polish can look very at-tractive and remains that way unless the bike gets into a salty atmosphere. Titanium is also an-odized or polished, while car-bon-fiber reinforced epoxy is generally pigmented throughout.

Another excellent frame finish is nickel plating, which can be used both on steel and aluminum frames. Popular around the turn of the century on high-end bicycles, this process was reintro-duced in the 1980s by several mountain bike frame builders. It

is highly scratch resistant, and although it is less shiny then chrome, it is more durable than either chrome or paint. In fact, to this day, the highest-quality chrome-plated components are first nickel-plated before the chrome plating is applied.

FRAME INSPECTION

The two most heavily loaded points of a frame, and therefore the most important ones to check for any damage, are the front fork and the area of the downtube just behind the lower headset. If you see any bulging or cracking, check with a bike shop (whose advice is probably to discard the frame or the fork). If there is no obvious damage, check for distortion of frame and fork, as per the following procedures.

FRAME ALIGNMENT CHECK

It's not safe to ride a bike with a frame that is misaligned, meaning that the front and rear wheels don't exactly follow one another in the same track. It negatively affects the balance of the bike, both when going straight and makes its cornering unpredictable. Here's how you can check the frame's alignment. You'll need 3 m (10 ft.) of twine and calipers to measure.

1. Wrap the twine around the frame from the right-side rear dropout to the head tube, pull it around and run it back to the left-side dropout, pulling it taut.

2. Measure the distance between the twine and the frame's seat tube on the right and the left and record the results.

3. If the two measurements differ, the frame is misaligned.

Just how much misalignment is permissible is up for debate, but we would say that any difference in excess of 3 mm (1/8 inch) is probably unsafe. In that case, it's

best to take the bike to a bike shop and ask for advice.

On steel frames it may be possible to force the frame back into alignment using a technique called cold-setting. That does not work on frames made of the highest quality steel tubing, nor those made of aluminum, titanium, magnesium, or carbon-fiber.

DROPOUT ALIGNMENT CHECK

The dropouts should be parallel for the rear wheel to align properly. You'll need a 45 cm (18-in.) metal ruler and calipers.

1. Hold the metal ruler flush against the outside surface of one of the rear dropouts, extending in the direction of the seat tube, and measure the distance between ruler and seat tube.

2. Do the same on the other dropout.

3. Compare the measurements. Consult a bike mechanic if the difference is more than 3 mm (1/8 in.).

The alignment of front forkends can be checked in a similar fashion, and this subject is covered in Chapter 10.

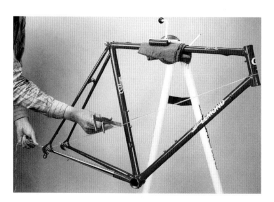

Left and above: Figs. 8.40 and 8.41. Frame inspection and caliper measuring detail. This is how you can check a frame for alignment.

9

THE WHEELS

THE BICYCLE WHEEL is a minor technical miracle. With a minimal weight of its own, the wheel not only carries a heavy weight by comparison, it also has minimal rolling resistance and even provides some shock absorption. Fig. 9.1 shows such a wheel, consisting of hub, spokes, rim, tire and inner tube.

PARTS ASSEMBLY OR INTEGRAL SYSTEM?

In recent years, more and more manufacturers have started capitalizing on the idea that the wheel can be treated as a integrated whole rather than as the assembly of individual components. There is something good and something bad in this trend. The good part is that indeed, those custom wheels are perfectly attuned structures, offering a combination of low weight and near-perfect rotation.

The downside is that maintenance, repair, and parts replacement are more complicated, because the individual components are often simply not available. Most of those lightweight wheels don't have enough spokes for anything but high-speed riding on smooth road surfaces. And... most of these wheels are very expensive. This too is one of those objects that are perceived as being high-tech. But realistically, a

Right: Fig. 9.1. The parts of a typical (spoked) bicycle wheel.

wheel that is durable and repairable is no less convincing a technological achievement.

THE HUB

The hub is the heart of the bicycle wheel, covered here only in its general form, while some

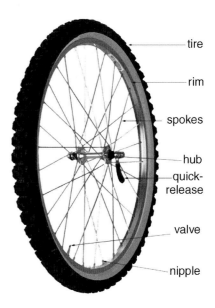

tire
rim
spokes
hub
quick-release
valve
nipple

special types, with integrated gearing, brakes, or generators will be described in Chapters 13, 16, and 20 respectively. Since the entire wheel is removed and installed by means of the hub, this section will cover this work as well as the technical details of the hub proper.

Fig. 9.2 shows a cross-section through a typical hub. The two main types of attachment are by means of axle nuts and by means of a quick-release device. In the latter case the hub axle is hollow, with a quick-release spindle installed through it, with a small thumb nut at the other end. Other bikes have hubs with axle nuts,

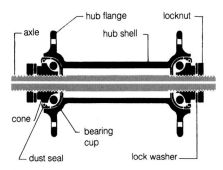

Left: Fig. 9.2. Cross-section through a typical hub, in this case with a hollow axle and adjustable ball bearings.

Right: Figs. 9.3 and 9.4. Classic high-flange (top) and low-flange hubs (bottom).

BIKE WHEEL VERSUS WAGON WHEEL

The first use of the modern tension-spoked bicycle wheel was in 1869, on the historic Meyer-Guilmet bicycle. It was a significant departure from earlier wheel designs.

Whereas earlier wheels were essentially wagon wheels, on which the entire load rests on the one or two spokes that are vertically, or almost vertically, down from the hub, the tension-spoked wheel is different. Here the load is distributed over all the spokes, though reduced for the one or two that are vertically, or almost vertically, down from the hub. And the load is not applied in compression ("pushing") but in tension ("pulling"). That means that much thinner, and therefore lighter and more flexible materials can be used. In fact, it is possible to make a tension-spoked wheel using flexible wire instead of metal rods.

The first bicycles to benefit from the tension-spoked design were the high-wheel bikes of the 1870s and 1880s. The 5- to 6-foot diameter front wheels on those machines could be made remarkably light with this method. And even though disk wheels and bladed wheels are sometimes used today for aerodynamic reasons, they are invariably heavier than their tension-spoked counterparts.

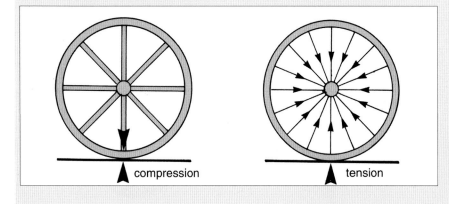

Fig. 9.5. Resulting forces for compression- and tension-spoked wheels compared.

often with a tab-plate between hub and fork to prevent the wheel from falling out when the nuts are loosened.

Another distinguishing factor for different hubs is based on the size of the flanges in which the spokes are attached into high- and low- (or big- and small-) flange models, as shown in Figs. 9.3 and 9.4. Although structural virtues are sometimes claimed for the high flange type, low flange hubs are lighter (although much of the weight difference is offset by the need for longer spokes) and equally strong (except in a radially spoked wheel, as described in the section *The Spokes*).

Another myth surrounds the use of quick-releases: Hubs with them are not inherently better

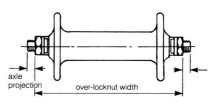

Above: Fig. 9.6. The width of a hub is measured as its "over-locknut" dimension, which should correspond to the clear width between the dropouts or forkends.

AERODYNAMICS OF THE BICYCLE WHEEL

The wheels are quite critical to the bicycles overall aerodynamic drag. Most critical is the front wheel, which is fully exposed to the air velocity (the rear wheel being located in the frame's and rider's slipstream).

The wheel not only moves forward, but it also turns around on its own axle. In addition, the top of the wheel actually moves forward at twice the bicycle's speed, whereas the bottom of the wheel, where it is in contact with the road, "stands still," and any point on the horizontal centerline of the wheel moves at the bicycle's riding speed.

Because so many different conditions apply to various parts of the wheel, it is not possible to accurately predict the overall aerodynamic drag even without considering the effect of a side wind. The only way is simply to try and make each component of the wheel as aerodynamically slick as possible, and test the result in a wind tunnel.

Specific measures that can be taken to achieve favorable aerodynamics for a standard, spoked wheel include the following:

❑ Use an airfoil-shaped rim profile, in the shape of a deep slightly convex V-shape;

❑ Minimize the number of spokes and avoid crossing spokes (i.e. use radial spoking);

❑ Use "bladed" spokes, which have an airfoil cross section;

❑ Use a low-flange hub with smooth contours;

❑ Install a narrow tire without tread pattern and smooth sidewalls.

Fig. 9.7. Wind tunnel testing of a Zipp Speed Weaponry aero bicycle wheel on a bike with rider.

Additionally, a smaller wheel, though it rotates faster, will have less overall aerodynamic drag than a larger one. If side winds are not a problem, significant advantage can be gained by using disk wheels, made either as an integral unit or by installing smooth disks on a spoked wheel.

than those without, even though most quality hubs are made with hollow axles and quick-releases for easy installation and removal (so, unfortunately also for theft). A solid axle of the same material and the same diameter is somewhat stronger than the hollow one used with a quick-release, and its overall weight is about the same.

Early mountain bikes had solid-axle wheels, and most tandems and "fixies" come with solid axles. The best ones have axle nuts with integrated washers to reduce friction resistance between the nut and the forkend or dropout, and axle torque when they are tightened with a wrench. They are becoming more readily available on account of their use on "fixies" and single-speeds.

Fig. 9.6 illustrates the width of the hub. It is measured between the outside faces of the locknuts and must correspond to the

internal dimension between the dropouts or forkends. The over-locknut width is typically 100 mm for a front wheel, 124–126 mm for a rear wheel with 6- or 7-speed freewheel for regular drop-handlebar derailleur bikes, 130 mm for 8-, 9-, 10-, and 11-speed freewheels. Hubs intended for mountain bikes and tandems tend to be even wider—most commonly 135 mm.

Some builders space them somewhere in between—e.g. at 132 mm—so either a road bike or a mountain bike hub can be used with minor bending in or out of the rear stays.

Often the use of solid axles is structurally justified, especially on the rear wheel, which would be more prone to the axle bending or breaking. The greatest risk of breaking an axle is when the bearings lie rather far inward relative to the dropouts or forkends.

The pre-built wheelsets that have become so popular—and profitable—in recent years, often incorporate quite special hubs, rims, and spokes. Some have holes for straight spokes (as opposed to the bent heads of the

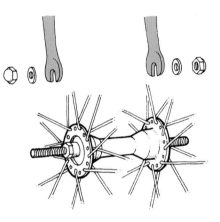

Above: Fig. 9.8. Partial cut-away view of a Shimano cartridge bearing hub.

Top Left: Fig. 9.9. Quick-release skewer detail. Note the orientation of the coil springs that go on either side of the hub.

Bottom left: Fig. 9.10. Quick-release hub with hollow axle and quick release skewer.

Right: Figs. 9.11–9.13. Details and overview of "bolt-on" axle, with solid axle and axle nuts.

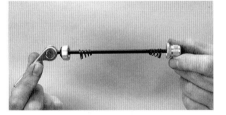
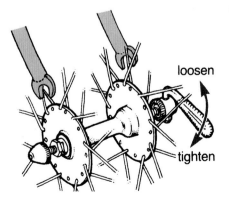

standard spokes); some are specifically designed for a pre-determined combination of some tangential spokes and some radial spokes; some are designed for spokes that screw into the hub instead of a nipple at the rim. All of these special wheels are all difficult to service, and their parts are difficult to replace.

One of the oddest wheels that were recently introduced has 6 mm (¼ in.) diameter tubular carbon spokes, screwed into one nipple at the hub and another nipple at the rim. Advertised as being stronger and lighter than other wheels, it may be a case of one feature defeating another:

The aerodynamic drag of those 24 cylindrical spokes slows the bike down more than the weight savings speed it up.

Fast moving cylindrical cross-sections are aerodynamic disaster areas, and it is not for nothing that "aero" wheels come with bladed spokes instead of round ones. If indeed their weight is less than it is for a regularly spoked wheel, the only benefit will be faster acceleration, not higher speed.

HUB BEARING ADJUSTMENT

If the hub does not turn freely or is too loose, the problem can generally be solved with bearing adjustment. Only if adjustment does not do the trick, will a general overhaul be necessary, although this work is recommended on a yearly or even half-yearly schedule, certainly if the bike is used frequently especially in a dusty or moist environment.

The hub bearings must be tightened if the wheel can be moved sideways relative to the fork or the frame in the vicinity of the rim. They must be loosened if the wheel does not spin lightly, finally coming to rest after some pendulum movement (with the

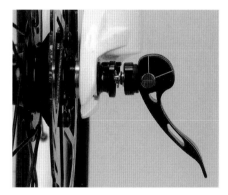

Above: Fig. 9.14. A clever way to overcome "lawyer's lips." With this special quick-release, the parts that sit against the forkends can be pulled back once the lever is opened, allowing wheel removal and installation without the need to unscrew the thumbnut.

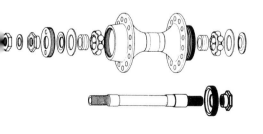

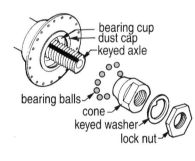

Above: Fig. 9.15. Cup-and-cone hub bearing adjusting detail.

Bottom left: Figs. 9.16. Exploded view of a Maxicar micro-adjustable hub with sealed cup-and-cone bearings.

Top right: Fig. 9.17. Adjustable bearing with the bearing balls exposed for lubrication or adjustment.

Bottom right: Fig. 9.18. Typical cartridge-bearing hub with the quick-release skewer and the locknut removed.

valve at the bottom, unless its weight is offset by e.g. a magnet sensor for a bicycle computer), when allowed to turn freely.

The hub bearings should be overhauled if you notice rough spots or crunching noises when the wheel is turned or if adjusting for too loose a bearing results in notable tightness. A loosely adjusted hub bearing that allows the wheel to turn freely may still have high resistance. It may turn freely only without load, and the resistance may become quite

significant when the bike is loaded with the rider's weight.

However, most modern hubs are no longer adjustable. Although most manufacturers and cycle magazine writers make cyclists believe that "sealed-bearing," or cartridge-bearing, hubs are somehow more "high-tech" than hubs with cup-and-cone bearings, this is not necessarily so (notwithstanding the fact that there are some excellent hubs of either type).

The reason manufacturers like to use cartridge bearings is that they are easier, and thus cheaper, to install. Their greatest drawback

Left: Fig. 9.19. Classic cartridge-bearing hubs by Phil Wood, who has been making these since the 1970s.

is that they cannot be adjusted for wear, nor easily lubricated. When they're not performing well, they have to be taken apart and new bearing cartridges installed, which requires special tools, but can be handled by any well-equipped bike shop.

THE TIRES

The tires not only cause the most misery on the bike, they also directly affect how lightly the bike runs, so it is well worth selecting and maintaining them properly. In this section we will cover both practical matters and the theory that determines tire rolling resistance.

There are three types of bicycle tire in use today: the common

TIRE ROLL-OUT TEST

Tire rolling resistance can be compared, though not quantified, by means of this simple test. Let the bike run down a ramp onto a level surface and measure how far it rolls out before it stops. These tests will be most accurate if you build a simple recumbent, with almost 100 percent of the rider's weight

over the rear wheel, which is the one with the tire to be tested.

If the bike rolls out further with tire A than with tire B, or with a tire inflated to pressure X than the same tire inflated to pressure Y, then tire A or pressure X cause less rolling resistance. It is even possible to conduct the same test on different road surfaces to establish the effect of surface conditions.

Most of the recommendations in this chapter are based author Van der Plas's experiments using this simple testing technique. However, it is also easy for anyone else interested in optimizing tire choice and pressure for him or herself.

Fig. 9.20. Setup for a simple roll-out test to compare tire performance.

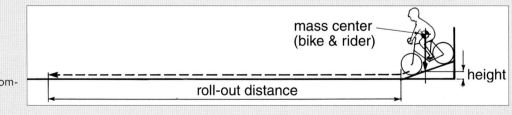

wired-on type, usually referred to as "clincher" in the U.S.; the tubular tire, often called "sew-up" in the U.S., or "tub" in the U.K.; and the tubeless tire (easily the rarest of the three). Their respective cross-sections are illustrated in Figs. 9.21 and 9.22. The wired-on tire is held around a separate inner tube on a deep-bedded rim by means of metal wires (sometimes these are replaced by aramid, such as Kevlar, to save weight and provide flexibility for easy folded storage). The tubular

tire is sewn around the inner tube and is literally glued onto a much shallower rim. In case carbon-fiber rims are used instead of

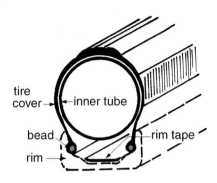

aluminum or wood rims, special carbon-compatible tire adhesive must be used to achieve adequate adhesion of the tire to the rim.

The probable reason why modern wired-on tires are referred to as clinchers is that they are held onto the rim by a hook bead, as shown in the illustration, keeping the tire in place under the effect of the tire's inflation pressure. The original clincher tire had a similarly (though much bigger) bead keeping the tire in place.

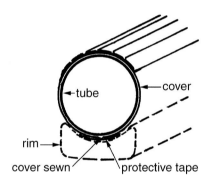

Above: Fig. 9.21. Wired-on, or "clincher" tire. and matching rim

Left: Fig. 9.22. Tubular, or "sew-up" tire and matching rim.

Right: Fig. 9.23. The first pneumatic-tired cycle: This is presumably the John Boyd Dunlop's son's tricycle, which the elder Dunlop equipped with pneumatic tires in 1887.

TIRE IMPROVEMENTS

Though not as widely publicized as some of the other technical developments, there has been significant improvements in the quality of bicycle tires over the last 40 years or so. Tires and tubes withstand higher pressures and are often lighter, more flexible, and even more puncture resistant than they were when the authors first took up cycling seriously.

The subject would bear more thorough investigation, but

based on several manufacturers' claims, the likely contributing factors include the following:

❏ Tire carcass construction has been refined resulting in greater flexibility;

❏ The fabrics used are often more densely woven, using thinner and more consistent fibers;

❏ Tread compounds have been optimized, often using different compositions for

the different parts of the tread (harder for the surface, more flexible for other areas);

❏ The shape of the hook bead and the wired used have been optimized for a close fit with the rim at minimum weight;

❏ Better compounds are used for the inner tubes, resulting in lower weight and greater flexibility.

Certainly at speeds below 16 km/h (10 mph), tire rolling resistance plays a major part in determining how easily a bicycle runs. Only at higher speeds (or strong head winds) does aerodynamic drag become increasingly important. But even at those elevated speeds, tire rolling resistance may make the difference between comfortable cycling and plodding along—if higher speeds are ever reached at all on a bike with poor wheels.

TIRE COMPRESSION AND DROP

The contact area between the road and the tire is easy to calculate, and it is the same for any tire, whatever its size or design: It's the quotient of wheel loading force and tire pressure.

Here's an example based on our standard bike and rider of Chapter 3, weighing 90 kg together. We'll assume a weight distribution that puts 55 kg (61%) on the rear wheel and 35 kg (39%) on the front wheel, and both tires inflated to 6 bar, which is about 6 kg/cm². So the rear tire's contact area will be 55/6 = 12 cm², and the front tire's will be 35/6 = 6 cm². It will be clear that halving the load or doubling the pressure has the same effect on the contact area, which is halved either way.

An argument can be made that "drop," i.e. the amount by which a tire compresses between its unloaded and loaded condition may be the most accurate indicator of tire rolling resistance. Unfortunately, the amount of drop is not so easy to determine.

It's however far the tire has to be compressed to reach that contact area. It depends on the tire diameter as well as its width, being less for a large-diameter tire than it is for a small-diameter tire and less for a wider tire than for a narrower one. So a 700 C tire (with an outside diameter of about 685 mm) requires less drop than e.g. the 20-in. tires used on most folding bikes. And, get this: a wider tire of the same wheel size, if inflated to the same pressure, will have less drop, and consequently less rolling resistance than a narrower one.

Although the information is not published, several tire designers confirmed that, in-house, they design tires for optimal performance when inflated to achieve a drop of 20% of the tire's nominal height (which is generally the same as its width). At this figure, the tire is believed to provide an optimum balance of rolling resistance, handling, and shock absorption. The only way to establish that figure is by trial and error: Measure the inflated tire height and the height of the hub above the ground of an unloaded wheel. Then apply a representative downward force to the wheel, and measure the height of the hub under these conditions.

The difference between the two figures is the amount of actual drop. If it is more than 20% of the tire height, the pressure should be increased, if it is less, it should be decreased until the 20% figure has been achieved. Make a note of that pressure, and keep the tires inflated to that figure. And clearly, the more heavily loaded rear tire should always be inflated to a higher pressure than the front.

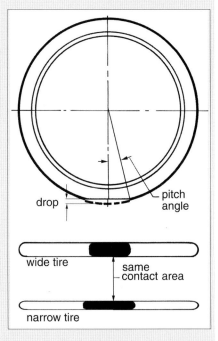

Fig. 9.24. Under a given load, at a given pressure the tire compresses to have a fixed contact patch, or area, with the road. Consequently, the contact patch will be shorter for a wider tire than it is for a narrow tire, resulting in lower rolling resistance.

In recent years, several manufacturers have introduced tubeless tires. These are similar in design to those used on automobiles and rely on a special rim (obviously without any spoke holes poking through) with a tightly sealing lip. They are reputedly slightly lighter, and probably more puncture-resistant, than regular wired-on tires with inner tubes. The weight difference is not significant, and in our humble opinion they don't serve any other purpose than to make the bicycle more expensive and harder to fix.

TIRE ROLLING RESISTANCE

Tire pressure is the most important factor in rolling resistance. Technically, it is easier to make a tire withstand a high pressure by minimizing the cross-section width, but it can be achieved with a wider tire too. The condition of the road also enters into the equation, increasing rolling resistance for more uneven surfaces. Also important is the load, increasing the tire rolling resistance proportionally for heavier overall loads.

Fig. 9.26 shows the principle of the pneumatic tire as a suspension element that minimizes energy losses due to road unevenness. The idea is to provide a very flexible layer that forms around the obstacles, balancing out the forces on either side, so no retarding component force results. To approach this ideal, the tire must be both highly compressed (to minimize deformation on level ground) and highly flexible (to minimize the forces required to deform the tire around the obstacles).

On an inflexible tire, the higher resistance is mainly due to the energy that goes into lifting

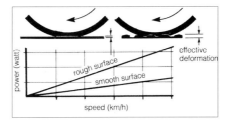

the bike up over the obstacle. On a soft tire (or on soft ground), the energy equivalent to raising the bike over the height of the deformation is consumed with each wheel revolution.

TIRE PRESSURE

To optimize the tires' suspension effect, and to minimize rolling resistance, many tire manufacturers recommend inflating the tire to the pressure by which the tire drop (see page 116) is 20% of the tire diameter. Thus, if the tire is 25 mm wide, and the bike is loaded under the weight of the rider (and any luggage to be carried), each tire should sag by just 5 mm. Although that is a nice starting point, it is only valid if the bike is ridden on a smooth, hard road surface.

In practice, rolling resistance is minimized if they are inflated to the maximum pressure *compatible with the road surface*. Fig.

Above: Fig. 9.25. Tire rolling resistance is higher on rough surfaces than on smooth, hard ones.

Left: Fig. 9.26. Ideally, as a pneumatic tire rolls over an obstacle, it should deform around it so that the reaction forces around the obstacle are equalized, minimizing rolling resistance.

Top right: Fig 9.27. On soft ground, the tire sinks into the soil, increasing rolling resistance.

Bottom right: Fig. 9.28. Check the tire pressure frequently and inflate the tires to minimize both rolling resistance and puncture resistance.

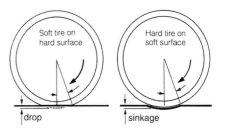

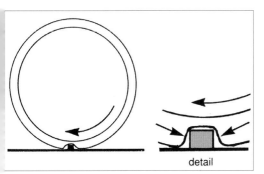

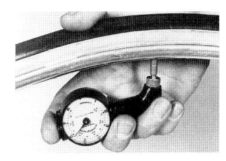

9.25 shows the effects of different road surfaces relative to the tire pressure. In order to keep close to the 20% drop condition, it is obviously also necessary to choose a tire width compatible with the given pressure and road surface: You need wider tires for a rougher or softer road surface than for a smooth, hard road surface.

The pressure of front and rear tires should reflect the differences in loading, meaning that the rear tire should have up to 50% more pressure than the one in the front. The narrower tires do not only allow higher pressures, they usually *require* it, because they don't have as much protective cushioning as the thicker ones. However, even mountain bike tires are now available that withstand quite impressive pressures without being blown off the rim.

The following values are based on the use of road racing tires with a cross-section of up to 25 mm. For the rear tire, the optimal value for use on smooth asphalt is about 7–8 bar (100–125 psi). A rough asphalt or brick road surface would require 5–6 bar (70– 85 psi), while a cobblestone road can only be mastered

at any respectable speed with much wider tires inflated to 3–4 bar (30–45 psi). Off-road, soft soil, sand, and snow may require pressures as low as 1–2 bar (15–30 psi), and again, much wider tires. In each case, the front tire should be inflated to about two-thirds of those values.

Only relatively fat tires, such as mountain bike versions, allow use at very low pressures. (A 50 mm wide tire will reach its 20% drop at half the pressure at which that is achieved for a 25 mm tire.) Narrower tires do not have enough cushioning to protect the rim or prevent the tire and the

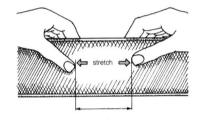

Above: Fig. 9.29. A tire with a flexible carcass is more compliant, minimizing rolling resistance, especially on rougher road surfaces.

Left: Fig. 9.30. Whereas on a hard road surface it is the tire that deforms, it is primarily the ground itself when riding on soft ground that deforms, and depending on the softness of the ground, that may result in a great amount of sinkage (the equivalent of drop).

Right: Fig. 9.31. This is how the phenomenon of losses on rough surfaces is illustrated by Wilson in *Bicycling Science.*

tube from getting caught between a rock and a hard spot, so to say—the rim and the road respectively.

Special tires with protective layers between the tread and the casing, usually made with aramid (e.g. Kevlar), will prevent puncturing upon impacting in the thread area, but will generally not help if the tires are so soft that the tubes get pinched (resulting in a "snake bite" puncture).

Most people who have investigated rolling resistance under the pretense of science have done so in a rather inconsistent manner. Rather than comparing similar tires under different circumstances or different tires under the same circumstances, they have compared different tires, each inflated to some arbitrary pressure that differed widely, all ridden on a perfectly smooth, hard surface—of course using the fanciest electronic measuring equipment. Not surprisingly, the results simply favored whichever tire was inflated the hardest, because that is all that really counts under such favorable conditions.

What's needed is less hocus-pocus and more common sense. In a consistent series of simple comparative tests, published in

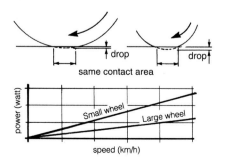

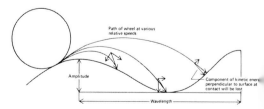

Bike-Tech back in 1984, author Van der Plas has established the criteria that determine the ease of rolling when all are inflated to the same pressure. This is of course not the full story. After all, the bicycle wheel is part of the total handling and suspension system of the bike (so the tires on a suspension bike should only be tested in combination with it), and even the relative flexing of the front fork and any lateral steering forces increase rolling resistance. Even so, this simple test has brought to light a number of significant conclusions about the tires themselves:

❏ A cross-section that minimizes the volume contained inside the rim relative to the volume projecting outside the rim.

❏ The lightest and most flexible side wall design and construction possible.

❏ A flexible carcass, which can be tested as shown in Fig. 9.29.

❏ The use of the lightest and most flexible inner tube.

❏ At least in theory, a larger diameter wheel also rolls more easily than a smaller diameter wheel (at least given the same tire pressure, see Fig. 9.30). Fig. 9.31 illustrates the effect of the wheel size on the way the bike travels

AVOIDING PUNCTURES

For most riders, punctures are the most common technical problem encountered, and generations of tire manufacturers have worked in vain to eliminate them. Even with the same tires mounted, and riding on the same roads, one rider may have many more punctures than another. Heavy riders, and bicycles loaded with luggage are more likely to get punctures, and all cyclists have more punctures in the (more heavily loaded) rear tire than in the front tire.

Two distinct categories of punctures can be distinguished: penetration punctures and pinch punctures (sometimes referred to as "snake-bites").

In most environments, it seems pinch punctures are more common than penetrating punctures. They can be minimized by maintaining adequate tire pressure, especially in the rear. And if you see a bump in the road coming up, you can try to steer around it with the front wheel. As for the rear wheel, it will be a good idea to shift the balance of weight forward to reduce the load on the rear wheel when approaching a bump in the road.

Concerning penetration punctures, it's again largely a matter of keeping an eye on the road surface ahead and steering around any patches with sharp objects.

A special case of penetration punctures are those caused by

Fig. 9.32. Tire inflation is one of the keys to preventing most punctures, especially the dreaded snake-bite, which is caused by the (under-inflated) tire being caught between the edge of the rim and an irregularity in the road surface.

thorns. A thorn can penetrate the tire and tube, but may be hard to locate because it soon wears off on the outside, making it hard practically invisible from the outside. Tires with a protective strip help prevent many such punctures. There are also "thorn-proof" inner tubes available. They're very thick and rather inflexible, resulting in a less comfortable ride with probably more rolling resistance (although we haven't measured it, it certainly feels that way).

through any unevenness (in the absence of a separate dampened suspension system).

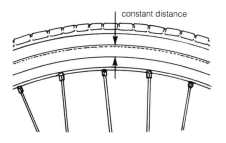

Above: Fig. 9.33. The tire should be mounted concentric to the rim.

Tire Sizing

Although it is still customary to give tires sizes by some figure in mm or inches (which often turn out not to correspond to any measurable dimension on the actual tire), there is also a more logical system for tire (and rim) size designation in use. This is the ETRTO method, developed by the European Tire and Rim Technical Organization. This method is now integrated in the internationally applicable ISO standards for bicycle components, and referred to as Universal Tire Marking System. This method is illustrated in Fig. 9.35.

The ETRTO/ISO size designation applies to both rims and tires. It references the rim bed, or shoulder, diameter in mm. A second dimension quoted is the tire cross-section for tires, the inside rim width for rims. Thus, the tires are identified by a code consisting of a 2-digit number followed by a

Those Awful Tires of the Past

Before the now familiar wired-on tires were introduced in America, most bicycles sold there were equipped with one of two different tire types: clincher tires and the single-tube tire.

The clincher tire (sorry about any confusion, but they are not the same as modern wired-on tires, even though most American cyclists call them "clinchers") and the single-tube tire.

The original clincher tire, patented in 1887 by Thomas Jeffrey in the U.S. and William Bartlett in the U.K., had outward protruding edges that fit into grooves at the sides of the rim,

and enclosed a separate inner tube. Because it was rather expensive to make, most American manufacturers chose to use a competing design, the single-tube tire.

This design was introduced in 1890 and belatedly patented by Prudon W. Tillinghast in the U.S. (while a similar patent had been issued in the U.K. to I. W. Boothroyd). Described as "composed of an inner tube, an intermediate layer of structural fabric, and an outer rubber covering, all vulcanized together into an integral annular ring." It was, in essence a glorified loop of heavy-duty garden hose.

They had a slew of disadvantages: hard to install and remove, even harder to repair, heavy, and incredibly sluggish to ride. Nevertheless, they remained the staple of the American bicycle trade until 1933, when Ignaz Schwinn introduced the (European) detachable balloon tire on his epoch-making B 10-E bicycle, which another 50 years later would spawn the mountain bike revolution.

Fig. 3.34. Original clincher tire mounted on profiled wood rim (left) and single-tube tire mounted on bent steel rim (right).

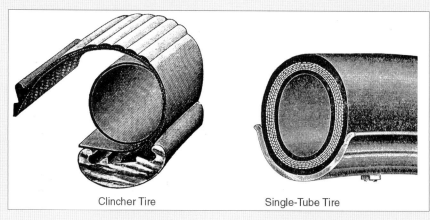

Clincher Tire   Single-Tube Tire

3-digit number, separated by a dash. The 2-digit number represents the inflated tire cross-section, while the 3-digit number is the diameter of the rim bed in mm. Similarly, rim sizes are quoted as the same three-digit code, followed by a two-digit code referring to its inside width in mm, separated by an X.

The outside diameter of a wheel is the sum of the rim bed diameter and twice the tire cross-section. For mountain bikes, the usual rim size is 559 mm, while it is either 622 mm or 630 mm for conventional derailleur bikes.

The last set of figures betrays the absurdity of the archaic tire size designation method still generally used for anything except road bikes: The 622 mm rim used for 700 C (28-inch) tires is actually *smaller* than the 630 mm rim used

on what is called a 27-inch wheel. Thus, given tires of the same cross-section, the 27-inch wheel is actually bigger than the 700 C (28-inch) wheel. In the ETRTO system, within reason, any tire with 622 in its code fits any rim of that size, while any tire with 630 matches a corresponding 630 mm rim size.

In recent years, several mountain bike manufacturers have introduced what they call 29-inch wheels. What these actually are is 622 rims (i.e. the rim size for 700 C road tires) with fat tires. Putting a 2.125 mm tire on a 622 mm rim results in an outside diameter of 622 + 2 * 54 = 730 mm, which is 28¾ in.—considered close

enough to get away with calling it a 29-inch wheel.

TIRE TREAD

The tread of a bicycle tire is generally profiled. Certainly in the case of high-pressure tires, this is of dubious benefit, because the idea of tread profile is strictly unique to the low-pressure condition found on cars. Car tires are inflated much less than bicycle tires for comparable road surfaces. Consequently, the contact pressure (i.e. force per unit area) is much less—it is indeed the same as tire pressure. The low pressure and large surface area on a car tire allow water to build

Left and right: Figs. 9.36 and 9.37. Similar tires, one with, the other without a tread pattern.

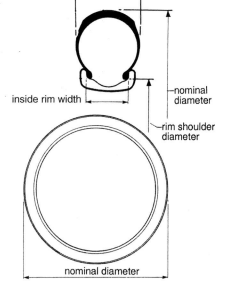

Above: Fig. 9.35. ETRTO tire size designation system.

TIRE VERSUS SPOKE FLEX

There have been claims and counter claims concerning the amount of flex, or suspension, provided by the spokes. It is easy enough to put the theory to the test" push on the axle of a wheel with tire installed and correctly inflated, and check how much it deflects; then do the same for a wheel without tire, and compare the results.

We found that, under a load of 50 kg (110 lbs.) a tire at 6 bar (90 psi) deflects about 5 times more than the spokes. So spoke flex does not seem to account for much. Yet, subjectively, a spoked wheel just feels nicer than a rigid wheel, so perhaps we've been missing something that does not come out clearly in the numbers of the test?

up between tire and road when it is wet, causing aquaplaning in rainy weather on smooth asphalt.

Bicycle tires do not have this problem, because they are inflated to pressures that are up to four times as high as car tires (at least for road use) and have much smaller contact areas. Consequently, there is no need to remove water through channels in the tire tread. Only toward the sides of the tires, where the contact is angular in a curve, is there any justification for a rougher surface to prevent skidding when cornering in wet weather.

TUBE AND VALVE

The inner tube used with the conventional wired-on tire is generally made of butyl, or synthetic

rubber. Natural rubber is also still in use but it is rather uncommon these days. The lightest and most flexible tubes, chosen to minimize rolling resistance, are of latex, i.e. pure unvulcanized rubber. This flexible material is not particularly puncture-prone either, but it allows air to pass through rather easily, and thus latex tubes may require daily re-inflation.

Butyl tires also lose air, but less so: road bikes with butyl tires may require inflation once a week, while mountain bike tires will go at least two weeks without fresh air. Depending on the material, the size of the tube must match that of the tire within certain limits. Latex tubes must match the tire dimension to within the closest tolerances, while butyl tubes can be stretched e.g. from 47 mm to 54 mm cross-section (typical mountain bike sizes).

Fig. 9.41 shows three valve types, used for letting the air into the tube. In the U.S., only the Presta and Schrader models are commonly used: the former for road bikes, the latter for most

mountain bikes and utility machines. Each type requires a different valve hole diameter in the rim.

Although Schrader valves can be inflated at a gas station, the Presta type is preferable, requiring less force to overcome the resistance of the valve mechanism. When inflating a Schrader-valve tire at a gas station, it must be done very carefully to avoid over-inflating the tire.

Tubes with Presta valve type are available for any tire size, although more readily so for narrow tires than for mountain bike tires. Make sure the valve has a section of screw thread on the shaft, because valves without this feature tend to disappear back

Left: Fig. 9.38. A historic gadget: a "Puncture Detector," available around 1900.

Right. Fig. 9.40. Inner tube with Presta valve.

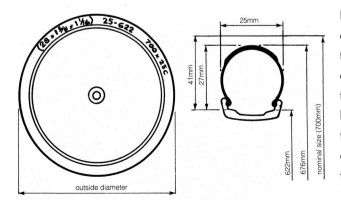

outside diameter

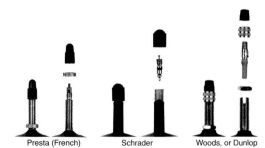

Left: Fig. 9.39. An example of the tire-sizing system as it applies to a typical 700 C road bike tire. Note that the actual outside diameter is less than the quoted 700 mm.

Presta (French)   Schrader   Woods, or Dunlop

Above: Fig. 9.41. Three valve types for bicycle tires. The Woods, or Dunlop, valve, though rare in the U.S., is quite common in Europe.

into the rim when you try to in-flate them, making it very hard to do so. If the tires are to be used on deep-section "aero" rims, the valve stems have to be long enough to penetrate through.

RIM TAPE

Rim tape wrapped around the rim bed, should be used to protect the tire from the spoke ends and the sharp outlines of the nipples in the rim bed. Its width must be selected to match the interior width of the rim bed. Adhesive-backed cloth tape appears to give better protection than flexible butyl tape.

THE RIM

Although aluminum rims are pretty much standard issue for bikes sold at bike shops, there are other materials in use as well: steel, carbon composite, and even wood. Steel rims are common on utility bikes and some of the throwaway bikes sold at big box

stores. They should never be used on bikes with rim brakes, because the braking deteriorates sharply when steel rims are wet (much more so than for aluminum rims).

Steel rims are not usually stronger than aluminum ones, even if the latter are significantly lighter. This is due to the box pro-file that can be used for extruded aluminum sections, while the cross-section shape of the steel rim is much less structurally sound. Figs. 9.42 and 9.44 show the various cross-sections used.

Most steel rim manufacturers try to increase wet-weather brake performance by serrating the sides of the rim. The only pattern that seems to do this trick—though at the price of noisy brak-ing and high brake block wear—is an arrangement with al-ternating sections of opposing di-agonal grooves.

Wood rims don't work with brakes either, because they would wear too fast, don't offer

predictable friction, and don't transfer heat away from the brak-ing surface. They are only found on track bikes. As such, there has been some demand for them for the rear wheels of fixed-wheel bikes, which don't need brakes in the rear.

Carbon rims do exist, and they are remarkably light, but you can't buy just a carbon rim. They come integrated with carbon spokes and special hubs in an "all-carbon" package. These don't work with rim brakes either, be-cause of inadequate friction and heat transfer. So they should only be used with disk brakes. More common is an aluminum rim em-bedded in a carbon "aero" struc-ture, which can also be used with rim brakes.

Some rims have ceramic sides, forming highly efficient and long-wearing brake surfaces. Ex-pensive, but worthwhile if you're going for the lightest wheels that will wear well anyway.

Aero

Above: Fig. 9.42. Sprint rims, as used for tubular, or sew-up, tires.

Left: Fig. 9.43. Rim tape. This is a type made of butyl. There are also adhesive-backed cloth tapes available.

Right: Fig. 9.44. A selection of different available rim profiles for wired-on, or clincher, tires.

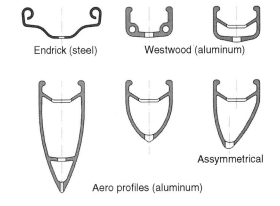

Endrick (steel)   Westwood (aluminum)

Assymmetrical

Aero profiles (aluminum)

SPOKE HOLES

The spoke holes in the rim are usually installed alternatingly off-set to the left and the right of center, corresponding to the direction the spokes run in the assembled wheel. Several manufacturers offer rims with spoke holes that are accurately aligned, which may result in a wheel that maintains its shape and tension because the spokes and nipples run in a straight line.

An even cleverer idea (if you're willing to leave the world of interchangeable componentry behind altogether) is that of an asymmetrical rear wheel rim, with the spoke holes located in such a way that the left and right spokes run under practically the same angle, even on the rear wheel, and thus are tensioned the same. This insures greater rear wheel stability and less chance of buckling.

In order to prevent cracking of the rim at the spoke holes, these points should be reinforced by means of ferrules, or bushings. These should connect inner and outer sections on the box-section, or "double bottom"

design. At a minimum, a washer should be installed between the nipple head and the inside of the rim to distribute the spoke forces around the hole.

RIM SIZE

The size of a rim is determined in accordance with the ETRTO designation and corresponds closely to the size designation for the matching tires. To give an example, a rim with designation 622 X 18 has an inside width of 18 mm and a rim-bed diameter of 622 mm. Most tires with 622 in their designation will fit on this rim.

RIM STRENGTH

The strength of the rim is only relevant within the total assembled structure of the wheel. In fact, most kinds of rim deformation are not really the result of a weak rim, but of insufficient spoke tension. Even so, strength and rigidity of the rim itself do matter, because they help distribute the forces over more spokes.

Very, very few rims are made of heat treated aluminum, which is stronger than regular aluminum. Although some of these models are dark gray, it is not generally true that all dark gray rims are heat treated, or particularly strong for that matter. The color is not due to heat treating, but to anodizing with a dye. Anodizing to significant depth increases the surface hardness of the rim, but has no significant effect on its strength. It should also be noted that anodized rims tend to provide poorer wet weather braking than plain aluminum ones.

The easiest way to test the lateral rigidity of a rim is to place it halfway on a flat table, with the other half projecting. Holding

Above: Fig. 9.45. Special rim for use with screwed-in carbon-fiber spokes.

Left: Fig. 9.46. Rim with ceramic coating on the sides for improved braking.

Right: Fig. 9.47. An old (ca. 1900) wood rim with a single tube tire installed.

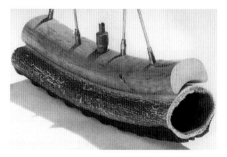

it down firmly, while pushing the overhanging part down, will indicate how easily it is deformed (but don't apply so much force that permanent deformation is caused, as may happen on a weak lightweight rim).

The radial rigidity can be verified by standing the rim on end and pushing it down from the top. By and large, assuming the same material, heavier rims are stronger; higher profiles lead to more radial rigidity; and wider profiles have more lateral rigidity.

THE SPOKES

Unlike most other types of wheels, the spokes in a bicycle wheel are not loaded in compression but in tension. This allows the total forces to be distributed over all spokes (though the tension is reduced in the ones near the bottom of the wheel). On any other

wheel—whether cartwheel or bicycle disk or bladed wheel—the entire load is by one or two spokes at the bottom of the wheel.

This is the reason why disk wheels and most bladed wheels are heavier than tension-spoked wheels. The spokes of the conventional bike wheel can also be kept very thin because the tension loading does not transfer a bending moment on the spokes. Fig. 9.49 compares the loading cases for the wagon wheel and the bicycle wheel.

Despite the obvious technical advantage of the wire-spoked wheel, some manufacturers and would-be innovators never give up on reinventing the wheel. Consequently, we regularly see the (re-)introduction of such abominations as cast aluminum or cast plastic wheels built on the basis of the cart wheel. Though they may be suitable for some limited applications, they

are not suitable for regular cycling use: They are heavy, rock hard, impossible to straighten when they get bent, and they provide rather miserable riding qualities.

Most spokes are steel, circular in cross-section, either straight gauge (constant in thickness) or butted (thinner in the center than at the ends). Only three gauges are in common use: 14, which has a diameter of 2 mm; 15, 1.8 mm; and 16, 1.6 mm. However, a 16-gauge spoke end would be too weak, so the only varieties commonly seen are 14 straight gauge, 14–15–14 butted, 15 straight gauge, and 15–16–15 butted, the latter being recommended only for the front wheel, which does not have to sustain pedaling torque.

Fig. 9.50 shows two versions of the spoke with the nipple that connects it to the rim and by which it is tightened. In fact, the higher the tension, within

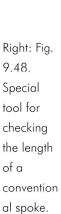

Right: Fig. 9.48. Special tool for checking the length of a conventional spoke.

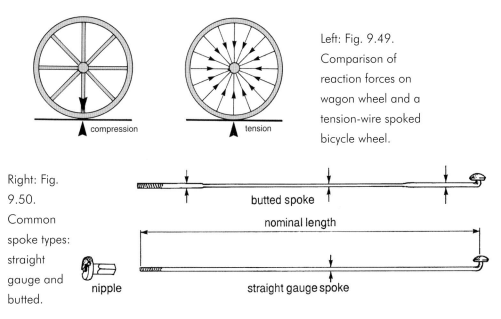

compression

tension

Left: Fig. 9.49. Comparison of reaction forces on wagon wheel and a tension-wire spoked bicycle wheel.

Right: Fig. 9.50. Common spoke types: straight gauge and butted.

nipple

butted spoke

nominal length

straight gauge spoke

reason, the stronger the wheel. When the tension is lower, the sequence of stress variations through which the material goes is more demanding, as the spokes are intermittently loaded and released during the rotation of the wheel. This tends to induce metal fatigue, leading to breaking, usually directly at the bend near the head.

The illustration also indicates how the spoke is measured. Its size is quoted as the length from the inside of the bend to the end, while the thickness is usually quoted as a gauge number. Recently, spoke thicknesses are, more logically, referenced in mm. When two gauge numbers are quoted, the spoke is butted, meaning the ends are thicker than the middle section. This leads to greater flexibility and consequently to greater overall wheel strength than a spoke that has the same thickness over its entire length—despite the reduced cross-section. Any associated weight savings is insignificant.

Wheels built for riding at speed may have bladed, "aero" spokes instead of the normal round cross-section. Of course they are still round at the ends, but they have been flattened out to give them an airfoil shape in between.

Nowadays, stainless steel is commonly used for spokes. Even though this is a fine material, it is not necessarily correct to assume them to be stronger than spokes made of galvanized or cadmium-plated steel. The advantage of stainless steel spokes is that they don't corrode. Corrosion not only weakens the spokes over time, it also makes it harder to turn the nipple, often causing the spokes to break when an attempt is made to tighten or loosen them.

Even carbon-fiber spokes are in use, but not for conventionally built wheels. They are occasionally used for aerodynamic pre-built wheels, with price tags of over $1,000 a pop. We've already mentioned the tubular spokes and their questionable aerodynamics.

Carbon spokes are possibly not strong enough in this kind of application. One ad claims its composite spoke is tested to withstand "over 400 pounds" of tension, but because stainless

Above: Fig. 9.51. Some spokes are threaded in at the hub, instead of at the rim. This one dates from 1875.

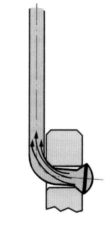

Right: Fig. 9.52. Stress concentration at a spoke head may cause conventional spokes to break at this point.

Left: Fig. 9.53. Spokes in the making. View inside a spoke-making facility.

Top right: Fig. 9.54. Roval straight-pull spokes with matching rim.

Bottom right: Fig. 9.55. Vectran flexible replacement spokes.

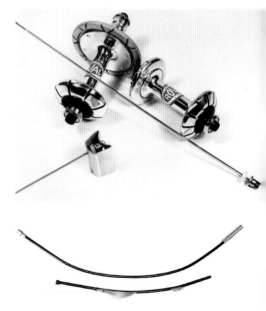

steel spokes have been tested at 600 pounds or more, that statement is hardly a ringing endorsement.

In addition to the conventional hooked-end spokes, there are straight-pull spokes, which of course require special hubs. These are often used on aero wheels. Technically seen, the straight-pull spoke is advantageous because no bending stresses are caused, which often lead to failure of conventional spokes.

SPOKING PATTERNS

The spokes are installed according to a certain spoking patterns, some of which are shown in Fig. 9.57. The simplest pattern is that of the radially spoked wheel, where the spokes do not cross each other. Because this pattern does not lend itself very well to the transfer of a torque (the application of a rotating force on the hub, tending to twist it relative to the rim), the various tangential patterns have been

introduced. This makes sense on the rear wheel and on any wheel with a hub brake, but for the front wheel radial spoking works very well, providing the hub flanges are strong enough to withstand the resulting radially oriented spoke forces.

The various tangential spoking patterns are identified by the number of spokes that each spoke crosses on its way from the hub to the rim: 1-cross, 2-cross, 3-cross and 4-cross.

The whole spoking pattern is actually simpler than it appears, because it is repeated every fourth spoke on the rim, every second spoke on either hub flange. The place to start looking is at the valve—it should lie between two nearly parallel spokes, leading to the left-hand and the right-hand hub flange respectively.

These days, most road bike wheels have 28 or 32 spokes, while essentially all mountain bikes have 32 spokes. Utility, touring, and comfort bikes are more likely to have 36 spokes, whereas tandems and carrying

bikes may have even more. In Britain it was customary until the late sixties to use 40 spokes on the (more heavily loaded) rear wheel, and 32 on the front wheel. Smaller wheels require fewer spokes, down to 20 for a 16-inch wheel.

In recent years, the craze for lightness and reduced air resistance has brought back full-size wheels with fewer spokes, requiring matching rims and hubs. For the rear wheel, reducing the number of spokes would only be suitable for light riders, riding on smooth road surface. Bladed spokes, which are oval in cross section over much of their length, and even more radically sectioned spokes have been introduced to further reduce the air resistance of lightweight road racing bikes.

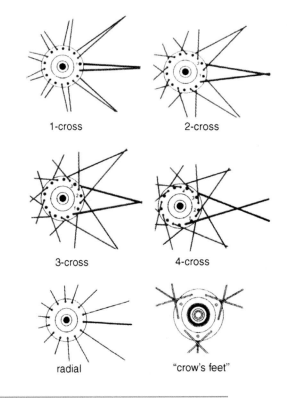

1-cross   2-cross

3-cross   4-cross

radial   "crow's feet"

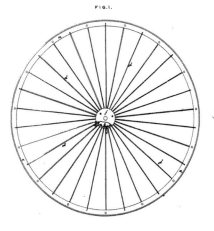

Left: Fig. 9.56. Eugène Meyer's 1869 patent drawing for the invention of the modern tension-spoked wheel.

Right: Fig. 9.57. Common spoking patterns.

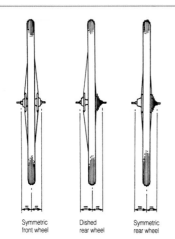

Symmetric front wheel   Dished rear wheel   Symmetric rear wheel

Whatever the number of spokes and crosses, the spokes generally run alternatingly to the left-hand and the right-hand hub flange. Depending upon whether a particular spoke lies on the inside or the outside of the flange,

Left: Fig. 9.58. Wheel symmetry and resulting spoke angles left and right compared.

it is referred to as an inside or outside spoke respectively. In the case of a radially spoked wheel, all spokes should be outside spokes. On all other wheels, inside and outside spokes alternate on each hub flange. Since the outside spokes wrap furthest around the hub flange (and because they stand under a slightly less acute angle), they are

MOMENT OF INERTIA VERSUS AERODYNAMICS

Because the smaller the moment of inertia of its wheels, the faster the bicycle can accelerate or decelerate, a step taken to reduce the moment of inertia is a step toward improved performance. This step usually entails choosing a lighter tire, a lighter rim, and fewer and thinner spokes. However, this is also a step toward reduced reliability: more frequent truing, shortened useful life, greater likelihood of road damage, probably greater likelihood of flats.

The rider must be careful to choose wheels and tires sturdy enough for the load they must carry and the road surfaces they will encounter. It will be a trade-off between performance and maintenance. This is done by trial-and-error, based on one's own experience and the advice of one's riding companions and shop personnel.

Another consideration, however, is aerodynamics. Most

wheels are designed for a good strength-to-mass ratio without regard to drag. Though standard wheels are perfectly adequate for most uses, the availability of aero versions raises new questions. A rim with a tall parabolic cross-section no doubt improves the aerodynamics of the wheel, but it is also heavier than a standard rim, and its extra mass is far from the hub—the worst place to put it as far as moment of inertia is concerned. Do the improved aerodynamics offset the increased mass and inertia? Aerodynamic carbon-fiber composite wheels with a few blades instead of standard spokes are supposed to be very effective in reducing drag, but they are invariably heavier, as are disc wheels and wheel covers. Under what conditions are aero wheels improvements?

If the terrain is flat, or nearly so, and if the application is time trialing or similar riding at a nearly constant speed, the answer is simple: aero wheels unquestionably improve per-

formance. Mass and moment of inertia under such conditions make little difference, because the bicycle is seldom climbing or accelerating. What matters most is a low drag coefficient. Disc wheels (or wheel covers, if permitted) usually give the lowest C_D, followed by aero composite wheels, then aero rims with fewer-than-usual bladed spokes. Unfortunately, precise coefficient of drag figures for these options are not available, and the best aerodynamic wheels are often very expensive, but at least the qualitative answer is straightforward.

When mass matters, the answer may be different. Here the lack of precise C_D data hurts, and though wheel mass may be known, moment of inertia can only be estimated. But estimation is exactly what we have to do to assess how effective different wheels may be in improving performance. Suppose we take one of the severest tests of acceleration: a 200-meter sprint.

generally less prone to breaking. Consequently, the spokes that take twisting forces (from the drivetrain or from a hub brake), should preferably be outside spokes.

In cross-section, the spoked wheel may take any of the shapes depicted in Fig. 9.58. Obviously, the front wheel is generally symmetric (an exception might be a front wheel with hub brake), while the rear wheel is generally offset to accommodate the freewheel cluster with its sprockets, which forces the

Right: Fig. 9.59. Radially spoked wheel with straight-pull spokes.

(Continued)

We will assume a light bike and rider, beginning at a total of 80 kg, perhaps more typical of sprint conditions. We will also give the rider sprinter horsepower: 1,120 W, or about 1.5 hp, to accelerate from an initial 11.2 m/s (25 mph) to whatever speed he can reach by the finish. Our standard wheels will be very light ones, with particularly low-mass tubular rims and tires suitable for a smooth track but strong enough (we hope) to stand up to a sprint—moments of inertia 0.0528 and 0.0534 kgm² at front and rear respectively. Nothing aerodynamic, however; our rider and bike have a C_D of 0.88 with these wheels. When we run them through their paces, we find they complete the 200 meters in 13.54 seconds, accelerating to 16.71 m/s (37.38 mph) by the finish line.

The next option will be very similar, the only difference being aero rims. We will suppose the aero-profile rims add 360 grams to the bike and have moments of inertia of 0.0699 and 0.0705 kg-m² respectively. (These numbers are based on actual rims available on the market.) The resulting C_D, however, can only be a guess; we'll try 0.87. The corresponding time for the same sprint is also 13.54 s, the final speed 16.74 m/s: a photo finish against the lightweight standard wheels. If our guess is only a little pessimistic, these wheels could win easily despite their considerable extra mass.

Finally, we'll make some wilder guesses about composite aero bladed wheels, again based on a model actually available. These are very light for such wheels, adding only 160 grams to the bike—better than the aero rims above. Judging from the distribution of carbon-fiber and aluminum, their moments of inertia may be about 0.0782 kg-m² each, not quite as good as the other wheels in this example, but better than a lot of wheels used by recreational riders. C_D is more problematical. Ads for one model of such composite wheels estimate a certain time savings in a time trial; assuming that their time trial is flat (not downhill!) and that their reference bike and rider are similar to ours, it is easy to calculate the drag coefficient which could produce such savings all by itself. Doing so, however, yields a number near 0.78, a C_D so low it is frankly unbelievable: it is almost recumbent bike territory! Even though the ads are almost certainly exaggerating their product's performance advantage, we will go ahead and use that drag coefficient value. The sprint then takes 13.37 s, ending at 17.10 m/s: not surprisingly, the best by far.

While the results hinge on data that is difficult to come by, it should still be clear that it takes only a modest improvement in aerodynamics to offset a hefty quantity of rotating mass. Already some sprinters are showing up with wheels that were formerly reserved for time trialists and triathletes. Their numbers are bound to increase.

spokes on the right-hand side into a much steeper angle relative to the axle (or a more acute angle relative to the wheel centerline). This asymmetry is referred to as wheel dishing, or simply "dish," and leads to proportional differences in spoke tension with attendant breakage probability. Cassette rear hubs have a more favorable bearing configuration and allow for a more symmetrical spoking configuration, which reduces the risk of broken spokes and of the wheel going "out of true."

Many of the modern pre-built wheels deviate from the rather straight-forward patterns described here, mainly to save

weight and minimize aerodynamic drag. Amongst these, you may find wheels with as few as 12 or 18 spokes, and there may be more spokes on one side than on the other, or a radial pattern on one side and tangential on the other. All these wheels will have very deep, so-called aero rims. Those aero rims are indeed strong, at least radially, but they do not necessarily result in a lighter wheel, because the extra metal in the rim weighs more than the weight savings that result from using fewer spokes.

With a conventional wheel of 32 or more spokes, if a spoke should break out in the boondocks, even if the rider cannot replace the spoke right there or adjust nearby spokes to bring the wheel closer to true, it is usually possible to open the brake quick-release and ride home carefully on the warped wheel. With a wheel of fewer spokes, often in a paired pattern, if a spoke breaks, not only can't the rider make a repair, but the wheel is likely to be so warped that it will not clear the brake pads even with the quick-release wide open. A bike with a wheel

that does not turn cannot be ridden anywhere.

WHEEL ALIGNMENT AND SYMMETRY

In the assembled bike, the two wheels must be perfectly aligned one behind the other with the centerline through the bike, so it stays on track without undue steering and balancing corrections. One factor that comes into play here is the wheel dish on the rear wheel: it must be just

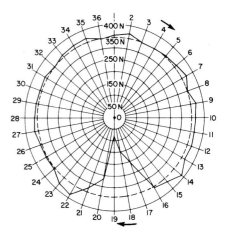

Above: Fig. 9.62. Distribution of forces on a spoked driven wheel. All spokes were pre-stressed to 350 N (77 lb-force). The load on the spokes near the bottom of the wheel is reduced but still positive. The irregularities are due to the driving force of 800 N (170 lb-force).

Left: Fig. 9.60. Wheel builders at work, using a wheel spoking machine (top) and by hand (bottom).

Right: Fig. 9.61. The components and tools used for building a wheel.

enough to place the rim on the centerline through the front wheel and the rest of the bike. If necessary, the wheels are centered correctly to achieve this. If the wheels are not in line, the bike may be dangerous to ride due to balancing problems.

The wheel must also be correctly centered when mounted, before the quick-release is tightening and that's what the derailleur adjustment screws are there to help you do.

Someone riding behind you can usually confirm the problem when he tries to visually align the two wheels. To establish how much correction is required, it is best to use a wheel alignment gauge, which may be bought ready made. The idea is to

correct spoke tension so that the rim is centered between the lock-nuts over the entire circumference (check in at least three locations equally spaced around the circumference).

Above: Fig. 9.63. On this wheel, from Kindler, the spokes are in the form of Kevlar wires.

Left: Fig.9.64. Wheel truing options and procedures.

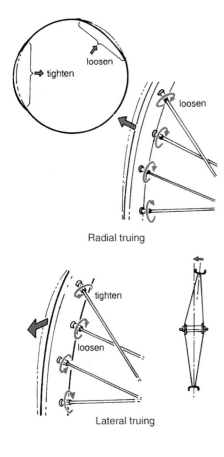

Radial truing

Lateral truing

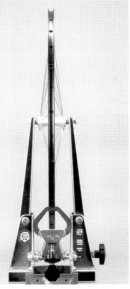

Right: Fig. 9.65. While it is being built, and later to make sure it is trued properly, the wheel is held in a truing stand.

DISK WHEELS

Since the mid eighties, disk wheels have been all the craze in time trial events. They offer markedly reduced air resistance compared to the conventional tension spoked wheel, especially at higher speeds. Since the upper portion of the wheel actually moves against the air at twice the bicycle's speed, it can be seen that this factor is more significant than may appear at first.

Interestingly, disk wheels had been on the market as early as 1893, and their benefit was established even at that time, although few people realized their potential. Only after various manufacturers introduced all sorts of other supposedly aerodynamic components in 1980, and it was soon established that none of them did anything significant, did one begin to realize how much more could be gained by

Above: Fig. 9.66. Tioga Tension-Disk, or Disk-drive, wheel with an aramid (Kevlar) web instead of spokes.

using such aerodynamic disk wheels.

The international sanctioning organization for bicycle racing, the UCI, did not allow the use of aerodynamic fairings on the bike or its components, but did not object to wheels constructed as one piece—as the disk wheel is. Thus, the disk wheel was given an artificial boost, even though, from a technical standpoint, these wheels were inferior to spoked wheels with added light-weight covers (which remained illegal in sanctioned races). At astronomical prices and at first excessively heavy, disk wheels soon appeared on any bike used for time trials. Ironically enough, this also became customary in

Above: Fig. 9.67. A set of disk wheels.

Right: Fig. 9.68. Ultralight, aerodynamic bladed wheels such as these are quite good, but they don't hold up as well as conventional wheels in case of an accident. With a failure like this, you're lucky to get away with your life.

triathlon, where the UCI regulations did not apply and where wheel covers would be more economical.

The technical disadvantage of the disk wheel is obvious: it is essentially the same heavy construction as the wagon wheel, which was so elegantly overcome by the tension-wire spoked bicycle wheel. A disk wheel is difficult to construct so that it stays true, or can be trued, and its weight [really mass] is relatively high.

Oddly enough, the high weight has sometimes been used as an argument in favor of disk wheels, because the increased momentum is supposed to act as a flywheel. Actually this is correct, but it is no advantage, because these heavier wheels first have to be accelerated to the desired speed, which requires more energy than is needed to bring a lighter wheel to the same speed.

Perhaps for some track races, such as time trials and pursuit races, where the bike is only accelerated up to speed once or twice, while subsequent

accelerations and decelerations are minor, the disadvantage is minimized. However, it would make no sense to use disk wheels for other events, where changes of speed and direction are more common, and weight is a more important factor.

The other disadvantage of the disk is its sensitivity to cross winds, or any kind of wind on a curved course. One way around this is the three-, four- or five-bladed wheel. This too is a design that was available as early as 1893, and at the time advertised with the same arguments as today. It is about as heavy as a full disk of the same materials—and even more expensive.

Recently, more sophisticated materials and construction methods have produced disk wheels of remarkably light weight that begin to compete with tension-spoked wheels, although they are still less flexible and less durable—and *a lot* more expensive.

Finally, the Tioga *Tension-Disk* wheel (which was also sold under the Sugino brand name), should be mentioned. In this now abandoned design, the conventional spokes were replaced by a kind of spider's web of tensioned aramid (e.g. Kevlar) fiber, embedded in a lightweight plastic membrane with a pretty good aerodynamic shape. However, in practice, most riders who used these sophisticated wheels seem to report more problems than benefits.

The Steering System

THE COMPONENTS that make up the bicycle's steering system are illustrated in Fig. 10.1. It comprises the front fork, the top and bottom head set bearings that hold it in the frame's head tube, the handlebars and the handlebar stem.

Before proceeding to the technical details of these components, the steering principle will be described. This will greatly aid in gaining an understanding of the way frame geometry and the steering components act together to influence the bicycle's handling characteristics.

The Steering Principle

The steering system not only serves to control the bicycle in curves, it is equally essential for going straight and for balancing the bicycle under all circumstances. Anybody whose front wheel has ever been caught in a parallel groove, such as a street-car track and survived it, can confirm that even going straight is an impossibility with locked steering. Actually, the bicycle never goes in a completely straight line. Instead, it always follows a more or less curving path, always deviating a little to one side or the other, corres-

ponding to similar deviations in the vertical position of bike and rider.

When the center of gravity is to the right of the point of contact between wheels and road, the bike leaning in that same direction, the rider regains his

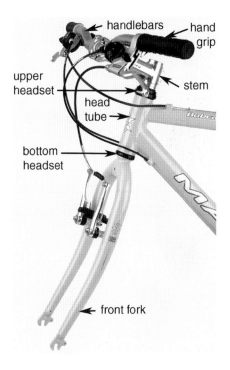

Right: Fig. 10.1. The parts of the steering system, shown here on a flat-handlebar bicycle.

balance by pointing the steering further to the right. This causes the bottom of the bike to move back under the center of gravity, restoring equilibrium—but only temporarily, because the bike now starts to lean in the opposite direction. In turn, this lean is countered by steering slightly in that same direction, causing it to move back under the center of gravity and beyond, ad infinitum.

At low speeds, this serpentine-action is quite distinct, with considerable steering deviations. At elevated speeds, the deviations are smaller, although the lean relative to the vertical plane tends to be greater at any steering angle than it is at lower speeds. To get a feel for this movement, low speed riding,

consciously trying to follow a straight line, is educational.

NATURAL VERSUS FORCED CURVES

To ride a curve, the simplest way is to use the natural lean. To follow a curve to the right, wait until the bike is naturally leaning in that same direction, and then don't do anything for a while. Thus, the bike is not brought back upright, but continues to lean further and further, until quite a distinct lean angle is reached. Now it is time to steer noticeably in the same direction, avoiding the crash that would

have followed the excessive lean, while forcing the bike in the desired direction.

This method of steering is referred to as the *natural* turn and is illustrated in the right-hand detail of Fig. 10.4. It has one drawback: it requires a lot of time and room to maneuver. If there is not enough of either to follow this method, use the technique referred to as the *forced* turn. This

BIKE HANDLING TEST

An enjoyable way of testing bicycle steering, balancing, and handling skills is in a "slow race." Here the object is to be the *last* one at the finish line without putting a foot down.

In off-road cycling, there is also a type of competition that emphasizes handling skills at slow speed. Called technical trials, it's still a race for first place, but also here you get penalized for putting a foot down.

Above: Fig. 10.2. Setup for measuring steering variables while the bicycle is ridden and steered at controlled speed.

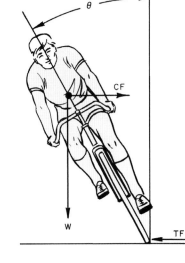

Above: Fig. 10.3. Body lean and resulting reaction forces while riding through a curve.

Fig. 10.5. Off-road bike handling as demonstrated in a observed trials competition.

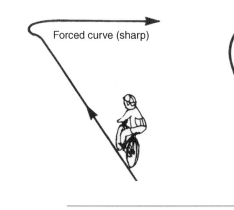

Forced curve (sharp) Natural curve (gradual)

Left: Fig. 10.4. Natural (gradual) versus forced (quick) curve..

method is illustrated in the left-hand detail of Fig. 10.4.

To carry out the forced turn, the cyclist first steers in the direction opposite to his intended path. This causes the bike to lean in the opposite direction. Rather than correcting this right away, the bike is first allowed to drift further with increasing lean in the direction of the intended curve. When a significant lean is reached, the rider finally steers in that same direction, resulting in a tight and sudden curve.

Most of this is usually done subconsciously, although this is the very thing that makes learning to ride a bike confidently so difficult at first. It also explains why beginning cyclists, or riders who use a bike with drastically different steering geometry for the first time, feel and act so insecure and often ride so unpredictably.

BICYCLE STABILITY AND THE "UNRIDABLE BICYCLE"

It had long been assumed that the gyroscopic effect of the spinning wheels is what keeps the bicycle upright, a theory first put forward by Timoshenko and Young in 1948. To check that theory, E. H. Jones in 1970 built a presumably unridable bicycle, in which the gyroscopic effect was cancelled out by means of a disk rotating in the opposite direction.

It turned that that, though the bicycle's stability was indeed decreased without a rider, it was no problem to ride it when loaded with the rider's mass. Jones established that the combination of bicycle and rider was inherently stable and mainly balanced by what he called the "caster" effect of the fork trail.

Since then, several researchers have tried to establish a more comprehensive theory of bicycle steering and balancing, but for all practical purposes, the simple explanation still holds true. As long as the fork has enough trail, it will tend to self-correct rather than fall over.

Left: Fig. 10.6. The spinning bicycle wheel has a gyroscopic effect. When it is leaned one way, the gyroscopic effect works to balance it out with an opposing force. But no, that is not the force that keeps bike and rider upright.

Left: Fig. 10.7. E. H. Jones demonstrating that a bicycle without gyroscopic effect of the wheels can be balanced, even with "no hands."

Right: Fig. 10.8. Diagrammatic steering and lean representation.

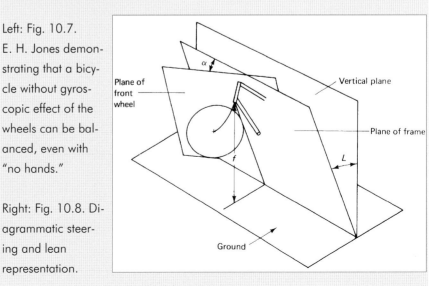

FRAME ANGLES, YAW, AND HANDLING

A road racing bike handles quickly by virtue of its relatively short wheelbase. That short wheelbase is achieved not only by shorter chainstays but by steeper frame angles and shorter fork rake. But that does not mean that any bike with steeper angles or shorter rake will handle more quickly. Surprisingly, neither of these assumptions is the case; in fact, the opposite is true. The figures and equations that follow will illustrate these points.

Figure 10.7 shows a top view of the steering geometry. The distance labeled f is the horizontal length of the fork (projected onto the ground) as it rotates through a steering angle θ. The distance c is the constant portion of the wheelbase, back to the rear wheel; W is the actual wheelbase, equal to f + c when θ is zero but a little less when θ is greater than zero. The angle

between the two wheelbase lines is labeled φ (phi), and is referred to as yaw.

Figure 10.8 shows the side view. Here α is the head tube angle, R is the fork rake, and r is the wheel (and tire) radius. R (rake) is shown as a short line perpendicular to the steering axis and ending at the fork dropout. The radius r is the vertical distance from that dropout to the ground, and also the distance from the dropout to the point at which the steering axis and the circumference of the tire meet. The following formulas apply, with angles expressed in degrees:

$$f = r \sin (\arctan R/r + 90 - a)$$

$$\phi = \arcsin [(f \sin \theta) / W]$$

It means that yaw decreases as head tube angle steepens. For example, given 700C wheels, a constant trail of 5 cm, a steering angle of 10 degrees, and a constant wheelbase of 99 cm measured when the front wheel is

pointing straight ahead, yaw is about half a degree more (over 40% greater) with a 70-degree head tube angle than with a 75-degree angle.

Similarly, with a constant head tube angle, say 73 degrees, if everything else is held constant except for the rake (and the corresponding trail), yaw decreases with decreasing rake: it is almost 30% greater with 7 cm rake than with 3 cm.

Even if we allow the wheelbase to shorten solely on account of the steepening frame angle and shortening rake, keeping the quantity c constant, yaw decreases as head tube angle steepens.

The quick handling of the road bike is thus the result of the short wheelbase only. While steep angles and short rake contribute to that short wheelbase, they slow the steering more than the short wheelbase quickens it. Shallower angles win the quickness contest.

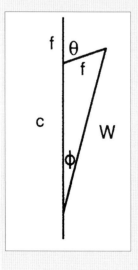

Left: Fig. 10.9. Steering geometry, top view.

Right: Fig. 10.10. Steering geometry, side view.

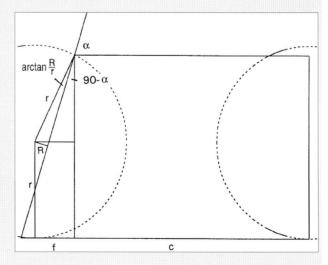

STEERING GEOMETRY

How accurately and predictably a bicycle steers and handles, and how comfortable it is to ride and maneuver, is largely affected by its steering geometry. This is the relationship between angles and dimensions of the parts of the steering system as they relate to the total bike.

Although the manufacturer of a ready-made bicycle has predetermined the steering geometry, it is quite useful for the technically competent rider to know how a certain characteristic is achieved. This is all the more important if one considers that a remarkable number of manufacturers and bicycle sales people haven't the faintest idea how it is done correctly. The result is that they finish up producing or selling bikes that are less (or sometimes more) stable than they should be.

Fig. 10.11 illustrates the most important concepts that play a part in determining the bicycle's steering geometry, and indirectly its handling characteristics. How predictably a bike handles and how much stability it has are largely determined by the dimension called *trail*.

This is the distance between the contact point between the wheel and the road (point A) and the point at which the imaginarily extended steering axis crosses the road (point B).

Right: Fig. 10.11. Handling is largely determined by the dimension called trail, which in turn depends on head tube angle and fork rake.

At any head tube, or steerer, angle of less than 90° (and typical values are far below that, namely 66—74°), combined with a straight fork, point A lies well behind point B. Thus the amount of trail, dimension X, would be quite big. This would result in a distinct tendency of the bike to follow a straight course, requiring relatively strong steering

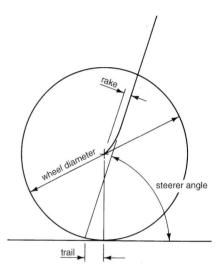

EFFECT OF STEM EXTENSION ON HANDLING

Proper stem extension reach (that is, forward length, not height) places the handlebars at the correct distance in front of the rider. But because the distance depends on the sum of the top tube length and stem extension, any given distance can be achieved with a variety of combinations.

Before buying a new bike or ordering a custom frame, you should be aware of the tradeoffs. A shorter top tube gives a shorter wheelbase, the effects of which are discussed elsewhere. However, it must be counteracted with a longer-reach stem. This increases the length of the lever arm effecting steering corrections, which makes the steering more stable, or (viewed another way) more sluggish. Minor road jitters transmitted to a long stem cause only small changes to the steering angle, and a given steering angle change requires a longer sweep of the hands. Conversely, a long top tube may require a short-reach stem, which could seem either responsive or nervous, depending on your point of view.

Reach should not be a serious handling concern unless you are forced to use a very short or very long stem. In that case, if your physical dimensions and the models available permit, you should consider a different frame, i.e. a model of the same size with a different top tube length, or perhaps a slightly bigger or smaller version of the same model. Good fit should override all other considerations.

forces, or significant external effects, to deviate from this straight path.

As the illustration shows, the fork is usually bent forward—the distance over which this is done is referred to as *rake*. This brings point A forward, closer to point B, decreasing the amount of trail. Thus, the more raked the fork is for any given head tube angle, the less trail it achieves, decreasing the bike's inherent stability and increasing its agility. Obviously, the same amount of trail, and essentially the same stability, can be achieved with different head tube angles, providing the rake is selected correspondingly to provide the desired trail with each angle.

Even so, there is a difference between the way bikes with the same trail but different head tube angles handle. The bike with a shallow angle is somewhat more sluggish and only responds predictably up to a certain steering deviation, after which a phenomenon called *wheel flop* sets in. This means that the bike oversteers abruptly beyond this point. The advantage of the bike with

the shallower head tube angle lies in the increased comfort due to the greater flexibility of the more inclined and more distinctly bent fork, making this solution more desirable for touring on rough surfaces. Trail values typically fall between 50 mm for a quick-steering criterium racing bike to 65 mm for a stable touring or mountain bike.

Of course, the head tube, or steerer, angle for any given frame is fixed. These days, most manufacturers supply that information for the bikes they sell. Road racing bikes typically have a head angle from 73.5—74°. Touring bikes have an angle of around 72°, while older mountain bikes and many utility bikes may have one as shallow as 66—68°, although the trend in mountain bikes is toward steeper head angles, 71—72° being more typical these days.

Fig. 10.12 shows how the fork rake can be chosen to match any head tube angle, while still arriving at the required trail. Fig. 10.13 simplifies the selection of the appropriate fork rake that gives a certain amount

of trail once the head tube angle is known. These graphs are based on the following formulas:

$$T_1 = (d \cos \alpha - D) / (2 \sin \alpha)$$

$$T_2 = T_1 (\sin \alpha)$$

where

T_1 = Projected trail (mm)

T_2 = effective trail (mm)

D = front wheel diameter (mm)

α = head tube angle (degrees)

r = rake (mm)

The difference between the two values T_1 and T_2 bears some

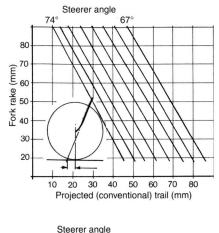

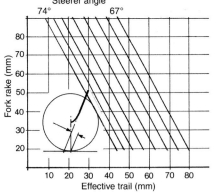

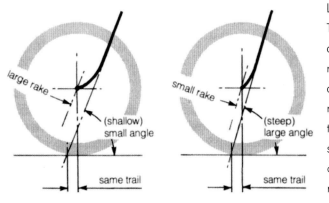

Left: Fig. 10.12. The desired amount of fork rake can be achieved (almost) regardless of heat tube angle: shallower angles call for more fork rake.

Above: Fig. 10.13. Graphs to determine trail for any given head tube angle and fork rake for different steerer, or head tube, angles.

explanation. The value T1 is the one commonly used, but does not give as accurate an impression of actual stability as T2. The latter, which we refer to as *effective trail*, is what some authors call *stability index*, creating the impression that this is a dimensionless number (which it should not be).

However, it can easily be determined, as we have done above, and should be used in preference to the conventional value T1, which we refer to as *projected trail*. The difference between the two values increases as the head tube angle decreases, making it critical to use the right one, especially on mountain bikes and touring or utility machines with a relaxed geometry.

The formula also makes it clear that the wheel radius enters into the calculation. Small-wheeled bikes should consequently be built with less rake than the values indicated in the table for 650 to 700 mm wheels (nominal sizes 26 in. to 28 in.). As the formula and Figs. 10.13 and 10.14 suggest, even a completely straight fork barely provides enough trail for adequate stability on a bike with 20 in. or smaller wheels—important on folding bikes and children's bikes, as well as on recumbents and some other special designs. Essentially, such bikes with small wheels should have very little or

no rake at all if they are to provide adequate directional stability.

THE HEADSET

The headset bearings provide the rotational support for the steering system in the frame. Two types of headset are in use, referred to as conventional (or threaded) and Aheadset (threadless) types respectively. In recent years integrated headsets have become popular, but these work essentially the same as threadless headsets

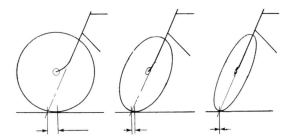

Above: Fig. 10.16. As the steering is turned further, the amount of rake decreases, changing the steering characteristics.

Right: Fig. 10.17. For a given head tube angle and fork rake, trail is less for a small-wheeled bike than it is for a standard bike. For that reason small-wheeled bikes need *less* rake (or even *no* rake).

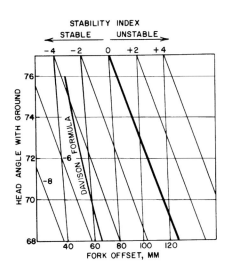

Above: Fig. 10.14. Diagram by Fred DeLong to determine relative stability at different head tube angles and fork rake values.

Right: Fig. 10.15. Another one of DeLong's diagrams, this one showing relative handling qualities on different road surfaces.

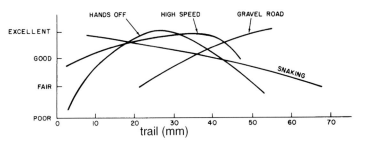

CONVENTIONAL HEADSET

This is the traditional type of headset that was in use on all bikes until about 1990, and is still installed on touring, city, and folding bikes. Its advantage is that it allows for an adjustable handlebar height. Fig. 10.17 shows how the conventional headset is built up, consisting of a fixed bearing in the bottom and an adjustable one at the top.

Above: Fig. 10.18. The parts of a conventional, or threaded, headset. This is an oversize headset (1 ¼ in diameter), which provides superior directional stability for e.g. tandem or mountain bike use.

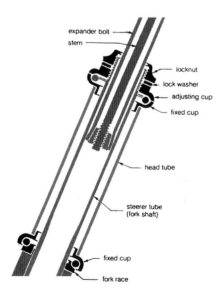

The lockring may either have the form shown or it may have projecting teeth that match similar teeth in the top of the upper bearing cup.

On bikes with high handlebar position, the locknut may be built up with a high collar that stabilizes the handlebar stem. On bikes with cantilever or center-pull brakes, an anchor for the brake cable may be installed between the locknut and the adjustable cup, replacing the lockring.

The ball bearings of the headset are loaded differently than those of most other bicycle applications. Whereas most other bearings rotate constantly and are loaded radially, i.e. perpendicular to the axle, the headset bearings hardly rotate and are loaded axially, i.e. in line with it. This is an unfavorable condition for ball bearings, because impacts from the road are transferred to the balls which remain in the same location, causing pitting of the bearing surfaces in those spots, referred to as *brinelling*. This is the reason mountain bikes are nowadays

Left: Fig. 10.19. The parts of a conventional (threaded) headset.

Right: Fig. 10.20. This illustration shows how a conventional headset's "stacking height" (the sum of the parts projecting from the head tube) is important in determining the length of the steerer tube.

often equipped with so-called oversize headsets, requiring an oversize head tube and a fork with a matching steerer tube as well.

The standard size for conventional headsets is 1 in. (25.4 mm), and oversize headsets, which are more resistant to abuse, are either 1¹/₈ or 1¹/₄ in. Beware of these differences when it comes to part replacement and repair.

Since the headset bearings are so unfavorably loaded, it is quite important to keep them well adjusted and lubricated, and to overhaul them occasionally. You can check whether it is too loose by lifting the wheel off the ground and checking whether the fork can be moved relative to the frame at the fork crown.

In order to establish whether the headset is too tight, again lift the front wheel off the ground and check whether the steering can be turned from the fork crown (where there is less leverage than at the handlebars) without noticeable or irregular resistance. Unfortunately, the

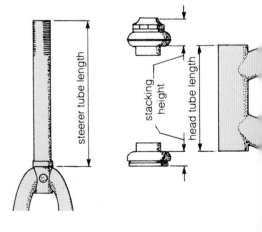

problem of a rough or tight headset can rarely be solved by means of adjustment, although that is the first step. Only too often, it is the result of damage that can only be eliminated by completely overhauling, and perhaps replacing, the headset.

CONVENTIONAL HEADSET ADJUSTMENT

Usually, this can be done without removing anything from the bike. On mountain bikes it may be helpful to remove the straddle cable of the front brake if it is of the cantilever type—just make sure it is replaced again afterwards. It is preferable to use special matching headset wrenches, although it can usually be done with the aid of a large crescent wrench.

Procedure:

1. Unscrew the locknut on top of the upper headset by about two turns (models with toothed lockring: far enough to disengage the teeth).

2. Lift the lockring up enough to free the adjustable cup.

3 Screw the adjustable cup in or out a little, as required to tighten or loosen the bearing respectively.

4. Push the lockring down on the adjustable cup again.

5. Tighten the locknut, making sure the lockring and the

adjustable cup do not turn with it.

6. Check operation of the headset and repeat adjustment if necessary.

THREADLESS HEADSET

This is the type of headset, also called Aheadset, is found on essentially all modern road bikes and mountain bikes. There is a particular version of this referred to as integrated headset, which however is the same thing on which the manufacturers have made life a bit easier on themselves (and harder for whoever has to maintain it later) by placing the bearings straight in the head tube. Not a good idea, but very fashionable.

Fig. 10.25 shows how the threadless headset is built up and installed. It requires a fork that does not have screw thread on

Above: Fig. 10.21. The conventional headset is adjusted, tightened, or loosened using two wrenches.

Left: Fig. 10.22. A conventional headset mounted on a bicycle.

Right: Fig. 10.23. Threadless headset installed on a bicycle.

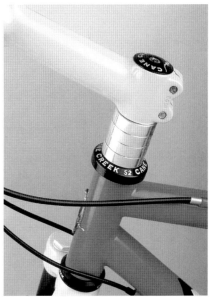

the steerer tube. The bolt on top of the stem does not hold the parts together but is merely there to adjust the bearings.

Above: Fig. 10.24. Inside detail after the cap has been removed, showing the "star-fangled washer (which is really a nut, with screw thread) into which the adjusting bolt on the cap is screwed.

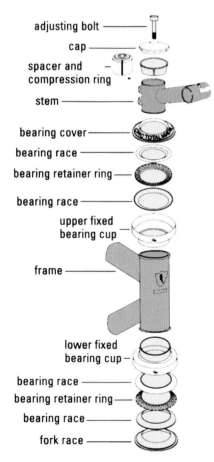

adjusting bolt ——

cap ——

spacer and compression ring ——

stem ——

bearing cover ——

bearing race ——

bearing retainer ring ——

bearing race ——

upper fixed bearing cup ——

frame ——

lower fixed bearing cup ——

bearing race ——

bearing retainer ring ——

bearing race ——

fork race ——

Any instructions below for the threadless headset also apply to the integrated headset, which is nothing more than a variation on the same theme as the thread-less headset.

THREADLESS HEADSET ADJUSTMENT

The threadless headset tends to stay properly adjusted longer, but there may still be a need for adjustment from time to time. The only tool required is a matching Allen wrench.

Procedure:

1. Loosen the clamp bolts that hold the stem around the fork's steerer tube by about one turn each.

Left: Fig. 10.25. Exploded view of a threadless headset.

Right: Fig. 10.26. On the integrated headset the (threadless) headset bearings are embedded in the oversize head tube.

2. Tighten or loosen the Allen bolt on top of the stem—this is not a binder bolt taking force but solely serves as an adjustment bolt (and the plastic or aluminum cap underneath would break if too much force were applied to it by that bolt). Tighten by turning the bolt clockwise, loosen by turning it counter-clockwise.

3. When the adjustment feels right, tighten the stem clamp bolts, making sure the handlebars are straight.

Left: Fig. 10.27. Loosening or tightening the cap nut on a threadless headset. Don't force it!

Right: Fig. 10.28. Loosening or tightening the stem clamp bolts.

THE FRONT FORK

Fig. 10.29 shows the construction of a typical front fork. It comprises the steerer tube, or fork shaft, two fork blades, a fork crown that connects them together, and forkends, also-called front dropouts.

The steerer tube is either threaded, for use with a conventional headset, or threadless, for use with an Aheadset type headset. The way the fork blades are attached to the steerer tube may vary. Two special types are referred to as unicrown and switchblade fork respectively, both initially developed for the mountain bike.

The two latter versions were developed for mountain bike use, before front suspension forks took over.

The unicrown is easier to build, and thus used to save cost on some bikes. The idea behind the switchblade fork, which has now all but disappeared, was to allow repair of a fork if one of the blades got bent.

In the past, and to some extent still today, steel, aluminum, and titanium frames are usually equipped with forks of the corresponding material. However, more and more bikes now come with carbon-fiber forks.

Indeed, carbon forks are lighter than forks made of more conventional materials. This is not only due to the fact that carbon-fiber is inherently lighter, having a higher strength-to-weight ratio. The other reason is that it is relatively easy to vary the thickness of the material to correspond to the force distribution along the length of the blades and at the junction of fork crown and steerer tube.

But before jumping to the conclusion that all bikes should have carbon forks, consider that there is a serious downside to the use of carbon for front forks. Since the fork is the most likely part of the bike to suffer damage in a frontal collision, it should be resilient enough to withstand significant forces. Unfortunately, carbon is strong only in the direction of tensile force, and is hopelessly inadequate when it comes to handling "sheer forces" which are typical of accidental impact. Though they may be unequaled in lightness, which is fine in an actual racing situation, for general use (including training rides), carbon forks can be considered accidents waiting to happen.

FORK BLADE SHAPE AND PATTERN

The front fork is a particularly heavily loaded part of the bike. Being cantilevered out, it is not loaded only in tension and compression as most other parts are, but in bending. It is also the first one to be damaged upon collision impact. Even so, it should not be too heavy, to provide adequate shock absorption. Ideally,

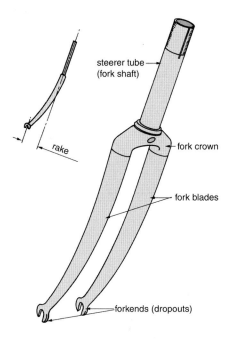

Left: Fig. 10.29. The parts of a traditional front fork. This model is made much the same way as a traditional lugged frame, with the various parts brazed together, and the fork crown acting like a lug.

steerer tube (fork shaft)

rake

fork crown

fork blades

forkends (dropouts)

Right: Fig. 10.30. A selection of different fork designs. From left to right: a Unicrown fork (tops of the blades curved in and welded to the head tube), a straight-bladed fork, and a one-piece carbon fork.

the fork blades should flex only parallel and remain linearly aligned, while lateral flexing should be minimized, all of which is best achieved with round fork blades.

However, most fork blades are made of oval cross-section, probably justified only by questionable aesthetic and aerodynamic arguments. Internal reinforcement of the steerer tube and the fork blades is appropriate. Unfortunately, the shaping process with which the fork blade diameters are made less at the bottom, where the load is minimal, than at the top, where it is greatest, results in increased wall thickness in the area with the smaller outside diameter. To compensate for that, high-quality forks are made of taper gauge tubing, which starts out thicker at the top and finishes up having a nearly constant wall thickness all the way down after forming.

There are several different solutions to the problem of providing the required fork rake needed to achieve the desired amount of trail. Most commonly, the forks are bent forward in a curve, but it is also possible to simply offset the fork blades under an angle pointing forward relative to the steerer tube angle. For mountain bikes, with their fat shock-absorbing tires, it doesn't matter much what shape is used (if rigid forks are used there at all any more), but the story is quite different for road bikes and other machines with (relatively) skinny tires.

It turns out that a properly designed fork can provide significant shock-absorption without noticeable energy loss. Tests conducted by *Bicycle Quarterly* have confirmed that a fork with curved fork blades transmitted significantly less road shock to the handlebars than those

Above: Fig. 10.31. Fork blades being tapered.

Below: Fig. 10.32. Fork blades being bent into the desired curved shape.

FORK SPRING CONSTANT

The spring constant of a fork, or any other spring, can be determined as shown in this illustration. With the fork clamped in at the fork crown and held horizontally, the fork ends in the same horizontal plane as the crown, apply a downward force, or weight, at the fork ends.

Now measure the deflection, i.e. the distance by which the forkends "sag" below their original position. If, for example, the force F = 200 N and the displacement s = 7 mm, or 0.007 m, the spring constant is 200 / 0.007 = 29,000 N/m.

In practice, of course the fork is not loaded in this direction, and the angle of the fork relative to the horizontal plane needs to be taken into account.

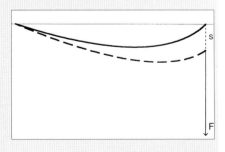

Fig. 10.33. Measuring fork deflection to determine the fork's spring constant.

fashionable straight-bladed forks. And, what most high-tech-obsessed cyclists may find hard to believe, the increased shock absorption actually increased overall efficiency.

Of course, there are other ways of providing shock-absorption, even on a non-suspension, or "rigid" front fork. One of the methods used is to embed flexible pads inside a recess in each, specially formed, fork blade. Tests by a German bike magazine revealed that removing the inserts does not change the damping effect, so it seems to be just a gimmick, although the special shape with recess does seem to do the trick.

Beyond this, there is the use of suspension forks, which will be covered in some detail in Chapter 18.

OTHER DETAILS

The forkends, or dropouts, in which the front wheel hub is

Above and right: Figs. 10.34 and 10.35. What happens in an accident depends largely on the material of the fork. The carbon fork (above) broke catastrophically, whereas the steel fork got bent out of shape, but stayed in one piece, with much less risk to the rider.

held, should be relatively thick and accurately flat and square to the wheel axle. Other than that, what was said about the (rear) dropouts in Chapter 8 applies here too.

The steerer tube of a replacement fork is usually provided long enough to fit even the

FORK OSCILLATION AND "SHIMMY"

Even a "rigid" fork has some flexibility, it is in effect a spring, held at one end (the headset) and loaded at the other (the dropouts). Like any other spring, the fork's characteristics can be defined by its spring constant The sidebar on this page shows how the spring constant is determined.

For every spring constant, there is also a natural frequency, where a repeated impact causes

an ever-increasing buildup of oscillations, which may lead to loss of control of the bike. This repeated impact may be caused by a slight imbalance of the wheel, such as out-of-true, a tire that is not perfectly mounted and balanced, or simply the weight of the valve. Mot of the time, it is no problem. However, in some cases these impacts may arrive at the fork in just the frequency at which the fork, with its particular spring constant, would oscillate.

If that happens, some of the things you can do is slow down (or speed up) to shift the frequency of the impacts, or to change riding posture to shift the load on the handlebars. And in the long run, to minimize the chances of this happening it is worthwhile to check the following points:

❏ headset adjustment;

❏ wheel bearing adjustment;

❏ wheel trueing;

❏ tire seating.

largest frame, so it may have to be shortened to provide the right length to match a smaller frame. The screw thread, in the case of a threaded headset, may then have to be recut, a job for which any bike shop should be equipped. Appendix 7 summarizes the different common thread types.

When cutting a steerer tube down to size, the stacking height of the headset must be considered, measured as shown in Fig. 10.21, and adding 2 mm (3/32 in.) clearance. The fork race, which is part of the lower headset, should match the collar, or shoulder, on the fork crown, which may have to be machined for an accurate fit.

The forkends are similar to the rear dropouts described in Chapter 8, but do not have an adjusting feature. The slots in the forkends point down almost vertically. For the last twenty years or so, most bicycles have been supplied with forks that have ribs at their ends—so-called "lawyer's lips," to prevent the wheel from coming out of the fork when the wheel quick-release is not tightened.

Unfortunately, these things also make the quick-release into a "slow-release." You have to unscrew the thumb nut to get the wheel out after the quick-release

lever is opened up, and of course, you have to tighten it again before you can tighten the lever when reinstalling the wheel. Ways to get around this problem can be found in Chapter 9, which is devoted to the bicycle wheel.

Disk brakes pose a special problem: when the brake is applied, the reaction force on the wheel tends to push the wheel down and back. This can lead to the wheel being pushed out of the dropouts if it is not held in firmly enough. In this case those pesky "lawyer's lips" can prevent the worst from happening, but it is still important to make sure the quick-release is tightened properly.

Above: Figs. 10.36 and 10.37. Aluminum fork with blades that are bonded to the fork crown (left) and carbon fork on which the blades are integral with the crown. On some carbon forks even the steerer tube is part of the one-piece construction.

Left: Fig. 10.38. A sample of investment-cast steel fork crowns.

FORK INSPECTION

The front fork may get damaged when the bicycle runs into an obstacle. Any of the distortions depicted in Fig. 10.39 may result, depending on the nature and direction of the impact. It should be inspected after any collision, and whenever the steering characteristics seem to have deteriorated. On steel bikes, it is sometimes possible to bend a fork blade back into shape if the damage is not too severe. Otherwise, the fork will have to be replaced. For the inspection procedure, a long metal straightedge is required.

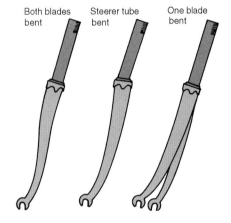

Above: Fig. 10.39. Different types of fork damage. Although a bent blade (either one or both) can be straightened on low-end steel forks, there is no way to rescue a fork with a bent steerer tube. And forget about trying to straighten any high-end forks, whether made of high-alloy steel, titanium, or aluminum. And of course, carbon does not bend, it just breaks.

Inspection Procedure:

1. With the fork still installed in the frame, sight along the fork blades from the side, to verify whether any damage as shown in Fig. 10.40 is apparent. If so, the fork should usually be replaced, although a straightening suggestion is given below, which sometimes works, depending on the strength of the fork.

2. Leaving the fork in the bike, place the straightedge in line with the center of the head tube and check whether there is a less pronounced bend of the fork blades relative to the steerer tube. If the distortion is slight, you may be able to continue riding the bike only if the steering does not have a rough spot—check carefully as described in the headset maintenance section above.

3. If necessary, remove the fork from the bike, following the procedure. Place the fork exactly perpendicular to the edge of a perfectly straight,

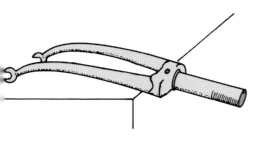

Above: Fig. 10.40. Method for checking alignment of the fork blades.

level surface as shown in Fig. 10.41. Verify whether all four points actually make contact simultaneously: the forkends and one point each near the top of the fork blades. In case of deviation, measure the difference: if it is more than 2 mm, measured at the forkends, the fork must either be replaced or straightened by a competent bike shop mechanic.

HANDLEBARS AND STEM

Most modern bicycles use handlebars that are connected with the rest of the steering system by means of a separate stem, as shown in Fig. 10.43. The handlebars proper, often referred to as the handlebar *bend* on a road bike, are clamped in the collar at the end of the stem. The stem is clamped either inside or outside the fork's steerer tube. It depends whether the bike has a conventional headset or the type usually referred to as Aheadset.

Left and right: Figs. 10.41 and 10.42. How the stem is held inside the steerer tube with a threadless headset (left), and how it is clamped around it with a threadless headset (right).

On bikes with a conventional headset, the stem is clamped inside the fork's steerer tube by means of either a wedge- or a cone-shaped clamping device that is tightened with the expander bolt which is usually an Allen bolt, recessed in the top of the stem.

Of the two methods shown in Fig. 10.43, the one with the wedge is more popular these days. It has the larger contact area, and thus applies less local stress to the steerer, and is recommended for applications in which the handlebar height is frequently adjusted. The method with the cone, though harder to loosen, does not deform the steerer tube's roundness,

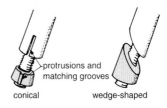

protrusions and matching grooves

conical   wedge-shaped

Above: Fig. 10.43. The two types of stem clamping devices for bikes with a conventional (threaded) headset.

allowing a more accurate angular alignment of the handlebars.

On a bike with a threadless headset, the stem is clamped around the non-screw-threaded steering tube protrusion. The stem should not be tightened until *after* the headset is properly adjusted.

In order to avoid the possibility of either breaking or loosening the stem, it should never be clamped in less than 65 mm (2½ in.). Many manufacturers mark this point of minimum insertion, and if this is not done, you can take care of it yourself with the aid of an indelible marker. Both the height and the reach (or forward length) may vary, as shown in Fig. 10.45, and should be selected to match the desired posture on the basis of the rider's size. Many "standard" bikes are sold with stems that have too much reach to be comfortable for most women, whose arms tend to be shorter in proportion to overall body height, and should be replaced by one that fits at the time of purchase.

Triathletes and time trial cyclists, who typically ride considerable distances without need for difficult maneuvering and braking, like the aerodynamic advantage offered by special aero bars that point far forward and support the arms on pads. They allow a different, more stretched and forward-leaning body posture, which does reduce wind resistance. A special type of gear shifter is available that is installed at the ends of such bars. Instead of full-blown aero bars, it's also possible to use a separate extension, referred to as "clip-on bars," attached to conventional drop handlebars.

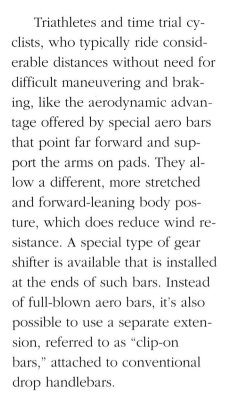

HANDLEBAR DIMENSIONS AND TYPES

Handlebars are also available in many different shapes, even within the two main categories of drop bars, for road bikes, and flat bars (for other kinds of bikes).

Width

On a road racing bike, it is usually recommended that the width should be such that the arms are parallel all the way from the shoulders to the wrists when the rider holds the drops (the ends of the drop handlebars). On mountain bikes, the arms spread out slightly, and the width should be no more than 15 cm (6 in.) greater than the rider's shoulder width. Wider handlebars, popular on early mountain bikes, require too much upper body movement when maneuvering at low speeds.

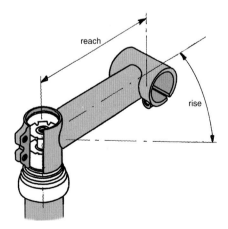

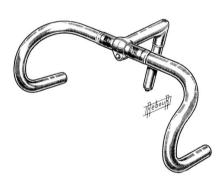

Above: Fig. 10.44. Traditional handlebars and stem for bike with threaded headset.

Left: Fig. 10.45. Stem dimensions, shown on a bike with threadless headset.

Right: Fig. 10.46. Triathlon handlebar and stem for a stretched-out, aerodynamic riding position.

Drop

On drop handlebars, drop is the difference in height between the nominally straight horizontal part in the center and the ends of the bars, referred to as the drops. Although the term is not used on flat handlebars, their shape too may bring the ends at a different height as the center section.

Reach

On drop handlebars, reach is the horizontal distance between the nominally flat center section and the forward-most part of the curved section. On some flat handlebars, the ends are curved forward and then point back under some angle that will vary from one model to the next.

Diameter

The diameter of the handlebars is greater in the middle portion than over the remainder of their length, to provide a point where they are clamped, while still allowing insertion in the stem. This thickened section usually contains a reinforcing sleeve or insert. The ends of the reinforcing sleeve cause a so-called *stress raiser*, which sometimes leads to fatigue cracking, causing the handlebars to suddenly break apart. This kind of damage is least likely if the reinforcement is put around the outside, even if this is aesthetically less pleasing. Whether inside or out, it should be at least 7.5 cm (3 in.) long to distribute the stresses far enough away from the most sensitive location at the ends of the stem

clamp. The bar itself has a smaller diameter, and for small riders, or rather riders with small hands, there are models available with a diameter that's less than the customary

TAPE AND GRIPS

Drop handlebars are usually finished off by winding handlebar tape around them. As an alternative, foam plastic sleeves can be used, requiring the brake levers to be removed first. Handlebar tape is available as adhesive cloth, as non-adhesive plastic and in fancy versions made of leather. The ends of the tape are tucked into the handlebar ends, after which the handlebar plugs are installed. Tape is also available in a padded version. Another quite comfortable type is made of cork.

Mountain bikes and other flat-handlebar bikes usually have plastic handgrips at the ends. And you can be really stylish on

Above and below: Figs. 10.47 and 10.48. Mountain bike handlebars old and new. Bullnose-style bar-and-stem combination by Tom Ritchey (above) and modern Shimano flat handlebar.

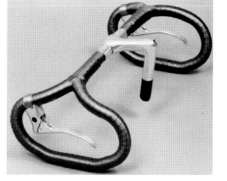

Above: Fig. 10.49. European touring handlebars, allowing a wide range of hand positions.

Top right: Fig. 10.50. Handlebar-end plugs for use with handlebar tape.

Bottom Right: Fig. 10.51. Probably the most comfortable type of tape is cork.

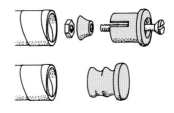

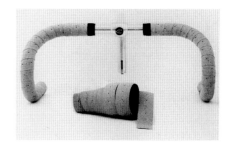

a high-end city bike with cork handgrips.

SUSPENSION STEMS

The simplest, and surprisingly effective way of adding front suspension is a suspension stem. You can replace a normal rigid stem by one of these. Usually, preload is the only factor that can be adjusted on a suspension stem. This and other suspension-related concepts are covered in more depth in Chapter 18 under *Suspension Terminology*.

ADJUSTABLE STEMS

These devices allow adjustment of the angle of the stem reach relative to the horizontal plane. They range from quick-release-operated clamps for conventional (threaded) headsets to micro-adjusting clamps with Allen bolts for use with threadless headsets. This angular adjustment also affects the

handlebars themselves, meaning that e.g. the brake lever position is also affected and may need to be readjusted.

Another related item is a German device called Speedlifter. It is a height-adjustable stem with a clamp that holds it to the top of a non-threaded steerer tube. It is tightened and loosened by means of a quick-release lever. Its advantage over regular quick-release adjustable stems is that adjustment in height does not affect the angular orientation of the handlebars. Thus, brake and shift levers, and anything else, mounted on the handlebars do not have to be re-oriented.

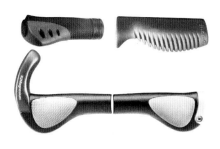

Above: Fig. 10.52. Ergonomically contoured handlebar grips for flat-handlebar bikes.

Left: Fig. 10.53. Adjustable-rise stem, popular in Europe for use with city or comfort bikes.

Right: Fig. 10.54. Adjusting the tension on a simple suspension stem.

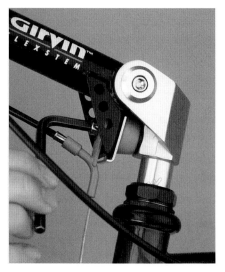

HANDLEBAR AND STEM MATERIALS

Most bicycles sold these days have handlebars and stem made of aluminum alloy. Usually the stem is forged and the handlebars themselves are bent from a tubular profile. On top-quality bikes, the handlebars may be made of titanium or even carbon-fiber, both options resulting in a lighter product with the same strength.

As for the stem, a welded stem made of either high-alloy steel or titanium is likely to be stronger and lighter than those made of forged aluminum. Presumably welded aluminum versions are also available; however, the only thing welded is the connection between the horizontal and vertical part, while the main components are still made of forged aluminum.

THE DRIVETRAIN

11

THIS CHAPTER deals with the components that transmit the rider's effort to the rear wheel. It comprises the pedals, the crankset (which in turn is made up of cranks, bottom bracket spindle, and chainrings), the chain, and the rear freewheel or cassette with cogs, or sprockets.

Not included in this chapter is the selection of the sizes of chainrings and sprockets, because this subject will be covered fully in Chapters 12 and 13, for derailleur gearing and hub gearing respectively.

THE CRANKSET

Known as chain-set in Britain, the crankset forms the heart of the drivetrain. It is made up of the bottom bracket (comprising the bearings with a spindle, or axle), the cranks, or crankarms, and the chainrings that are mounted on an attachment device incorporated in the right-hand crank.

Although it is generally sold as a unit of components made by the same manufacturer, a certain degree of interchangeability remains. Bottom brackets can be purchased separately from the cranks and various models from of different manufacturers are available that may match the

Left: Fig. 11.1. Bottom bracket detail, with outboard-mounted bearings.

Right: Fig. 11.2. Drivetrain on a hardtail mountain bike. This photo also shows the derailleur gearing system, which will be covered in Chapter 12.

original model installed on the bike. Individual cranks (as opposed to the entire crankset) are also available for replacement.

On bicycles without derailleur gearing, a single chainring is used, which on simple bicycles may be permanently attached to the right-hand crank.

THE BOTTOM BRACKET

The bottom bracket is installed in the frame's bottom bracket shell, where downtube, seat tube, and chainstays come together. Although there are several different types in use worldwide, most quality bicycles now have either conventional (adjustable) BSA bottom brackets or similar units with cartridge bearings. Two other bottom bracket types are the Fauber system (better known in the U.S. as one-piece, or Ashtabula crankset) and the Thompson bottom bracket. The former is still found on some utility and BMX bikes; the latter

mainly on low-end European bikes.

On the BSA-type bottom bracket, the bearing cups are open toward the center and are screwed into the bracket housing from both sides. The spindle is forged out of one piece with integral cones facing out, the bearing balls (usually in retainer rings) lying between cup and cone. The right-hand cup is screwed in all the way, whereas the left-hand one is adjustable and locked in position by means of a lockring. The space between the two bearing cups is usually bridged by means of a plastic sleeve to keep

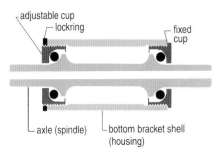

Above: Fig. 11.3. Cross-section through BSA-type bottom bracket.

Top left: Fig. 11.4. Cartridge bearing unit to fit BSA bottom bracket shell.

Bottom left: Fig. 11.5. High-end cartridge bearing unit for hollow spindle crankset from bearing manufacturer SKF.

Top right: Fig. 11.6. Cross-section through bottom bracket for one-piece crankset.

Bottom right: Fig. 11.7. Cross-section through Thompson bottom bracket.

dirt and water out. The BSA bottom bracket is the most universally available type, and consequently recommended for anyone who plans to cycle far from home: In case of damage, it can be repaired or replaced almost anywhere with minimal tools and parts.

The cartridge bearing, often referred to as sealed bearing unit, is not adjustable, being based on conventional machine bearing, or Conrad bearing. On most models, it is installed in the bottom bracket as an integral unit and held in position either by means of lockrings. Their design is quite critical, because the fixed bearings used are essentially only suitable to support radial loads, and significant wear and resistance could result if the design does not prevent the application of an axial load when tightening the unit in the bracket.

On many of today's high-end bicycles, a variant of the cartridge bottom bracket unit is used, in

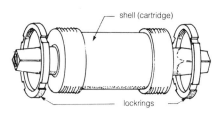

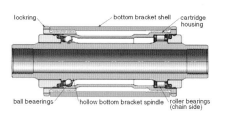

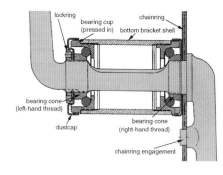

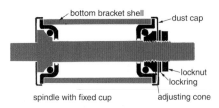

which the bearings are placed farther apart, essentially outside the bottom bracket shell. On these, the spindle itself is typically hollow and may be split with the two halves splined together. On all hollow-spindle models, the right-hand crank is permanently connected with the spindle (or spindle half in case of a split spindle), and the right-hand crank is clamped around the spindle.

The Thompson bottom bracket has cups that are press-fit into the ends of the bracket shell with the open end facing out, while the cones installed on the spindle face in. Theoretically, this is the right way of doing it, because the offset pedaling forces are supported most effectively this way. Unfortunately, the construction of this item is generally so crude that any theoretical advantage is more than outweighed by the practical drawback caused by inaccuracy and the lack of a seals against the penetration of dirt and water.

The predecessor of this bearing type, the German *Glocken-lager* ("bell bearing") combines

the outward-facing bearing with a labyrinth seal for protection—and a cotterless crank attachment. Unfortunately, it is now virtually extinct.

The one-piece design is perhaps the most interesting—not on account of its bearings, but because here both cranks and the spindle form one unit (the crank-to-spindle attachment causes headaches on all other versions). As is the case on the Thompson bracket, the bearings face the right way here. However, unfortunately, the lack of seals make this an item that rarely works satisfactorily for very long.

Above: Fig. 11.8. Cotterless cranks on a 1930s bike with a *Glockenlager* (see text), with labyrinth-sealed outward-facing bearing arrangement.

Left: Fig. 11.9. 1980s mountain bike with a cartridge bearing held in the bottom bracket shell by means of spring clips.

Right: Fig. 11.10. Modern cartridge bearing unit with outboard mounted sealed bearing unit and hollow spindle.

All bottom bracket types are available in several different versions. In the first place, the spindle length has to correspond to the bracket shell width and the number of chainrings installed. Besides, the way the crank is attached to the spindle comes into play. Cotterless and cottered attachments are each made in different dimensional variants depending on make and model. In addition, the screw thread diameter and other details of the installation in the bottom bracket shell may vary.

For BSA and threaded cartridge bearings, there are at least four different standards: English, Italian, French, and Swiss. Apart from differences in dimensions, the English and Swiss versions have left-hand thread on the right-hand (or fixed cup) side; Italian and French versions have right-hand threading on both sides, the former otherwise closely corresponding in size and thread details to the English standard, while the Swiss type has

dimensions that are similar to those used on the French standard. The only foolproof way to avoid mismatching parts is to take the entire old unit to a bike shop when buying replacement parts. These problems are more common on older bikes, because most bikes sold these days have the same (English) standard threading.

BOTTOM BRACKET ADJUSTMENT

Maintenance will be necessary if the crankset turns poorly—either too tight, too loose or too irregular. On bikes with cartridge unit bottom brackets (i.e. almost every bicycle sold these days), there's nothing you can do except replace the entire bearing unit, a job best left to a bike shop mechanic.

On all other types, it is possible to adjust the bearings. The adjustments are made on the left-hand side. To establish whether the bracket bearings are too loose, try to move the end of a crank in and out relative to the frame. If there is noticeable resistance when you try to turn the spindle by hand after the cranks

have been removed, it is too tight. Unfortunately, if the latter is the case, it is usually necessary to do more than adjust the bearing: you may have to overhaul the whole unit, but adjustment should remain your first step.

To adjust a Thompson bottom bracket, the cranks can remain on the bike. The only tool usually needed is a large wrench that fits on the locknut underneath the left-hand crank. Refer to Fig. 11.13.

One-piece crankset bearings can be adjusted essentially the same way as the Thompson type. Being one piece with the spindle,

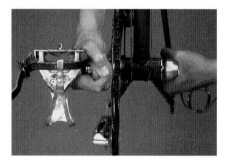

Above: Fig. 11.11. Checking for bottom bracket bearing looseness on a bike with adjustable bottom bracket.

Bottom left: 11.12. BSA-bearing adjustment detail.

Below: Fig. 11.13. Thompson bearing adjustment detail.

the cranks obviously don't have to be removed. All you need is a large adjustable wrench. Refer to Fig. 11.14 for this work.

THE CRANKS

Except on one-piece Fauber units, the cranks are separate parts that are attached to the ends of the bottom bracket spindle. On older bikes, they are often held by means of a cotter pin, illustrated in Fig. 11.20. The torque transmitted by the cranks on the connection, calculated as the pedal force multiplied by the quotient of the crank length divided by the distance of the cotter pin to the center of the spindle, is quite considerable at this point. Consequently, the force on the connection can be 20 times the cyclist's pedaling force, and cotter pins, with their small contact area, may not hold up unless kept scrupulously tightened.

Cotterless systems avoid this problem by offering a larger contact area. Whereas the contact area of a cotter pin is only about 1 cm^2, it is typically 8 times larger on a cotterless crank. The spindle here usually has square tapered ends, matching square tapered holes in the cranks. A bolt, or on

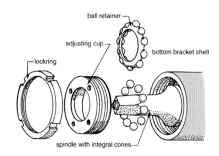

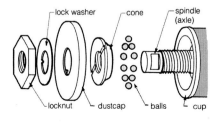

Right: Fig. 11.14. One-piece crank bottom bracket bearing adjusting detail.

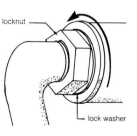

cheaper versions sometimes a nut, pushes the crank sideways onto the end of the spindle. Many modern cotterless systems use a splined connection instead of the square taper, resulting in more predictable and consistent seating of the crank on the spindle.

When replacing any parts of either the cottered or the cotterless crank assembly, keep in mind that there are several different versions of each. Cotter pins come in different dimensions, matching different cranks and spindles. Cotterless connections may have slightly different angles for the tapered ends, or different spline patters. Take care to get matching components.

An interesting variant of the cotterless connection is the one-key attachment depicted in Fig. 11.17. This type does not require a special crank extractor tool but is removed and installed by means of a single Allen key and can sometimes be retrofitted on a crankset that did not

originally come equipped that way. Especially touring cyclists find the one-key design particularly useful.

Most cranks have a length of 170 mm, measured per Fig. 11.21 from the center of the spindle hole to the center of the pedal hole, long-legged riders may wish

to use slightly longer models, and short-legged riders will be better off with shorter cranks. Some makes come in quite an array of different sizes between 160 and 185 mm, while the cheaper models do not offer much choice. More about this subject can be found in the sidebar on page 157 and in Chapter 22, *Bikes for the Short and the Tall.*

Cottered cranks should always be made of steel, because

Above: Fig. 11.15. Campagnolo uses a split hollow bottom bracket spindle, each half permanently connected with its respective crankarm. The two halves are joined by what is known as a Hirsch coupling.

Top left: Fig. 11.16. Conventional square-tapered crankarm attachment detail.

Bottom left: Fig. 11.17. One-key coterless attachment detail.

Top and center right: Figs. 11.18 and 11.19. Shimano's modern cranksets use either a splined connection (top), or a serrated connection and a split crank that is clamped tight around it by means of a binder bolt (center).

Bottom right: Fig. 11.20. Cottered crankarm attachment detail.

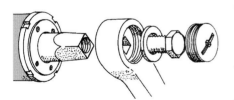

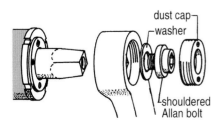
dust cap
washer
shouldered
Allan bolt

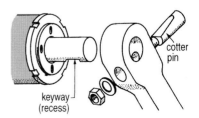
cotter pin
keyway (recess)

aluminum is so soft that the hole (which is much smaller than it is on the cotterless crank) would deform and the connection would not hold up. The largest European crank manufacturer paid a high price to learn this after it introduced aluminum cottered cranks in the early eighties. Even cotterless cranks can be made of steel, with the advantage that their connection is very reliable, while aluminum cotterless connections have to be re-tightened several times on a newly installed one.

Apart from the kind of deformation of the hole due to insufficient tightening, the most common problem is a crack extending from one of the corners of the square hole. This is typically a fatigue failure, usually leading to sudden fracture across the crank.

Another problem is that the crank can get bent in a fall. Don't try to straighten the crank

yourself, because it only works without damage if you use the right bending tool, which most bike shops have. If the thread with which the pedal is screwed onto the crank gets seriously damaged, the hole can be drilled out and a Helicoil insert can be installed, essentially providing a new screw thread (Fig. 11.22).

The right-hand crank has an attachment flange for the chainring or chainrings. On low-end cranksets, a single chainwheel may just be swaged (pressed) on, while they are simply inserted between the right-hand crank and the bearing on one-piece cranks. On quality bikes with cotterless cranks, the right-hand crank is a forged unit with a star-shaped attachment onto which the chainrings are held with special bolts, typically following the kind of detail depicted in Figs. 11.25 and 11.28.

the cranks properly. Consequently, they should be fastened on a regular basis (every 25 miles during the first 100) at first, and checked once a month afterwards. To carry out this simple maintenance job, there is a crank extractor tool that corresponds to the make and model of cotterless crank in question (several tool manufacturers offer models that universally fit all).

THE CHAINRINGS

Depending on the kind of gearing used on the bike, the right-hand crank will be equipped with either one, two or three chainrings. The choice of the number of teeth will be treated in the chapters devoted to gearing. Replaceability criteria include both the construction and the attachment details: bolt circle diameter (covered above) and the number of bolts.

CRANK MAINTENANCE

The connection between spindle and cranks may come loose, especially on a new bike or one on which the cranks were recently replaced. Left unchecked, this leads to deformation, eventually making it impossible to tighten

Right: Fig. 11.23. Probably the first "modern," sleek looking crankset was introduced 1980 by Edco, of Switzerland.

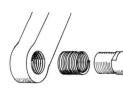

Right: Fig. 11.22. Helicoil insert to repair threaded pedal hole in crank.

crank length

Above: Fig. 11.21. Definition of crank length. The most common size is 170 mm, but other sizes are also available.

CRANKARM LENGTH

There is nothing inherent in the physics of the bicycle that makes any particular crank length best, but when we consider physiology, it is a different story. It should be obvious that short-legged people will have a more difficult time spinning long crankarms than will long-legged people. Many experts recommend choosing crankarm length based on the rider's inseam (crotch to floor measurement). The formula for adult riders usually comes out something like this:

Recommended crankarm length in mm = inseam in inches + 139.5 mm.

For example, a rider with a 30.5-inch inseam would, according to this rather unscientific formula, find 170 mm cranks perfect; a rider with a 27.5-inch inseam should select 165 mm.

Another, all metric, formula is:

Recommended crankarm length in mm = 0.5 x Upper leg length (see Fig. 11.24).

Unfortunately, physiology is far more complex than a single inseam measurement. Musculature, bone length, flexibility, and other factors vary considerably from one individual to another. A definitive physiological study on the topic of optimum crankarm length may never be performed. Meanwhile, the tests that have been conducted are inconclusive, showing no significant correlation between crankarm length and performance.

From all the nebulous data available to date, we can draw some conclusions:

1. First, the basic crankarm length is 170 mm, and is suitable for most riders.

2. Tall, long-legged riders may prefer longer crankarms.

3. Short-legged riders may be better off with shorter crankarms.

With few choices available, and the knowledge that the length isn't critical, this task shouldn't be difficult. Perhaps in case a knee injury or some other condition has made one or both of the legs less flexible, the prospective buyer should reduce this initial choice of length, on the advice of a qualified therapist. Riders who like to pedal gears at high RPM's ("spinners") may opt for something a little shorter; riders who prefer a lower cadence and higher gears ("pushers") may like something longer.

There are two additional concerns:

1. On bikes with low bottom brackets and long cranks, it may be unsafe to pedal through a curve due to the inside pedal hitting the ground when the crank is down.

2. On short-wheelbase bikes (read: any modern road bike) the rider's toe may dangerously overlap the front wheel.

As long as the rider is aware of these potential problems, they really are not serious safety hazards.

Longer crankarms are of course also marginally heavier. An extra 5 mm length of aluminum alloy on each arm adds a whopping 7 or 8 grams to the bike—can you stand it?

Finally, a longer crankarm is not a sensible substitute for lower gears, and most coaches advise their riders to develop a fast, smooth spin, something that (though never easy) is at least a little less difficult with shorter crankarms.

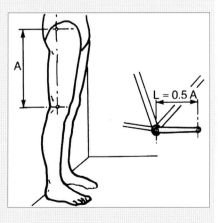

Fig. 11.24. Crankarm length determination.

As concerns the quality of chainrings, traditionally the best ones are not simply stamped but machined (sharp contours and a regular, fine groove pattern are telltale signals). However, today's forming techniques have evolved to the point where it is possible to make highly accurate stamped-out and formed chainrings. This technique is more suitable for fine-tuned tooth shapes, such as those that lead to improved, and quieter, derailleur gear shifting. Machining allows the use of stronger (i.e. more wear resistant and less easily deformed) aluminum alloys.

Amongst aluminum chainrings, the most durable ones are those made of the hardest material. The surface hardness can be enhanced by deep-anodizing. Although author Van der Plas's own hardness tests date back nearly 20 years now, the picture probably has not changed much since then: in general, high-end chainrings

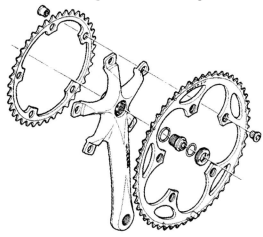

Left: Fig. 11.25. Typical crankset with 5-arm attachment for two chainrings, sometimes referred to as a "double."

Right: Fig. 11.26. A single-chainring crankset, as used on singlespeeds and "fixies" (fixed-wheel bikes).

CHAINRING BOLT CIRCLE DIAMETER

Chainring and crankset interchangeability depends on the bolt circle diameter. This dimension can be determined by first measuring the distance between the centers of two neighboring holes, and then using the appropriate formula below, based on the equation BCD = s / sin(180/n):

3-hole attachment:

BCD = 1.15 s

4-hole attachment:

BCD = 1.41 s

5-hole attachment:

BCD = 1.70 s

6-hole attachment:

BCD = 2.00 s

where:

BCD= bolt circle diameter

s = spacing, or center-to-center distance between neighboring holes.

Fig. 11.27. Attachment bolt patterns for 3-, 4-, 5-, and 6-hole chainring, showing bolt circle diameter (BCD) and hole-to-hole center (H-H) dimensions.

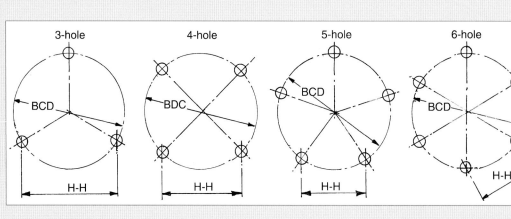

tend to be significantly harder and thus more wear-resistant, than superficially similar looking items that cost a little less.

Chainring and sprocket teeth tend to wear according to Fig. 11.29, and the smaller ones wear fastest, as do models with teeth that are specially shaped to ease shifting (actually, the very simple solution of cutting back a few teeth, as done on Shimano's SuperGlide and HyperGlide chainrings, does not by itself increase wear; it is merely the use of thinner teeth that does).

Wear of chainrings, chain, and sprockets can be minimized by selecting the former and the latter

with such numbers of teeth that prime numbers (numbers that are not multiples of some other whole number except one) result. This minimizes the repeated correspondence of particular teeth, which is one of the major reasons for wear. Special shaped teeth that are designed to ease shifting work very well, especially for the less experienced cyclist when new. However, they also tend to wear faster, due to the fact that they are thinner in certain points of contact with the chain. Some French chainrings can be flipped around, which effectively doubles their useful life, a feature we'd like to see more manufacturers adopt.

The introduction of stainless steel chainrings (used as the smallest chainring on some mountain bike cranksets) has been a big step forward, because they are much more wear-resistant and not significantly heavier than aluminum chainrings.

In the 1980s, there was a craze of non-round chainrings. Even before that time, oval chainrings had been around for a long time, based on the idea that cycling would be more efficient if the inherently uneven application of power during the pedal cycle could be evened out more. In 1983, Shimano took this concept one step further and introduced an irregular chainring shape that it called BioPace. It proved to be more convincing as a marketing tool than as an aid to efficient cycling. The marketing success forced some of the other manufacturers to introduce their own, usually just elliptical, chainring designs.

Curiously, every few years after, Shimano would come out with a "new" or "newer" biopace

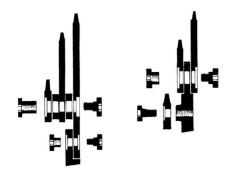

Above: Fig. 11.28. Two chainring attachment methods, shown here for triple chainring cranksets.

Below: Fig. 11.29. Typical pattern of chainring tooth wear, resulting in "hooked" teeth.

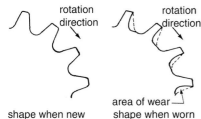

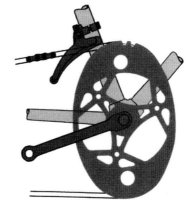

Above and right: Figs. 11.30 and 11.31. Elliptical chainrings have long been available, but in 1983, Shimano went beyond elliptical and offered chainrings of a more refined shape to improve the efficiency at low pedaling speeds.

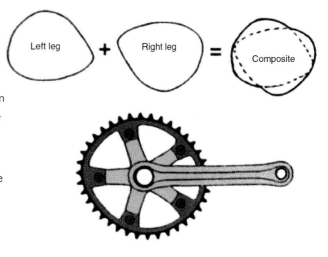

version, which became progressively rounder until around 1993, when all chainrings offered by all the major manufacturers, including Shimano, were once again round.

Today, it is generally agreed that the most efficient shape (if there is any difference at all) is round. This also eliminates the question in just what orientation the off-round chainrings ought to be installed for greatest efficiency, which there has been in the past. If you still have non-round chainrings on an older bike, there's no need to worry: the difference is minimal, once you get used to the slightly different pedaling motion, and you can always change to round chainrings with the same

bolt-hole pattern when the old non-round ones are worn.

CHAINRING MAINTENANCE

Check, and if necessary tighten, the chainring attachment bolts once a month. Prevent chainring wear by keeping chainrings, sprockets, and chain clean and lubricated on a regular schedule—once a month, plus whenever you have used the bike in inclement weather or muddy or dusty terrain. See the section *The Chain* for comments on establishing when to replace the chain. To clean the chainrings in the area of

Top left: Fig. 11.32. Shimano XTR high-end mountain bike crankset with hollow cranks.

Bottom left: Fig. 11.33. Stronglight, a French company that seemed to be losing out to the bigger drivetrain makers, has made some impact in the high-end, superlight arena. This is their hollow carbon-fiber composite road bike crankset.

Right: Fig. 11.34. Although Leonardo da Vinci did not invent a bicycle, he did have the idea for a drive chain. Practical application had to wait until late 19th century manufacturing techniques made it possible to produce the consistently identical components needed for efficient transmission of power.

the teeth, wrap a rag around a small screwdriver and work around each of the teeth.

THE CHAIN

The bicycle chain drive is a remarkably efficient transmission system. This explains why other, technically more complicated drive systems have never made it to success on the bicycle, however often they have been tried. However, the superior efficiency only applies to a well maintained, cleaned and lubricated chain. Whereas such a chain delivers 98% of its input as output, this figure can drop to 80% for a rusty, dirty, unlubricated chain.

All modern bicycle chains have a link length of ½ in. (measured between two consecutive link pins). The width is measured between the inside of two inner link plates and measures a nominal $3/32$ in. for derailleur chains, $1/8$ in. for non-derailleur chains. Even so, there are some differences in construction resulting in

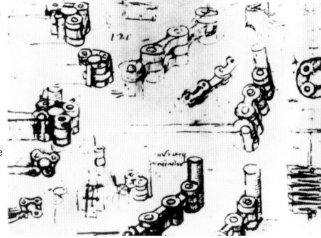

slightly narrower chains, measured on the outside, and sometimes with slightly narrower inside dimensions. These are necessary for use with gearing systems with 8, 9, 10, or even 11 sprockets.

The wider ½ in. x ⅛ in. chain for the utility bike without derailleur is usually equipped with a master link, or connecting link, to join the two ends. As shown in Fig. 11.37, this device must be installed so that the closed end of the spring link faces in the direction of rotation. Since the master link projects further than the other links, it cannot be used on derailleur bikes, where it would hit the derailleur cages. For this reason, an endless chain is used there, which is formed by attaching the outer link plates of the one end with the inner link plates of the other by means of a regular pin. A chain extractor tool is required

to remove, install or shorten such a chain.

Recent narrow derailleur chains from several manufacturers include a clever master link with slotted link plates to connect the two ends. It's usually finished in a different color to distinguish it from the regular links. Although this is a convenient solution, touring cyclists still prefer to use conventional chains without master link, using a simple chain tool to deal with any emergencies out on the road.

Fig. 11.35 shows the two basic chain designs. On the Sedis design, which is now used by most other manufacturers as well, since the patent ran out long ago,

the inner link plates are shaped to carry out the same function provided by the inner bushings on the conventional chain construction.

With the ever-increasing number of sprockets on the rear wheel, sprockets, chainrings, and of course also chains have been getting narrower and narrower. That does have some disadvantages, the most obvious one being wear. It also has led to a situation that every drivetrain seems to need its specific proprietary chain. Don't try using a 10-speed chain on a 9-speed gearing system, and vice versa.

CHAIN CARE

Cleaning, lubrication and replacement are the jobs occasionally required on the chain. Replace the chain if it is (seemingly) stretched so far that it can be lifted off the chainring as shown in Fig. 11.44. Alternatively, you can remove it and measure a 100-link section hanging down: it is worn too far if it measures more than 51 in., representing a 2% increase in length.

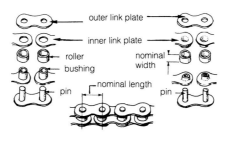

Above: Fig. 11.35. Details of the two types of bicycle chain in use today.

Left: Figs 11.36 and 11.37. Simple connect and disconnect options by means of a master link. A conventional master link as used on ½ x ⅛ inch chains for utility bikes without derailleur gearing (top) and the modern version as used on narrow chains for modern derailleur chains (bottom).

Right: Figs. 11.38 and 11.39. Narrow chains from SRAM (top) and Shimano (bottom).

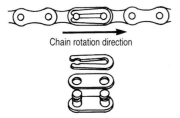

Chain rotation direction

Actually, what seems to be stretch is nothing but the wear of the pins and bushings, which can be minimized with regular cleaning and lubrication. A well maintained chain can last 5,000 km (3,000 miles) in road cycling, or about half as long in off-road use, and even less if mainly used off-road under unfavorable weather and terrain conditions.

CHAIN LUBRICATION

There are handy aids available to clean the chain without taking it off the bike. Here the chain is run through a bath of solvent between rotating brushes. Alternatively, remove the chain from the bike and rinse it in a bath of solvent containing about 10%

Left and right: Figs. 11.40 and 11.41. Chain lubrication, once with a bottle dispenser over the chain, an once with a special tool that can be used to clean as well as to lubricate the chain.

mineral oil to prevent rust, then let it drip out briefly and wipe dry, followed by lubrication.

There are effective chain lubricants on the market that do not attract as much dirt as the old-fashioned types. The ultimate in lubrication, hardly known in the U.S., used to be Castrol chain

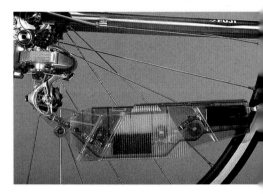

CHAIN LINE AND CHAIN LOSSES

Chain line is the path of the chain from the chainring to the sprocket. It had long been universally assumed that anything short of a direct chain line, i.e. without any offset, would be inefficient. In fact, English manufacturers and riders alike adhered to this so strictly that they continued to prefer internally geared hubs, with a single sprocket over derailleur gearing well into the 1960s. And many attempts were made to develop derailleur systems with sliding sprockets to keep the chain line direct.

In recent decades, several efficiency tests have confirmed that there is no justification for this belief. It turns out that the modern bicycle chain is equally efficient when run under a slight offset as it is in a straight line. Even 10- and 11-speed rear sprockets, when combined with a double chainring have a maximum angular deviation of about 2.4 degrees. At that angle, the chain is laterally

flexible enough to transmit 100% of the force applied to it.

It is still a good idea not to "cross-chain," i.e. run the chain from the inside chainring to the outermost sprocket or vise versa from the outside chainring to the innermost sprocket. The reason for this recommendation is not so much chain losses as concern about the chain rubbing against the cage of the front derailleur.

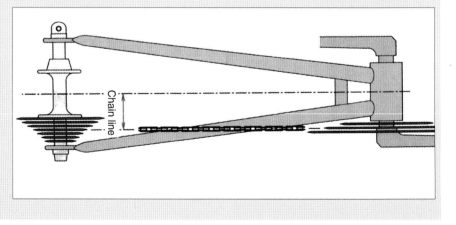

Fig. 11.42. Chain line defined.

grease. This is a waxy grease containing graphite particles, which is melted in a pan of hot water (i.e. *not* directly over the stove), after which the chain is dipped in. The chain is left to soak in the hot lubricant and then removed to drip and wiped clean on the outside.

Modern chain lubes are also typically wax-based lubricants, sometimes containing molybdenum disulfide (like graphite, this material works well on journal bearings, i.e. the kind of bearings represented by the chain's pins and bushings). They come in spray-cans, and therefore may tempt the user not to clean the chain first.

CHAIN SKIP

Sometimes during pedaling the chain of a derailleur bike will suddenly jump forward with a jolt, as if a gear tooth has broken off. This phenomenon, known as chain skip, can have one of several different causes. Certainly if the chain was recently replaced, chances are it is merely due to a stiff link. To check whether this is the cause, set the derailleur to engage the smallest sprocket in the rear, then turn the cranks back

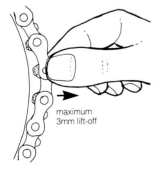

maximum
3mm lift-off

slowly, while watching what happens as the chain runs over the rear sprocket. In one position, the chain will lift off the sprocket—check this link for stiffness, with the loosened, e.g. by lifting it off the chainring.

If the problem cannot be eliminated this way, it is usually due to the use of a new chain on an old sprocket, and virtually always happens only on the smallest sprocket, which tends to wear down faster than the others. Since the chain pitch (distance between link pins) does not correspond to the worn and therefore changed pitch of the sprocket, it will ride up and give a jerking action. The

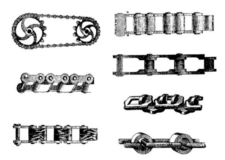

Above: Fig. 11.43. Historic chains: a collection of 1-inch pitch chains in use at the turn of the 20th century.

Left: Fig. 11.44. A simple method to check for chain wear on the bike. If the chain can be lifted more than 3 mm ($^1/_8$ in.) off the chainring, it should be replaced.

Right: Fig. 11.45. In 1976, Shimano introduced the Dura-Ace 10 mm pitch chain for track use. It never caught on. Here's an illustration of the special crankset for the 10 mm pitch system.

only solution is to replace the sprocket.

THE PEDALS

The pedals, which are shown in cross-section in Fig. 11.46, are installed at the ends of the cranks. Figs. 11.47 and 11.48 show two standard versions. Especially on road and mountain bikes, so-called clipless pedals are now pretty universal. Actually, these are far from clipless: they integrate their own patent clipping device instead of the formerly conventional separate toeclip with strap. Whereas the latter can still be ridden with any kind of shoes, the clipless pedals cannot, confining you to the particular type of matching shoes. Interestingly, the recent popularity of "fixie," or single-speed bikes has led to a resurgence of conventional toeclips.

Those conventional toeclips may come either with straps to tighten them around the shoes or open strapless types, which lend

themselves well to city riding. The ones with straps are available in several sizes: small, for shoe sizes up to 7 (European size 40), medium up to shoe size 8½ (European size 43), and large for anything bigger than that. When installing the strap through the pedal housing, twist it one full

turn between the pedal's side plates so it does not slip.

Clipless pedals come in an astonishing range of shapes and

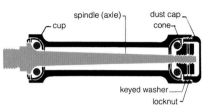

Above: Fig. 11.46. Cross-section through a pedal with adjustable bearings.

Left and right: Figs. 11.47 and 11.48. Conventional pedal (top) and clipless pedal (bottom). Both are mountain bike versions; road bike pedals are shown in Fig. 11.51. and 11.52.

flavors, each requiring proprietary matching cleats to be mounted to the soles of the shoes. On Shimano's SPD pedals, and similar designs from other manufacturers, the matching cleats do not project below the shoe sole, making it possible to walk in them, which means they are a good solution for any form of cycling other than road racing.

PEDALING FORCE AND STYLE

How much force a cyclist exerts on the pedal depends on the type of riding. Whitt and Wilson report the following ranges:

Touring: 70–145 N

Road racing: 200–240 N

Track sprint: 370–535 N

Motor-paced: 155–165 N

Particularly impressive are the results for track sprinters, especially considering that these high forces were reached while pedaling at cadences between 136 and 182 RPM (though for a very short duration). All racing cyclists together averaged 82 RPM.

These high pedaling speeds require a technique referred to as "pedaling circles": the force on the pedal should not be merely down, but forward and down near the top crank position, back and down near the bottom, and possibly even slightly negative on the "upstroke."

The technique referred to as "angling," which was widely

Fig. 11.49. Of the total force the rider exerts on the pedal, only the portion perpendicular to the crank is turned into driving force.

advocated before the advent of clipless pedals has been discredited. That technique would require the foot to be oriented heel down near the top and heel down at the bottom of the pedal stroke. It has been found that successful racing cyclists did not naturally orient their feet this way, and did not gain in output or efficiency when they did.

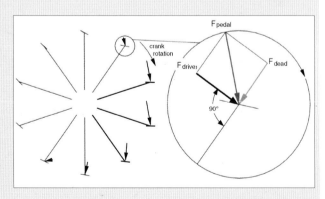

There are different thread standards for the pedal-to-crank connection, summarized in Appendix 7. Whether English, French, or American (only found on older American bikes), the left-hand pedal always has left-hand thread and the right-hand pedal normal right-hand thread, whereas non-conforming thread sizes, introduced by

Shimano during its brief flirtation with aerodynamic pretense in the early eighties, have disappeared as fast as they were introduced (meaning both pedals and cranks may have to be replaced if you should run into one of these on an older bike—and don't throw

them away, because they are now valued collector objects).

An important dimension for pedals, certainly if intended for fast riding, is the one that determines under what angle the bike can lean when cornering without scraping the pedal on the ground. Since this also depends on the bottom bracket height and the spindle length, comparative values are not very reliable except

up to left

L

left-hand thread
left-side pedal

up to right

R

right-hand thread
right-side pedal

Above: Fig. 11.50. Pedal screw-thread orientation.

Left: Fig. 11.51. Conventional pedal disassembled.

Right: Fig. 11.52. Cartridge bearing pedal disassembled.

FOOT, PEDAL, AND CLEAT POSITION

If performance were the only goal, the only consideration in choosing a cleat system would be to ensure that the foot is held fast to the pedal, a criterion easily met by older slotted cleats and straps and all clipless systems. However, there are additional considerations, including avoidance of stress on the knees whether the rider is seated or standing, ease of entry and release, compatibility with other shoes and other bicycles, reliability in muddy conditions, shoe fit, style, and cost.

Knees easily eclipse Achilles's legendary tendon as a human body design weakness. Particularly because the knees are such a notorious trouble area, cyclists should take great pains both in selecting a cleat system and adjusting it to perfection. Any setup pains sidestepped now may easily return manifold when permanent knee problems set in a few years later. Some people have such sensitive knees that they cannot seem to find any comfortable cleat position. If that is the case, uncleated shoes with clips and tightened straps incur only a modest loss of potential power,

a small price to pay for healthy knees. However, most riders and their knees readily adapt to clipless pedal designs that allow a bit of angular play.

Any motion that does not help the bicycle move forward can be considered a waste of energy. While it may be true that sideways foot motion diverts a small amount of power from the pedaling motion, even minor discomfort during pedaling is certain to rob power. If discomfort occurs while using fixed cleats but not while using cleats with built-in play, the choice should be clear.

when comparing models by the same manufacturer. By and large, low and narrow pedals clear the road in a sharper corner better than high and wide models.

The pedal bearings must be adjusted if there is play or they turn poorly. If adjusting does not solve the problem, the pedals will have to be overhauled or replaced.

FREEWHEEL AND SPROCKETS

Except on fixed-gear bikes, all regular bicycles have a freewheel mechanism on the rear wheel hub to allow the wheel to turn forward while holding the cranks still. On utility bikes and other bikes with hub gearing, the freewheel is usually an integral part of the hub
(together with the gear mechanism and sometimes a brake).

On older derailleur bikes and on touring-specific bikes, it is usually a separate freewheel block that is screwed on to the right-hand side of the hub, and on which the sprockets are installed. On all other derailleur bikes it is a unit that, though removable, is part of the so-called cassette hub. To ease shifting, specially designed tooth shapes and sequences are incorporated in most modern designs, such as Shimano's HyperGlide, providing

Above: Fig. 11.53. Conventional pedal, with toeclip and strap, in a modern look.

Top left: Fig. 11.54. Typical modern clipless road bike pedal.

Bottom left: Fig. 11.55. Cinelli's 1960s clipless pedal. It wasn't so easy to unclip, for which reason it was used mainly in track racing rather than road racing.

Top right: Fig. 11.56. Conventional (screwed-on) freewheel and sprocket cluster removed from rear hub.

Bottom right: Fig. 11.57. Freewheel cassette with sprocket cluster removed from cassette rear hub.

specific locations around the circumference where the teeth are cut down so that the chain is eased over sideways very easily.

For use with single-speeds, there are also similar freewheels with only a single sprocket. Whatever the number of sprockets, and whether built-in or screwed on, the principle of these freewheel mechanisms is always as depicted in Fig. 11.58. Turning the internal body relative to the fixed outer part in one direction engages the pawls, causing the two to turn together.

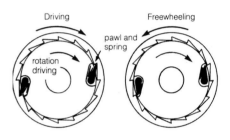

Above: Fig. 11.58. Operating sketch of a typical modern freewheel.

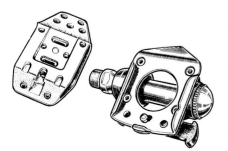

Turning it in the opposite direction, the pawls ride over the teeth against their spring tension, resulting in the familiar freewheeling sound. Only on some bikes with a coaster brake is a different type of freewheel used, which will be described in Chapter 16. The most important consideration in selecting a freewheel or freehub cassette is the number of sprocket teeth. This subject will be extensively covered in Chapter 12, which is devoted to derailleur gearing.

The other considerations mainly concern the kind of screw thread: here too, there are different standards, even for screwed-on freewheels. Most bikes in the U.S. and Britain with screwed-on freewheel (i.e. mainly older bikes) have rear hubs with Italian standard thread, while some may have French standard threading. These do not fit one

another without doing serious damage.

Above: Fig. 11.59. Singlespeed bike drivetrain with two-sided, or "flip-flop" rear hub, with a freewheel on one side (shown here) and a fixed sprocket on the other. Another way of achieving this is with the SRAM Torpedo hub, which can be switched from fixed to freewheeling without removing the wheel.

Right: Fig. 11.60. Cassette freewheel, with individual sprockets disassembled.

Top left: Fig. 11.61. Shimano's HyperGlide sprockets (and similar designs from other manufacturers) provide direct shifting paths.

Bottom left: Fig. 11.62. Exploded view of cassette hub assembly.

Most modern cassette hubs are designed for matching 9-, 10-, or 11-speed cassettes, although in low-end gruppos may have 7- or 8-speed cassettes. In either case, the freewheel mechanism itself is a (removable) part of the hub, while the sprockets and the spacers are installed on splines, with the last one or two screwed on. The two parts of a cassette hub can be separated with a special tool (although it is rarely done), while the conventional freewheel is unscrewed with a compatible freewheel tool.

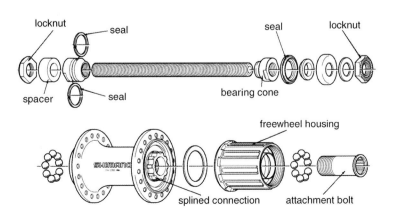

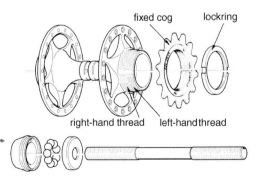

Above: Fig. 11.63. Exploded view of fixed wheel hub assembly, showing cog and lockring installation detail.

DERAILLEUR GEARING

FIG. 12.1 SHOWS an overview of a typical derailleur system. The rear wheel hub is equipped with a cassette or a screwed-on freewheel with a range of different-sized sprockets in the rear, while two or three different-sized chainrings, or chainwheels, are attached to the right-hand crank in the front.

The front derailleur, or changer, as it is called in Britain, shifts the chain sideways between the chainrings, while the rear derailleur, called mechanism or "mech" Britain, selects the appropriate sprockets in the rear. These derailleurs are operated by means of handlebar-mounted shift levers, usually integrated with the brake levers on modern road bikes, or on the down tube. The shifters and derailleurs are connected by means of Bowden cables.

GEAR RATIO

Since the various sprockets and chainrings each have different numbers of teeth, the ratio between the rate at which the

Left: Fig. 12.1. Overview of a derailleur drivetrain. This one has 3 front chainrings and 9 rear cogs, providing 27 different gear combinations.

Right: Fig. 12.2. Rear gear change in action, as the chain is moved to a smaller cog for a higher gear.

cranks are turned and that at which the rear wheel turns can be varied accordingly. Given a certain pedaling rate, the speed with which the rear wheel turns is proportional to the quotient of the number of teeth in the front and the number of teeth in the back:

$$RPM_{wheel} =$$
$$RPM_{cranks} \times T_{front} / T_{rear}$$

where T_{front} and T_{rear} represent the number of teeth on chainring and sprocket respectively.

The number of different gearing options is expressed by the product of the numbers of sprockets and chainrings: 2 chainrings and 10 sprockets gives 20 speeds, 3 chainrings and 9 sprockets 27. Actually, there is a certain overlap, so the number of significantly different gears may be less than these nominal figures.

Nominally, modern road bikes generally have 20 or 22 speeds (2 chainrings up front, 10 or 11 rear dogs), while mountain bikes and touring bikes usually have 24 or 27 speeds (3 chainrings, 8 or 9 rear cogs). On cruisers and other simple bicycles, 7- or 8-speed systems are often still used. These have but a single front chainring, thus eliminating

the need for a front derailleur—a sensible approach for most casual cyclists.

GEARING THEORY

The principle of the gearing system is the idea of adapting the transmission ratio between cranks and rear wheel to the difficulty of the terrain. Under favorable conditions—when the resistances are low—the driven rear wheel can be made to rotate significantly faster than the cranks, propelling the bike at a high speed without pedaling excessively fast. This is referred to as a high gear and is achieved when a large chainring is combined with a small sprocket.

Under unfavorable conditions, when resistances are high, a low gear is selected; that is achieved with a small chainring and a large sprocket, so the rear wheel does not turn much faster (or sometimes even slower) than the cranks.

It will be instructive to compare the situation on a level road with that on an incline. The example will be based on a cyclist who can maintain an output of 133 W (i.e. about 0.18 hp). On a level road without head wind, this will suffice to progress at 30 km/h (19 mph). If the road goes up by 5%, the same output only allows a speed of 10 km/h (about 6 mph).

If the gearing ratio were fixed, the pedaling rate would

Left and right: Figs. 12.2–12.4. Combining chainrings and sprockets of different sizes provides higher or lower gear ratios. In the highest gear the biggest chainring drives the smallest sprocket (upper right); in the lowest gear, the smallest chainring drives the biggest sprocket (lower right).

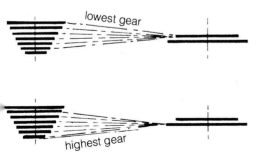

have to be three times as high in the first case as it is in the second. Conversely, at a constant speed, the forces applied to the pedals would be three times as high when pedaling uphill as they would be pedaling on the level road. However, the muscles and joints work better if the pedal force is limited, even if this requires a higher pedaling speed. Thus, the uphill ride is particularly tiring, even though the same total output is delivered— not because of the output, but because of the high forces at low muscle speeds.

This predicament is solved with the use of gearing: it allows selecting the ratio between pedaling and riding speed in such a way that the pedaling force remains within the limits of comfort by allowing an adequately high pedaling speed, regardless of the riding speed. Conversely,

BEFORE THE DERAILLEUR

The wish for variable gearing on the bicycle is almost as old as the concept of the pedal-driven bicycle itself—or even older, because it had already been used on treadle-driven tricycles in the 1850s. Frank Berto's book *The Dancing Chain* (see Bibliography) describes the complete history of gearing into the minutest details, but here and on the next page is a very brief synopsis of it is origins and development.

Before variable gearing was achieved by means of shifting the chain between different size cogs and/or chainrings, several other methods had been in use.

The first geared bicycle was probably James Starley's 1871 Geared Ariel (shown in the left-hand image below). In the following years, many hub gearing systems were introduced, most of them limited to two gears.

With the spread of the safety bicycle around 1890, manufacturers started offering interchangeable chainrings and/or sprockets, usually requiring lengthening or shortening of the chain. About the same vintage are the first double-chain-drive systems, using a freewheel and clutch to select one or the other combination of chainring and sprocket (center image below).

Although experiments with derailing devices date back as early as 1895, many other gearing methods were introduced. Yet very few bicycles were actually equipped with multi-speed gearing. One of the impediments to derailing systems remained the relative lateral stiffness of the chains in use at the time.

Probably the most common method used before World War I, other than epicyclic hub gearing, was the "retro-direct," a system with a chain looped around two sprockets, each with its own freewheel. Pedaling forward drove the small sprocket (high gear); pedaling backward the large sprocket (low gear).

Left: Fig. 12.5. Geared Ariel of 1871.

Center: Fig. 12.6. Bi-chain, or double-chain drive, 1908.

Right: Fig. 12.7. Retro-direct, 1900.

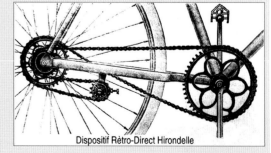

Dispositif Rètro-Direct Hirondelle

it is possible to keep the pedaling rate within the comfortable range when conditions are so easy that one would otherwise have to pedal extremely fast to deliver the available output.

To maintain the comfortable pedaling rate, a cyclist might select a gear in which he maintains a pedaling rate of 70 RPM while each crank revolution brings him forward by about 7.15

EARLY DERAILLEUR DEVELOPMENTS

Almost all early derailleur development, starting shortly after the turn of the 20th century, took place in France, and its greatest proponent was Paul de Vivie,

known under the pen name Vélocio. After experimenting with various gearing methods, he hit upon on the very simple idea of several sprockets side-by-side and a chain long enough to handle the largest. Thus the chain hung slack in the lower run. The chain could be shifted sideways, either by hand, by foot, or by means of a frame-mounted derailing fork. This system became known as *chaine flottante,* or floating chain.

Eventually, Vélocio and other French touring cyclists adopted devices to take up the slack chain by means of a spring-loaded pulley, a system that had first been used on the English Whippet a decade earlier.

Top left: Fig. 12.8. Vélocio with bichain.
Bottom left: Fig. 12.9. Vernon Blake with floating chain.
Below: P.d'A. 3-speed derailleur, 1908.
Bottom right: Fig. 12.10. Nivex 5-speed derailleur, 1938.

In 1908, Prével d'Arley, another French inventor, devised a mechanism with two pulleys, one of which was spring-loaded to tension the chain; and a rod-operated device for shifting the pulleys and chain sideways. Over the next 20 years, several inventors and manufacturers came up with similar devices. Some of these men had been followers of Vélocio. By the outbreak of World War II, their efforts had led to the introduction of what were in essence modern derailleurs.

The main stumbling block, however, remained the relative lateral stiffness of the chains in use at the time. It was not until the 1970s that this problem was overcome, and other improvements to the sprocket teeth, as well as further refinement of the derailleur geometry eventually made today's multiple gearing possible.

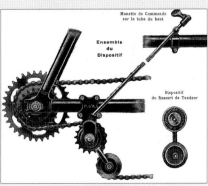

m. This results in a speed of 70 x 7.15 x 60 = 30,030 m/h, or 30 km/h.

On an incline, he may maintain the same pedaling rate and output level, but might select a gear that brings him forward only 2.40 m per crank revolution, which results in a speed of 70 x 2.40 x 60 = 10,080 m/h, or 10 km/h (6.2 mph). Either way, pedaling speed and muscle force remain unchanged.

Actually, it is unrealistic to assume that the same output level and pedaling speeds are always maintained. All riders put in more effort when climbing than when riding on the level. The example shows what is possible, even though the actually selected gears and speeds may vary a little one way or the other. To adhere to the example would require a very wide range of gears, even for rather moderate terrain differences.

A typical configuration for a road bike might include a range of 12 to 22 teeth in the rear and 52 and 42 teeth in the front, resulting in a top gear that is (52/12) / (42/22) = 2.2 times as high as the lowest gear. For a mountain bike, the range might

be determined by front chainrings of 46, 36 and 26 teeth, rear sprockets ranging from 13 to 26 teeth, resulting in a top gear that is (46/13) / (26/26) = 3.54 times as high as the lowest gear.

Virtually all bicycles except the mountain bike are equipped with gears that have an insufficient range of gear ratios for most uses. Even if you ride a road bike, the range between favorable and unfavorable conditions is much greater than can be comfortably mastered with the narrow range of gears usually installed by the manufacturer. It is simple enough to adapt the system to more sensible gearing by installing a freewheel with a wider range of sprockets.

GEAR DESIGNATION

Although one could refer to the particular gear ratio by simply stating the size of chainring and sprocket, this is not a satisfactory method. It would not easily reveal that e.g. 52/26 gives the same gear ratio as 42/21 (curiously enough referred to as 52 X 26 and 42 X 21 respectively, whenever this method is used). Obviously, it becomes completely impossible to compare

Upper left and above: Figs. 12.11 and 12.12. You've heard of it in stories about the early days of the Tour de France, and here you see it: the reversible wheel hub, for a small cog on one side, and a larger cog for climbing on the other side (left), and the men in action during the 1932 Tour.

Bottom left: Fig. 12.13. The gear ratio (i.e. the ratio between pedaling speed and riding speed) can be expressed either in "gear-inches" (the equivalent directly-driven wheel diameter) or as "development," the distance covered per crank revolution.

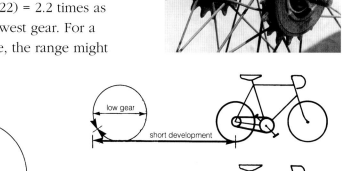

low gear
short development
high gear
long development

bikes with different wheel sizes and different gear ratios.

To overcome these problems, two methods are in use, referred to as *gear-inches* and *development* respectively. The two methods are illustrated in Fig. 12.12.

Gear-inches is a rather archaic method that is still used in the English-speaking world, (probably because it provides two-digit numbers that are easy to relate to). It references the

equivalent wheel size of a directly driven wheel that would correspond to the same gear. To calculate gear-inches, use the following formula:

$$N = D_{wheel} \times T_{front} / T_{rear}$$

where:

N = gear-inches in inches

D_{wheel} = actual outside wheel diameter in inches

T_{front} = number of teeth on chainring

T_{rear} = number of teeth on sprocket.

Typical high gears are in the vicinity of 100 inches, while low gears may be around 30 inches, or even lower for mountain bikes.

The internationally used method called development designation is easier to visualize: it

GEARS FOR CLIMBING

Back in 1975, when Ron Shepherd, of Australia, published his *Low-Gear Bulletin*, he

concluded: "Most bicycles are geared too high for comfort." Until today, not much has changed in that respect, and because comfort is critical for

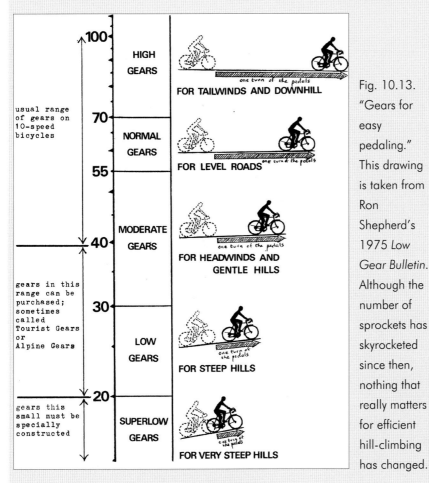

Fig. 10.13. "Gears for easy pedaling." This drawing is taken from Ron Shepherd's 1975 *Low Gear Bulletin*. Although the number of sprockets has skyrocketed since then, nothing that really matters for efficient hill-climbing has changed.

efficiency on the bicycle, most cyclists would be able to ride farther, longer, and faster if only they could select lower gears.

Shepherd developed a simple gear selection formula on the basis of empirical evidence to determine the optimum low gear:

A Comfortable low gear (in inches) is twice the gradient denominator.

Thus, if the gradient is one in twenty (or 5%), the low gear should be 40 inches. Of course, this also means that a comfortable gear for a 12.5% slope would be 16 inches (development 1.3 m), and it is hard to find a gear that low, so you may be more comfortable getting off and walking.

Under racing conditions, it may be more important to have enough high gears available, but even then, adding at least one really low gear will allow you to last longer and do better in hilly terrain.

represents the distance traveled per crank revolution, measured in meters (but it results in "messy numbers with a decimal point). To calculate it, use the following formula:

$$Dev. = \pi \times D_{wheel} \times T_{front} / T_{rear}$$

where:

Dev. = development in meters

$\pi = 3.14$

D_{wheel} = actual outside wheel diameter in m

T_{front} = number of teeth on chainring

T_{rear} = number of teeth on sprocket.

A typical high gear may be around 8–9 m, while a typical low gear may be 2.5–3 m.

Neither of these gear designations needs to be calculated once you know how they are determined individually, because Appendix 1 provides a quick reference on the basis of 700 C and fat-tire 26-inch wheels, while they can be determined for other wheel sizes by multiplying with the following ratio:

$$X_{wheel} = X / 0.675 \times D_{wheel}$$

where:

Left: Figs. 12.14 and 12.15. Narrow-range gearing (on a road bike, top) versus wide-range gearing (on a mountain bike, bottom).

Below and right: Figs. 12.16 and 12.17. Narrow-range rear derailleur, with a short cage (below) versus wide-range rear derailleur, with a long cage (right).

X_{wheel} = the required value for the wheel size in question

X = the value for development or gear-inches for 27-inch or 700 C wheels

0.675 = the wheel size in meters on which the tables are based

D_{wheel} = the actual outside diameter in meters of the wheel in question.

GEAR RANGE

The overall gear range is an indicator of the spread between the highest and lowest gear available to the rider. Typically, it will be smaller for racing conditions than for e.g. mountain biking or touring conditions. But even for a road racing bike, the range should be selected depending on the terrain and weather conditions. In very hilly terrain, or in an environment where very strong winds will be encountered, a wider range should be selected than for conditions with only moderately steep hills and/or less extreme winds.

A typical modern road bike may come standard with 52- and 42-tooth chainrings and a 12- to 23-tooth cassette in the rear. With 700-C wheels, this translates to a gear range of 49 to 117 in. (3.90 to 9.25 m development), a range of about 117 / 49 = 240%.

For hillier terrain, it may be wiser to select a different combination. From the same manufacturer, that same bike may be ordered with e.g. 50- and 34-tooth chainrings and a 12- to 27-tooth cassette. The gear range of that bike would be 30 to 113 inches, and a range of 113 / 30 = 375%. This latter arrangement gives more choice of gears in the low range, for climbing, without sacrificing high gears for speed.

Within limits, it is possible to adapt a bike for different types of terrain by installing a wheel with a different cassette. Even in professional stage races, such as the Tour de France, riders may switch either entire bikes or rear wheels depending on the terrain.

Mountain bikes and touring bikes typically come with wider-range gearing than road bikes. The former usually have lower gears all-around and especially a very low bottom gear. Such low gears may dip below a 1-to-1 ratio, whereby the rear wheel actually turns slower than the cranks.

Make sure the bike is equipped with derailleurs that can handle all the gearing options you may want to use. Not all derailleurs are suitable for the same gear range. There are specific "long-cage" (wide-range) and "short-cage" (narrow-range) derailleurs, both for the front and the back. Most long-cage derailleurs will also handle narrow-range gearing, but a short-cage derailleur may not be able to handle the wider range. If you wonder why not just use wide-range derailleurs on all bikes, that's because they don't shift as crisply on narrow gear ranges as do short-cage derailleurs. And of course they're also a bit heavier and more fragile.

GEAR PROGRESSION

Ergonomically, it is best to select the gears in such a way that the difference between them is larger in the range of low gears than it is in high gears. This is achieved by selecting the sprocket sizes so that the smaller sprockets differ less from each other than the biggest sprockets. The best ratio is obtained when the percentage steps of the sprocket sizes remains approximately the same. Thus, the high gears are closer together than the low ones.

SPROCKET SIZE SELECTION

Take, as an example, a series of 9 sprockets from 12 to 28. At first, it may seem logical to assign them as follows: 12, 14, 16, 18, 20, 22, 24, 26, and 28. The

Above: Fig. 12.17. Example of a useful gearing progression on a cassette with 10 sprockets. Note the big difference between the largest sprockets, compared to the small steps between the smaller ones.

Left and center: Figs. 12.18 and 12.19. The optimal gearing progression has the high gears more closely spaced than the low gear (left), requiring smaller steps between small sprockets than between the big sprockets (right).

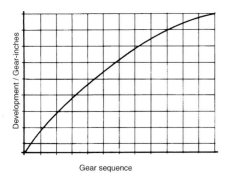

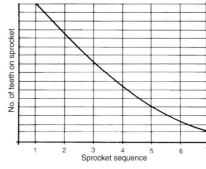

difference is always 2 teeth. However, between 12 and 14 that amounts to 2/14 = 0.14, or 14%, while between 26 and 28 it is only 2/28 = 0.07, or 7%. This incongruity becomes even more dramatic as wider-range gearing is used.

It will be more comfortable to adhere to a progression that keeps the percentage steps similar throughout the range, using smaller steps between small sprockets than between big ones. Mathematically expressed, you want a geometric progression, rather than an arithmetic progression. An example for the range between 12 and 28 would be 12, 13, 14, 15, 17, 19, 22, 25, 28. In this case, the steps can be calculated to be 8%, 7%, 7%, 11%, 11%, 14%, 13%, and 12%.

This too can easily be selected with the use of a graph, referring to Fig. 12.21 Place a copy of the strip over the graph in such a way that the first and last arrows (depending whether it is a freewheel with 8, 9, or 10

sprockets) coincide with the values for the smallest and biggest sprockets. At the intermediate points, read off the closest intermediate sprocket sizes, deviating slightly to the left or the right only if done consistently to the same side.

CHAINRING SIZE SELECTION

There are several different theories for the selection of the chainring sizes. In the days before 10- and 11-tooth sprockets (and for touring bikes still today) our preference goes toward something referred to as *half step* for systems with two chainrings, and *half step plus granny* for systems with three chainrings (see sidebar below). In both cases, the term *half step* refers to the principle of selecting the smaller chainring of such a size that intermediate gears between steps with different sprockets are achieved (this is done by

choosing the second chainring only a few teeth smaller than the biggest). The term *granny* refers to a very small third chainring, that makes an entirely different low range available when it is combined with any of the sprockets.

The more common selection of chainrings results in achieving

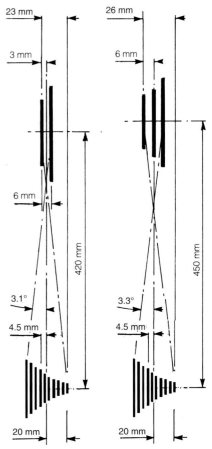

Above: Fig. 12.20. The extent to which the chain gets deflected on a typical 20-speed road bike with 420 mm chain stay length (let) and on a mountain bike with 450 mm chain stay length (right).

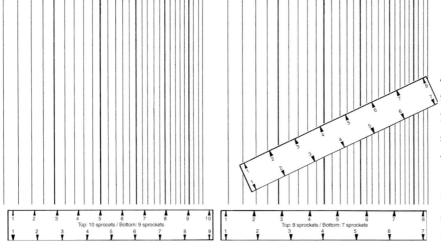

Left: Fig. 12.21. Gear progression selection graph (left) and example (right). See text for an explanation.

a different range of gears with the smaller chainring than with the larger. On mountain bikes, often ridden under conditions where shifting with the front derailleur must be avoided, this makes perfect sense. However, we find it a crying shame that many touring bikes and fitness machines are also equipped with the kind of gearing that provides such overlaps that fully 40% of the theoretically available gears are wasted.

When selecting chainrings and sprockets, keep in mind that they wear less if they are selected with numbers of teeth that represent prime numbers. This is the reason why 41, 43, 47 or 53-tooth chainrings and 11-, 13-, 17-, 19-, or 23-tooth sprockets might be selected in preference to slightly different sizes. They

not only wear better, they also run more smoothly.

The extreme gears that cross over the chain from the smallest sprocket to the smallest chainring, or from the largest sprocket to the largest chainrings, should be avoided (see Fig. 12.20). The resulting lateral chain deflection causes both high wear and noise in the drivetrain (even though there is no discernable decrease in efficiency). It will be virtually impossible to adjust the derailleurs in such a way that the chain does not rub against the derailleur cage in the extreme gears.

TOURING GEARS

Touring cyclists often have to cope with more extremes in

conditions than other cyclists, and in response a touring-specific gearing method has been developed. Although today's mountain bike gearing setups are usually adequate, the reader should at least be made familiar with another option, which is referred to as "half step plus

Above and below: Figs. 12.23 and 12.24. Two examples showing the two main derailleur types. The double-pivot parallelogram (above) was used by Campagnolo and other European manufacturers until the 1980s. Since then, the Japanese slant-parallelogram design (below) has become the standard for modern derailleurs.

HALF-STEP-PLUS-GRANNY GEARING

This is a system with three chainrings. The endearing term "granny" refers to a very small smallest chainring, which results in a very low set of gears when it is engaged. The "half-step" refers to the use of two larger

chainrings that are so close in size that the resulting gearing steps are half as big as those between adjacent sprockets.

An example of a half-step-plus-granny gearing setup would be chainrings of 53, 51, and 39 teeth, combined with a 12- to 28-tooth cassette.

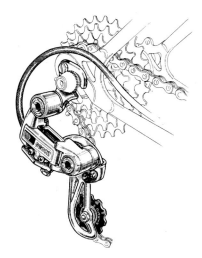

Fig. 12.22. Half-step-plus-granny gearing, shown here with only 7 sprockets. Many closely spaced gears achieved with the two large chainrings, and a separate range of low gears achieved with the small

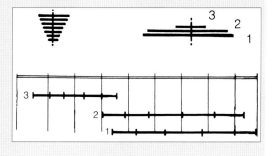

granny" gearing, and is explained in the accompanying sidebar and Fig. 12.20.

THE REAR DERAILLEUR

Essentially every rear derailleur consists of a hinged, spring-tensioned parallelogram mechanism with which an, also spring-tensioned, cage with its two chain guide wheels can be moved sideways, shifting the chain from one sprocket to another. The most significant difference in design is that between models with a hanging parallelogram and a more horizontal one, between models with long cages and short ones, between the location at which the cage is pivoted, and between straight and slanted parallelogram mountings (referred to as slant pantograph design).

Figures 12.21 and 12.22 show the two major types. In general, the models with nearly horizontal cages, referred to as pantograph models, lend themselves better to indexing (although the indexing is contained in the

lever, rather than the derailleur). The slant design minimizes the distance between the chain and the sprocket teeth, making for more positive shifting. The models with a long cage, preferably pivoted at a point between the two chain guide wheels, or pulleys, are better at handling large differences between sprocket sizes (i.e. wide-range gearing). These are referred to as long-cage or wide-range models, while derailleurs with a regular

Above and left: Fig. 12.25 and 12.26. Frank Berto's 1980s derailleur shifting tests (left) revealed that the smoothest-shifting rear derailleur design was the slant-parallelogram (above), which was at the time available only from SunTour, the patent holder. Since the patent expired, most manufacturers now use this design for their derailleurs.

Right: Fig. 12.27. Chain gap defined. For quick and predictable shifting action, this distance should remain small (no more than about 40 mm (1½ in.) throughout the range of gears.

cage may be called short-cage or narrow-range models.

The manufacturer's technical specifications for most derailleurs list the range of sprocket sizes and the amount of chain wrap for which they are suitable. In some cases, the cage can be attached to the body in several different locations, each representing a certain range of sprocket sizes. The amount of chain wrap for which a derailleur is suitable indicates how big the difference between the combinations *largest chainring, largest sprocket* on the one hand, and *smallest chainring, smallest sprocket* on the other may be.

The most important adjusting device for the modern derailleur is the cable tension adjuster. In addition, the extreme limits of travel are adjusted with the set-stop, or limit, screws. In addition, on the now almost universally used slant pantograph models, there is an adjusting screw with which the angle between the parallelogram and the horizontal plane can be adjusted, as described in the manufacturer's instruction leaflet, to achieve the

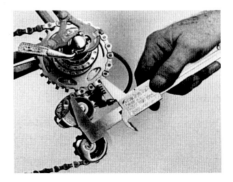

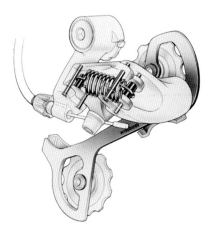

Above: Fig. 12.28. Partial cut-away view of a modern rear derailleur.

Below: Fig. 12.29. Rear derailleur adjusting detail.

greatest degree of chain-wrap around the sprocket consistent with smooth shifting.

Although most derailleurs nowadays are installed directly to a threaded lug on the right-hand rear dropout, simple bikes may lack this feature. In that case, the derailleur is mounted on an adaptor plate that is held between the dropout and the wheel axle nut or quick-release. Both adaptor plates and dropouts are sometimes designed for specific derailleurs, which work best when certain distances are adhered to.

Above and bottom left: Figs. 12.30 and 12.31. Modern rear derailleur in the position for high gear, small sprocket (above) and low gear, big sprocket (left).

Right: Fig. 12.32. Exploded view of a slant-parallelogram rear derailleur.

CHAIN GAP AND EASE OF SHIFTING

In the days before indexed shifting, the advice on gear shifting was to first shift beyond the desired gear position, and then "trim" back for the gear to engage properly. That advice was based on the use of "late-shifting" derailleurs and large (and inconsistent) gaps between the sprockets and the derailleur's jockey wheel (called "chain gap"). Some of today's cheap derailleurs still have such shifting problems.

The first derailleur to offer smooth, early, and consistent shifting, even with wide-range gearing, was SunTour's then patented slant-pantograph design. That patent ran out in 1988, and since then, almost all derailleur manufacturers have based their derailleurs on that design.

Meanwhile, that still leaves the possibility of large chain gap, depending on several factors, including chain length, derailleur cage design, sprocket cluster, and how the derailleur is

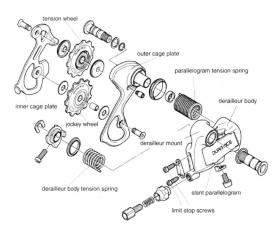

oriented. Fig. 12.25 shows how the chain gap can be measured, and it has been found that the gap should not exceed 4 cm (1½ for quick and predictable shifting.

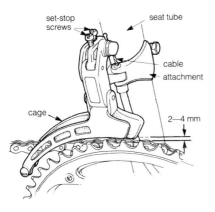

Above: Fig. 12.33. The front derailleur. Not much has changed in front derailleur design since the 1970s.

THE FRONT DERAILLEUR

Fig. 12.33 shows a typical front derailleur. It consists of a hinge mechanism that moves an otherwise fixed cage sideways to guide the chain over one chainring or another. The differences between the various models are primarily the size of the cage and the lateral travel: there are distinct differences between models suitable for triple chainrings and those suitable only for double chainrings.

A long, low dropped cage indicates that it will shift down to a really small chainring, as is necessary for touring and mountain bikes. The adjustment mechanism is usually limited to a set of set-stop screws to adjust the range of lateral travel.

Most modern versions have a hinge mechanism that does more than just move the cage sideways. Instead, they tend to lift the chain toward the larger one as they move to the right, and drop down as they move to the left. Especially for triple chainring use, the (long and thus sensitive) cage should be ruggedly constructed.

Nowadays, most road bike models (for twin chainrings) are designed to be installed on a lug attached to the seat tube, while mountain bike models always

REAR DERAILLEUR PULLEY RESISTANCE

On any modern rear derailleur, the chain is routed over two small wheels, or pulleys, installed in the spring-tensioned derailleur cage. It had long been argued that this arrangement resulted in inefficiency of the drivetrain in the form of "passive resistance." Until World War II, most racers chose single-pulley derailleurs out of fear for this presumed resistance.

More recently, some manufacturers have offered pulleys with ball bearings instead of the conventional bushings that were essentially journal bearings. With today's dynamometers it is possible to do accurate measurements comparing the power input and power output of a drivetrain to establish the passive resistance of the drivetrain (including pulley friction as well as chain friction and bearing friction).

When researchers at Australia's University of Melbourne made such a set-up, they found that the difference between input and output power did not depend on the type of pulley bearings. They found that the entire drivetrain losses of a non-geared bicycle (chain and bearings) were typically about 0.8%, and that the two regular derailleur pulleys together added less than 1 W, or about 0.3% for a racing cyclist, a number that was not affected by the choice of pulley bearings.

To summarize, there's no need to go out and spend extra money on after-market ball-bearing derailleur pulleys, or for that matter on a more expensive derailleur in the hope of improving your performance.

Fig. 12.34. University of Melbourne engineering students with their set-up for testing passive drivetrain resistance.

have a clamp with which they are attached to the seat tube, a solution that allows more flexibility, because the lugs brazed on to the frame tend to be suitable only for a limited number of front derailleurs and a limited range of chainring sizes.

Instead of a regular front derailleur, there once was a system on the market that does the same job in a more sophisticated manner. This is the Browning system, which for some time in the 1990s was available from SunTour under the name BEAST. It is an electronically controlled system in which sections of the chainrings are hinged and move sideways to deliver the chain to the next chainring.

Although one may object to battery-powered technology on the otherwise perfectly manually operated bike, there is no doubt something to be said for the ease with which this system shifted the chain even under the most

difficult conditions (all other front derailleurs shift only very reluctantly when the chain is under tension, as when cycling uphill).

Of course, the recent introduction of digitally controlled derailleur systems by Shimano also relies on electricity to power the shifts, as did earlier versions made by Mavic in the 1990s, which were unreliable due to their sensitivity to moisture. These electronic shifting systems now work very well, but not noticeably better than a well-tuned mechanical system.

Most high-end front derailleurs these days are designed for installation by means of a bolt attaching it to a lug provided on the frame. However, some front derailleurs—including essentially all cheaper ones—are installed with a clamp that fits around the bike's seat tube. The advantage is adjustability in height and

orientation, allowing you to fine-tune it for optimal performance.

There are four possibilities for the cable operation, with the cable either coming from below or above, and with the neutral (spring-tensioned) position either in (large chainwheel) or out (small chainwheel). There are an equal number of theories as to why one method would be preferable to the other, but having tested bikes with all four options, I'd say their performance is about equal.

Above: Fig. 12.36. Campagnolo Veloce front derailleur for "double" (2-chainring) cranksets.

Below: Fig. 12.37. And the matching version for triple (3-chainring) cranksets, with a larger inside plate.

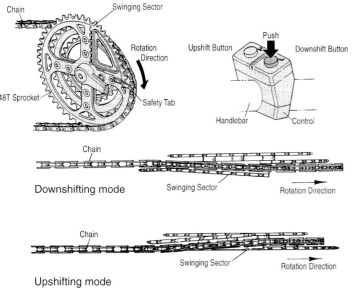

Left: Fig. 12.35. The Browning swinging gate front shifting system, which was available from SunTour under the name BEAST during the 1990s, was electrically activated and delivered the chain seamlessly from one chainring to the next.

DERAILLEUR QUALITY

All the major manufacturers—and there are others besides Shimano, SRAM, and Campagnolo—make excellent derailleurs that shift predictably and reliably. Yet, derailleurs vary greatly in price. Cheap models from the same manufacturers often shift well (though perhaps over a more limited range of gears) but are heavier and not as nicely finished.

Limiting the discussion to mechanically operated high-end road bike derailleurs for now, the major manufacturers each offer similar derailleurs at several distinct price points. The ones in the highest category are functionally identical to those in the middle category. The differences are usually as follows:

❏ minor weight savings due to use of titanium and/or carbon parts, and sometimes small cutouts;

❏ prettier finish, with more finely polished aluminum body.

If it is functionality you're interested in, a Shimano 105 derailleur will do the job just as well as its Ultegra and Dura-Ace sisters, and the weight difference is small enough to go unnoticed when riding the bike. Perhaps the main reason for choosing the top-of-the-line model is that it gives you more owner's pride, and that may provide enough of a psychological boost to give you more joy riding, which in turn may well improve your performance.

There's a saying that cyclists are like dogs: they sniff the rear end first, meaning a bike's rear derailleur. That may explain why

many bicycle manufacturers choose the higher-level derailleur for a bike that is otherwise equipped with lower-level components. Thus, you may find Shimano Dura-Ace rear derailleur on a bike equipped with everything else from a "lower" gruppo. It's not a clever way to keep the price down, but an effective way of making buyers think they've got a Dura-Ace-equipped bike at a bargain price.

Of course, the rider can always upgrade most components to a higher level. Co-author Baird likes to point out that even his cheapest bike is "Campy-equipped": it has Campagnolo adjusting screws in the rear dropouts.

DERAILLEUR CONTROLS

Both front and rear derailleurs are generally operated by means of shift levers via Bowden cables. The shift levers may be installed on the down tube, on the

Above: Fig. 12.38. 1960s Shimano Lark and Archery 3- and 5-speed derailleurs were shifted by means of either a full twistgrip or a nifty thumb-operated twistring.

Left: Fig. 12.39. Simplex front derailleurs were lever-operated until the mid 1950s.

Right: Fig. 12.40. The double-lever-operated Campagnolo Corsa of the 1940s.

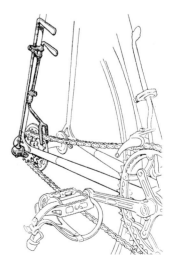

handlebars, on the stem, or at the handlebar ends. The stem-mounted location is convenient for riders who habitually ride with their hands on the top of their drop handlebars.

Whatever design is used, the shifter for the rear derailleur is mounted on the right, the one for the front derailleur on the left. The Browning system (which only works in the front) is operated by means of a double push button switch.

Finally, on the subject of controls, there are other methods that can be used to transmit the force from the lever to the derailleur mechanisms. Some early derailleurs were directly operated by means of a long lever installed on the derailleurs themselves.

Later, both rod and cable controls have been used to connect the derailleurs with their control mechanism. Simple levers have been used as well as rotating twistgrips. Until about 1990, the most common way was by means of cables and levers mounted either on the frame's downtube or the handlebars or, less frequently, the handlebar stem. The twistgrip was reintroduced in the 1980s, first for use on triathlon bikes with tri-bars, then for mountain, and finally for commuter bikes, where they are still in use today.

A more modern alternative is the use of electronics, by which the shift lever is essentially a multi-position electric switch and the derailleur has a little electric step-motor, as used with Shima-no's digitally-controlled top-of-the-line Dura-Ace Di system. An extension of this is a fully automatic setup in which the rider does not do the shifting, leaving the decisions about which gear is best to a micro-computer. Already, there are some city and comfort bikes that successfully incorporate such automatic shifting, but as yet it is limited to 4-speed systems for non-competitive cyclists.

INDEX VERSUS FRICTION SHIFTING

The difference between the modern index derailleurs and old-fashioned friction models lies mainly in the shifters and the cables. These index shifters have a

Left, right, and below: Figs. 12.41–12.46. A selection of shifters. Clockwise from upper right: flat-handlebar under-bar trigger shifter; flat-bar twistgrip; downtube shifter; handlebar-end shifter ("bar-con"); above-the-bar thumb shifter; and integrated brake-shift lever.

stepped ratchet mechanism inside, which stops the cable in predetermined positions, coinciding with derailleur positions for particular sprockets. Most of the older versions have a supplementary lever that allows shifting between the index mode and a mode in which intermediate positions can be reached (to allow full use of the gears even when the index system is out of adjustment).

The cables used for index gearing are thicker and stiffer than conventional cables, so as to eliminate real or apparent stretch, which would throw the system out of adjustment. Their length is usually preset for a certain configuration, because they are very hard to cut. These cables also have a nylon low-friction liner and do not require lubrication.

Since 1990, most mountain bikes come with double levers

mounted under the handlebars. These allow operation without moving the hands: push the top lever to shift up, the bottom one to shift down. There are some differences between the available models, but most are so complicated that the manufacturers rightfully warn against taking them apart when they don't work properly: you'll have to replace the whole unit.

Most shifters no longer have a friction mode to allow for maladjustment. And of course for road bikes, the use of integrated brake-shift levers has become

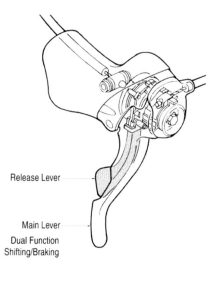

Release Lever

Main Lever
Dual Function
Shifting/Braking

Above, left, and right: Figs. 12.47–12.49. Three different brake-shift levers, respectively Shimano STI (the original, above); Campagnolo Ergopower (different, but close enough to require a license from Shimano, left); and SRAM's very cleverly designed Double-Tap (right).

almost universal. Shimano was first off the block with their STI system as early as 1988, and it has taken the competition some 20 years and a number of patent infringement law suits to catch up with systems of their own that work as well.

In fact, the most recent SRAM versions, called Double-Tap, which elegantly appear to steer clear of any Shimano patents in that the shift levers are operated in the same direction for upshifts as for downshifts, have become the preferred components for many racers. In fact, in the 2009 Tour de France, riders on SRAM-equipped bikes for the first time took the highest honors (for the 10 years prior, Shimano-equipped bikes had dominated, and for the 50 years before that, Campagnolo had been the choice of champions).

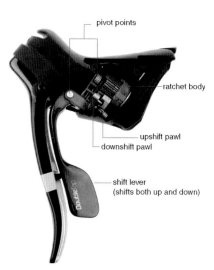

pivot points

ratchet body

upshift pawl
downshift pawl

shift lever
(shifts both up and down)

13

HUB GEARING

ALTHOUGH DERAILLEUR GEARING is used on most bicycles sold in the U.S. and Britain, hub gearing also bears some mention. Instead of moving the chain sideways between different sprockets and chainrings, this system uses an epicyclic gear incorporated in the rear hub.

The advantages of hub gearing include uncomplicated shifting, fewer external parts to get damaged, and the possibility to enclose the chain. All these add up to enough reasons to choose this system for a wind-and-weather utility bike, as indeed it is in countries like Holland and Germany, where the bicycle is to this day seen as a means of transport.

HUB GEAR OVERVIEW

Fig. 13.1 shows the parts that typically make up a hub gearing

drivetrain with—in this case—three speeds. Systems with 2, 4 and 5, 7, 8, 9, 11, 12, and even 14 speeds are, or have at one time or another been, available as well. A shifter on the

Right: Fig. 13.1. Hub gearing gives the bike a clean look, without the clutter of derailleurs. Although the chain is enclosed here, it can even be fully enclosed for protection against the elements.

handlebars operates a mechanism connected to the pull-rod in the hub via a Bowden cable.

Hub gears are available from at least three manufacturers: Sturmey-Archer, SRAM (formerly Sachs, and before that Fichtel & Sachs), and Shimano. If you ever encounter one that says SunTour, it is actually made by Sturmey-Archer. There was even a brief period when Sturmey-Archer built 3-speeds with coaster brake for their main competitor, Fichtel

& Sachs, which explains the difference between some of those old hubs sold under the same name.

THE EPICYCLIC PRINCIPLE

The guts of a typical 3-speed hub are shown in Fig. 13.2. All internal hub gears used these days are based on the epicyclic, or planet, gearing principle illustrated in Fig. 13.2. This section will explain the principle by which these systems operate. The rear wheel axle holds a fixed central, so-called sun gear.

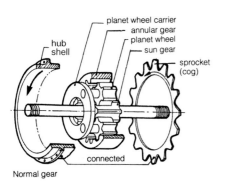

Normal gear

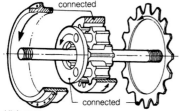

High gear

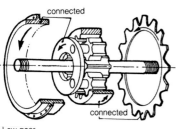

Low gear

At some distance from this sun gear, on the inside of the hub shell, is an inward-facing annular gear. The space between these two gears is bridged by a set of mutually connected small gear wheels, referred to as planet gears. The teeth of the planet gears mesh on one side with the central sun gear, on the other side with the annular gear.

The axle is hollow and contains a clutch mechanism that is operated by the pull rod that connects certain parts of the system. The sprocket, or cog (which is the term we shall use throughout this chapter to prevent some confusion in the abbreviations used in the formulas that follow, even if sprocket is used in the rest of the book) driven by the bicycle's chain can be connected by this same clutch mechanism to particular parts of the system, while a freewheel mechanism sees to it that the wheel can rotate forward while the cog is stationary.

In the normal gear position, the clutch is set so that the entire

Left: Fig. 13.2. The epicyclic gear principle. See the text for an explanation.

Top right: Fig. 13.3. The internals of the most famous gear hub, the original Sturmey-Archer three-speed.

Bottom right: Fig. 13.4. Beyond the three-speed: This is the new Shimano 11-speed hub.

planet system is by-passed: the cog is connected via the freewheel to the wheel hub. This way, the hub turns just as fast as the cog and there are no mechanical losses—it corresponds to what used to be an overdrive on older cars. Expressed in a formula, the wheel rotation speed in this gear is:

$$V_n = V_c$$

where:

V_n = wheel rotation speed in normal gear

V_c = cog rotation speed.

When the high gear is selected, the clutch mechanism connects the cog with the cage on which the planet gears are mounted, while the hub shell is connected with the annular gear. Consequently, the planet gears turn forward as they move together around the sun wheel and drive

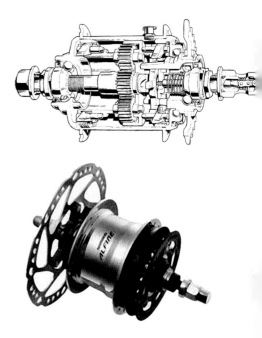

the annular gear. The speed with which the annular gear—and consequently the whole wheel—turns can be determined as follows:

$$V_h = V_c (T_a / T_s)$$

where:

V_h = wheel rotation speed in high gear

T_a = number of teeth of annular gear

T_s = number of teeth of sun gear.

In the low gear position, the clutch mechanism connects the cog with the annular gear, while the wheel hub shell is connected with the cage holding the planet gears. Consequently, the planet gears turn backwards and drive the hub shell more slowly than the speed of the cog. The wheel rotating speed will be:

$$V_l = V_c (T_s / T_a)$$

where:

V_l = wheel rotation speed in low gear.

HUBS WITH MORE THAN THREE SPEEDS

Today's 5-, 7-, 8-, 9-, 11-, and 14-speed systems consist of two or three planet gear systems. Two different methods have emerged here. One way is to have two or three separate planetary gear system, the other one

Below: Fig. 13.5. Not just Sturmey-Archer: This are just some of the many different hub gears available in Great Britain at the turn of the 20th century.

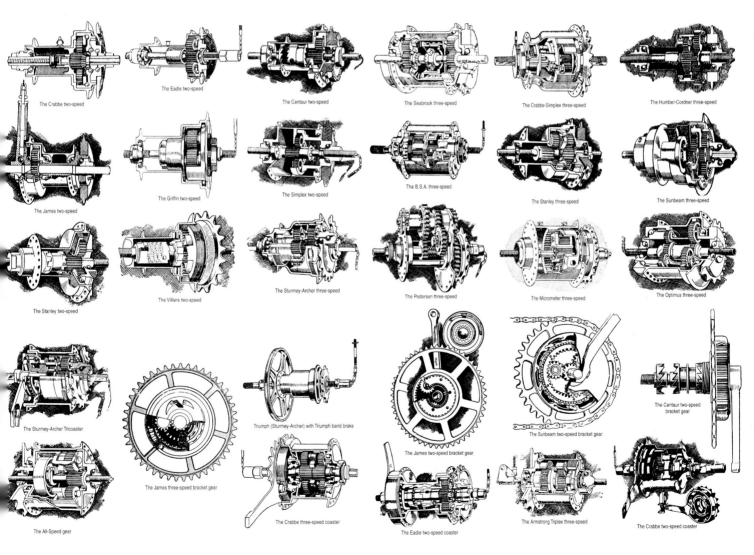

The Crabbe two-speed

The Eadie two-speed

The Centaur two-speed

The Seabrook three-speed

The Crabbe-Simplex three-speed

The Humber-Cordner three-speed

The James two-speed

The Griffin two-speed

The Simplex two-speed

The B.S.A. three-speed

The Stanley three-speed

The Sunbeam three-speed

The Stanley two-speed

The Villiers two-speed

The Sturmey-Archer three-speed

The Pedersen three-speed

The Micrometer three-speed

The Optimus three-speed

The Sturmey-Archer Tricoaster

The All-Speed gear

The James three-speed bracket gear

Triumph (Sturmey-Archer) with Triumph band brake

The Crabbe three-speed coaster

The Eadie two-speed coaster

The James two-speed bracket gear

The Sunbeam two-speed bracket gear

The Armstrong Triplex three-speed

The Centaur two-speed bracket gear

The Crabbe two-speed coaster

is to drive one system via the other.

In the former method, one planet gear system gives normal, normal-high, and normal-low gears. A second planet system gives the same normal, but now with a higher high and a lower low gear, and a third system may give normal, moderate-high and moderate low gears. Because this methods results in friction being generated in only one planet system at any time, it is relatively efficient.

The maximum (theoretical) number of available gears can be calculated with the following formula:

$$X = 1 + 2 \times N$$

Where:

X = number of gears

N = number of planet systems

With two planet systems, you could have a maximum of: $1 + 2 \times 2 = 5$ speeds. With three planet systems, you can have up to $1 + 2 \times 3 = 7$ speeds. Each additional planet system would provide 2 additional gears.

The second system, which results in lower efficiencies but

greater gearing choices, places the planet gear systems in series. Thus, normal high, normal, and low gears can each be connected to a second planet gear system that gives the choice between a normal, a higher and a lower gear.

The maximum (theoretical) number of available gears can be calculated with the following formula:

$$X = 1 + 2^N$$

Where:

X = number of gears

N = number of planet systems

With two planet systems, you could have a maximum of: $1 + 2^2 = 5$ speeds. With three planet systems, you can have up to $1 + 2^3 = 9$ speeds, and for 4 planet systems you could theoretically get up to a whopping 17 speeds.

In practice, for either method, there would be some overlap of gears. So you'd probably finish up with fewer than the

theoretical maximum number calculated above. On some models, a combination of the two methods are.

In the most efficient multi-speed hub-gearing systems, such as the Rohloff Speedhub, the planets and other parts run on low-friction needle bearings, whereas the simpler models use journal bearings, which reduce their efficiency, but also keep the price down.

GEAR RANGE AND PROGRESSION

For simplicity, we'll just look at the three-speed for now. When the annular gear has three times the number of teeth as the sun wheel (and each of that sun wheels the same number of teeth), the resulting gear combinations are $-33\frac{1}{3}\%$, 100% and $+50\%$, or $66\frac{2}{3}\%$, 100%, 150%.

The above relationship is a geometric progression. That means that the steps between higher gears are bigger than

Left: Fig. 13.6. Shimano 7-speed hub.

Right: Fig. 13.7. Exploded view of a Shimano 4-speed hub. Note the 2-step planet gears and sun gear, required for any epicyclic system with more than three gears.

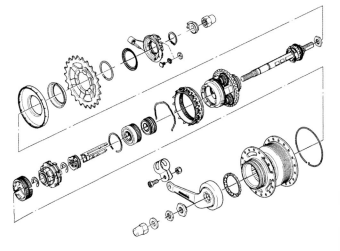

those between lower gears. Although such an arrangement works well when more gears are relatively narrowly spaced, it doesn't feel so good with only three rather widely spaced gears.

In the past, narrower-range three-speeds have also been available, and they are now sought-after collectors' items. Today's multi-speed gearing systems often space some of the gears closer together as well. On the narrow-range model, the highest gear was $33\frac{1}{3}\%$ higher and the lowest 25% lower.

The range of gears can be described by the ratio between the extreme gears. For the common wide-range 3-speed, it is $150 / 66\frac{2}{3} = 2.25$: the high gear is 2.25 times as high as the low gear. (In the case of the narrow-range hub, the highest gear is $133 / 75 = 1.78$ times as high as the lowest.)

Used with a chainring with 46 teeth and a cog with 19 teeth, the common wide-range three-speed setup the normal gear will have a development of 5.20 m (a 65-inch gear). The low gear will have a development of 0.67 x 5.20 m = 3.50 m (a 43-inch gear),

while the high gear will have a development of 1.50 x 5.20 m = 7.80 m (a 97-inch gear). On a 2-speed system, the low gear would be missing, meaning that the available gears have developments of 7.80 m and 5.20 m (97 and 65 gear-inches) respectively.

The table below gives the gear ranges for the current crop of 7-, 8-, 9-, 11-, and 14-speed hub gear systems. Depending on typical usage patterns, a larger or smaller range may be appropriate. In flat terrain, the range should preferably not exceed 200%, while in mountainous terrain the sky is the limit.

On systems with more than three speeds, which incorporate a double or triple planet gearing systems, the progression for a five-speed is usually as follows: 67%, 78%, 100%, 122%, 150%. Consequently, the individual gears, assuming the same set-up with 46-tooth chainring and 19-tooth cog, would be as follows: 3.60, 4.20, 5.40, 6.60, 8.10. Thus, these gears do not lie quite as far apart as is the case on the 3-speed, making this a more comfortable arrangement with adequate range.

Ergonomically, the disadvantage of the geometric progression applies here too, but it should not be overlooked that in reality derailleur gearing usually does not allow perfect progression either. Fig. 13.10 shows a comparison between the two gearing systems, which is clearly not all that unfavorable for the 5-speed hub. On the other hand, the mechanical losses are greater in the extreme gears.

The examples listed above were based on a 46-tooth chainring and a 19-tooth cog. Although the ratio between the gears remains the same whatever cog and chainring are selected, the whole range can be made higher or lower to match the user's preference. This is done by installing a cog (or a chainring) with a different number of teeth: either a smaller cog (or a larger chainring) to increase all gears, or a larger sprocket (or a smaller chainring) to reduce them.

Above: Figs. 13.8 and 13.9. Replacing a cog to achieve a different gear range.

Left: Fig. 13.10. Comparison of gear range for a 5-speed hub gear and a 24-speed derailleur system, both intended for use on city bikes.

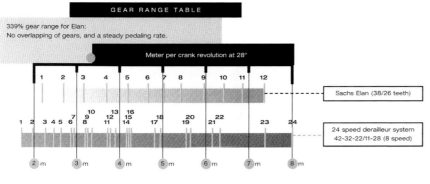

GEAR RANGE TABLE

339% gear range for Elan:
No overlapping of gears, and a steady pedaling rate.

Meter per crank revolution at 28"

Sachs Elan (38/26 teeth)

24 speed derailleur system
42-32-22/11-28 (8 speed)

HUB GEAR CONTROLS

Generally, the three-speed hub is operated by means of a handle-bar-mounted shifter, which operates a little chain or a hinged device connected with the clutch mechanism in the hub via a flexible cable that runs over rollers or guides.

Fig. 13.11 illustrates a typical 3-speed gear shifter. Five-speed hubs may either be controlled by means of a double lever, a twistgrip or a twistring, or by means of a single lever. The modern 7-, 8-, and 9-speed hubs are usually controlled from a twistgrip or a twistring. The two-speed comes in two versions, one controlled by backpedaling briefly, the other by an internal centrifugal clutch, which automatically switches from one gear to the other depending on the speed.

The hub axle is hollow and carries the operating rod on which the clutch mechanism is held. On most models, the clutch rod is attached to a little chain, while other models connect it with a hinge mechanism screwed on in the location of the axle nut. The cable is attached to the little chain or the hinge-device by means of a cable adjuster which serves to correct the adjustment of the gears.

When shifting into a lower gear, the pull rod is pulled further out of the chain and sets the clutch in the appropriate position.

The simplest adjusting mechanism is the one used by SRAM.

In conjunction with the mechanical superiority of the gears themselves, this is a good reason to choose this make in preference to some of the others—certainly now that this manufacturer has finally introduced models without a coaster brake.

HUB GEAR EFFICIENCY

Traditionally, English touring cyclists were great believers in hub gearing, while the French favored derailleur gearing, calling hub gears "friction boxes," because of all the rotating parts involved. we think the difference mainly depended on the typical weather conditions: the English had to deal with a lot more rain and mud than the French, so to them it was more important to have an enclosed mechanism and be able to protect the chain.

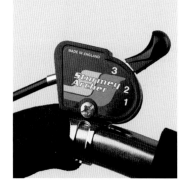

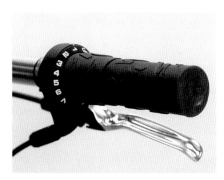

Above: Fig. 13.11. Traditional Sturmey-Archer 3-speed trigger shift lever.

Upper left: Fig. 13.12. Adjusting 3-speed hub.

Lower left: Fig. 13.13. SRAM twistgrip.

Upper right: Fig. 13.14. Shimano 7-speed control mechanism at the hub.

Lower right: Fig. 13.15. Shimano 8-speed twistgrip.

Meanwhile the English thought that derailleur gearing could not be as efficient as hub gearing because the chain would not be perfectly aligned (except in the middle gear).

In 2002, Chester Kyle and Frank Berto tested a collection of different gear trains, and reported on their findings in the Proceedings of the International Cycle History Conference. As it turns out, derailleur gearing was tested to be more efficient—as long as the various parts are kept clean and lubricated—but the difference was not big enough to go to war over.

In direct drive, all hub gears are about as efficient as derailleur gearing. For a three-speed that is the middle gear. The extreme gears were progressively less efficient, but in most cases not enough so to become noticeable. I had supplied several of the hub gears that were tested, and the authors were surprised to find that my well-worn (and well lubricated) old (pre-SRAM)

Fichtel & Sachs threes-peed outperformed most of the other drivetrains.

What makes hub gears potentially less efficient is the fact that there are a bunch of load-bearing journal bearings inside and a lot of meshing teeth. Straight out of the factory, most of those meshing teeth have rough edges, causing excessive friction, but after extensive use and with proper lubrication, they run like clockwork.

Overall the most efficient hub gear was the Rohloff Speedhub 14-speed hub, which costs about as much as any top-of-the-line component gruppo

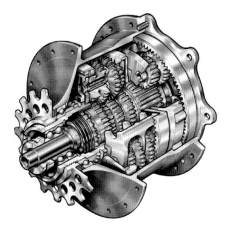

derailleur drivetrain with all the other parts thrown in. The Rohloff's efficiency is probably due to the use of needle bearings instead of journal bearings, as well as higher accuracy in overall and detail design and manufacture.

BOTTOM-BRACKET GEARS

The wheel hub is not the only possible place for epicyclic gearing. Right back to the beginning of gear drives, some manufacturers have chosen to put them in front, around the bottom bracket. In general, the disadvantages of this arrangement are:

1. It usually required a custom frame with an oversize bottom bracket shell.

2. The gears are at the point of higher forces rather than higher speeds, and thus had to be made sturdier and heavier.

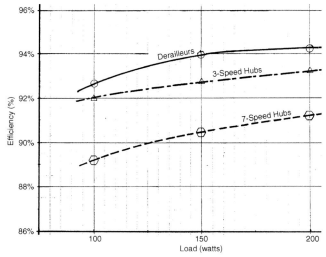

Above: Fig. 13.16. Rohloff 14-speed Speedhub, with roller bearings.

Left: Fig. 13.17. Average efficiencies from Kyle and Berto tests, 2002.

Right: Fig. 13.18. SunTour V-Box bottom-bracket gear.

On the other hand, bottom-bracket gears are in a fixed location on the bike, making it easier to operate them and less sensitive to damage.

Even today, some variants of the bottom-bracket gear are available. Most notable of these are the Schlumpf Mountain-Drive and the SRAM HammerSchmidt. Both consist of a special crankset with a 2-speed epicyclic gear inside.

These gears can be operated either by depressing a button in the crank with the ankle or by means of a handlebar-mounted shift lever. These devices are used on some downhill mountain bikes, as well as on folding bikes and recumbents. Their main use is as an alternative to the front derailleur and double chainrings, and they're indeed easier to shift.

For downhill mountain bikes, SR SunTour makes the V-Box. This is a 9-speed bottom-bracket gear with a range of 610%, making it the widest-range gear setup available, while eliminating the need of both front and rear derailleurs. It weighs an amazing 4.5 kg (10

lbs.), but that is no object in downhill racing, where gravity is the source of speed.

HYBRID GEARING

It is quite possible to combine gear hubs (or bottom-bracket gears) with derailleur gearing, which is referred to as hybrid gearing. Sturmey-Archer, Fichtel & Sachs, and Shimano all have offered such systems in the past. Currently the most readily available is a system called Dual-Drive, from SRAM.

Above: Fig. 13.19. SRAM Hammer-Schmidt bottom-bracket crankset.

Left: Fig. 13.20. Schlumpf Mountain-Drive bottom-bracket crankset.

Top right: Fig. 13.21. Hybrid gearing: SRAM DualDrive combines a gear hub with a 9-speed cassette for derailleur gearing.

Bottom right: Fig. 13.22. SRAM Dual-Drive shifter, for control of hub gear and derailleur with a single twistgrip.

Although such systems are usually marketed to the commuting segment of the market, similar systems sometimes crop up on mountain bikes and recumbents as well. One such system is created by combining any rear derailleur (or, for that matter, a hub gear) with the MountainDrive or the SRAM HammerSchmidt.

INFINITELY VARIABLE GEARS

However many gears you have with a conventional hub gear, there are always definite steps and gaps in between. Eliminating those steps and gaps calls for an infinitely variable gear system. Many ideas have been floated in the past to achieve this, but in the last few years a promising system has finally emerged. It's Fallbrook Technologies' Nu-Vinci hub.

In this system, a set of ceramic spheres transmits the power from

one disk to another. The first disk is connected with the freewheel, and the second one to the hub shell. Depending on the spheres' position relative to the center, the second disk turns faster or slower than the first. A twin-cable control with a non-indexed rotating twistgrip allows the rider to adjust the gear ratio. With a 350% range, this hub is about as versatile as the best 8-speed hubs on the market today.

The only serious drawback of the NuVinci is its weight, which, at 4 kg (9 lbs.), far exceeds that of any other gear system on the market. However, the manufacturer has already shaved about a pound off compared to the first year of production, and presumably these things will become available in models with less weight in the near future. In all fairness, though, for the kind of bikes on which they are likely to be used, weight may not be such an issue. The Dutch Batavus company installs it on a city bike that already weighs 20 kg (44 lbs.) without the Nu-Vinci, so the extra weight is not such a big issue there.

HUB GEAR MAINTENANCE

Whenever hub gearing does not work properly, it is generally not due to the mechanism itself, but rather to the controls. Slipped cable guides or pinched cables are the most frequent causes of control problems. Consequently, these points should be checked

before attempting to adjust the mechanism.

By way of regular maintenance, it's most important (and often enough) to clean around the gear hub, especially the control mechanism of today's more complex multi-speed units.

If the hub features an oil nipple (most newer models do not, being lubricated for life and sealed), it's recommended to give it about 10 drops of light oil, such as SAE 30 motor oil, sewing-machine oil, or a bicycle-specific lubricant.

Cleaning and lubrication are not the only aspect of hub gear maintenance. Here is a list of frequent causes of improper shifting with their respective solutions:

❏ Hub, adjusting mechanism, cable or handle does not run freely: lubricate;

❏ Cable (seemingly) stretched: adjust;

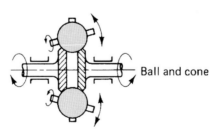

Ball and cone

Above: Fig. 13.23. Ball-and-cone friction drive, the operating principle of the Nu-Vinci infinitely variable gear.

Right: Fig. 13.24. Nu-Vinci hub installed on a bike. Though slightly less efficient than epicyclic gears, it is easier to use, especially for inexperienced cyclists.

❏ Hub defective: overhaul or replace;

❏ Control part (shifter, cable, cable guide, hinge mechanism) defective: repair or replace.

Most often, the cause is one of the first two points, so it can simply be corrected by means of adjustment or lubrication.

On the three-speed, the adjustment is generally correct when the cable is taut, but not under tension, when the shift lever is set for the high gear. However, the procedure is slightly different for each of the various makes and models.

On hubs that are controlled via a little chain protruding from the axle (Sturmey-Archer and Fichtel & Sachs 3-speeds), this chain must be perfectly aligned with the cable—that may mean that it is not fully screwed in but backed off a little.

Modern multi-speed gear hubs come with their own adjustment instructions, which differ from one make to another.

RIM BRAKES

THE OVERWHELMING MAJORITY of all bicycles sold in the U.S. are equipped with some kind of rim brake. Even on bikes with a coaster brake on the rear wheel, the rim brake usually finds application on the front wheel, except in those countries where only one brake is required by law.

The laws that govern bicycle brakes vary from country to country and in the U.S. from state to state. Generally, the laws require a certain maximum braking distance starting out at a specified riding speed on a clean, dry, level road surface.

Left: Fig. 14.1. Overview of brake, lever, and cables, shown here on a mountain bike with linear-pull brakes.

Right: Fig. 14.2. The two types of rim brake action: lateral (left) and radial (right).

THE RIM BRAKE PRINCIPLE

All rim brakes are based on one of two principles, which are depicted in Fig. 14.2. By means of a lever and usually a cable (sometimes a pull rod or even a hydraulic system), two brake pads of a wear-resistant high-friction material are pushed against the wheel rim.

In the U.S., only the type that applies force from the sides, i.e. laterally, is used. It is also possible to apply the force radially outward toward the rim, something that is still found on the

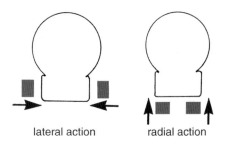

lateral action   radial action

THE RIM BRAKE PRINCIPLE

roller-lever (or stirrup) brakes used on utility bikes in many parts of the world. Neither system is inherently superior to the other. The roller-lever system is less trouble-prone, but it is heavier and not suitable for use with lightweight rims.

BRAKE DESIGN AND CONSTRUCTION

In order to brake more forcefully, it does not suffice to pull the brake lever more firmly. In addition, the components must be able to convert the force into friction between the wheel rim and the brake pads. The following factors come into play:

❏ Maximum coefficient of friction between the materials of brake pad and rim;

❏ Stiff (as opposed to deformable, or "spongy") construction of brake, cable, lever, and braking surface;

❏ Favorable relation between brake lever travel and brake caliper travel (mechanical advantage).

The coefficient of friction between natural rubber (as well as most synthetics and composites used for brake pads) and steel or aluminum used for the rims is quite adequate when dry. However, the harder and smoother the surface of the rim, the more severely the friction is reduced when wet.

Smooth hard anodized rims brake poorly when wet, and chrome-plated steel rims are a catastrophe when used with natural rubber or most synthetics. Even unanodized aluminum suffers greatly when wet: with the same applied force, the effective braking force on the wheel is reduced to less than 50%, resulting in half the deceleration or twice the braking distance.

DECELERATION

Car magazines often publish braking performance data in terms of g: some number (such as 0.8) times the acceleration due to gravity. This assumes that deceleration under braking is nearly linear (a good approximation), and implies that other drivers ought to be able to expect similar results.

Comparable performance figures for bikes are not to be found. Although bike braking is much the same, several factors make it inadvisable to list a typical braking deceleration number. as motorists do most of their braking on level ground, but most bicycle braking is done on downhills, where the grade must be taken into account because gravity reduces the effective deceleration and affects the weight distribution between front and rear wheel. On steep grades, bicycle braking is further limited by the danger that the rear wheel may lift, vaulting the rider over the handlebars—a concern automobile drivers do not have.

Whereas the weight of the driver of a car is only a small fraction of the car's weight, bicycle rider weight is very significant, and greatly affects the rate of deceleration. Finally, airspeed is almost always high on a downhill, and the coefficient of aerodynamic drag is higher for a bicyclist than a car, so air resistance is a significant decelerating force; it also varies with speed.

It helps to deal with force, rather than some number of g's.

Typical forces from braking, considered in the direction of motion rather than (for example) from the brake onto the rim, range up to 450 N on a level paved surface, somewhat less on a steep downhill, much less off-road or under wet conditions. (These figures were obtained from a few trial runs, although probably higher figures are possible.)

Summing this force with those from rolling and aerodynamic resistance and dividing by mass gives acceleration—in this case, deceleration, or negative acceleration.

Most legal bicycle braking requirements can be met with a deceleration of approx. 0.5 g.

The stiffness of the brake, the lever, the cable, and any anchor points is important because all these factors could otherwise limit how much force can be applied. If the components bend, rather than transmitting the force directly to the contact point between rim and brake pad, the amount of lever travel may not

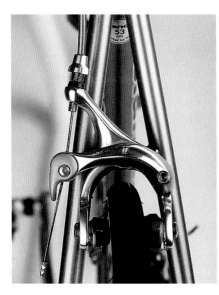

suffice to apply the force necessary for effective braking (note that neither force nor power gets lost, as is often suggested: it just limits how much force can be applied and consequently how powerful the resulting braking is). The first step to take when brakes feel "spongy" is to replace the cable with a version that has a thick core and a stiff mantle.

The effective leverage, or mechanical advantage, between lever and brake should be selected with the dimensions of both parts in mind, as well as the size and the force the rider is able to apply to the lever. Not enough leverage is just as bad as too much: in the first case not enough force is applied; in the latter, the distance of caliper travel is inadequate to apply the available force.

RIM BRAKE TYPES

Rim brakes can be divided into two distinct categories: squeezing and pulling. The pulling type, represented by the roller-lever, or stirrup, brake with pull rod operation, is becoming increasingly rare, even in Britain, where it used to be standard equipment on most roadsters and utility bicycles. All other brakes, referred to as caliper brakes, operate by squeezing against both sides of the rim simultaneously.

Several different types are shown in Figs. 14.4 through 14.9 On all caliper brakes, the brake arms must return to the inactivated position when the handle is released. This is done by means of one or more springs. As will be explained more fully under *Brake Controls*, these springs are not always powerful enough to overcome the friction in brake, cable, and lever. This has something to do with the fact that some manufacturers use the method first introduced by Dia-Compe, integrating a spring in the lever as well. In this case, the spring in the brake need not do all of the work—but this

Above: Fig. 14.3. Dual-pivot sidepull brake on the rear wheel of a road bike. Some manufacturers (notably Campagnolo) use the dual-pivot type only in the front, preferring to use a conventional sidepull brake in the rear, thus minimizing the risk of rear-wheel lockup.

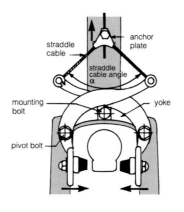

Above: Fig. 14.4 Centerpull brake.

Left: Fig. 14.5. Conventional (single-pivot) sidepull brake.

Right: Fig. 14.6. Dual-pivot sidepull brake.

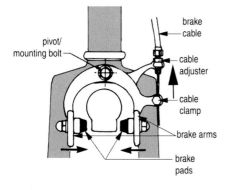

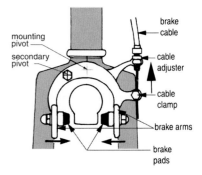

brake must be used with the matching lever.

Most rim brakes incorporate a quick-release device that is used to open up the brake so that the wheel can be removed and installed without changing the adjustment. After the wheel is installed, the quick-release must be fully closed again for the brake to function properly.

THE SIDEPULL BRAKE

On the sidepull brake, the two brake arms pivot simultaneously around a common central mounting bolt. It is illustrated in Fig. 14.6, while Fig. 14.23, on page 205, defines the critical dimensions that determine whether a particular brake will fit a certain bicycle. The inner cable is attached to one brake arm, while the outer cable is connected to the other. When applied, the cable pulls the lower brake arm up toward the other, causing the lower ends of the brake arms with the brake pads to push from both sides against the sides of the rim. Generally, a quick-

release is installed on one of the brake arms to un-tension or tension the cable for adjustment or wheel removal.

The inherent disadvantages of the sidepull brake are twofold: the distance between pivot and brake pad is relatively great (with given overall dimensions), and the brake is hard to center. The first is overcome by building the bike on which this brake is used to such close clearances, using narrow rims and tires, that the dimensions remain small enough to assure adequate rigidity: fine for racing and fitness bikes. But this problem becomes apparent when a big version is used on a bike with fat tires and big clearances, as it is done on cruisers.

THE DUAL PIVOT BRAKE

The dual pivot brake is essentially a modified version of the sidepull brake. On this type of brake, the pivot point between the brake arms does not coincide with the mounting bolt but is offset to one side on a short yoke. This method reduces the effective brake arm length that is free to flex, as well as making the brake more effective on account of improved mechanical advantage.

This and some other models are sometimes equipped with ball bearings in the pivots.

Above: Fig. 14.10. An elegant centerpull brake from the (now defunct) Spanish manufacturers Zeus.

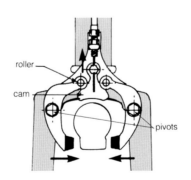

Above: Fig. 14.7. Cam-operated brake (also called roller-cam brake or Parapull brake).

Left: Fig. 14.8. Cantilever brake.

Right: Fig. 14.9. Direct-pull brake (also referred to as V-brake).

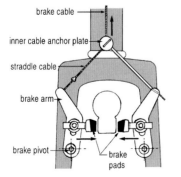

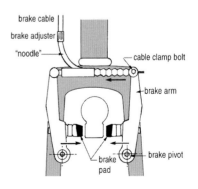

Although at first this may seem an unlikely location for a ball bearing, because of the high loading force and very slow rotation, an axial bearing turns out to be quite effective here. It does not support the brake arm around the pivot bolt but the two brake arms relative to each other, where otherwise high contact forces cause considerable friction when the brakes are applied.

THE CENTERPULL BRAKE

The centerpull brake, illustrated in Fig. 14.4, is a symmetrical model. Here the brake arms each pivot on their own bushings mounted at opposite ends of a common yoke, which in turn contains the central mounting bolt. The upper ends of the two brake arms are joined by means of a transverse (or straddle) cable, to which the inner brake cable is attached, while the outer cable is anchored against an adjustable stop mounted on the frame.

When the lever is applied, the upper ends of the brake arms are pulled together, causing the lower ends with the brake pads to squeeze from both sides against the rim. The adjustment mechanism is contained in the anchor that holds the outer cable, which is generally installed at the headset or the saddle binder bolt, for front and rear

BRAKING THEORY

Braking is done either to limit the speed, such as on a steep downhill or in preparation for a steep curve or other maneuver, or to come to a standstill. In the moving bicycle, a certain amount of so-called *kinetic* energy (the product of mass and the square of the speed) is stored, which is absorbed when the bike is brought to a standstill. This can be done by letting it roll until friction losses have depleted this energy, which may take a long time. Or it can be done by crashing into a fixed object, which will do the job much faster, but possibly with detrimental results to bike and rider.

To stop before an accident happens, the rider has to use the brakes. They apply friction between a moving and a fixed part (in the case of rim brakes, between the rim and the brake pads) to dissipate the energy at a rate controlled by the rider via the force he applies to the brake lever. The energy absorbed by the brakes is converted to heat (rim and brake pads become hot). The amount of energy to be absorbed is calculated as follows:

$$W = 0.5 * m * v^2$$

where:

W = energy in J (equivalent to Nm)

m = mass of bike, rider and luggage in kg

v = initial riding speed in m/sec.

The relationship expressed by this formula explains why it is harder to stop a heavily loaded bike than an unloaded one, and why it is so much harder to stop it from a higher speed, as evidenced by longer braking distances.

The speed is reduced more or less gradually. Just how gradually is expressed by the deceleration in m/sec^2. A deceleration of 1 m/sec^2 means that the speed is reduced by one m/sec after each subsequent second of braking. When rolling to a gradual stop, the deceleration is very low (in the order of cm/sec^2), while it is very high (several thousands m/sec^2) when crashing into a fixed object, the damage being roughly proportional to the deceleration.

During controlled braking, decelerations of several m/sec^2 are achieved. If the brakes apply a deceleration of 1 m/sec^2 (either because they are not more effective or because the rider does not apply more force), it will take 8.3 sec to stop from an initial speed of 30 km/h (20 mph, or 8.3 m/sec). The braking distance can be calculated as

$$S = (v_o)^2 / 2 * a =$$

$$S = 8.3^2 / 2 * 1 = 34.5 \text{ m}.$$

brake respectively. This brake works best if the angle of the straddle cable α is about 120°.

Generally, the centerpull brake is designed for larger clearances and wider rims and tires, due to the more favorable (i.e. shorter) distances between the brake pad and the pivot for each brake arm. It is important to keep the angle between the two legs of the transverse cable at least 120° to achieve adequate leverage. It is unfortunate that in recent years the centerpull brake has been largely ignored: the fashion of using sidepull and dual pivot brakes overlooks the fact that even a simple centerpull brake offers superior braking and

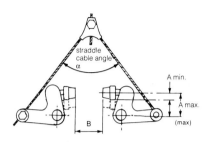

Right: Fig. 14.11. Cantilever brake: straddle-cable angle and other critical dimensions.

BRAKING THEORY (CONTINUED)

If the deceleration is increased by more powerful braking, the braking time and distance become proportionally less. In practice, decelerations of 1–6 m/sec^2 are typical for the range from gentle speed reduction to hard braking, resulting in braking distances that range from 35 to 6 m from an initial speed of 30 km/h (19 mph).

Another situation occurs when riding downhill. In this case, the bike also has a certain amount of *potential* energy, expressed as the product of weight and height (or mass, height and mass constant, or gravitational acceleration, g). Part of this energy is absorbed by the resistance of the air, mechanical friction and rolling of the tires. Any difference that remains between the resulting "free fall" speed and the desired safe handling speed has to be taken up by the brakes. The steeper the slope, and the heavier the bike and rider, the more energy has to be absorbed (or the more power has to be applied) to maintain the same speed, in addition to any speed reduction that may be required.

While braking, the effective mass center of bike and rider is transferred forward as shown in Fig. 14.15 on page 201: The front wheel is loaded more, the rear wheel less. Due to the relatively high mass center and short wheelbase, this imposes a severe limitation on the deceleration possible as distributed over the wheels, at least on the conventional bicycle.

The maximum deceleration that can be reached with the front brake is approx. 6.5 m/sec^2, while it is approx. 3.5 m/sec^2 with the rear wheel. Anything in excess of those figures would lead to tipping forward or skidding of the rear wheel respectively, both causing loss of control. To limit this effect as much as possible, the cyclist should place his body weight as low and as far back as possible during sudden braking, as shown in Fig. 14.12.

The braking force required to achieve a certain deceleration can be calculated. The interesting thing is the insight gained that braking, like so many other bicycle phenomena, is not some kind of black magic, but can be rationally determined.

If the system does not provide enough mechanical advantage, the rider may not be able to bring the bike to a stop. If it has too much, the brakes may grab too directly.

Fig. 14.12. Avoiding rear-wheel liftoff by transferring the body weight back and down.

ease of maintenance to what can be achieved with most sidepull brakes.

THE CANTILEVER BRAKE

The cantilever brake, mainly used on touring bikes and cyclo-cross machines, was also the most common brake on the first generation of mountain bikes. Illustrated in Fig. 14.8, this symmetrical brake consists of two separate brake arms that are each mounted on a pivot bushing brazed or welded to the frame or the fork. The ends of the brake arms to which the transverse cable is attached reach outward, which makes these

Above: Fig. 14.13. Typical modern cantilever brake. Note the angle of the straddle cable, which optimizes the mechanical advantage.

Right: Fig. 14.14. Shimano XTR direct-pull brake with parallelogram action to keep the brake pads moving in to the rim along a straight path.

brakes protrude laterally beyond the rest of the bike. The critical dimensions are illustrated in Fig. 14.11.

Just about everything said about the centerpull brake applies to the cantilever brake as well. Once again, the angle between the two ends of the straddle cable must be at least 120° to allow enough leverage. This is particularly critical on so-called low-profile versions, on which the brake arms do not protrude outward as much. If a brake like this does not seem to work, just check and correct this feature and you will not believe how much difference it makes.

The adjusting mechanism for the cantilever brake is usually integrated in the brake lever. It is also possible to use an adjuster on the anchor that holds the end of the outer cable, as is the case on the centerpull brake. Most cantilever brakes have no quick-release as such: instead they are released by lifting one of the cable nipples out of the open-ended one of the brake arms,

which can be done once the brake pads are simultaneously pushed against the sides of the rim.

On many modern cantilever brakes, the brake arms do not protrude laterally as much as vertically, and these are referred to as "low profile" cantilevers. Although indeed, they do not protrude as much as older cantilever brakes, they are very much less efficient, and only work reasonably well if the straddle cable is kept very tight, with an angle of about 150 degrees rather than the 120 degree angle that works best on regular centerpull and cantilever brakes.

DIRECT-PULL BRAKE

The direct-pull brake, often called V-brake, has become the most common brake type for all bicycle types except road bikes. In essence, it is a cantilever brake with long, straight brake arms that are pulled together from one side. Like the cantilever brake its brake arms are mounted on bosses welded to the fork and the seatstays. The control cable is fed into the brake via a short curved tubular guide, referred to as "noodle." The location of the bosses is different from the location needed for most cantilever brakes, so these brakes are not mutually interchangeable.

Operating very directly, it can be an extremely powerful brake.

Because the tops of the brake arms have to be pulled together over a longer distance than with other brake types, they require more cable pull than regular brake levers can supply. For that reason direct-pull brake-specific brake levers should be used. Because these are not available for drop handlebars, there are also gadgets available that can be installed in the cable near the brake to "multiply" the amount of cable travel of road bike brake levers.

In the hands of an inexperienced rider, the direct-pull brake's very direct action may result in sudden and excessive brake application, resulting in

BRAKING AND REAR WHEEL LIFT AND LOCKUP

It's pretty common knowledge amongst cyclists that when braking, the mass of bike and rider is transferred away from the rear wheel and toward the front wheel. The result is that the rear brake becomes ineffective and the rear wheel may lift off the ground, sometimes even tipping the rider forward. Many, however, live under the illusion that it only applies to use of the front brake, and therefore they may try to rely on the rear brake only. Wrong: the transfer happens regardless which brake is used.

This phenomenon was particularly serious on the high-wheel bikes of the 19th century, leading to something referred to as a header: the rider being catapulted over the handlebars. Those bikes had a very short wheelbase, and essentially all the weight rested on the front wheel. At the opposite end of the spectrum are tandems and recumbents, both of which have a long wheelbase, with larger proportion of the weight over the rear wheel. And within "

normal bikes," short-wheelbase road bikes are more susceptible to it than longer-wheelbase touring and city bikes.

If you're interested in the calculations involved, you are referred to contributing author Stuart Baird's book *Performance Cycling* (see Bibliography). Here is a summary of the conclusions.

❑ Do not rely on the rear brake only, because with the forward thrust, the front wheel is loaded more, and braking in the front becomes (even) more effective. Contrary to what may seem "intuitive," braking more with the front and less with the rear actually prevents rear wheel lockup.

❑ When braking, don't treat the levers like on-off switches, but "modulate" the force applied, paying particular attention to how the bike feels.

❑ In sudden braking, it is OK if the rear wheel locks up, as

Fig. 14.15. Rear wheel loss of traction and tip-over.

long as you avoid the wheel from lifting off the ground. Do that by both shifting your weight toward the rear and by reducing the lever force, both front and rear.

❑ All these effects are aggravated when riding downhill (and, conversely, reduced when going uphill).

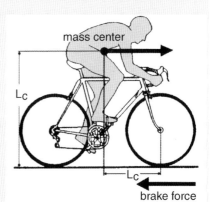

Detail A. Rear Wheel Unloading

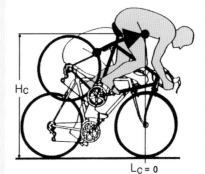

Detail B. Tip-Over

wheel lock-up. To prevent that, another gadget is sometimes installed, mainly on city bikes, that limits the brake force. It is essentially a flexible element installed between the outer cable and the "noodle."

THE U-BRAKE

The U-brake, illustrated in Fig. 14.18, is essentially a centerpull brake on which the pivots are not installed on a yoke but are brazed or welded to the fork blades or rear stays for front and rear brake respectively. In many ways, what was said about the cantilever brake applies here too, except that this model does not protrude as far on both sides of the bike. The mounting boss location is different from that for the cantilever, so these brakes are not mutually interchangeable.

THE CAM-OPERATED BRAKE

The cam-operated brake is based on an idea that resurfaces every so many years: the brake arms are pushed apart by a roughly triangular-shaped cam plate attached to the end of the inner cable.

In the late 1970s, it was available from Shimano in the form of a self-contained caliper unit and was not exactly a big success in that form. In the mid 1980s, another version was

introduced by that group of creative California mountain bike engineers that called themselves Wilderness Trails Bicycles, which for some years in the 1990s was available from Sun-Tour under license.

On this version, the brake arms are mounted on individual bosses, just like the direct-pull brake, the U-brake, and the cantilever brake. Illustrated in Fig. 14.7, the critical dimension are the same as those shown in Fig. 14.11 for the cantilever brake. Another version of this brake was the Odyssey, on which the brake arms were installed on a common mounting plate. It was very suitable for use on BMX-bikes and wherever space is limited, such as on other small-wheeled bicycles (it is the only brake suitable for the Moulton mountain bike with small wheels and suspension).

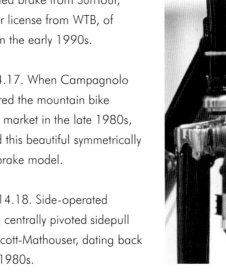

Above: Fig. 14.16. Fixed-pivot-mounted cam-operated brake from SunTour, made under license from WTB, of California in the early 1990s.

Left: Fig. 14.17. When Campagnolo briefly entered the mountain bike component market in the late 1980s, they offered this beautiful symmetrically pivoted U-brake model.

Right: Fig. 14.18. Side-operated lightweight, centrally pivoted sidepull brake, by Scott-Mathouser, dating back to the mid 1980s.

THE PIVOT-LINK BRAKE

Never heard of a pivot-link brake? It's the generic term we use to describe the rather rare models operating by means of a complex linkage mechanism as illustrated in Figs. 14.19 and 14.20. Campagnolo's Delta brake, which long formed part of that company's top-of-the line C-Record group, is one—very sleek and expensive. These brakes are in general not particularly effective. As the illustrations show, it is an old idea.

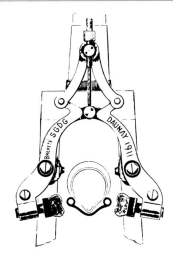

Above and right: Figs. 14.19 and 14.20. Pivot-link brakes old (above) and new. Campagnolo's Delta brake (right) had its mechanism neatly hidden behind a smooth cover plate.

THE STIRRUP, OR ROLLER-LEVER, BRAKE

This is the traditional brake used on heavy-duty English roadsters and the type of utilitarian bicycle

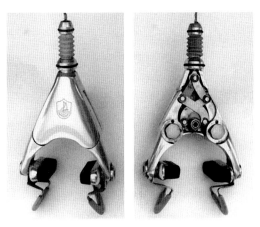

MECHANICAL ADVANTAGE

The term "mechanical advantage" is used to define the overall ratio of applied force between the brake lever and the brake arm. If a force of 1.0 N is applied to the lever and the effect is a 1.0 N force between the brake pad and the rim, the mechanical advantage is 1.0 (or 100%). A higher mechanical advantage brings more force to bear on the brake than is applied at the lever, a lower mechanical advantage would translate into less force at the brake than what the rider applies to the lever.

Of course, there is no magical force multiplier at work here: it's a matter of the effective leverage ratio. More leverage means less travel and therefore

more force at the receiving end (the brake) than what is applied at the point where the force is applied (the lever). The illustration shows how mechanical advantage of a certain combination of lever and brake is determined.

Different types of brakes may require more or less mechanical advantage. Specifically, direct-pull brakes require a greater mechanical advantage than other rim brakes. Consequently, direct-pull brakes should be used with levers that pull in more cable than is the case for other rim brakes. If suitable levers are not available, a special cam-shaped

Fig. 14.21. Mechanical advantage depends on the ratio between lever force and brake force.

device may be installed that increases the amount of movement at the brake.

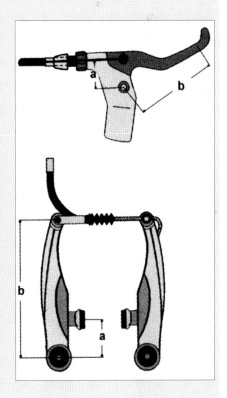

ridden in many third-world countries. It is operated by means of pull-rods (and hence it is sometimes also referred to as pull-rod brake). Instead of the brake pads pushing laterally against the sides of the rim, they are pulled up radially against the inside surface of the (differently shaped) rim.

The type of rim for use this kind of brake is referred to as Westwood, and is shown in the illustration and described in more detail in Chapter 9. Instead of cable-operation and two-sided force application against the sides of the rim, this brake, also known as stirrup brake, is characterized by pull rod operation and the application of force radially toward the inside of the rim, as illustrated in Fig. 14.21.

The rigid rods allow very effective force application, and little maintenance is required. On the other hand, the weight is

about twice that of typical side-pull brakes, each including their respective controls. You have to loosen and readjust the brake controls to adjust the handlebars—not to mention removing the wheel.

THE HYDRAULIC RIM BRAKE

Only readily available from Magura, the hydraulic rim brake is essentially a hydraulic disk brake that works on the wheel rim instead of on a solid disk. Although rarely seen in the U.S.,

this is an interesting alternative to conventional cable-operated rim brakes. Because the hydraulics transmit the force without perceptible friction, they are amazingly easy to operate.

On the hydraulic brake, the force is transmitted by compressing a liquid. The now obsolete Mathouser hydraulic rim brake used a flexible bellows unit contained in an unsealed cylinder, whereas some other hydraulic brakes use a hydraulic cylinder, often leading to leakage.

Compared to cable controls, hydraulics have the advantage of very direct, rigid and light operation, with negligible friction. The argument that damage to the liquid-filled tube connecting brake lever and brake unit seems far fetched: these tubes are not

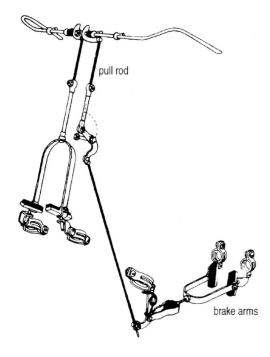

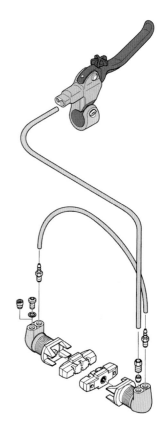

Above: Fig. 14.20. Magura hydraulic rim brake installed on a mountain bike.

Left: Fig. 14.21. Stirrup brake system, as used on heavy-duty roadster bikes, and still used on many bikes sold in Asia and Africa.

Right: Fig. 14.22. Overview of a hydraulic rim brake system.

particularly sensitive and should last a long time with normal use. After all, a regular brake does not work with a broken cable either. It should not be your choice for a world tour (because it may be difficult to repair or replace), but it is fine for normal use.

THE SPINDLE BRAKE

This is another rare item, illustrated in Fig 14.24. Here the cable turns a spindle with a helical groove that then pushes the brake pads against the rim. Since there is not less but more friction in this set-up than in conventional caliper brakes, there seems to be no technical justification for their use.

BRAKE CONTROLS

With the exception of the hydraulic brake and the roller-lever brake, all rim brakes are operated by means of a Bowden

cable that connects the lever with the brake mechanism. The end of the inner cable and the nipple are hooked through a recess in the lever, while the other end is clamped in at a movable part of the brake. The outer cable is anchored against the fixed part of the lever on one end, and either a stop on the frame or one on the fixed part of the brake mechanism on the other end. Sometimes the outer cable is not continuous but consists of

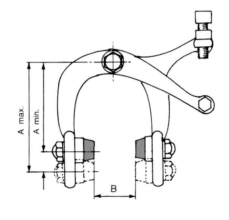

Above: Fig. 14.23. The critical dimensions on any caliper brake are the maximum opening width, B, and the minimum and maximum reach, A_{min} and A_{max}. Most modern road bike brakes don't offer enough of either dimension to fit on bikes with heavy-duty rims and tires (and fenders).

Left: Fig. 14.24. 1980s Spindle brake from Weinmann.

Right: Fig. 14.25. Most modern road bike brakes are operated by brake levers that are combined with shift levers for the derailleurs, like this Shimano Dura-Ace model.

interrupted sections installed between stops on the frame.

Brake cables can cause significant loss of brake force, especially in curves. It's not so much the radius that matters but the length of the curved section and the coefficient of friction. Lubrication helps, as does keeping much of the cable exposed rather than inside an outer sleeve.

There are several different brake lever types, each designed

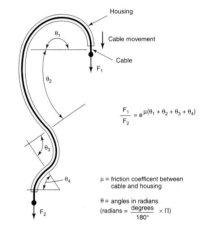

$$\frac{F_1}{F_2} = e^{\mu(\theta_1 + \theta_2 + \theta_3 + \theta_4)}$$

μ = friction coefficent between cable and housing

θ = angles in radians
(radians = $\frac{degrees}{180°} \times \Pi$)

Above: Fig. 14.26. Determining brake cable losses, which can amount to as much as 50 percent of the applied hand lever force in the case of poorly run and unlubricated rear brake cables.

for a particular model of handlebars. The most significant difference is between those made for drop handlebars and those for mountain bikes with flat handlebars, the latter being shown in Fig. 14.30. These would be suitable on any kind of straight handlebars, although cruisers, three-speeds and other utility bikes usually come with more primitive and less sturdy versions.

Since the introduction of Shimano's STI and other combined brake-shift levers, most road bikes now use these devices, but individual brake levers are still around, even for drop-handlebar bikes.

Amongst self-contained brake levers, there are also several variants. In the first place, there are models with a built-in retraction spring as mentioned before, intended for use with matching brakes with weaker return springs. Secondly, it has become fashionable to use so-called aero levers, on which the cables don't project from the front but are run along

the handlebars under the handlebar tape. For the retro crowd and single-speed riders, traditional drop-handlebar levers with protruding cables are still available.

Then there used to be those with extension levers, shown in

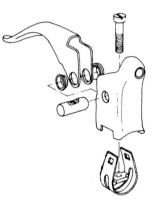

Above: Fig. 14.29. Brake lever mounting detail.

Top right: Fig. 14.30. Flat-handlebar brake lever with a trigger to use it as a drag brake for long descents.

Center right: Fig. 14.31. Drop-handlebar brake lever with a return-assist spring built in.

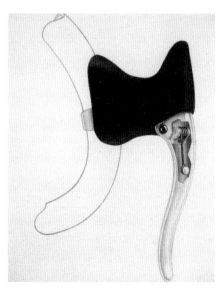

Above: Fig. 14.27. Extension levers, popular during the bike boom of the 1970s, don't allow adequate brake force to be applied.

Right: Fig. 14.28. A selection of traditional brake levers, including *guidonnet* models that can be operated from the top of the handlebars. Brake levers like these are making a bit of a comeback due to their use on fixed-gear and singlespeed bikes.

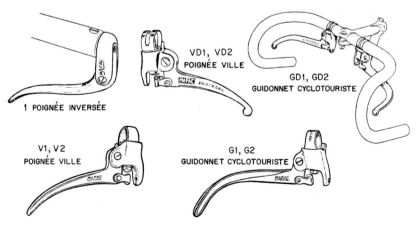

BRAKE CONTROLS

Fig. 14.27, and often incorrectly referred to as "safety levers." The auxiliary lever can be reached from the top of drop handlebars, a position frequently used by inexperienced cyclists. Unfortunately, these auxiliary levers are not rigid enough to allow the application of full force: they simply bend. Their other disadvantage is that they interfere with another, more suitable, hand position, namely "on the hoods"—i.e. on top of the brake lever mounts. A better solution for those who want to reach their brakes from the tops of the bars are the *guidonnet* levers, shown in Fig. 14.28, which have made a bit of a comeback with the popularity of single-speeds.

Finally on the subject of controls, a few words about the roller-lever brake. Operated by pull rods, it relies on a number of pivots mounted on the frame and several adjusting connectors between rods. The attachment of the pivot mechanisms to the handlebars, the frame and the front fork must be checked occasionally. These brakes are adjusted by means of the rod connectors.

BRAKE SHOES AND PADS

A distinction should be made between brake shoes and brake pads (also-called brake blocks): the latter are essentially only the pieces of friction material, while the brake shoe is the entire assembly, including its mounting hardware.

Nowadays, replaceable brake pads are not available very widely. More commonly on today's bikes, the entire brake shoe has to be replaced when the brake pad is worn. Not all brake shoes and brake pads fit all brakes. Some manufacturers design them to match, often precluding replacement by other makes and models. In addition, there are essentially two types respectively adjustable in a single plane or in multiple planes, referred to as directly and indirectly mounted.

On the directly mounted brake shoe, the mounting stud is screw-threaded and is held in the brake arm by a nut (or,

alternately, the brake shoe has a threaded hole and is mounted by means of a bolt). On the indirectly mounted version, the stud is plain and is held in a kind of eye bolt that is in turn mounted in the brake arm. Although the latter design allows more flexibility of adjustment, the use of concave and convex washers in combination with direct mounting can achieve similar flexibility and is used on many mountain bike brakes.

The material used for the brake pads is either natural rubber, a synthetic material, or a composite of several materials. Natural rubber is quite poor, especially in wet weather, as pointed out before. Some of the synthetics give higher friction coefficients, but those that work better in wet weather operate poorly when it is dry.

Very effective in both wet and dry weather are sintered brake blocks, but these are quite abrasive and may wear out the rims.

Brake shoes with cooling fins don't offer a noticeable improvement. While braking, the heat is mainly absorbed by the rim, which gives it off to the air. Although the brake pads get hot too, the measured effect of

Left, above, and right: Figs. 14.32–14.34. Fancy brake pads from Mathouser (left) with cooling fins, Kool-Stop (above), and Modolo (right).

external fins is just about zero: the heat transfer from the brake pad surface to the metal of the shoe is so poor that the fins do not provide effective cooling.

Another fallacy is the assumption that longer brake pads, or any other design that offers more contact area, would be more effective. The friction is a function of the force and the coefficient of friction, so, within practical limits, the area has no effect. Although the larger brake pad may wear better, the braking may actually be worse, because the contact pressure is inversely proportional to the area, which may lead to the build-up of water between rim and brake pad in wet weather.

Braking a bike with steel rims is a different kettle of fish altogether. When dry, this material works as well as aluminum, except that some of the homogeneous synthetics tend to leave deposits on it and are therefore not recommended. But when it gets wet, trying to brake such a bike becomes a true adventure: the coefficient of friction is reduced to about 25% of its dry weather value, resulting in

dramatically increased braking distances.

Although some manufacturers offer special brake pads for use on steel rims (which should never be used on aluminum because they are too abrasive), the use of disk brakes or hub brakes is a better solution for bikes with steel rims.

BRAKE MAINTENANCE

From a maintenance standpoint, the brakes should be considered as integral systems, each incorporating the levers, the control cables and the various pieces of mounting hardware, as well as the brake itself. In fact, brake problems are most often due to

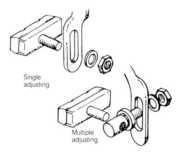

Above: Fig. 14.35. The two types of brake shoe mounting hardware.

Left: Fig. 14.36. Brake block testing at MIT, done with a spring-loaded device to compensate for rim unevenness.

Top right: Fig. 14.37. Adjusting centering of a dual-pivot brake.

Bottom right: Fig. 14.38. Adjusting a mountain bike brake at the lever.

inadequacies of some component in the control system. Consequently, it will be necessary to approach the problem systematically, trying to isolate the fault by checking off one component after the other.

When the brakes work inconsistently, often associated with vibrations or squealing, the cause is frequently found either in dirt and grease on the rims, or in loose mounting hardware. First check the condition of the rims, then the attachments of brake pads, brake arms, brake units, cables, anchors and levers. If the rim is dented, there is usually no other solution than to replace it, while all other causes can usually be eliminated quite easily.

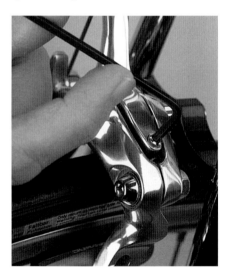

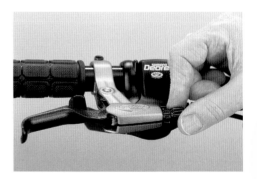

DISK BRAKES

ONE OF THE MOST SIGNIFICANT changes in bicycle technology in recent years has been the introduction and popularization of disk brakes. Of course, like so many other innovations, the idea has been around a long time, but not until the late early 2000s did disk brakes become generally available for mountain bikes, and have since trickled down to other types of bikes as well.

Modern disk brakes work great for road and mountain bike use, even on prolonged descents. Unlike other types of brakes, the disk brake can withstand high temperatures.

As so many other presumably modern developments in cycling, the disk brake isn't a brand new concept either. First patented in England in 1890, most designs were initially used for other vehicles, including trains and automobiles. Not until the early 1970s did they start making an appearance on production bicycles. Several models had been available in Japan from Araya, intended for tandem use as after-market installation, screwed onto a special hub. In 1972, Schwinn introduced a production bike with a disk brake made by Hope. American specialist component maker Phil Wood offered a very

fine, and expensive model, suitable for both front and rear wheel installation.

THE DISK BRAKE PRINCIPLE

Disk brakes have to do the same work as rim brakes do, and for the theory of braking you are

Fig. 15.1. Front brake on a mountain bike with front suspension and hydraulically operated disk brakes.

referred to the preceding Chapter 14, where this subject was covered in conjunction with its applicability to rim brakes.

In fact, disk brakes are very similar to rim brakes, except that they don't work on the rotating rim but on a flat disk, often referred to as *rotor*, connected to the center of the wheel. A pair of brake pads is held in a set of calipers mounted on the frame (for the rear brake) or the fork (for the front brake) in such a way that they can clamp down on the rotating disk to slow it down. The resulting reaction forces are taken over by a set of two attachment lugs that hold the brake caliper unit firmly to the fork or the rear stays.

The advantages of putting the braking action on a flat disk near the center of the wheel are quite significant: Not only is the disk far enough from the road not to get damaged and bent, nor influenced by moisture on the road, but also the gap between the brake pad and the

braking surface (the disk) can be kept quite small with the pad traveling only a short distance, allowing for maximum mechanical advantage. Unlike the rim, the disk does not get deformed under pressure from the brake, and the materials of the disk and the brake pads can be selected to accept much higher temperatures.

Operating at very high pressure between the brake pad and the solid disk, they are also significantly less sensitive to wet weather conditions than rim brakes. Since disk brake operation does not heat the wheel rim, they also don't heat up the air in the tire, which can blow a tire off the rim on a long descent in the case of rim brake use.

The only significant disadvantage of the disk brake is that the braking force is applied far from the most effective point (the circumference of the wheel). Consequently, the braking force is transmitted via the spokes, while the reaction force is taken up via a restraint that works on an inherently weak point of the bike—the fork blades or the rear stays. Consequently, disk brakes cannot be recommended as after-market replacement parts for bikes designed for rim brakes, but they are fine on any bike designed for their use, where these points are suitably reinforced.

ROTOR DESIGN

The rotor is attached to a special hub by means of 5 or 6 shallow-headed Allen bolts or Torx bolts (which have a star-shaped recess). Use only a matching wrench to make sure they are properly tightened about once a month.

There are two types of rotor designs: fixed disk and floating

Above: Fig. 15.2. 1970s mechanically operated disk brake from Shimano.

Left: Fig. 15.3. The disk brake operating principle.

Right: Fig. 15.4. Another 1970s disk brake, this one made by Phil Wood and intended for tandem use.

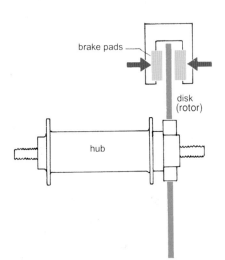

disk. The rotor itself has holes cut out, and the small holes near the circumference act to keep the brake pads clean. The larger cutouts near the center are to reduce the likelihood of deformation caused by the high temperature when braking. For the same reason, some manufacturers use a wavy circumference rather than a simple circular shape.

The rotor diameter has an effect on the brake's performance. Larger rotors allow more braking force to be applied, for which reason they are usually chosen for the front wheel. Of course, the larger disks represent a larger cooling area, so they can absorb more heat. However, smaller rotors allow better brake modulation and are less likely to lock up.

CALIPER DESIGN

The brake calipers come in two types, depending on make and model. They can either have the brake pads symmetrically

operated or asymmetrically, or one-sided. In symmetrical operation, the brake pads are pushed in toward the disk from either side, while in asymmetrical operation, one of the pads is fixed in its
position relative to the disk, whereas the other pad is pushed in when the brake is applied, pushing the rotor in until it engages the fixed pad as well. Most high-end disk brakes are symmetrically operated, although there's nothing inherently wrong

Above and left: Figs. 15.5 and 15.6. In the mid 1980s, Sachs offered this aftermarket disk brake with hydraulic operation from the lever to an intermediary reservoir (above) and mechanical (cable) control from there to the disk in the front wheel.

Upper right: Figs. 15.7 and 15.8. Hayes Prime brake lever and caliper unit, designed to be adjusted without the need for tools.

Bottom right: Fig. 15.9. Modern mechanically operated disk brake on the rear wheel from Shimano.

with asymmetrical operation either.

The caliper units are attached to matching lugs on the forks and the rear stays, of which there are, unfortunately, several different standards. The two main standards are IS (International Standard), which are drilled transversely without screw thread, and post-mount, drilled and threaded parallel to the wheel rotation plane. IS-mounts come in only one flavor, so any IS-mount caliper, front or rear, will fit any bike with IS-mounts.

Not so with the post-mount system, where the spacing can be anything from 21.5 mm (rear only), to 70 mm, to 74 mm, and to cap it all, post-mounted brakes come in versions that are mounted with or without an intermediate adaptor.

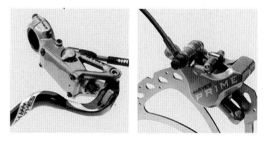

Older disk brakes—those made before 2000—may have an even more bewildering array of different mounting spacings, so don't try to put an old brake on a new bike or fork (or vice versa).

USING DISK BRAKES

When new, all disk brakes seem to work quite poorly, but their performance improves over time. This is because the (very hard) brake pads and the (very smooth) rotor must first get seated properly before they work effectively.

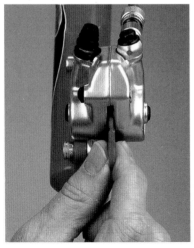

Oddly enough, they work better once metal particles from the disk are embedded in the brake pads (which may be an argument against cleaning them). They are extremely sensitive to oil or grease contamination (after all oil is a

Left and above: Figs. 15.10 and 15.11. Post-mount (left) and lug-mount (above) caliper units.

Above: Fig. 15.12. Modern Shimano cable-operated rear wheel disk brake. Note the frame reinforcement brace, to withstand the high reaction force when braking.

Left: Fig. 15.13. A pad protector should be installed between the brake pads when the wheel with the rotor is removed.

lubricant, and it is *friction* you need here).

Never apply the brake lever when the wheel (with the disk) is not in the bike. This would make the brake pads bind together, and it will become hard to separate them again in order to reinstall the wheel. To prevent this, insert the plastic protector plate that comes with the brake unit when removing the wheel.

Operation of disk brakes can be either by means of cables, like those used for rim brakes, or hydraulically. In the case of hydraulic operation, the brake lever incorporates a hydraulic oil reservoir with a piston to compress

Above: Fig. 15.14. Rotor installation.

Below: Fig. 1515. Hydraulic disk brake control lever.

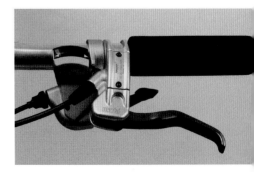

the liquid, and there is another such reservoir and piston at the caliper unit. The two are connected by means of hydraulic tubing.

HYDRAULIC SYSTEM DETAILS

Most hydraulic brakes rely on hydraulic tubing made of plastic with an outside diameter of 5 mm and inside diameter of 2.8 mm. On high-end versions, flexible braided steel hoses with plastic liner (and often a plastic outside cover) are used, which are typically greater in outside diameter. The flexible steel hoses are more resistant—whether on account of external impact or thermal expansion of the oil inside when it gets hot. Plastic hoses may spring a leak at the connection to the brake caliper

when the brakes themselves and the oil gets too hot on a long, steep descent.

Most hydraulic brakes have what is referred to as an "open" system. These systems have a compensating reservoir in which the excess oil can escape when it expands due to overheating. In a closed system, the built-up pressure would tighten the brake regardless of lever application, possibly leading to either sudden full brake application or sudden rupture of the tubing connection. To activate the open system and let expanded oil escape, the lever has to be disengaged and re-engaged briefly during a long

descent, something that should be done for just one brake (front or rear) at a time.

If a hydraulically operated brake starts to become less effective, with a "spongy" feel when the lever is applied, that is usually due to the presence of air in the system. To alleviate this problem, the system must be "bled" periodically—typically just once a year. Instructions for this operation can be found in any good bicycle repair manual.

There are two different types of hydraulic liquid in use for hydraulic brakes: DOT No. 4 automatic transmission oil and hydraulic oil. Both are available in automotive supply stores more cheaply than in bike shops (but be careful not to ruin the seals by using the wrong type for your particular brakes).

The discussion in this section applies equally to hydraulic rim brakes (described in the preceding chapter 14) as it does to hydraulic disk brakes.

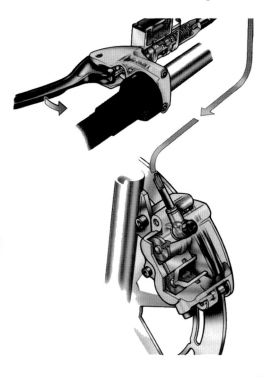

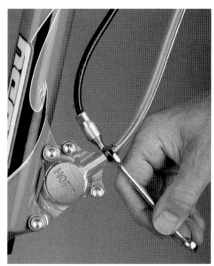

Above: Fig. 15.16. Avid Juicy hydraulic disk brake installed on the rear wheel of a mountain bike.

Left: Fig. 15.17. Workings of a hydraulic disk brake control system (Magura).

Bottom right: Fig. 15.18. Bleeding the hydraulic system in order to remove air bubbles.

16

OTHER BRAKES

IN ADDITION TO rim brakes and disk brakes, there are other brake types as well. The alternative way of stopping a moving vehicle by means of brakes contained in the wheel hubs remains of considerable technical interest. Used on virtually all other vehicles in some form or another, hub brakes can't be all wrong.

TYPES OF HUB BRAKES

In addition to disk brakes, there are other types of hub brakes as well, each with its own particular characteristics, which will be discussed in this chapter:

❏ coaster brake;

❏ drum brake;

❏ roller brakes;

❏ band brakes;

❏ expansion-contraction brake.

The advantage of any hub brake is its insensitivity to rain, sleet and snow. Tucked away nicely inside and protected from rainwater splashing up from the road, a hub brake is unaffected by conditions which compromise the performance of a conventional rim

Right: Fig. 16.1. Front end of a modern city bike equipped with drum brakes front and rear.

brake. The disadvantages of such brakes are mainly in the mind: it is not considered *cool* to have anything except what is in fashion, and clearly hub brakes are not. Technically, they all have minor problems, but they remain interesting alternatives.

The common technical disadvantage of all these hub brakes is

that, as also with the disk brake, the braking force is applied far from the most effective point (the circumference of the wheel). Furthermore, the braking force must be transmitted via the spokes, while the counter-force is taken up via a restraint that works on an inherently weak point of the bike—the fork blades or the rear stays. All these problems can be resolved through the correct selection of dimensions and components. They may not be suitable for use on a lightweight bike, but for many uses, you don't want a lightweight bike anyway. And let's not forget: all other components on the bike also have some problems.

For all these brake types, it can be said that the bigger the brake, the more satisfactory it will be. Bigger brakes have large cooling surfaces. On the rim brake, it is the wheel rim that acts as cooling surface, while on the hub brake, the cooling surface is the outside of the hub. Considering the small size of coaster brakes and roller brakes, one appreciates that these devices, designed for rear wheel

use, cannot be suitable for longer descents. So they should always be used in combination with another brake on the front wheel.

One method used to increase the cooling surface on some hub brakes is to add an external cooling disk, which may even be equipped with cooling fins.

Above: Fig. 16.2. Fichtel & Sachs Torpedo coaster brake.

Left: Fig. 16.3. Coaster brake operating sketch.

Right: Fig. 16.4. The Morrow was probably the best coaster brake available in the U.S. Early mountain bikers in Marin named their favorite descent in its honor, because the hub had to be overhauled (re-packed with grease) after every ride.

Below: Fig. 16.5. Exploded view of Torpedo coaster brake.

THE COASTER BRAKE

The coaster brake, known as backpedaling brake outside the U.S., is operated via the chain. It can only be used on the rear wheel, and consequently it is usually combined with another type of brake for the front wheel. Fig. 16.3 illustrates the principle of a common coaster brake. Although some models work differently, none appear to be as simple, powerful, and reliable as the Fichtel & Sachs Torpedo brake (now sold under the SRAM brand name) depicted here. It is shown in an exploded view in Fig 16.4 in its simplest form (other models have built-in multi-speed gear mechanisms). Modern versions of the Bendix brakes, the traditional U.S. make, work on the same principle.

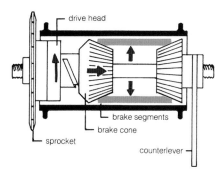

drive head

brake segments
brake cone
sprocket
counterlever

The Torpedo brake incorporates an interesting frictionless freewheel mechanism. When you stop pedaling forward, the rollers of the freewheel drop down into the lower position, disengaging the interior from the forward rotating hub shell. When pedaling back, this position of the freewheel rollers allows continued wheel rotation, but at the same time the backward rotation forces the brake cone up a helical groove toward the right, pushing out the segmented brake mantle against the inner braking surface of the hub shell. The resulting friction absorbs the energy and decelerates the wheel. The braking forces are countered by means of a counter lever that connects the fixed center with the left-hand chainstay.

Coaster brakes tend to run hot when used vigorously over longer distances. In extreme cases, the lubricant burns out of the bearings. If this happens, it is usually sufficient to partly disassemble the bearings and re-pack them, using the manufacturer's recommended special heat-resistant grease. Early mountain bikes

had coaster brakes, and the most famous downhill track in Marin County was referred to as "Repack" because the brakes had to be re-packed with grease after each descent.

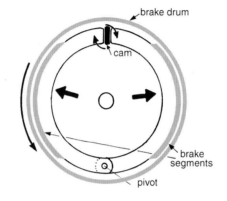

Above: Fig. 16.6. Drum brake operating diagram.

Bottom left: Fig. 16.7: A historic drum brake: the Sun tandem brake used on Gary Fisher's early mountain bike.

Below: Fig. 16.8. Exploded view of Sturmey-Archer drum brake for the front wheel.

THE DRUM BRAKE

Fig. 16.6 shows how the drum brake works, while an exploded view of a typical drum brake is depicted in Fig. 16.8. When the brake lever is applied, the attached cam pushes the brake segments apart against a brake liner in the interior of the drum on the hub shell. The resulting friction absorbs the energy, slowing the bike, while the counter lever fixes the interior against the fork or the chainstay. This counter lever must be quite substantial, as disastrous experiences with some early models have proven: they tended to crumple up, as did some of the frames that were not designed for the high local stresses.

The material of the brake segment linings should not come in contact with lubricants, because that reduces friction dramatically. This is often a problem on old Sturmey-Archer's models with built in hub gearing, because they lacked a seal between the two parts. If this happens, get the brake segments relined

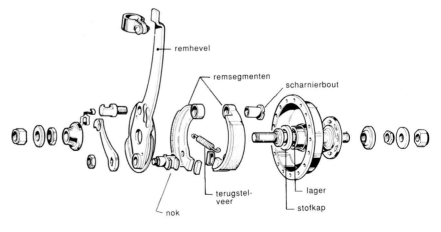

(or exchanged) by an automotive brake specialist. Fortunately, Sturmey-Archer's new Taiwanese owners have wasted no time in correcting this problem.

FADING

The drum brake, whether used on bikes, cars, or motorcycles, is quite sensitive to a phenomenon called fading. During long descents, the brake heats up and starts to lose effectiveness. It used to be assumed that the heat caused the drum to expand away from the brake liner, and as the diameter increased, the surfaces of the two would no longer match, leading to a drastically reduced braking effect.

Meanwhile it has been established that fading is actually due to a number of factors, mainly "gassing out" of the brake lining material, which deposits what is

effectively a lubricating coating on the contact surfaces of the brake segments and the lining inside the drum.

The problem is minimized by intermittent front and rear wheel braking, allowing the other one to cool off after every half minute of application. A related problem that applies to all commercially available drum brakes

is the fact that the liners wear asymmetrically, due to the one-sided pivoted arrangement. Since one of the segments spreads in the direction of rotation, the other one in the opposite direction, unfavorable wear results, and the brakes not only become less effective during long descents, but gradually become less effective over their lifespan as well.

DRUM BRAKE MAINTENANCE

The drum brake's effectiveness can verified by checking whether they can bring the bike to a full

Above: Fig. 16.9. The Dutch Gazelle bicycle maker uses its proprietary drum brake with cartridge bearings and symmetrically expanding brake segments.

Left: Fig. 16.10. Also from Gazelle is this commuting bike with rod operated drum brakes. Rod operation is more positive and reliable than cable operation. It's also heavier and more expensive.

Top right: Fig. 16.11. A typical drum brake taken apart, showing drum and brake segments.

Bottom right: Fig. 16.12. Arguably the finest drum brakes ever made, for front and rear, came from the French Maxicar company. This is a rear tandem brake.

stop from a normal riding speed. Other maintenance operations include adjustment of the cable (or in a control rod on models so operated) and bearing adjustment and maintenance, as well as exchanging the segments when the liners are worn or contaminated. In the latter case, disassemble and remove the old segments which can be exchanged by a brake specialist.

Brake adjustment is done as on any other hand-operated brake. The cable adjuster is used to increase the cable tension if the brake does not engage properly, and is loosened if it does not clear when the lever is released. As with the rim brake, the cable, the lever, the guides, and the anchors must be checked first, because these points are the most frequent causes of improper operation. If necessary they must be cleaned, freed, lubricated or replaced when adjustment does not have the desired effect.

OTHER HUB BRAKES

In this section, the other commonly used types of hub brakes will be described briefly.

SCREWED-ON DRUM BRAKE

This is a variant of the drum brake that is not an integral part of the hub but is screwed on the threaded end of a special hub by the same maker—usually Araya. It is intended only for use on the rear wheel, and its most common application is as a drag brake on tandems, operated independently from the main cantilever or direct-pull brakes. Everything said about the conventional drum brake applies here too.

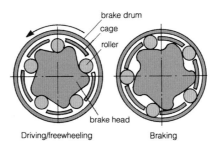

Above: Fig. 16.13. Roller brake operating sketch.

Left: Fig. 16.14. Counter lever attachment is needed to absorb the brake reaction forces of all hub brakes. But the frame and fork must also be designed strong enough to handle those forces.

Right: Fig. 16.15. SRAM's i-brake is essentially a small drum brake with an external cooling disk.

I-BRAKE

The i-brake is a new SRAM proprietary brake that is similar to a drum brake. However, here a floating aluminum ring is expanded into contact with the stainless steel surface of the hub shell. It is equipped with an aluminum cooling disk to dissipate generated heat. The manufacturer warns against use on heavily loaded bicycles and long descents.

THE ROLLER BRAKE

The roller brake is a very compact hub brake that comes in versions for the front and the rear (some of the latter are operated by backpedaling). Their application is powerful and well-controlled, though they are not suited for long descents. For most urban cycling, these brakes are probably the most reliable and wear-resistant brakes available today.

Some models are combined with a hub generator. The roller brake has gained in popularity in

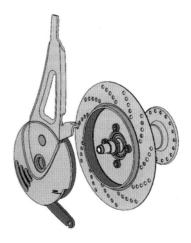

Europe and the U.S. with the introduction of comfort bikes. Its operating principle is shown in Fig. 16.13, and corresponds to that of the unique freewheel used in Fichtel & Sachs' coaster brakes. When driven backward, the rollers travel up the inclined recesses and contact the brake mantle. It works very well for short-time braking but is unsafe for longer descents due to overheating on account of the brake's small cooling surface.

THE BAND BRAKE

The band brake is essentially a drum brake turned inside-out. As shown in Fig 16.17, a strap is pulled inward against the exterior of a brake drum, causing friction. Although it is a

remarkably powerful brake, it suffers from overheating on longer descents because the surface that heats up is not directly exposed to the cooling air. This feature makes it inferior to the contracting drum brakes and most other rim and hub brakes.

THE CONTRACTION-EXPANSION BRAKE

The contraction-expansion brake is sold by Bridgestone in Asia and Europe under the designation Dynex. As illustrated in Fig. 16.18, it combines the principles of the drum brake and the band brake, simultaneously pushing and pulling brake shoes against both the inside and the outside of a heavy

brake drum directly connected to a mounting plate with cooling fins. It works very well, presumably due largely to the fact that the effect of fading in the one mode is compensated by increased braking force in the other.

Above: Fig. 16.19. Nothing new: 1890s American-made band brake.

Below: Fig. 16.20. Bridgestone Dynex expansion-contraction brake.

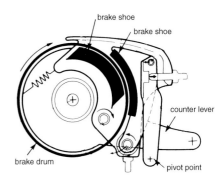

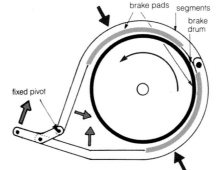

Above: Fig. 16.16. Band brake operating principle diagram.

Left: Fig. 16.17. Shimano roller brake for the front, with external cooling disk.

Right: Fig. 16.18. Expansion-contraction brake operating principle diagram.

17

SEAT AND SEATPOST

NOT A TECHNICALLY exciting subject, perhaps, but some sensible and necessary things can be said about the seat, or saddle, and its peripherals. Fig. 17.1 illustrates a typical seat and the seatpost, or seat pin, used to attach it to the frame, as well as the binder bolt used to clamp it in. Several different versions exist of all these parts, and they will be covered systematically in the following sections.

THE SEAT

The choice of a bicycle seat may be the most personal matter in all of cycling. They come in all sorts of shapes, sizes, and materials, and different riders have

Left: Fig. 17.1. Seat, seatpost, and seat clamp, as installed on a high-end steel-framed hardtail mountain bike.

Right: Fig. 17.2. Lightweight leather saddle on a Moots titanium seatpost.

strong opinions on what they perceive as the most comfortable choice.

Utility bikes and cruisers have models consisting of a metal frame with springs supporting a cover made of plastic (or sometimes leather). Racing, touring and mountain bikes typically have seats made with a stressed, self-supporting cover, usually of either leather- or fabric-covered polyamide (nylon) or another plastic on a metal-wire

frame, also called rails. Some "retro" saddles consist of stressed, solid leather on a wire frame.

The seats intended for mountain bikes and touring machines are generally padded and somewhat wider in the rear portion, while those commonly installed on utility bikes tend to have a shape that defies any ergonomic and anatomic principles—too wide and padded to allow enough leg rotation to pedal properly.

The authors, and many other touring cyclists, are firm believers in the benefits of leather saddles,

such as those made by Brooks. Unfortunately, they do require more care and many miles of "breaking in."

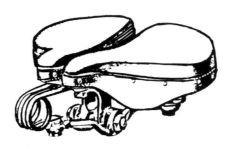

Above and right: Figs. 17.3–17.5. Some historic saddles: A 1912 split saddle, an 1898 Safety Poise ring saddle, and an 1897 leather saddle on a wood-framed bicycle.

BREAKING IN A LEATHER SADDLE

The following advice on treating and breaking in a leather saddle was written by Sheldon Brown (✝ 2009).

If a leather saddle is not oiled, and especially if it is allowed to get wet with water repeatedly, perhaps even ridden while soaked, it will eventually crack and disintegrate. The low-quality leather saddles that came on inexpensive ten speeds of the sixties and seventies would also often go out of shape under such conditions.

The easiest and fastest method to break in a new saddle is with a liquid leather dressing, such as neats-foot oil, Lexol, seal oil (a French favorite) or baseball glove oil.. These products are

available from shoe stores and sporting-goods stores. There are probably lots of other liquid oils that would work as well—RAAM pioneer Lon Haldeman uses SAE 30 motor oil. Paste or wax type leather dressings, such as Brooks Proofide, Sno-Seal, and saddle soap will work, but it takes much longer to break in a saddle that way.

You can just pour the oil on and rub it in by hand, or for a more drastic approach, you can actually soak the saddle. The easiest way to soak a saddle is to turn it upside-down on a sheet of aluminum foil, then form the foil up around the saddle for a snug fit. Pour in a whole 4-ounce can of neats-foot oil or whatever oil you prefer, and let the saddle soak for 30 minutes to an hour. Pour the remaining oil back into

the can, and wipe the excess oil off with a rag or paper towel. Install the saddle onto the bike, put on your black shorts, and ride. Even the most recalcitrant saddle will be substantially broken in within 200 miles or so.

The soaking technique is best for thick, hard-to-break in saddles such as the Brooks Professional. For most leather saddles, the pour-and-rub technique is adequate. A saddle only needs baptism by immersion once. After that, some oil should be poured onto the saddle and rubbed in by hand once a month. Once the saddle has become soft and comfortable, it is only necessary to oil it lightly twice a year to keep it from drying out.

If a leather saddle should get wet, you're not supposed to sit on it until it has been thoroughly dried. Besides, it should be treated with a special leather treatment (e.g. neat foot's oil or Brooks Proofide) to prevent it from drying out and becoming too absorbent.

The shape of the seat becomes quite critical when cycling over long distances, where the cyclist pedals rather fast and applies noticeable force to the pedals for a long time. To allow freedom of movement without chafing, a narrow front end is

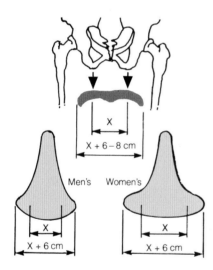

required, while the rear must conform to the rider's pelvic width. Women generally need a design that is rather wide in the back, as shown in Fig. 17.7, it should be about 6 cm (2½ in.) wider than the distance between the two bony protrusions.

Due to the generally more upright position used on mountain and touring bikes, these probably need seats that are modeled on the woman's seat, but more padded, as shown in Fig. 17.10. Excessive springiness, however comfortable it may seem, is not recommended, because it makes for a tiring lateral instability and inefficient pedaling.

It has long been a trick of female touring cyclists to increase the comfort of a leather saddle

for their specific use by making a cutout in the middle, as shown in Fig. 17.5. This same idea has recently been incorporated in some commercially available plastic seats, which have a recess in the center. If you can't get comfortable on another seat, it may be worthwhile to try one of these.

Some seats incorporate a form of gel padding that takes on the rider's shape, much like the filling of modern ski boots. This is still not the ultimate solution to the comfort dilemma, because even this material is eventually penetrated and then feels as hard as a rock. More promising is the

Above: Fig. 17.9. A narrow, grooved racing style saddle from Wilderness Trail Bikes.

Below: Fig. 17.10. A gel-padded saddle, suitable for city bikes and other upright-style bicycles.

Above: Fig. 17.6. Adjusting the tension on a Brooks leather saddle.

Top left: Fig. 17.7. Saddle width recommendations for touring saddles.

Bottom left: Fig. 17.8. Leather saddle with double wires and coil springs, held on a conventional tubular seatpost with a separate clip.

special gel material used e.g. as the seating cushion in modern wheel chairs, because this remains flexible even under enduring pressure.

Most seats with a stressed cover are based on a frame with two wires, or rails, usually made of steel. If you want a more lightweight solution, there are also seats with titanium wires. Aluminum wires, on the other hand, don't measure up, because their weight saving is paid for at the price of inadequate strength, often resulting in a broken wire—and a ruined expensive seat. The inadequate strength is easily explained by the fact that it is practically impossible to make the wires any thicker than they are when made of steel, resulting in less strength when weaker materials are used.

A few expensive leather models for touring, utility, and mountain bike use have a double set of wires and incorporate a set of coil springs in the back. Although we are not in favor of excessive springiness in seats, this is probably the most acceptable solution for those who like to ride in a rather upright position, which puts more weight on the seat. These models do require special matching support hardware.

Right: Fig. 17.13. Non-adjustable tubular seatpost and saddle clip, as installed on most low-end bikes.

THE SEATPOST

The conventional tubular seatpost, shown in Fig. 17.13, is mounted by means of the rather crude clip supplied with most cheap seats. This type does not allow very accurate angular adjustment of the seat relative to the horizontal plane, since the serrated clamp has notches that lie too far apart to find the optimum angle for some riders.

Typical adjustable seatposts are illustrated in Fig. 17.13. These either have an integrated fine-adjusting mechanism of some kind, or they are made up of separate parts: a tubular aluminum post and a separate, precisely adjusting head with clamp to hold the saddle wires. The simple one-bolt version shown in the right-hand detail of Fig. 17.12, is more prone to failure of the bolt, and therefore not recommended for riders who weigh more than 80 kg (170 lbs.).

Of all types available, the old Campagnolo model with two

Above: Fig. 17.11. Fatigue testing of saddles at a bicycle manufacturer's (Raleigh U.K.) test facility.

Right: Fig. 17.12. Three basic types of adjustable seatposts.

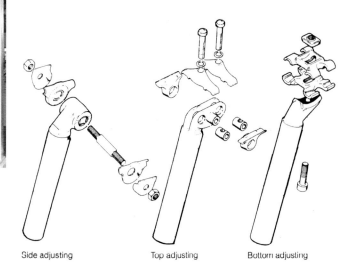

Side adjusting   Top adjusting   Bottom adjusting (hard-to-reach) bolts in the front and the rear, as shown in center detail of Fig. 17.12, is now more of a collector's item than a practical device. More recent versions have a more accessible adjusting mechanism.

As in the case of the handlebar stem, seatposts are not necessarily lighter when made of aluminum than when made of steel. Some of the fine-adjusting aluminum models are actually heavier than a simple steel tubular clamp with matching clip. Due to design and construction constraints, it is often easier to make a really light adjustable seatpost of steel alloy than it is to do so of aluminum. On the other hand, the manufacturing technique for the aluminum version allows mass production and thus a lower price.

The lightest seatposts available these days use carbon for the tubular section, combined with an aluminum head.

The diameter of the seatpost must correspond to the inside diameter of the seat tube. Although many utility bikes and cruisers use 25.4 mm (1 in.) diameter, the most common sizes for road bikes and mountain bikes are in the range of 26.8 mm to 27.2 mm. Even so, there are quite a number of different sizes to fit the various odd-size inside seat tube diameters, and the variety gets bigger from year to year due to the use of non-standardized oversize steel and aluminum tubing, often requiring a sleeve adaptor to fill the gap between the outside diameter of the seatpost and the inside diameter of the seat tube.

At least 65 mm (2½ in.) of the seatpost must remain clamped in at the top of the seat at all times. This requires a long model on mountain bikes and folding bikes. These days, most seatposts are marked to indicate the minimum insertion depth. If it was not marked by the manufacturer, you can mark it yourself using an indelible marking pen. The longer seatposts introduced for mountain bike and folding bike use, which are 30 cm (12 in.) long or more, also seem a nice solution for people with long legs, who previously could never find a frame big enough to achieve the desired seat height.

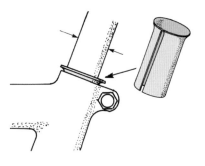

Above: Fig. 17.18. Use of shim to adapt a seatpost to an oversize seat tube.

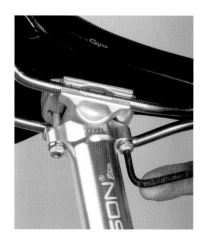

Above: Fig. 17.14. Adjusting detail on a seatpost with bottom adjustment.

Far left: Fig. 17.15. Easton aluminum seatpost. The same design is also available in carbon-fiber composite.

Near left: Fig. 17.16. Insertion depth markings on a Bontrager seatpost.

Right: Fig. 17.17. The seatpost must be long enough to allow a minimum insertion depth of 65 mm (2½ in.).

Unfortunately, the likelihood of these long seatposts being available in a size to match the bike in question is rather meager.

AERO SEATPOSTS

If you are concerned about aerodynamics at all, the seatpost may be a good place to start. The area between the rider's legs is perhaps the most aerodynamically disturbed are between bike and rider. These devices were first marketed on a large scale as part of Shimano's 1984 Aero gruppos. Although these gruppos were not a big success, they also were not as fully thought out as they might, with only minor ovalization.

The optimum airfoil shape should have a ratio between length and width of 4 to 1, and in recent times such seatpost designs have indeed become available. In combination with an aerodynamically optimized monocoque frame design and a

compact rider position, they can help achieve noticeably higher maximum riding speeds.

SUSPENSION SEATPOSTS

The idea of making life in the saddle a bit more comfortable by means of a sprung seatpost has been around for a long time. Today, these devices are often found on comfort bikes and city bikes. They work very well on any bike ridden in a rather

Above: Fig. 17.19. Simple suspension seatpost, with the spring element (either a coil spring or elastomer pads) contained inside the seatpost.

Left: Fig. 17.20. Aero seatpost, on which the insertion portion is round, the part above the seat tube is airfoil-shaped.

Right: Fig. 17.21. Internal parts of a simple coil-sprung seatpost. The spring's tension can be adjusted from the bottom of the (removed) seatpost.

upright posture, because this position puts more of the weight on the seat and does not allow the rider's legs and arms to absorb some of the shock impact from the road.

Several versions are available, ranging from simple spring-loaded plungers that simply go up or down to hinged parallelogram systems on which the movement upon impact is slightly back as well as down. Most come in 25.4 mm diameter, and shimming sleeves are

Right: Fig. 17.22. With suspension seatpost like this SunTour Shockpost, with a parallelogram linkage, the riders weight is transferred back as well as down when the spring is compressed.

available to adapt them to other seat tube diameters.

It is rather important that the spring device should also include a damping device, so the seat does not keeps bobbing up-and-down in response to every impact. This subject is covered in more detail in Chapter 18 under *Suspension Damping*.

The disadvantage of all these systems is that the distance between the seat and the pedals varies as the seatpost reacts to road shocks. For that reason, rear suspension systems built into the bicycle frame are considered superior for shock major absorption. However, for anything except mountain biking, the suspension seatpost is quite adequate at a reasonable price.

SEATPOST CLAMP AND BINDER BOLT

The seatpost is clamped in at the top of the seat tube. The seat tube is slotted in the back so it can be clamped tight around the seatpost by means of a binder bolt.

Virtually all quality bikes are equipped with an Allen key type binder bolt or a quick-release type clamp. Both methods have the advantage of allowing adjustment without the risk of either chipping the bike's paint or deforming the nut of the binder bolt. Unfortunately, some of these still require the simultaneous use of two identical size wrenches (most modern ones use a different size on either side), which may not always be available. Ideally, one of the two parts of which these bolts consist should have a prong that fits in a matching locating recess to eliminate rotation of that part, thus

Above: Fig. 17.23. Seat height adjustment by means of a quick-release seat clamp.

Left: Fig. 17.24. Seat height adjustment by means of an Allen bolt seat clamp.

obviating the need for a second wrench.

Reserved for folding bikes up to the late seventies, quick-release clamps, shown in Fig. 17.23, are also common on mountain bikes and city bikes. They are quite handy if you want to adjust the seat height frequently (such as for different riders on the same bike). However, they also make the seat more vulnerable to theft and vandalism. Actually, you'll rarely find a quick-release on high-end mountain bikes anymore, because most mountain bike riders don't use the adjusting feature on their bikes very much.

Seat height adjustment on the fly was common in the early days of mountain biking, which often consisted of laboriously pedaling to the top of a hill, followed by a fast, dare-devilish descent. The descent required a low seat position, so the rider could get a foot down to the ground when needed, while the seat was moved back to the normal, higher, position for pedaling uphill.

In the early days of mountain biking, there was also a clever adjusting aid, called Hite-Rite. This connected the binder bolt location with the seatpost under spring tension, as shown in Figs. 17.25 and 17.26, preventing theft and vandalism at the same time as easing adjustment while sitting on the bike. The seat is adjusted by loosening the quick-release binder bolt while applying your

body weight to bring the seat to the desired location, and then flip the quick-release to tighten the binder bolt again.

Lightweight bikes on which the seat height is frequently adjusted sometimes suffer from fatigue-induced cracking of the seat cluster. The cracks form either at the end of the split portion at the back of the seat lug or at the eye, or lug, through which the binder bolt fits. The former problem is minimized by drilling a 3–4 mm ($^{1}/_{8}$–$^{5}/_{16}$ in.) diameter hole at the base of the slot. The second problem can only be eliminated by correct design.

A relatively simple solution used on most aluminum bikes is to separate the clamping function in the form of an external clip that is more easily replaced than a cracked frame. If the clamping action does not work properly, the split end can sometimes be filed out just a little.

It is also possible to do away with adjustment altogether and put the seat in a fixed position at the top of the extended seat tube. This is sometimes done on custom-built bikes intended for time-trialing, saving the weight of a separate seatpost and binder bolt. Obviously, you'd better be very sure about the correct seat height before you buy such a setup.

SEAT HEIGHT

The best way to determine the optimal seat height is to sit on

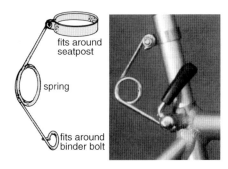

Above: Figs. 17.25 and 17.26. All but forgotten is the Hite-Rite seat height adjusting spring. It was used in the early days of mountain biking to allow quick changes in seat height.

the bike wearing cycling shoes (or other shoes without raised heels) while supported, e.g. holding on to a doorframe. Place the heels on the pedals and pedal back. The correct height is achieved when the legs are fully extended in the pedal-down position, but your pelvis remains steady (i.e. you don't wobble from side to side as you pedal backward). This method even applies to recumbents (although it won't be seat height but seat distance).

This method doesn't work for a bike with a fixed wheel or a coaster brake, because you can't pedal backward. You may want to establish the correct height on another bike, measure the distance between the down-pedal and the seat, and place the seat of the non-freewheeling bike to the same height.

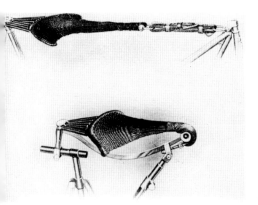

Left: Fig. 17.27. Designed around its comfortable "hammock saddle" was the Pedersen (later called Dursley-Pedersen) bicycle, built from 1897 until 1914. Replicas (of both the bike and the saddle) are built to this day.

Right: Fig. 17.28. Recumbent bikes are a different kettle of fish altogether. This is a typical modern recumbent seat.

18

SUSPENSION SYSTEMS

SINCE THE EARLY 1990s, there has been an accelerated trend toward the integration of suspension systems on bicycles. Nowadays, not only mountain bikes, where many modern systems were first used, but also city bikes, comfort bikes, and even some folding bicycles may have some form of suspension.

Although front suspension can be added to an existing bike by installing a suspension fork, in most cases, it means that the bicycle is designed specifically around a suspension system, Some of the more complex suspension systems result in an entirely different appearance of the bicycle.

Left: Fig. 18.1. Full-suspension bikes, i.e. bikes with suspension both front and rear as shown here, have become quite common in recent years.

Since it is the more common, front suspension will be covered first, followed by a section dealing with rear suspension systems and finally the integration of front and rear suspension into a system.

A well-tuned suspension system does not have to be an energy drain. The underlying concept is somewhat akin to that described for the pneumatic tire: to balance out the forces applied by road unevenness to reduce energy loss as the wheels move around the obstacle without subjecting the weight of the entire bike and rider to the shock impact.

SUSPENSION TERMINOLOGY

What's commonly referred to as suspension really comprises two different, though related, concepts: suspension and damping.

Think of the former as "springiness" and the latter as a way of reducing "bounciness" after the suspension's first response to an impact.

If the fork responds immediately to the slightest bump and then springs right up again, then bobs up-and-down several more times, it has inadequate damping. If it does not respond enough to an impact, it either has too much damping or the spring is too tough for the load. If it "bottoms out" even in response to moderate bumps, the spring element is too weak for the rider's weight.

The most important measure of suspension is called travel—the difference between the compressed and uncompressed state. You want more for downhill racing in rough terrain than for more modest use in urban or touring use.

Two other concepts are preload and stiction. Preload refers to the amount by which the spring element is compressed even before hitting a bump. Stiction is the initial resistance against movement. For rough terrain, you want more stiction than for a bike ridden mainly on relatively smooth paths. Preload should be no more than 25 percent of total travel.

SUSPENSION FORKS

The most common front suspension is by means of a telescoping front fork. The telescoping fork incorporates two sets of tubes that slide inside each other, the inner ones (the stanchion tubes) being guided in the outer ones (called slider tubes) and connected with spring elements. The spring elements are either elastomer pads, metal coil springs, or air cartridges; and different types may be combined on different sides of the same fork. The slider tubes are held at the top and connected with the steerer tube by means of a fork crown, which is referred to as a "triple clamp."

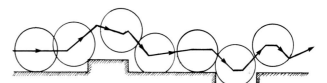

vertical movement of bike without suspension: jolting movements and wheel lifts off

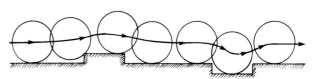

vertical movement of bike with damped suspension: gradual transitions and wheel stays on the ground

Above: Fig. 18.2. Whippet full-suspension bike, 1886. At the time, bikes still had solid rubber tires. After pneumatic tires were introduced, around 1888, suspension were considered no longer needed.

Top right: Fig. 18.3. Suspension should allow the wheels to stay in contact with the ground and reduce the energy loss due to the upward reaction forces as the wheel "climbs" in and out of surface irregularities.

Bottom right: Fig. 18.4. Around 1970, Captain Dan Henry converted his 10-speed to a full-suspension bike of his own ingenious design.

See Fig. 18.6 for the names of the parts of a suspension fork.

Although most suspension forks are indeed "forks" in that they have two legs, one on either side of the front wheel, it is also possible to use a single-blade construction, with the wheel hub anchored one-sided and cantilevered out to one side. Whereas this may be done for aerodynamic reasons on a regular fork, it is done here for purely technical reasons (primarily on some "heavy-duty" downhill bikes).

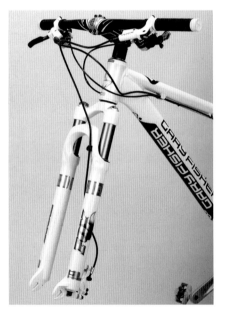

Depending on the specific fork, there may be adjustment devices for any of the following:

❏ Preload, which controls the response rate, i.e. how easy it is to compress the fork;

❏ Damping, i.e. how much it seesaws up and down after compression and release;

❏ Travel, i.e. how far the fork can go down and back up again (this can only be adjusted by opening the fork and replacing its internal parts, and only on certain models);

❏ Rebound rate, i.e. how quickly it recovers after compression.

Left: Fig. 18.5. Front suspension of a hardtail mountain bike with the front wheel removed.

Right: Fig. 18.6. Components of a typical suspension fork.

On different forks, there may be different methods and locations for making these adjustments, mainly depending on the type of spring elements used. By and large, simple forks, as may be found on comfort bikes and low-end mountain bikes, use only elastomer pads for the spring elements and have minimal adjusting options.

Higher-end forks are not only lighter (usually with magnesium alloy stanchions and triple clamp), but also use more sophisticated spring, damping, and adjusting mechanisms. These also tend to have more travel and better responsiveness and damping.

All telescoping forks (as well as most other types) do affect

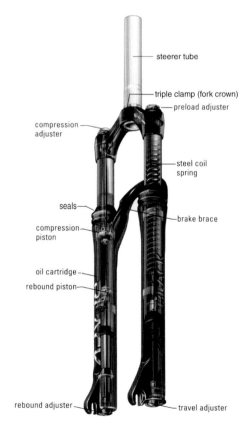

steerer tube

triple clamp (fork crown)
preload adjuster

compression adjuster

steel coil spring

seals

brake brace

compression piston

oil cartridge
rebound piston

rebound adjuster

travel adjuster

TABLE 18.1. COMPARISON OF SUSPENSION FORK SYSTEMS

TYPE	ADVANTAGES	DISADVANTAGES
Elastomer spring and damping	Light, cheap, bottom-out protection	Stiffens up in cold weather, poor damping
Steel coil spring / elastomer damping	Responsive, bottom-out protection, adjustability	More expensive, heavier
Steel coil spring / oil damping	Very responsive, good damping	Heavier, even more expensive
Air suspension / oil damping	Very responsive, good damping, bottom-out protection	Expensive, hard to adjust

the steering somewhat. As the fork arm length is effectively shortened, so is the effective fork rake (the distance over which the fork is offset forward of the steering axis). This results in an increase in trail as the fork is compressed, giving the bike slightly different steering characteristics in compressed than in uncompressed state. For this reason, bikes with very large fork travel, such as downhill bikes, benefit from a steeper steerer angle (which in turn requires less fork rake and results in less change in trail).

It is not impossible to design a suspension fork so that the suspension does not affect trail, as mentioned below under *Other Suspension Forks*.

A desirable feature of most high-quality suspension forks is a suspension lockout adjuster. This allows (temporarily) reducing the amount of travel and "stiffening up" the suspension, which is better for riding uphill. Some rear suspension systems incorporate a similar feature.

TRAVEL AND PRELOAD CHECK

The manufacturer's fact sheet (provided with the fork or available on the Web) states the maximum amount of travel a fork can provide. To get the maximum benefit from that fork, you need to set it up so that you actually use as much of that available travel as possible. To do that, first measure what we call the "active travel," i.e. the amount of compression you achieve under normal riding conditions. To

carry out this test, you need calipers (vernier gauge) and a zip-tie.

Procedure:

1. Strap the zip-tie tightly around the stanchion tube and push it up against the top of the slider tube.

2. Sit on the bike, distributing your weight the same way as you would riding it. This is the passive load and the zip-tie will be pushed down some distance.

3. Get off again and measure the distance between the zip-tie and the top of the slider tube. This distance should be no more than 25 percent of the total available travel (for example, it should not be more than 25 mm (1 in.) on a fork with 100 mm (4 in.) nominal travel).

4. Go for a fast 30-minute ride in the roughest terrain you would typically ride. The zip-tie gets pushed up

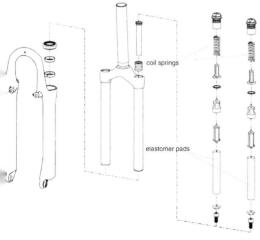

coil springs

elastomer pads

Above: Fig. 18.7. Establishing the effective travel of a suspension fork. (See text for explanation.)

Left: Fig. 18.8. Components of an elastomer-sprung and dampened front fork.

Right: Fig. 18.9. Geometry effect of a raked telescopic suspension fork. (See text for explanation.)

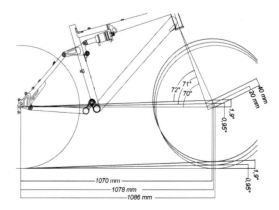

further, and the distance between it and the top of the slider is the fork's active travel. It should be close to the maximum quoted. In fact, it is about right if just once or twice during a demanding ride, you feel the fork bottoming out.

OTHER SUSPENSION FORKS

In addition to the commonly used telescoping type, there are several other types of front suspension, some of which are described in this section and/or in the captions to the accompanying illustrations.

On motorcycles, weight is not so much an issue as it is on most bicycles, and within limits, that also applies to downhill mountain bikes. That allows suspension designers for those bikes more latitude. The main issue is of course that they can (and

must) allow for more travel—up to 20 cm (8 in.) in some cases.

This can be achieved with regular telescoping forks, but of course it raises the frame's head tube much higher off the ground in the uncompressed state. That has led to experiments with other systems, including "up-side-down" telescopes, single-leg telescopes, trailing and leading pivot-link systems, external spring elements, etc.

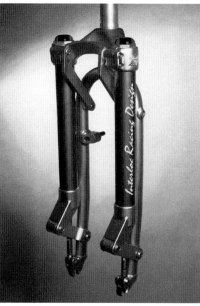

Most of these other systems are rather more intricate than even the most sophisticated telescoping forks. A very nice and quite sophisticated system, that is light in weight as well, is the one found on Alex Moulton's small-wheeled bikes. It is a trailing link system on which the top and bottom pivot links are selected in such a way that the fork's trail does not change as the suspension is activated.

One system that is not so intricate is the one referred to as "Headshok" and found on some Cannondale bikes. It is a single telescoping shock unit installed around the (special) steerer tube, between the lower headset bearing and the fork crown. Its travel is more limited than that of most telescoping forks, and it is rather more maintenance intensive.

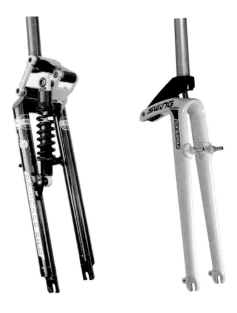

Above: Fig. 18.10. Girvin Proflex swinging-parallelogram front fork for downhill mountain bike use.

Left: Fig. 18.11. Schwinn front suspension fork of the late 1930s. This design leads to extreme changes in fork rake as the fork is compressed.

Right: Figs. 18.12 and 18.13. Another set of forks: GA Force Kilo, for mountain bikes (left), and the SunTour Swing for cyclo-cross bikes (right).

ACTIVE TRAVEL AND PRELOAD ADJUSTMENT

Referring to the information supplied with the fork in question, locate the preload adjuster (usually on top of the slider tubes). Turn it to reduce the preload to the lowest value. Then check the ride to see whether it bottoms out on rebound. If it does, adjust the preload up a little. This will give you the maximum amount of effective travel.

SUSPENSION FORK CHECK

Procedure:

1. Holding the bike firmly at the headset, try to wiggle the bottom of the fork at the forkends. If the fork ends move loosely, you have a problem, which should be referred to a bike shop mechanic.

2. Holding the bike from the front at the handlebars, push down with all your body weight and observe how the suspension fork reacts. If all is well, it goes down with increasing resistance but does not stop suddenly.

3. With the suspension fork pushed in as in step 2, release pressure and observe whether the recovery is smooth and quick.

If any of the criteria above are not met, you may have a problem, and it is recommended you refer it to a bike shop mechanic.

By way of preventive maintenance, the most important thing is to keep the seals and the stanchion tubes clean. Do this once a week and after every ride in wet weather or dusty terrain. With the bike supported from the handlebars and the front wheel lifted off the ground, wipe the seals and the exposed parts of the stanchions away from the seals. Then apply synthetic oil to these parts and push the fork in five times; finally wipe the stanchion tubes clean once more.

In addition, check the suspension fork at least once a season to make sure it is working properly, as described under *Suspension Fork Check.*

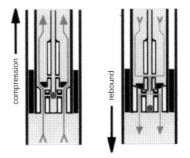

Above: Fig. 18.14. Oil damping principle diagram.

Right: Fig. 18.15. The unequal linkage arrangement of the front suspension on the current version of top-of-the-line Alex Moulton bicycles maintains a constant trail.

REAR SUSPENSION

Over the last two decades, rear suspension bikes have proliferated. Once reserved for downhill mountain bikes, rear suspension can now be found even on some comfort and city bikes as well as folding bikes and recumbents. As with front suspension, there are a number of different ways to achieve suspension of the rear end of the bike.

For the common terminology and general concepts that are common to all forms of suspension, refer to the preceding section, where they were described in conjunction with front suspension technology. Unfortunately, the more sophisticated, the more troublesome the rear suspension is likely to be. The most sophisticated ones, such as those used on downhill mountain bikes, tend to have many linkages and pivot points, which all add up to

potential loose connections, due to wear after some use.

Depending on the type of terrain for which the bike is designed, the amount of travel of the rear suspension can vary from as little as 50 mm (2 in.) to as much as 30 cm (12 in.). Especially for long-travel systems, it is desirable for the rear wheel to follow a straight up-and-down path, rather than a circular arc.

The major categories of rear suspension systems are single-pivot swing arm and multiple-linkage systems. The ideal of straight up-and-down movement of the rear wheel can be approached more easily with the various multi-linkage systems than with the single-pivot system. On the other hand, single-pivot systems are often less

troublesome because the one pivot point is large and therefore more robust than the many individual pivots and linkages on the other type.

From a maintenance standpoint, there are two important things to watch, and they're common on all those different types: the shock unit itself and the pivot points where the different linkage elements rotate relative to the frame and/or each other.

If you don't want to get more involved in rear suspension maintenance, at least keep all these parts clean, and regularly lubricate the pivot points, using a non-greasy, preferably synthetic, lubricant. Afterwards, wipe off any excess lubricant. Also tighten the pivot bolts once a month.

A desirable feature of some rear suspension systems is an inertia valve. It locks out the suspension (or at least stiffens it up) when it encounters a gradual force, such as in response to natural pedaling forces, and releases it when it is subjected to sudden impacts as from bumps in the terrain.

SUSPENSION SEATPOSTS

Some relevant words about these remarkably simple and effective devices are included in the preceding Chapter 17, which deals with general seat and seatpost issues. But you should never combine a suspension seatpost with a "real" rear suspension, because the two systems can counteract one another leading to unpredictable behavior and sometimes damage to the rear suspension system.

INTERACTION OF FRONT AND REAR SUSPENSION

There are a number of different ways to achieve a perfectly

Left and right: Figs. 18.16–18.19. Four different types of rear suspension setup: Santa Cruz (top left); Alex Moulton (bottom left); Specialized (top right); and a Breezer (bottom right).

tuned suspension system. Full-suspension bikes in the price range between $1,000 and $2,000 are usually set up by the manufacturer in a generally agreeable configuration that suits most riders—but without the opportunity to make many personalized adjustments.

For more sophisticated bikes, it is important to buy the bike from a bike shop with employees who understand the subject matter so well that they can set up the bike accurately to your personal needs, both when you first buy it and later as you become more experienced riding it.

In the long run it is preferable to familiarize yourself with the subject matter and learn enough about the physics of the moving bike and its suspension and damping systems to set it up correctly yourself. It is a matter of finding the correct balance between suspension and damping. Unfortunately, those two concepts are only too often confused, so let's try to understand them properly.

Let's look at suspension first. From a physics standpoint, suspension is a method of storing energy. When the wheel encounters an obstacle, the

suspension is pushed in, and the spring element (whether air spring, elastomer pads, or coil spring) is pushed in, storing the energy in the form of "potential energy." If undamped, the spring then would want to release this stored potential energy as soon as possible in the form of kinetic (i.e. movement) energy, making the bike bounce up.

Basically, the suspension isolates the sprung mass (the weight of the rider and the main part of the frame) from the unsprung mass (the wheels and the lower parts of the suspension elements). The unsprung mass should follow the contours of the ground as closely as

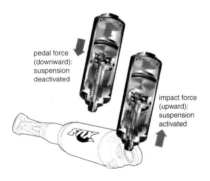

Above: Fig. 18.20. Fox Brain unit, an inertia valve that controls the rear suspension so that it responds to surface jolts without reacting to the rider's pedaling action.

Left: Fig. 18.21. The Rockshox lockout controller lets you control the front suspension lockout "on the fly."

Right: Fig. 18.22. Giant XTC 4-pivot system cleverly keeps the movement of the rear wheel strictly up-and-down.

possible, while the sprung mass should "float" above it with a minimum of jolts.

Two distinct advantages are associated with this separation of sprung and unsprung masses: rider comfort and traction. The well-suspended rider doesn't get knocked about so much, allowing him or her to concentrate on pedaling and steering the bike. Since the wheels closely follow the contours of the ground, the rider's input is immediately translated into reactions from the bike; after all, steering, braking, and accelerating only work when the wheels are actually in contact with the ground, and that is what suspension achieves.

Of particular importance for traction is what's referred to as "sag" (in essence, the amount of travel that is taken up with the rider just sitting on the bike). Sag represents the ability of the suspension to push the wheel back onto the ground when riding through a deep spot or after it has been raised up over a bump. On average, sag should be around 30 percent of total travel. For cross-country competition,

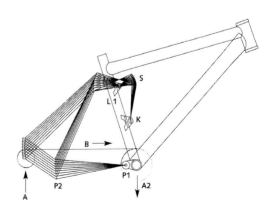

the amount of sag should be around 15 to 20 percent, while for downhill racing rear suspension sag should be as much as 40 percent, due to the forward displacement of the rider's weight on steep downhill sections.

On coil spring suspension units, front or rear, sag is adjusted by selecting a stronger or softer spring and by means of adjusting the amount of preload. The preload adjustment should only be used for fine-tuning within the target zone, and should not replace the selection of the right spring associated with the particular rider weight and the amount of desired sag. You're working with the wrong spring if you have to tighten the preload adjuster on the shock unit by more than five turns to get the amount of desired sag. Select a spring with a higher rating instead (coil springs are rated in lbs/in. and are available in 50 lb/in. increments in the range between 500 and 850 lb/in. for most models). On air-sprung units, sag adjustment is easier because there's no preload, and the spring rate can be adjusted gradually by increasing or decreasing the air pressure.

On most suspension forks, the preload adjuster knobs are located above the fork crown on top of the stanchions. To adjust for the correct amount of sag, first determine the maximum amount of travel.

But first a few words about damping. As mentioned before, a spring functions as an energy-storage device, and once it is moving, it tends to keep bouncing up-and-down. This is where damping comes in: Damping reduces the rebound reaction, and consequently the "bounciness" of the suspension.

On oil-damped units, that is achieved by connecting the two ends of the spring via a piston with one or more small openings that is forced through an oil-filled cylinder. It turns some of that stored energy from the spring into heat. The damper should be set up in such a way that the faster the movement of the spring, the bigger the damping effect.

On most elastomer-sprung forks, the damping is also achieved by means of some configuration of elastomer pads—a cheaper solution that is not as responsive and easy to adjust (a matter of replacing pads and bumpers inside the unit). This method requires little maintenance and is suitable for riders who don't want to bother too much with the mechanics of their bikes.

There are two distinct damping stages: compression phase damping and rebound damping. Compression phase damping slows the reaction when the suspension is pushed in, and rebound damping slows the bouncing back when released. Compression phase damping mainly serves to prevent bottoming out the suspension unit when it is compressed, so it doesn't really contribute much to traction control. Rebound damping, on the other hand, is very important for traction and safety, helping the wheel stay in contact with the ground after the initial impact. If the tire frequently loses contact with the ground, it is usually due to inadequate rebound damping, and the bike will tend to seesaw as it reacts to a bump. If the suspension gets less and less effective during a bumpy ride, it will be due to excessive rebound damping.

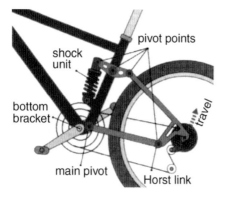

Left: Fig. 18.23. Common features of four-link rear suspension systems.

Right: Fig. 18.24. The Girvin Pro-Flex bikes are some of the designs that use single-pivot rear suspension, which, though less sophisticated, are more rugged than most multiple-link systems.

SUSPENSION FINE-TUNING

Unfortunately, there's not one optimal setting for damping that is best for any type of terrain and any rider. The basic setting to which the bike is adjusted in the bike shop is a good starting point, but beyond that, it is a matter of trial and error. Find a good stretch of varied terrain that will be representative of most of the kind of riding you plan to do. It should contain plenty of the real-life situations you expect to encounter on the trail: rippled surfaces, bigger bumps, gullies, jumps, steep downhill sections, climbing in even and bumpy terrain, compacted, rocky, and loose surfaces, plenty of curves, etc.

Once you've found the right test course, all you need is plenty of energy and determination—and a systematic approach with painstaking record-keeping discipline. First traverse the test stretch a couple of times with the bike set up the way it is. This will establish a point of departure to which you can compare any modifications you

carry out. Once you have a feel for it, make one adjustment, and only one at a time. The best place to start is by first increasing compression stage damping. If it improves the situation, try increasing it a little more, until things start to get worse, and then back off a little until you've found the optimum amount of compression stage damping.

Ideally, the bike should be set up to handle the most typical situations, and that means there will be "extreme" situations when e.g. the suspension "bottoms out." it is best when that happens just once during your traversing of the test circuit. If it doesn't bottom out even once, you've not set it up optimally for the most typical situations; and if it bottoms out several times, you're operating too close to the limit of the suspension's ability to absorb shocks.

Once you've found the optimum setting for compression stage damping, proceed to the next variable, e.g. rebound damping, working in stages the same way as before. An excellent way of establishing a good adjustment to start off with is to simply sit on the bike and let it

roll down a curb, keeping track of the number of times the bike bops up and down afterwards. If just once, you're pretty close to the optimum rebound damping; if it seesaws several times, rebound damping is inadequate and should be increased. Work on this, closing the rebound damping adjuster until it bops up just once. For fine-tuning, go back to the test circuit and work on it until you've found the right setting. There's too much rebound damping if the bike loses traction when traversing "washboard" rippled surfaces, with the suspension getting more and more compressed, and the amount of travel diminishing over time. If, on the other hand, the bike starts to swing out of control on longish surface bumps and dips, like waves, it will be an indication that you've got too little rebound damping.

When doing these various tests, try to retain a kind of balance between the front and the rear suspension; so each time, you should make the same adjustments to the front and rear

Left: Fig. 18.25. This German-built Expedition full-suspension bike has some very sturdy luggage racks that are isolated from road shocks by the suspension system.

Right: Fig. 18.26. Using a tire pump to increase pressure in an air-sprung suspension unit.

units. Usually any undesirable suspension system reactions are due to an uneven distribution between front and rear settings. So keep things even until you've found what seems like a good overall response, and only then try slightly increasing or

decreasing the settings of the front relative to the rear to establish whether this will give your settings the final touch—or until you are convinced that you have arrived at the best balance of suspension and damping.

Once you've set up the bike properly, give yourself enough time to get used to it set up that

Left: Fig. 18.27. Trailtronic is another, this time electronic, system to distinguish between pedaling action and road shock.

way. After a month or so, you will have become so aware of the bike's behavior that you can detect small changes. At this point, decide whether there are certain characteristics you want to fine-tune. If that is the case, go back to the same test circuit and repeat the tests, this time only adjusting what you think you want to improve. Work just as systematically until you're certain you've got the best settings for your current riding style.

SUSPENSION TROUBLESHOOTING

Here's a short list of the most common suspension problems and their solutions. These points apply both to front and rear suspension.

Problem: Suspension dips even on minor bumps and often bottoms out.

Cause/Solution: The spring is too weak. If air-sprung, increase air pressure. Otherwise, replace the coil spring or the elastomer pads by higher rated ones.

Problem: Suspension not responsive enough.

Cause/Solution: The spring is too stiff. If air-sprung, reduce air pressure. Otherwise, replace spring element by a lower rated one.

Problem: Suspension sags more and more as the ride progresses.

Cause/Solution: Insufficient recovery, or rebound. Adjust the rebound adjuster until the bike absorbs fast, repetitive impacts without loss of stability.

Problem: Suspension stiffens up progressively as the ride progresses.

Cause/Solution: Too much compression stage damping. Adjust for less compression stage damping.

Problem: Unequal responsiveness between front and rear suspension.

Cause/Solution: Non-compatible spring elements front and rear. Choose fork and rear shock with similar amounts of travel. You may be able to replace the front fork spring elements by ones with more (or less) travel.

Problem: Unpredictable behavior of rear end of the bike while turning.

Cause/Solution: Remove the shock unit and check for resistance. If it feels too soft, have it overhauled or replaced.

19

LIGHTING SYSTEMS

O F ALL BICYCLE ACCESSORIES, lighting equipment is probably the most important: lighting defects (or missing lights) are the only technical defects that cause a significant percentage of all serious bicycle accidents. Fortunately, probably no other bicycle component has seen more dramatic improvement over the last quarter century than lighting equipment

LIGHTING SYSTEMS OVERVIEW

There are four general types of bicycle lights in use today:

❏ battery lights with built-in batteries in the light unit;

❏ Battery lights with separate, central battery;

❏ Generator (dynamo) lights;

❏ Hybrid systems, using a generator and a battery back-up.

In the U.S. and England, battery lighting has been used almost exclusively in the past, while generator lighting has always

been more common on the European continent. However, many of today's city and comfort bikes available in the U.S. also rely on generator lighting systems.

From a practical standpoint, generator lighting should be taken more seriously than it usually is. Its great advantage is that

Right: Fig. 19.1. Technically, bicycle lighting may have come a long way over the last 120 years or so, but aesthetically, today's high-tech lights are no match for the old oil lantern.

it is always available when you need it—no need to make sure the batteries are charged or that you have proper spares with you. That's especially important for those who use their bikes frequently but not only for fixed-schedule commuting.

LIGHTING SYSTEM TYPES

The following sections provide information that is specific to the three different types of lighting systems that are used on the modern bicycle.

LIGHTS WITH BUILT-IN BATTERIES

These systems rely on separate light units for the front and the rear of the bike. The headlight, in the front, is usually clamped directly or indirectly to the handlebars, or in England often to a clip on the fork. In the rear, they

attach either to the seatpost or e.g. to a luggage rack or the seatstays. Usually, there's a clamp that stays on the handlebars once installed and the light just slides and clips into this clamp, so you can remove it when you leave the bike unguarded.

The taillight, or rear light, should be red, and point straight back (neither up nor down, neither left nor right). The rear light does not need to be quite so bright as the one in front. Especially for taillights, LEDs appear to be very suitable, mainly because they provide much longer battery life and do not need to be as powerful as the light in the front of the bike. The LEDs themselves also last much longer than light bulbs—however, they don't last forever either, and the light should be replaced if they, or individual LEDs in a multi-LED array, become dim.

The most common maintenance required on battery lights

is replacing the batteries and the bulbs. A battery charge typically lasts less than 4 hours, so it is a good idea to carry spares (and especially if you use rechargeable ones, recharge them at least once a month). Before you go on a longer ride that may take you into darkness (even if not planned), check the condition of both the batteries in the light and the spare batteries.

LIGHTS WITH CENTRAL BATTERY

These lighting systems are typically more powerful and often have high beam and low beam capabilities. Their larger battery, consisting of several cells wired up together, is either packaged in a pouch tied to the bike or neatly packed away in something that fits in a water bottle cage (actually, a real water bottle is often used, with the battery cells inserted and the space around them filled with some kind of compound to keep everything in place).

Again, the batteries and the bulbs need to be checked and

Above, left, and right: Figs. 19.2–19.4. The three types of lighting system: self-contained battery powered (above), generator-powered (left), and central-battery-powered (right) bicycle lights.

replaced if necessary (although the batteries are almost always rechargeable, in which case you just plug the unit in via its recharging adapter, which usually does the trick in about 2 hours). In addition to NiCad and NiMH batteries, there are still some models that use lead-acid gel batteries. The latter require different care: they have to be recharged *before* they are fully discharged, i.e. before the light gets dim, whereas the other types last longest if they are drained completely before they are recharged. See the preceding section *Battery Lights With Built-In Battery* for more information regarding spare bulbs and batteries.

In addition to bulbs and batteries, there is wiring to deal with. So, if the light doesn't work and you've checked the bulb and the battery, and found them to be OK, check the wiring. Usually it is a connection at the end of the wiring, so check there first and fix it with a soldering iron and solder. If there are any

exposed metal wire parts, use electrical insulating tape to fix it. You may have to replace the wiring completely if you can't identify the source of the problem.

GENERATOR LIGHTS

This type of lighting system also has a central power source and wiring connecting it to the light—either just a headlight or both a headlight and a taillight.

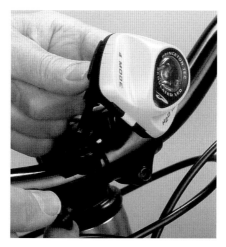

Above: Fig. 19.5. Installation of a typical modern high-output self-contained battery light with LED.

Usually, the electricity is carried by a single wire and returned to the generator via the metal of the bike, for which purpose each part—generator, front light, and rear light—has a pinch-screw to make what's called a mass contact.

It is also possible (and less trouble-prone) to use double, or two-pole, wiring instead of relying on mass contacts. In that case, the connections are made with little two-prong plugs and sockets.

It is important to match the generator output wattage to the bulbs used. If the generator is rated for 3 W at 6 V, it is intended for use with both a headlight and a taillight, rated at 2.4 W and 0.6 W respectively. If you use a separate battery-operated rear light, the headlight bulb should be upgraded to one that is rated at 6 V 3 W.

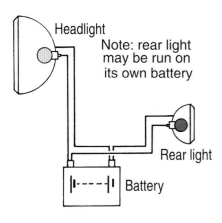

Left: Fig. 19.6. Schematic diagram of lighting system with central battery. Although the rear light is shown hooked up to the battery as well here, it is more common to use a separate self-contained battery light for the rear light.

Right: Fig. 19.7. Schematic diagram of generator-powered lighting system. While a tire-sidewall generator is depicted here, many systems now use a hub generator instead.

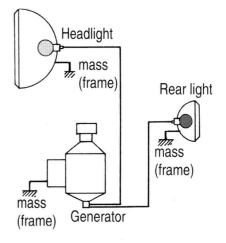

LIGHTING SYSTEM COMPONENTS

This section introduces the various components used for lighting systems. Further details can be found in the section that follows, which deals with the various systems.

BATTERY TYPES

If you use rechargeable batteries, note the difference between the two most common types. As rechargeable replacement batteries for standard-size cells, only NiCad (Nickel-Cadmium) and NiMH (Nickel-Metal-Hydride) are available. NiMH batteries last considerably longer but are more expensive. However, they're worth the extra money, because they also have a longer shelf life

Top left: Fig. 19.8. Halogen front light for Schmidt hub generator system, with an optimized light-bundling reflector-and-lens system.

Center left: Fig. 19.9. Cat-Eye three-LED light system with central battery.

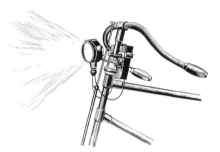

Right and above: Figs. 19.10 and 19.11. Electric bicycle lighting has been around for a while: 1886 tire-sidewall generator, by Weber (left) and an 1895 illustration of an electric headlight in use.

Bottom left: Fig. 19.12. The "guts" of an LED light. Unlike conventional incandescent bulbs, most of the energy is not turned into heat but into light.

(i.e. they will hold a charge much longer when not used).

BULBS AND LEDS

Incandescent (i.e. conventional) bicycle light bulbs typically don't last more than about 100 hours of use, due to running very hot (to maximize their light output) and abuse by road shocks and vibrations on the bike. Get some spare bulbs and carry one for each light on the bike, e.g. in the tire patch kit. If the system uses halogen bulbs (which are brighter than conventional bulbs), don't touch the glass with your bare hands, because the acidity will etch the glass dull, reducing their light output once they get hot.

In recent years, there has been significant development in the field of LED lights. LEDs with outputs of 1 Watt and even more challenge all but the most

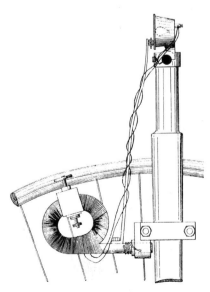

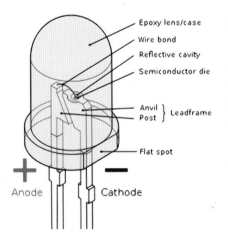

Epoxy lens/case
Wire bond
Reflective cavity
Semiconductor die

Anvil } Leadframe
Post

Flat spot

+   **—**
Anode   Cathode

powerful halogen lights. A 1-Watt LED is about as bright as a 3-Watt halogen light, resulting in increased battery life. Less powerful LEDs also have their place, especially for rear lights. In flashing mode, their batteries will last 100 hours or more (less when burning constantly, but still much longer than with standard bulbs)—and they are more visible in flashing mode. LEDs also have a much longer life expectancy than either conventional or halogen bulbs.

Many LED lights use several LEDs instead of a single one with more output. This is done because it is much more expensive to make one high-output LED than several smaller ones. The use of several LEDs complicates the reflector and/or lens design, because a single light source is easier to focus and bundle correctly than a combination of several sources.

LIGHT OUTPUT

Regardless of the type of lighting system used, the headlight

should be bright and produce a compact bundle of light that should be aimed at an area of the road about 6–9 meters (20–30 ft.) in front of the bike. Optimizing the light bundle is a surprisingly complicated issue, which some manufacturers have mastered better than others.

The British battery light standard defines the most desirable output bundling that can be achieved while still minimizing required light output and electricity consumption (read battery life). In modern days, most manufacturers have solved the problem by just throwing ever more power at it, resulting in lights that blanket the road with a pretty wide swath of light. This approach may be OK, but a bit wasteful, both in terms of initial investment (think $400 light

setups) and electric consumption, which at those output levels can only be available for a short time from a battery that doesn't weigh a ton.

GENERATORS

A generator, or dynamo, is a device that converts mechanical energy into electrical energy. Unfortunately, it usually does this rather inefficiently. Whereas an efficiency of 70% should be easy to achieve, most dynamos do not surpass 20—30%, meaning that 10—15 watts of mechanical output has to be produced by the rider to keep a 3 watt system operating. To put it into perspective: you'll be wasting 20—30% of the output required to keep a bike moving at 16 km/h (10

Above and right: Figs. 19.13–19.15. Three types of generators: tire-sidewall (above), bottom-bracket-mounted (top right), and hub generator (bottom right).

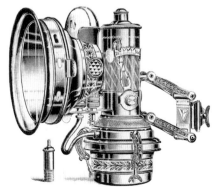

Left: Fig. 19.16. The most common form of lighting in the early days was the acetylene lamp, shown here in a 1909 illustration.

mph). Fortunately, modern hub generators are significantly more efficient than the run-of-the-mill, although even these waste more energy than they should.

There are three different types of generators:

❏ tire-wall, or side-mounted, generators;

❏ bottom-bracket mounted generators;

❏ hub generators.

By and large, hub generators are the most energy-efficient, turning one watt of power input into more electric power than the other models.

They also tend to have more sophisticated voltage control, resulting in a more stable light that is reasonably bright even at low cycling speeds without getting so bright at higher speeds that the bulbs burn out prematurely. The optimal output curve is shown in Fig. 20.18. In this graph, the non-shaded area defines the range within which the output

voltage should remain. The graph is based on a 6-volt system.

TIRE-SIDEWALL-MOUNTED GENERATORS

Side-mounted, or tire-wall, generators are still the most common and cheapest. The safest place for the generator is on the rear wheel, where accidental loosening does not impose the risk of a serious accident as much as it does in the front. Even so, keep it tightened properly. It should be mounted so that the longitudinal centerline points to the center of the hub.

Here too, the most common problem, other than burned-out

Above: Fig. 19.17. Luggage-rack-mounted rear light with integrated large reflector.

Left: Fig. 19.18. Generator output curve requirements. (See text for explanation.)

Right: Fig. 10.19. The tire-sidewall generator should be aligned as shown here.

bulbs, is wiring failure. Especially the point where the wires connect to the dynamo is subject to accidental disconnection. Check it frequently and be careful to route your wire in such a way that it is not likely to get caught when e.g. storing or parking the bike. There are two generator-specific problems: slip and mass connections.

❏ To prevent slip, which is most common in wet weather, make sure the generator is aligned as shown in Fig. 20.19, and with the roller running on a rubber part of the tire, rather than the almost bare sidewall of a skinny tire on the one hand or the thick "knobbies" on a mountain bike tire on the other.

❏ Mass connections are pinch screws that connect one side of the lights and of the generator to the metal of the bike's frame. They sometimes don't make a good contact, and you can restore the contact by loosening and

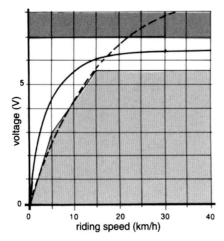

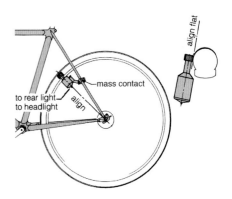

re-tightening the pinch screws.

BOTTOM BRACKET GENERATORS

Bottom-bracket-mounted, or roller, generators rub against the rear tire from underneath the chainstays. With the rotor supported between two bearings instead of pivoting from a single bearing, they tend to be more efficient than side-mounted generators. Usually, there is not enough room to install this type of generator on a bike with short chainstays, such as any modern road bike.

However, these generators must be installed in what is probably the messiest place on any bike, they are notorious for slippage problems in wet weather. You can increase the spring force by tying a little bungee cord between the roller mount and a fixed point on the bike close to the rear wheel axle.

HUB GENERATORS

Built into the front wheel, these devices not only aren't subject to slipping, they are also more efficient than regular tire-driven generators. They do cause a little extra drag (barely perceptible) even when the light is not switched on. When the light is turned on, they still have significantly less drag than other types of generators.

Unfortunately they are also significantly more expensive and require rebuilding the wheel. For that reason, they are mainly found pre-installed on certain bicycle models (mainly city and comfort bikes, as well as E-bikes). Hub-generator systems invariably use double wiring.

RETRO-REFLECTORS

In the U.S., and a rapidly increasing number of other countries, a

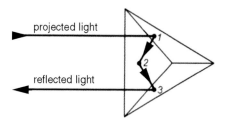

whole plethora of reflectors (more correctly called retro-reflectors) is currently prescribed—in some countries only when the bike is sold, in others when the bike is operated in the dark, and in some countries even by daylight. Reasonable though it may seem to require all those reflectors, the assumptions on which this type of requirement is based is totally unscientific.

The only reflector that is of any use is the one mounted in the rear facing straight back (although pedal reflectors may be a useful supplement, on account of their movement). All other reflectors do not serve any purpose that is not better met by other forms of lighting equipment. The two things to keep in mind with reflectors—more correctly called retro-reflectors—is that they are only visible to those whose headlights are directly aimed at them. Of course they also do not help the cyclist see any better, whereas lights are visible from a wide arc, and help the cyclist see his way and anything in his path.

Only a headlight can protect the cyclist from running into obstacles *and* being visible to approaching or crossing drivers and

Left, above, and right: Figs. 19.20–19.22. The difference between a retro-reflector and a mirror (left); the way a retro-reflector prism works (above); and why a flat reflector is more effective than one divided into three panels (right). (See text for additional explanations.)

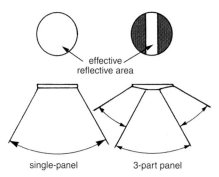

pedestrians. An additional white reflector does not help one bit (if the headlight does not work, the cyclist should not be riding in the dark).

To traffic approaching from side roads ahead, again only the headlight is visible. Spoke reflectors and reflecting tire sidewalls remain invisible to those who could endanger the cyclist, because the crossing driver's headlight is not aimed at them until it is too late. From the rear, either a rear light or a reflector aimed straight back gives adequate protection. All drivers approaching the cyclist have headlights that are aimed straight at the reflector, which lights up brightly.

Totally inept is the concept of dividing the rear reflector into three smaller panels aimed under angles offset to the left and the

right, as shown in Fig 20.17. Drivers whose lights are aimed at the bike under the angles to the sides are not on a collision course with the cyclist, so they do not need to see him: they will cross the point where the cyclist is now—but the cyclist will be gone by then.

There are a few points to consider in the selection and maintenance of reflectors. In the first place, bigger is better: larger reflectors are more visible than smaller ones, all else being equal (that is the reason why it is a bad idea to divide the rear reflector into three panels, only one of which faces back). Secondly,

Above: Fig. 10.23. An LED rear light for installation around a seat stay. Like a reflector, it must be kept firmly installed and aimed properly straight back.

Left: Fig. 19.24. Rear end with rear light and reflector on a utility bike from Gazelle.

lighter colored reflectors are more visible than darker ones. Amber reflects about twice as much of the light as red. Consequently, amber reflectors should be selected for the rear wherever it is legal to do so (the argument that it might be confused for a side-reflector is invalid, because lateral movement distinguishes side reflectors unambiguously from those mounted in the front or the rear).

As for maintenance, reflectors only do their job properly when they are kept clean: wash them regularly with plenty of water. However, if water should leak inside the reflector, it condenses on the inside, making the reflector virtually blind. For this reason, a cracked or broken reflector should be replaced immediately. To check a reflector's operation, aim a light at it from a distance of 10 m (33 ft), observing from a point close to the light source whether the reflector appears to light up brightly. But if your eye is too far from the straight path between the light source and the reflector, you will not notice the retro-reflection.

20 LOAD CARRYING EQUIPMENT

WHAT ONE NEEDS in the way of luggage carrying equipment varies widely with the load to be carried. For significant loads, the most common solution is on a luggage rack mounted over the rear wheel. However, there are actually quite a number of different solutions to the load carrying dilemma, which are covered in this chapter:

❏ luggage racks and panniers

❏ handlebar bags and supports

❏ saddle bags and supports

❏ rear frame extension systems

❏ trailers and sidecars

❏ custom-made carrier bikes

load-carrying components of the bicycle, rather than as mere accessories. Consequently, they should be designed, constructed and attached with the same considerations in mind as the major components of the bike. The support stays should run straight to their mounting points and must be firmly attached. Additional stays should be triangulated in such a way that lateral rigidity is achieved. The illustrations show some satisfactory racks for front and rear and a stay arrangement that achieves adequate lateral rigidity.

LUGGAGE RACKS AND PANNIERS

Luggage racks are available for the front and the back of the bike. They should be regarded as

Right: Fig. 20.1. 1920s carrier bicycle, with the load between the wheels for greatest stability.

The racks should be shaped to properly support the bags that are carried and they need to be firmly attached to the bike. They should allow the bags to be firmly attached and prevent them from shifting either sideways toward the wheel or back or forth toward the rider. Straight support stays from the front and the back to the wheel axle are not enough to support a bag, so an additional lateral frame running below the rack along the length of the bag will be required. Another important detail for a rear rack is a restraint on the top platform to stop the load from pushing against the rear brake

As important as the construction of the racks themselves is their location and mounting arrangement on the bike. From a stability standpoint, the most favorable load distribution is as shown in the middle detail of Fig. 20.2. Thus, the front rack

should be designed so that the load can be carried low and in line with the steering axis (i.e. just behind the front wheel axle). The rear rack should carry the load as far forward as possible—attempts to lower the load invariably also require it to be placed further back for heel clearance, which deteriorates the bike's handling.

Probably the finest material for racks is tubular steel with a diameter of at least 7 mm. Since this kind of construction is rather labor-intensive, with lots of brazed joints, most racks are made of aluminum alloy rod. It should have a diameter of at

least 6 mm, while racks made of steel rod may use material that is only about 4.5 mm in diameter. Recently, tubular aluminum racks have also become available, but their durability has not yet been convincingly demonstrated.

For moderate loads, there are racks that are attached to the seatpost. These racks may either have a bolted attachment or they may be clamped around the seatpost by means of a quick-release mechanism, making them easy to install and remove. Most are only suitable for top-mounted packs not exceeding about 8 kg (15 lbs.). Usually designed for use on

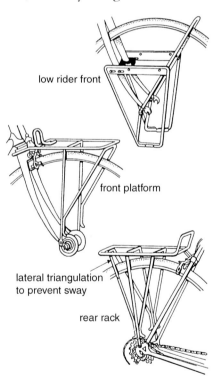

low rider front

front platform

lateral triangulation to prevent sway

rear rack

Above: Fig. 20.3. Seatpost-mounted rack with pannier supports.

Left: Fig. 20.4. To check the loaded bike, shake it at the front end to find out whether bike and luggage sway out of control.

Right: Fig. 20.5. A sampling of luggage racks for front and rear mounting.

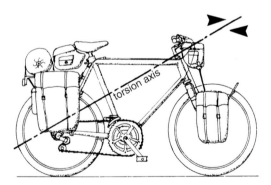

torsion axis

Right: Fig. 20.2. Back in the mid-1970s, Jim Blackburn tested various loading configurations. He found that the one shown in the middle offers the best stability.

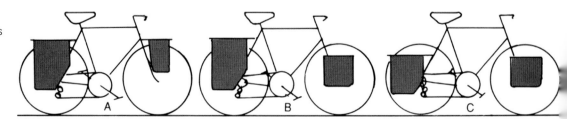

A   B   C

standard 27.2 mm diameter seatposts, they can be adapted to installation on smaller diameter seatposts by means of a neoprene sleeve. In either case, it is critical to make sure the clamp is very tight, requiring significant hand force on the quick-release lever to open or close.

Some seatpost-mounted racks have side frames that allow the use of small pannier-type bags as well. Topeak makes a racktop bag with side pockets that can be opened up to form panniers for this type of rack.

Anything tied to the luggage racks should preferably be secured with a firm webbing strap rather than a conventional hooked bungee cord, because the latter are prone to get caught in the spokes, potentially leading to an accident. Meanwhile, some rack manufacturers avoid such problems by equipping the racks with permanently attached bungee-like devices that do not rely on hooks.

PANNIERS

Panniers are bags that are attached on either side of a luggage rack. There is a wide variety of materials and sizes available. Probably the most durable are those made of traditional materials such as canvas or ducking, sewn with cotton thread. When the material of these bags gets wet, the fibers swell up and close up any gaps that would let in rain water.

Presumably waterproof "modern" materials, on the other hand, almost always leak at the seams. Exceptions are bags made of tough plastic-coated material with welded seams (as opposed to sewn seams). This construction is borrowed from water-sports equipment, and even the closures are often truly waterproof, using a roll-up technique.

The bags must include hardware to attach them securely on the luggage rack, well away from the turning wheel, the rider's feet, or any other moving part of the bike. On rear panniers, the front should be cut back to allow heel clearance when pedaling.

As for mounting the bags, it is preferable to mount them as far forward as possible without interfering with the rider's foot. That usually means they should be mounted rather high, rather than low. French touring cyclists to this day can't believe that, thinking that the bike is better balanced if the bags are low to the ground. That works if the bike has very long seatstays, but not for standard bikes of any type available today—including dedicated touring bikes.

Front panniers are essentially smaller versions that can be attached to the front rack. In the front it is more important than in the rear that the mass center of the load is close to the wheel axle, and for this reason so-called "low-rider" racks provide the best mounting position for the front

Above: Fig. 20.6. Tubus tubular steel rear rack.

Left: Fig. 20.7. Delta panniers for installation on a seatpost-mounted rack.

Right: Fig. 20.8. Moots Tailgator seatpost-rack bag and support frame.

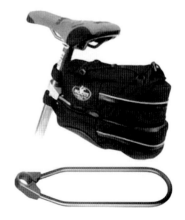

bags. Make sure they are attached in such a way that they do not sway sideways, because that would greatly affect the steering and balancing of the bike.

As for loading the panniers and other luggage, it is OK to put as much weight in the front as in the back, assuming low-rider racks are used in the front. Consequently, small, heavy items should go in front, while bulkier items should go in the back. It is preferable to balance the load between the left and right side. A balanced load does not sway as long as the panniers and their contents are firmly attached through a rigid rack to the bike frame (as they should be). It is almost certainly better from a fatigue and safety standpoint for the rider to be vertical than constantly leaning to one side, as would be necessary if the load is not balanced.

HANDLEBAR BAGS AND SUPPORTS

Small loads can conveniently be carried in a bag attached to the handlebars. Because of its location there, these bags should be carefully selected and installed to prevent interference with the steering and operation of the controls.

Bags that just dangle off the handlebars without any additional support are not suitable for serious use. The bag should be supported either by a U-shaped bracket that wraps around the bag and clips around the handlebars and stem, or by means of a solid frame built into the bag and clipped into a

Above: Fig. 20.9. Individual low-rider frames. Unlike other models, these do not come with a brace that connects the two sides but each side is clamped to the fork-end and the fork blade only.

Left: Fig. 20.10. Home made 3-sided package support with great flexibility for carrying anything bulky.

Right: Fig. 20.11. Bailey Works insulated front bag on a bag support frame.

matching clip support permanently attached to the handlebars.

If the bag is supported by a U-shaped bracket, it will be helpful if it is also tied down with straps running down to the front wheel axle or so me other point on the fork. It is critical to make sure that any bungee cords used for this should not get caught in the spokes of the wheel.

SADDLE BAGS AND SUPPORTS

The traditional way to carry loads used by English touring cyclists in the past used to be a saddle bag. Mounted behind the rider, it puts the weight in the most neutral position on the bike from a weight-distribution standpoint. In that position, it also does not add significantly to the aerodynamic drag. They are attached to eyelets in the back of the saddle, with one additional strap around the seatpost.

Saddle bags are still available from a few specialty suppliers, in sizes up to 24 liters (6 u.s. gal.), and they can carry up to 16 kg (35 lbs). The main problem these

days is that it has become hard to find suitable saddles to carry them. You need a saddle with metal eyelets in the back, where the bags are attached with short leather straps. The only saddles designed for that are the very expensive and rather heavy (and rather hard) Brooks leather touring saddles.

A gadget is available to convert a saddle without eyelets to carry a saddlebag. Basically, it is a metal strap mounted laterally to the back of the saddle rails, with eyelets for the bag's straps.

For large, heavily loaded bags, there are also supports that lift the bag up to prevent them from interfering with the rear wheel and/or the rear brake. These are usually mounted from the seatpost.

OTHER SYSTEMS

There are a number of other ways to carry luggage on a bicycle, and

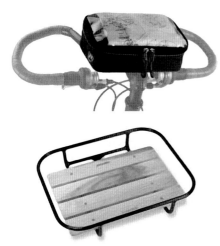

a few of those will be briefly described in the following sections.

REAR FRAME EXTENSION SYSTEMS

The load-carrying capacity of a conventional bicycle can be significantly increased if the rear wheel is placed further back. Indeed bikes designed for touring usually have longer chainstays (and of course, as a result also longer seatstays), placing less of the load behind the rear wheel

Above: Fig. 20.12. Wedge-shaped saddle bag for minor items. Traditional English large saddle bags, which require attachment to a heavy-duty saddle with eyelets, are also still available.

Top left: Fig. 20.13. Top-mount handlebar bag. It also fits on most regular handlebars.

Bottom left: Fig. 20.14. Front tray for large items. Fixed to the frame, it does not negatively affect the steering.

Right: Fig. 20.15. XtraCycle is an extension that can be attached to any hardtail bike to increase the bike's wheelbase and offer lots of carrying capacity.

axle. This concept is taken a step further by something called XtraCycle: a frame extension with a luggage rack that brings the rear wheel back by as much as 30 cm (12 in.).

XtraCycle first showed up around 2000 outside the Interbike bicycle trade show: a couple of teenage guys with what looked like skateboards attached to the back of their bikes. Although the concept seemed to be sound, nobody at the show took them seriously, and most of us were surprised that they were back a few years later with a booth of their own. Meanwhile, they have expanded their business to offer quite a variety of products based on their frame extension, including a complete long-wheelbase bike (that can be converted back a to "regular" bike).

TRAILERS AND SIDECARS

Bicycle trailers and sidecars have been around for a long time, and in recent years they have made a bit of a comeback. In the U.S.,

Burley has long been supplying trailers that can easily be attached to almost any bike, either at the seatpost or at the rear wheel axle. Several other manufacturers also offer similar devices.

A special case is the single-wheel trailer, designed purely for luggage, and considered by many touring cyclists as the best way to go. Their advantage is that they leave the bike itself essentially unencumbered. Known in France since before the Second World War, they were copied by an American manufacturer under the name BOB. Although early models suffered many failures, the current offering is

reputed to be quite reliable. Some models even include a suspension, which promises to significantly improve both handling and durability.

Another possibility for carrying loads is by means of a sidecar. They're not very common, but several manufacturers have introduced such devices in recent years. For transporting a child, they have the advantage that rider and passenger can communicate. The problem, of course, is that the combination of bike and sidecar becomes rather wide (though still a lot narrower than any car) and cumbersome to handle, park, or carry.

Fig. 20.16. 1934 sidecar that is pivoted so that the contents stays upright, while the wheel tilts with the bike.

LUGGAGE AND AERODYNAMIC DRAG

A touring cyclist can spend a lot of time fighting the wind. Consequently, it's not unreasonable to try and minimize aerodynamic drag. The effect of luggage dangling off the bike is quite significant and can be reduced by carefully selecting and mounting the various bags.

All bags, regardless of their mounting position, should preferably be compactly packed and smooth-contoured. Too many side pockets and loose straps may not seem like a big thing, but due to interference drag, they significantly affect the overall aerodynamics of the bike.

One surprising advantage of low front panniers is that the

bicycle may become slightly more aerodynamic. The front panniers are positioned in front of the rider's shins, ankles, and feet, adding little frontal area but diverting air away from the aerodynamically messy pedaling going on behind them.

Rear panniers, usually larger, extend a bit more into the airstream at the sides, but are partially shielded by the rider's legs. Though they probably have little effect on the drag coefficient, at least rear panniers do not add much to frontal area. Saddlebags and rack trunks are usually completely out of the airstream.

Probably the least drag are provided by saddle bags and rack top bags. Compactly packed and high-mounted rear

panniers are next. Although not very comfortable in the long run, a backpack carried on the rider's back is also an aerodynamically sound choice.

And then there is the rider him- or herself. Wearing tight-fitting cycle clothing really does cut down the aerodynamic drag compared to wearing loose fitting casual wear. Another factor is the rider's position on the bike: you will suffer less resistance if you keep your profile low in a semi-crouched position, rather than fully upright position. You can always straighten up when the scenery gets very pretty or bend down further when the headwind gets too severe.

Sidecars are universally attached at or near the rear wheel axle, being clamped around the chainstay. They are designed so that only their attachment frame tilts with the bike, while the sidecar itself remains horizontal.

CARRIER BIKES

it is not impossible to carry significant amount of luggage on a bicycle, as was adequately demonstrated by the Viet Cong during the Vietnam war. But even more can be carried on a machine that is specially designed for the purpose. The history of the bicycle includes a plethora of examples of this. But even today, the carrier bike is not dead; if anything, there's been a renaissance of such machines. Several such examples were shown in the illustrations in this chapter and in Chapter 2.

The load can either be carried over the front wheel, over the rear wheel, or somewhere in between. For a front-carrier, it is advantageous if the front wheel size is reduced. Although few

machines of this type are very sophisticated, it would seem desirable to add some front wheel suspension if the load is carried that way.

In order not to effect the steering negatively, it will be best to keep the steering separated from the load. Thus, the load platform or container should be rigidly attached to the frame tubes, not to the fork.

If carried over the rear wheel, the bicycle's wheelbase should be increased to avoid the forward imbalance and to maximize load-carrying capacity. Here too, the addition of a small amount of suspension, even if it has only about 2.5 cm (1 in.) of travel would make it possible to carry heavy loads without excessive strain on uneven road surfaces.

It is also possible to carry the load between the wheels. The Long John, a Danish design now

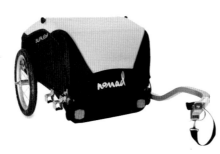

also available from U.S. frame builders, is an example of such a configuration. In this case, the bike has to have indirect steering, to bring the handlebars close enough to the rider.

The greater mass of bike, rider, and load suggests that the brakes should be particularly powerful, and both direct-pull brakes and disk brakes seem to be well-suited for this application. As for the drivetrain, it should be geared low enough to overcome the bike's higher momentum when starting off and when climbing hills. With the higher torque resulting, a heavier-duty chain, probably a $1/8$ in. wide one, should be installed with matching wider chainring and sprocket(s).

The load-carrying capacity of a cycle can be significantly increased if three wheels are used instead of two. That subject is explored more thoroughly in Chapter 26, which is devoted to cycles with more (or even less) than two wheels.

Above: Fig. 20.17. Burley Nomad bicycle trailer.

Left: Fig. 20.18. Bakfiets longjohn-type cargo bicycle from Holland.

Right: Fig. 20.19. Cargo-Lite carrier bike with the load over the front wheel.

21

OTHER ACCESSORIES

Although there is little doubt that an uncluttered bike is the more enjoyable one to ride on a sunny day, circumstances often dictate a need for one accessory or another. In this chapter, we deal with those other accessories that were not covered in Chapters 19 (lights) and 20 (luggage carriers).

Left: Fig. 12.1. The accessorized bicycle. In some societies, this kind of machine, with all its bells and whistles, is considered a normal bike. Most of the accessories on this machine are indeed useful, though not for every kind of bicycle use.

ACCESSORY CRITERIA

The first rule of accessory selection should be "if you don't really need it, don't buy it." It not only saves a lot of money, but also potential frustration.

As regards selection and maintenance of accessories, the most important advice is to select only items that can be firmly attached to the bike and are in themselves structurally sound. Basically, everything that is not attached in at least two points will tend to come loose, although very light items may be clamped less firmly—but only if they are held very close to the member they are attached to.

Simply clamped items are likely to slip down along the tubes of the frame if they are not specially secured. This problem will be avoided if the manufacturer has supplied a neoprene or other plastic sleeve to fit around the bike's frame tube. If not, you can stick a patch from the tire patch kit around the location where the accessory will be mounted, as shown in Fig. 21.2. Use rubber solution on the tube just as though you were patching a tube. It will prevent not only slip, but also damage to the frame. The same effect cannot be achieved by means of self-adhesive tape (e.g. handlebar tape), because this tends to slip because the adhesive never hardens enough to form a permanent bond.

For accessories that should be easily removed from the bike, be it because they are not always needed or to avoid theft, it is often possible to make some kind of quick-release attachment. In cases where this is not practical, it is still possible to ease installation or removal by means of e.g. wing bolts, which may be made by soldering a sizeable washer in the slot of a screw bolt per Fig. 21.3, if not commercially available in the right size.

Remove any removable accessories, such as water bottles, lights, computer, whenever you transport the bike, and even when you leave it unattended.

PUMPS

There are two types of bicycle pumps. For workshop use, we suggest using a big floor pump with an integrated pressure gauge, making sure it has a connector for the kind of valves on your bike (Schrader and Presta valves each require a different nipple, while Woods, or Dunlop, valves can be inflated with the same connector as the one designed for Presta valves).

For on-the-road use, get a frame-mounted pump that can be installed along one of the bike's frame tubes, again with the appropriate connection for the valves on your bike. With their relatively small volume, frame pumps should be of the kind without connector hose, because too much air gets trapped

in the hose to allow adequate inflation of high-pressure tires.

Instead of the frame pump, there are also "mini pumps," very small hand pumps that are small enough to fit in a jersey pocket or a small bag on the bike. They take a lot more time and effort to inflate a tire than a regular frame pump.

In recent years, the pump is being edged out by devices with CO₂ cartridges. Though small and handy, they are rather wasteful, especially considering their volume is inadequate to fully inflate even one set of mountain bike tires. And if you get a second flat, or merely fail to seat the cartridge properly on the valve, you're sunk, whereas pumps always have a ready air supply.

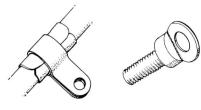

Above: Figs. 21.2 and 21.3. A sleeve between a clip and a frame tube, both for protection of the paint and to prevent slip (left); a home-made wing-bolt for easy installation and removal of accessories.

Left: Fig. 21.4. Make sure any accessories are securely fastened.

Right: Fig. 21.5 and 21.6. Floor pump (top) and mini pump (bottom).

LOCKS

Unfortunately, the lock is one of the most essential accessories. And even the best are inadequate to keep pace with the developing means to crack them. As a minimum, lock the frame and both wheels together with a fixed object big enough so it cannot be lifted off. The familiar U-lock, though not completely foolproof, is generally the most satisfactory. Use a bracket to attach it to the top tube or the seat tube of the frame.

Practical European-style locks have finally found their way to the United States and are often found on city bikes. These remain attached to the bike, and the key stays in place as long as the lock is not engaged (so don't ever forget to lock it when you leave the bike unguarded). The best ones also have a strong cable with which the bike can be locked to a stationary object.

By way of maintenance, it may occasionally be necessary to lubricate the lock. Do that very sparingly, using one or two drops of light oil on the key and on each of the points where the

shackle disappears into the lock housing. Then open and close the lock a few times and wipe off any excess lubricant.

WATER BOTTLES AND HYDRATION SYSTEMS

On all recreational and sports bikes, the most common accessory is probably a water bottle cage with a soft plastic bottle. Most bikes come with bosses for one or more bottle cages, but if your bike doesn't, there are also

Above: Fig. 21.7. Built-in lock on a modern city bike. Because it only locks the rear wheel, you should also use a cable to secure the bike to a fixed piece of street furnishing, such as a lamp post.

Left: Fig. 21.8. Although most U-locks, like this one, form pretty good protection against theft, they are not "pick-proof" either.

Right: Figs. 21.9 and 21.10. Water bottle cage (top) and Camelback "hydration system" to be carried on the rider's back. (bottom)

clip-on brackets available for mounting a cage to a frame without bosses. The bottles themselves should be washed and rinsed thoroughly inside and out after every day's use, especially if they are filled with anything more potent than plain water, such as energy drinks.

It has been found that the plastics used for regular soft plastic water bottles contain materials that may be cancer-inducing, and certainly don't taste good. For that reason many riders have switched to aluminum bottles. Their problem is that they don't squirt the water out, so you finish up sucking on them, which can't be too hygienic, considering that the bottle is exposed to flying insects and dirt spraying

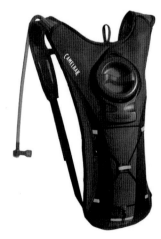

up from the road. By the way, a regular PET plastic bottle of mineral water also fits in a bottle cage; these can be squeezed for a hygienic squirt of water, and they can be washed out and reused.

Another solution is what's billed as a "hydration system," a flexible bladder carried as a backpack and equipped with a flexible hose with drinking nozzle. Once again, you'll be sucking on something that is exposed to the outside world, though not as close to the road as a water bottle. These too need to be cleaned, rinsed, and dried after every use.

BICYCLE COMPUTERS AND TRAINING AIDS

The digital revolution has not spared the bicycle. Computers have revolutionized speed recording, as well as several aspects of performance monitoring, training and navigation. This section will cover the following gadgets:

❏ bicycle computers;

❏ navigational aids;

❏ rollers and turbo trainers;

❏ heart-rate monitors;

❏ output metering devices.

BICYCLE COMPUTER

Bicycle computers have become common accessories, and they have been getting both smaller and smarter from year to year. Select one that has the minimum number of knobs consistent with the functions you desire. Follow the manufacturer's instructions for installation, calibration and maintenance.

Generally, it must be calibrated for the wheel size, measured accurately between the road and the center of wheel

Above: Fig. 21.11. Bottom view of a bicycle computer, showing the mounting clip. In addition, there is a sensor to be installed on the front fork.

Left: Fig. 21.12. Typical simple bicycle computer from Avocet.

Right: Fig. 21.13 and 21.14. Two GPS-based bicycle computers from Garmin.

with the bike's rider and any additional load in place. It pays to look for a model that is advertised as being waterproof and comes with a guarantee to back up this claim. If it is not, put a plastic bag over it in the rain.

The authors' pet peeve with computers (more a comment on ignorant owners and manufacturers) is that though most show a number labeled as average speed, they are auto stop-start computers that are turned off whenever the bicycle is stopped; consequently, their average speed numbers are artificially high (unless the bike doesn't stop). Some computers allow the choice of either auto or manual start-stop; the latter mode will give true average speed—*if* the rider remembers to turn it on and clear it at the start of the ride.

NAVIGATIONAL AIDS

Navigational aids are bicycle computers that acquire data from GPS (global positioning satellites) can determine position within a few feet, show that position on a

map, and calculate speeds and distances accurately independent of the size of the bicycle's wheels. And, of course, their primary function is to help you figure out where you are and how to get where you are going.

TURBO-TRAINERS

The concept of roller training is perhaps almost as old as the pedal-driven bicycle itself, and such devices are used both for indoor training and pre-race warmup. Place the bike on a set of rollers, and pedal away while staying in place. They provide a useful way of practicing, and improving, pedaling speed and endurance. In their basic configuration, they don't include any significant resistance, so they don't help in muscle strength development.

More sophisticated devices, which do include a variable resistance, allowing muscle training as well, are referred to as turbo trainers. They can be designed to simulate real-world cycling

conditions. Mechanically, that is achieved by means of finned rotors to induce an aerodynamic resistance. Because their resistance increases with the speed, they are indeed representative for actual riding conditions. The problem is the noise factor: when pedaled flat-out, they sound like a jetliner taking off.

More modern versions achieve the same goal electromagnetically, by means of an electric generator and digital control circuitry. These are a lot less noisy, more expensive, and much more flexible, because you can program the controls to provide the ride profile for any conceivable riding situation. They can even be connected to a TV

monitor displaying a video of an actual ride on the road.

HEART-RATE MONITORS

Strictly speaking, heart-rate monitors are not a bicycle accessory, because they are worn by the cyclist to measure his or her heart rate during exercise. It is a useful device if you understand the various training and fitness concepts involved. These days, most of them work without wires, and can be equally wirelessly hooked up with sensors that provide cadence, road speed, and gear ratio information.

The information can be downloaded to a computer after the ride and used to analyze the efficacy of the training regimen. For the casual rider in pursuit of mere fitness, they are useful to

Above: and left: Figs. 21.15 and 21.16. Electro-magnetic turbo-trainer (above) and fluid trainer (left), both from Blackburn. These devices are used with the rider's bicycle installed on it.

Top right: Fig. 21.17. Flywheel detail of mageneto-electric turbo-trainer.

Bottom right: Fig. 21.18. White Thunder permanent turbo-trainer: no need to bring your own bike.

make sure the rider stays in a safe range of heart rate that can be maintained long enough to avoid "bonking."

OUTPUT MEASURING DEVICES

There are quite expensive gadgets that calculate how much output the rider is providing to propel the bicycle. They use stress gauges to measure the force the rider applies to the drivetrain. Usually, they are built into a (special) pedal. Ideally, they should measure the force on both pedals, because these

can be quite different for some riders.

Even more than heart-rate monitors, these devices can be very helpful for scientific training, but only if someone—be it the rider or his or her coach—really understands all the implications of scientific training methods.

PROTECTIVE ACCESSORIES

In the following sections, we'll introduce some utilitarian devices that, though rarely installed on road or mountain bikes, may be useful for one purpose or another.

FENDERS

Fenders, or mud guards, are useful items in most climates. Though it may not be as much fun to ride in the rain as it is in sunshine, it is a lot more endurable on a bike with fenders. because they protect against water and mud splashing up from the road. Fig. 21.25 shows the typical spray pattern of water off the wheels, and the effect well-designed fenders should have.

In recent years, as more city and comfort bikes have entered the mix, fenders have become more common in North America than they've been in the past. However, they are still rarely used on most other kinds of bicycles. Suitable fenders for lightweight bikes are made of plastic

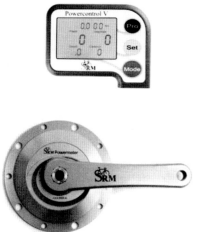

Above: Fig. 21.19. Heart-rate monitor, from Kinetic. The strap goes around the rider's chest.

Left: Figs. 21.20 and 21.21. SRM power meter (top) and typical output graph (bottom).

Right: Fig. 21.22 and 21.23. Full fenders for permanent installation (top) and short mountain bike clip-on fenders (bottom).

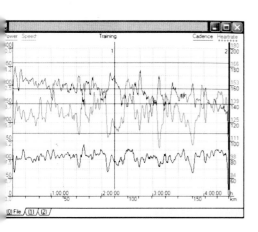

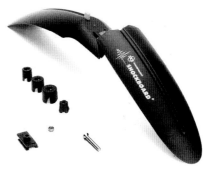

or aluminum, each attached to the bike with stays made of steel rod and clips.

Unfortunately, there have been a number of liability claims against bike shops due to accidents caused by either the fender itself or a item that gets caught in the fender causing an accident. That has made bike shops reluctant to install them on a bike. To avoid such problems, most fenders available in the U.S. now come with attachments that disengage when significant force is applied to them.

To make easily removable fenders, it is possible to attach the stays to the dropouts by means of wing bolts. On older sidepull brakes, it is also possible to make the fender clip easily removable by using two nuts on the brake's central pivot bolt. Replace the acorn nut by two (thin) locknuts, and tighten both nuts against each other, so the brake

is held adequately, which could not be done with only one thin nut.

Some fenders, especially those meant for mountain bikes, simply clip on to the fork or the frame. They keep some spray off your back and your face, but they don't keep the water from splashing every other part of the bike and your body.

At the bottom of every good front fender should be a mud flap, which stops spray from hitting your feet. If you can't find fenders with a mud flap, it is

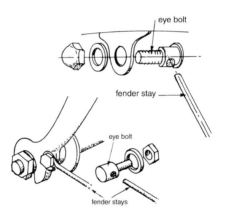

possible to make one yourself, using e.g. a piece of rubber from an old mountain bike tire or tube.

CHAIN GUARD

Chain guards are not "in." And even those that are used, generally don't serve their purpose very well. However, good chain guards that protect both the chain and the rider's clothing do exist, and are installed on just about every utility bicycle in countries like Holland, where cycling is as common as inclement weather is.

They usually limit you to the use of bikes without derailleur gearing, although the Dutch importer of the Japanese Miyata bicycles and Shimano components has dug out some components that actually make it possible to use derailleur gearing with a

Above: Fig. 21.24. A common type of fender attachment detail.

Left: Fig. 21.25. Splash-protection patterns for typical fenders. Clearly, a mud flap at the bottom of the front fender is also needed to keep road-splash from hitting the rider.

Top right: Figs. 21.26 and 21.27. Mud flap (left) and safety-release fender attachment detail.

Bottom right: Fig. 21.28. Chain guard; this model will protect the rider's clothing, but not the chain.

fully enclosed chain guard. These rather costly and heavy bikes are imported into the U.S. under the name Koga Miyata.

The bare minimum a chain guard should do is protect the rider's pants and shoe laces from getting caught in the chain. That purpose can be served by a simple cover plate attached to the right-hand crank, covering the chainwheel and the chain. There's even a European standard for the area that should be covered by such a device.

FAIRINGS

Fairings may be used for two reasons, but both derive their benefits from the same principle: aerodynamics. On the one hand

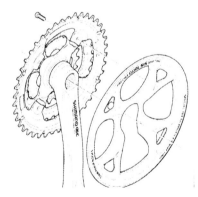

they may be installed to protect the rider (or in case of a front-mounted child seat, the passenger) from the elements. On the other hand they may be installed to speed up the bike by reducing aerodynamic drag. A properly designed fairing should be able to kill both birds with one stone, so to speak.

KICK STAND

More correctly known as prop stand outside the U.S., this

Above: Fig. 21.29. Zipper aerodynamic fairing. In crouched position, it also protects the rider from the elements.

Left: Figs. 21.30 and 21.31. Minimum and maximum drivetrain protection: chainring cover (top) and fully enclosed chain guard as used on most Dutch city bikes (bottom).

Right: Figs. 21.32 and 21.33. Two reliable types of kickstand: two-legged model (left) and rear-dropout mounted model (right).

device is typically only used on simple bicycles. Although few are any good, some models work better than others. The Japanese model that is attached on the rear stay, close to the rear wheel axle, is much more effective than the more common type that is attached just behind the bottom bracket. Besides, it does not get in the way while wheeling the bike backwards, as the conventional kick stand does.

Another interesting model is the two-legged version. Its advantage is that the bicycle can be balanced on it so that it does not lean over. With this model, either the rear wheel or the front wheel can be raised off the ground to work on the bike. You can also use a cheap shop display stand—nothing to install on the bike, but handy for in the home workshop.

Some utility bikes use a stand shaped like an inverse letter U. When not in use, they are clipped under the luggage rack. When in use, they support the bike in steady balance. Similar models are also available for front wheel of cargo bicycles with a loading area over the front wheel.

CHILD SEAT

Not your everyday accessory perhaps, child seats may be important for parents of a young child. They exist for installation in the front and the rear. The former type is only suitable for mountain bikes and other machines with flat handlebars and a rather long top tube, because on other models the child would interfere with handling and balancing of the bike (or the other way round). These must be attached to the top tube, not to any part connected with the steering system. Children above the age of 4 are generally too big to be carried in the front. Bigger children are better carried in the rear than in the front.

A child seat is not suitable for a child who is sleepy or not yet old enough to remain attentive during the ride. The child sits high above the ground, making a properly-fitting helmet mandatory. A bike pulling a trailer has to be a safer option for both parent and child, and then only if the child is both old enough to

hold up his or her head and small enough to fit in.

The type for installation in the rear comes in two versions: for independent installation and for attachment to a luggage rack. Only the very strongest and rigid racks lend themselves to the installation of a seat. Models for direct attachment to the bike are more common in the U.S., while luggage-rack mounted models are often seen in Europe. Any child seat should meet the following criteria:

❑ Very sturdy, stiff construction and attachment to the bike;

❑ Integral support for the child's back and sides;

❑ Seat belt to tie the child in securely;

Above: Fig. 21.34. Handlebar-mount map support.

Left: Figs. 21.35 and 21.36. Child seats for front mounting (left) and rear mounting (right).

Right: Fig. 21.36. Keep your hands warm: cycling muffs for winter riding.

❑ Adequate support and protection for the feet to stop them from getting caught in the spokes, a frequent cause of bicycle-related child injury.

A final word of warning on the subject: don't ever leave a child in the seat when you are not holding the bike—always take the child out of the seat first, before you do anything else.

AND EVEN MORE ACCESSORIES

There are many other accessories, ranging from map clips, thermometers, rear-view mirrors, to cell-phone holders and umbrella mounts. Other items are introduced from time to time, some of which hardly warrant mention due to their simplicity. Most of these gadgets are taken off the market as quickly as they were introduced, because few are really as practical or well-conceived as may at first appear.

22. Bikes For the Short and the Tall

The chapters of this last part of the book are devoted to the perhaps 1% of all bicycles on the road that differ from the run of the mill. Here we shall cover the special bicycles, machines that are technically different for one or more reasons. The present chapter covers machines for riders whose physical size makes off-the-peg bikes impractical or uncomfortable.

The most common reason for choosing a bike that differs from the norm is that no standard design comfortably fits the particular rider. Long ignored by the industry and large segments of the bike trade, some riders just can't find a standard bike to fit them.

Often, the answer to the need for such a machine has simply been either to modify an existing bike somewhat, or at best to build a version that is either scaled up or down a little.

Many women have problems finding a bike to fit. That is not only due to their overall size, but also to the fact that most bikes are still made with the typical male proportions in mind. Fig. 22.2 shows in what respects even an average female physique may differ from that of an average male of the same size.

Left: Fig. 22.1. There is more than frame size to the question of bicycle fit, especially for those who are significantly taller or shorter than others.

BEYOND FRAME SIZE

Tall riders typically not only need seat and handlebars that are higher, they also need a frame that achieves these positions without requiring excessively long (and therefore flexible) extensions of seatpost and handlebar stem. The length of the top tube should probably also be longer than on an average bike.

In addition to the frame, crank length (and consequently bottom bracket height), handlebar width, and quite a number of other items should also be adapted to the rider's proportions. Achieving all this while maintaining proper steering and handling is no mean feat.

For short riders—be they small adults or children—the problems are at least as severe. Only too often, the height of the frame is all that is reduced, and that just isn't enough: they need a shorter top tube while maintaining adequate steering tube length, shorter cranks (and consequently a lower bottom bracket) and quite a few other modifications.

Even the best-intentioned attempts to accommodate short or tall riders often go amiss. To give an example, merely scaling down a regular bike to achieve a design with smaller wheels will likely result in insufficient trail for proper steering stability. In recent years, some manufacturers have taken these problems a little more seriously, with the result that more choices are available today—at least among high-end (and thus high-priced) machines. Even when ordering a custom-built frame, it is good to consider the points that will be explained in this chapter,

because not all frame builders have a thorough enough grasp of the ergonomic needs of small and big riders.

Often quite minor points may matter a lot. Take the brake cables for example: it is common to run them over the top of the top tube. But that adds about 6 mm (¼ in.) to the effective top tube height when trying to straddle the frame. That does not seem like much, but a few minor points like that soon add up to a significant difference when you are trying to minimize frame size for a short rider.

THE FRAME

From a design standpoint, it is often just as difficult to accommodate tall riders as it is to design a good frame for a short rider. For most tall riders, it is not only necessary to make the frame bigger, it also needs to be stronger. There are two reasons for this: in the first place, the

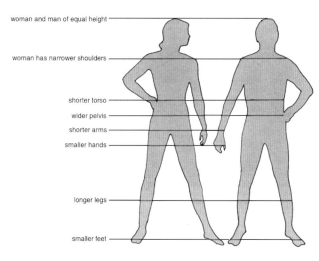

Above: Fig. 22.2. Bianchi Junior 24-inch wheel bike.

Left: Fig. 22.3. The average female is differently proportioned than the average male, even if they're equally tall. And, of course, there is plenty of variation in both groups as well.

woman and man of equal height

woman has narrower shoulders

shorter torso
wider pelvis
shorter arms
smaller hands

longer legs

smaller feet

Above: Fig. 22.4. Rivendell Bombardier bike for tall (and heavy) riders. But see our reservations about the frame design.

longer tubes of the bigger frame (assuming top tube and down tube are also longer) tend to flex more under the same load; in the second place, the taller rider is likely to be heavier and stronger.

All this must be achieved using standard wheel sizes, because larger ones are just not available. In addition, the distribution of weight and the correct steering geometry must be maintained. Numerous frame builders have had to disappoint their tall customers, some of whom got nearly unridable machines as a result of the vagaries of oversize frame design.

The greater frame length that may be required for a tall rider may be accommodated either by using frame tubes of greater diameter and/or wall thickness, or

by adding bracing tubes. Fig. 22.7 shows two common solutions for frames that exceed a size of 65 cm (26 in.).

Other methods to achieve increased frame strength and stiffness include the use of thick-wall and oversize tubing. Obviously, bikes for large riders should not be made with the lightest tubes, and there may be good reasons to choose mountain bike tubing with its greater diameters and wall thicknesses for such frames if they will be subjected to hard use.

Whether big or small, different size frames often involve different angles between the various tubes. Thus, the use of precision cast steel lugs is often not possible for such frames. So

if you like the retro look of a traditional lugged steel frame, that can only be achieved with pressed, welded lugs. These lugs, though not as accurately dimensioned and often not as pretty, at least allow some bending without doing damage. If the difference becomes more than 3°, a lugless construction should be used instead, so as not to stress the lugs excessively.

Large or small frames can of course also be built using titanium and carbon-fiber. However, because these materials and methods are usually selected for weight savings, you're unlikely to find anyone who can build you an oversize frame that is strong and stiff enough. Hydroformed aluminum has another problem: it is a mass-production technique that can't be applied to one-off production or even small-scale batch manufacturing.

Left: Fig. 22.5. Dimensioning sketches for bikes with large (above) and small (below) frames.

Right: Fig. 22.6. Two possible frame-bracing methods for large frames.

Below: Fig. 22.7. A "supersize" city bike from Utopia, in Germany, with an 88 cm (35 inch) frame.

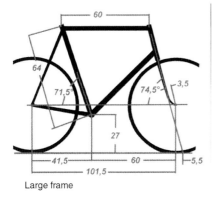

Large frame

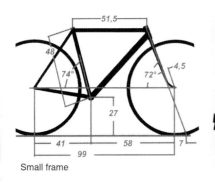

Small frame

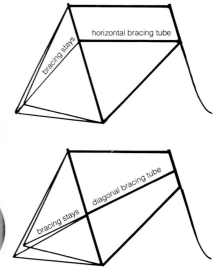

SMALL FRAMES

Obviously the frame should be small for short riders. Yet that usually can't be achieved by either shortening only the seat tube or by scaling all dimensions down. The first solution does not achieve the required shorter top tube length, nor does it address the need for an adequate head tube length—the most important criterion for overall frame stiffness and steering predictability. The second solution can't be carried out within the constraints of the required minimum clearances around parts such as the wheels.

The use of smaller wheels is an obvious choice for smaller bikes. The 650 B wheel size, using 584 mm rims, allows for a smaller frame that doesn't look as though it's a child's bike.

Another solution for a small bicycle is the design pioneered by frame builder Bill Boston, later successfully implemented by Georgina Terry in her production bicycles for women. This design uses a smaller front

wheel, providing adequate head tube length even in the smallest frame sizes, as shown in Fig 22.9. Other methods that can be successfully used include those that use a steeper seat angle and a shallower head tube angle (providing the other steering dimensions are adjusted to suit).

Often frames designed for women use either a lowered top tube or twin diagonal tubes that run straight, or sometimes even curved, from the top of the head tube to the rear wheel dropouts. Neither of these are particularly good solutions, and are more a

Above: Fig. 22.8. Small touring bike from Jitensha Studio in Berkeley, California. Custom built in Japan.

Left: Fig. 22.9. Conceptual sketch for Georgina Terry's women's bike with small front wheel.

Right: Fig. 22.10. Kimori Cross 200 bike for small riders. Yes, it looks a bit like an Alex Moulton spaceframe bike, but it is specifically proportioned for small riders. Also from Japan.

tribute to the days when women cyclists wore skirts. Anatomically, there is no reason why a woman should have more difficulty straddling a regular top tube than any man.

Fig. 22.12 shows the forces that apply in the case of a lowered top tube without bracing. It should be clear that, while all other forces on the bike frame are balanced by supports in two directions, the lowered top tube runs to the middle of the seat tube, where it is not countered by any other frame member. Thus a bike frame of this type requires an additional pair of

Above: Fig. 22.11. Not so good for a small frame: The small-diameter twin tubes that take the place of the top tube in this design don't provide enough resistance to torque loads.

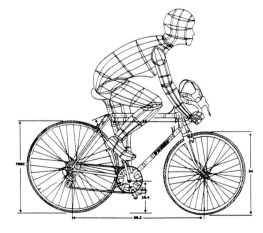

rear stays that run from that point to the rear dropouts.

The design on which the top tube is replaced by two thinner tubes running all the way to the rear dropouts is usually referred to as "twin lateral" or "mixte" (and "Berceau" if those tubes are curved). It does not suffer the same problem as the lowered head tube design. But here the problem is a lack of lateral stiffness. Those two thin tubes don't provide anything like the resistance to torsional flexing that a single large-diameter tube does.

THE WHEELS

Normal wheel sizes for adult bikes are nominally 26, 27 and

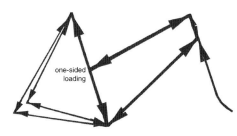

Above: Fig. 22.12. Unsupported forces in a frame with lowered top tube without bracing.

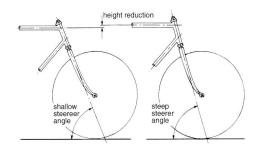

28 inch (again nominally: 650, 675 and 700 mm). In reality, these usually do not differ very much from each other, due to the fact that the nominally smaller wheels are frequently equipped with wider tires, the larger ones with very narrow tires. As we've seen in Chapter 9, wheels called 700 mm (28 in.) actually have smaller rims than those referred to as 675 mm (27 in.).

For small riders, there are some 26 in. wheels available with narrow 1¼ in. tires. This size is still readily available in France, Italy, and to a lesser extent in Britain, while they are hard to find in the U.S. The next step down is the 24 in. wheel, available both with relatively wide tires, as used on some dirt bikes, and with moderate tire widths.

Even more serious than the tire situation is that of the rims. In the U.S., it is often very hard

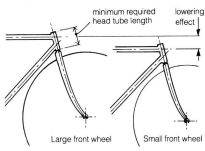

Above, left, and right: Figs. 22.13–22.15. Three factors that effect top tube height:
Above: Effect of smaller front wheel.
Left: Effect of shallower frame angles.
Right: Effect of slanted top tube.

to obtain strong aluminum rims in any size other than those that fit 700 mm road bike or 26 in. mountain bike tires. When my children were so small that their bikes required 22, 24, and 26 in. tires, I stocked up on those rims and tires on trips to Italy, but I can't seriously suggest you go there to buy rims and tires on a regular basis.

Most of these smaller rims come with fewer than the standard number of 32 spoke holes: usually 24 or 28. That means you also need matching hubs, which are hard to find, although they are now more readily available—at a price—thanks to the recent craze for light and supposedly aerodynamic equipment.

Tall cyclists can't count on finding bigger wheels, but the recent introduction of 29-inch wheels for mountain bikes (actually, they're 700 C rims with fat tires) offers at least bigger wheels for mountain bike riders. Other types of bike wheels still need special attention. Heavy riders require particularly strong wheels, calling for relatively heavy rims and more than the usual number of spokes. This also affects the

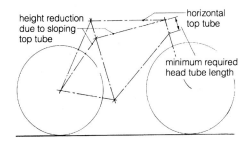

need for special hubs, which are available (usually intended for tandem use).

The spoking pattern should be selected to match the number of spokes. On wheels with 36 spokes, 3- and 4-cross patterns are optimally strong, while fewer crossings are required for (smaller) wheels with fewer spokes, more crossings for wheels with more spokes.

OTHER COMPONENTS

In addition to the frame itself, also many of the other components of the bicycle may need to be specially selected for a bike that is smaller or bigger than the run of the mill. The following sections will deal with those issues.

THE STEERING SYSTEM

To steer a bike with a big frame properly, it has to be long enough so the rider is not too close to the steering axis. On small bikes, sufficient trail must be provided, even if the front

wheel is smaller than usual, or if the head tube angle is different. This means that the fork rake should not be the same on bikes with different wheel sizes or with different head tube angles. A small front wheel requires less rake, as does a steeper head tube angle, to achieve the same trail. The effect of wheel size on steering stability was discussed in Chapter 10.

Drop handlebars appear to be readily available to fit any male gorilla, but to find one that matches a small rider with relatively narrow body build may be next to impossible. The correct posture keeps the arms parallel if the bars are held at the drops. There are some children's size bars that may do the trick, but very few of them seem to be available in the quality that is justified in the price category where one lands when getting a custom-built bike. Mountain bike handlebars can at least be cut short, assuming they are not bent too far from the center. Even the handlebar diameter

Left: Fig. 22.16. 24-inch wheel bicycle. Although it is intended for children, the proportions appear to be quite suitable for small adults as well.

Right: Fig. 22.17. 29-inch wheel bicycle. Those wheels are actually 700 C rims with fat tires, but the result is a wheel that's quite close to 29 in. (725 mm) in outside diameter.

should be reduced for riders with small hands.

THE SEAT

Very small or big riders often differ in that part of the anatomy that contacts the seat. Although there are now quite a number of reasonably comfortable women's seats available, people who are both heavy and broadly built may have difficulty finding something to match. Although it looks weird on an otherwise fine road bike, the kind of leather saddle with spiral springs in the (very wide) back seems to be the only comfortable solution for many women and quite a few older males.

For big riders, the seatpost may have to be rather long if the frame is not perfectly matched to the leg length. In recent years, very long seatposts have become available—but only in diameters to match the typical inside diameters of mountain bike seat tubes, which are slightly smaller than those on most road and touring bikes. It is possible to install a shim around the seatpost in the seat

lug, but this had better be quite long: at least 10 cm (4 in.) are required for adequately secure clamping.

DRIVETRAIN AND GEARING

Even small cyclists generally want to keep up with others as much as possible. Consequently, the drivetrain had better be adjusted to their special needs, especially if smaller wheels are installed. The biggest problem occurs on small bikes, especially those for children.

Manufacturers often overlook the fact that the smaller wheel already provides a lower gear. This effect is illustrated in Fig. 22.18. Instead of equipping the bike with the right gearing to compensate for this, they tend to install scaled-down versions of the chainring, with fewer teeth, aggravating the

Below: Fig. 22.18. Effect of wheel size on gearing. For a bike with small wheels, you need smaller sprockets (or, theoretically at least, larger chainrings).

problem even more. True, a tiny bike with small wheels and a big chainring may look a little odd, but it is technically required to obtain useful gearing.

Another solution is to choose a cassette with smaller sprockets. Sprockets with 11 teeth are readily available these days, and even smaller ones (all the way down to 9 teeth, though not easy to find) do exist. In that case, it will be quite essential to make sure that the chain wraps around the smallest sprockets as far as possible, by selecting the chain length and the derailleur orientation appropriately.

Cranks must match the rider's leg length as well as possible. Expensive cranksets are available in a variety of crank lengths ranging from 165 mm to 180 or for a few makes and models from 160 to 185 mm. This may be satisfactory for most big and small adults, but it still does not satisfy the needs of children, who may require even shorter ones. It also leaves those on a budget without

consolation, because the more modest quality found on affordable bikes is just not available in enough different sizes to satisfy all. Really small children's cranks are usually of very inferior quality.

Pedals are available in a limited number of sizes, but most high-quality pedals in only one size. Actually, this is often not a problem on road bikes, because size is not an issue on clipless pedals (if you can find the right size shoes). The problem is really most severe on touring and utility bikes for large riders, where few pedals will prove wide enough. One solution may be to install mountain bike pedals, which tend to be rather wide. Toeclips for conventional pedals also are available in a number of different sizes, although they rarely match children's or small women's feet. If it suits your kind of riding, the use of clipless pedals will solve most problems.

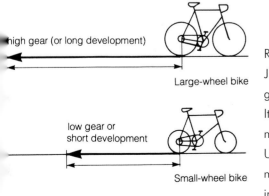

high gear (or long development)

Large-wheel bike

low gear or short development

Small-wheel bike

Right: Fig. 22.19. Junior component gruppo from the Italian component maker Miche. Unfortunately, these may be hard to find in the U.S.

THE BRAKES

Although the brakes themselves are not really a problem, the real issue here is brake levers. The use of brake-shift levers on almost all modern road bikes leaves most smaller riders out in the lurch. And most mountain bike levers don't seem to be designed with small hands in mind either.

If you are willing to go "retro," using conventional brake levers and separate shifters, it is possible to find something that fits. There are small and/or adjustable brake levers, both for drop handlebars and for flat-handlebar bikes. Fig. 22.21 shows the critical dimension for reach of the lever.

Another beneficial design for small riders is the brake with return springs in the lever (and, on some models, also in the brake calipers). This feature makes brake operation very light and accurate, even for riders with relatively weak hands.

Finally, in this respect, hydraulic brakes should be mentioned. Their operation is really an experience to behold, requiring absolutely minimal force. Unfortunately, there is not a suitable range of brake levers for these brakes available to date: small or adjustable versions are sorely needed.

ACCESSORIES

Whereas things like locks and lighting units are no different on a small or big bike than on any other machine, some other accessories may pose particular problems, especially for small bikes. Finding a good small frame pump, light fenders for smaller wheels, or a sturdy luggage rack to fit a small bike can be very hard, because many of such items are not available off-the-shelf in any other than "standard" size.

If you are willing and able to pay the price, the problem may be less severe. Anyone who is prepared to buy a custom-built bike should also investigate the possibility of matching accessories, which many frame builders will gladly design and produce. It does leave those on a budget out of luck.

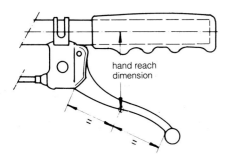

Left: Fig. 22.20. Brake levers need to be proportional to the rider's hand, so they can apply full force when held at the center of the lever.

Right: Fig. 22.21. Even handgrips should be available in proportional sizes.

hand reach dimension

23
THE TANDEM BICYCLE

Tandem is the Latin term for *at length*, and it is used to describe bicycles for two or more riders sitting in line behind each other, each contributing to the propulsion. Although just about every tandem you see these days is designed for two, machines for three or more riders do exist as well.

The longest tandem on record accommodates 36 riders, who, according to amy old edition of the *Guiness Book of Records*, have not yet managed to cover the distance of the machine's own length. The modern two-man tandem, by contrast, is a highly efficient bicycle.

TANDEMS TODAY

Interest in the tandem has increased significantly in recent years, so that it is now relatively easy to buy a quality machine of this kind in a wide range of sizes. And just as important, tandem parts and accessories are

Above: Fig. 23.1. Probably the first tandem bicycle: Michaux tandem, 1870.

Left: Fig. 23.2. A modern tandem. This is the Cannondale road tandem, a surprisingly light bicycle made for two.

becoming more readily available. That is one essential factor for keeping a tandem on the road, because many of the parts used differ from those installed on other bicycles.

TANDEM PROS AND CONS

Although tandems are efficient, enabling two riders to cover greater distances at higher speeds than they could individually, they are a bit of a nuisance in other respects. Sheer size makes it hard to live with them. Transporting one is at least as difficult as finding a convenient place to store it, and when it does break down, the second rider is stranded as much as the first, making it hard to get help. All these are mere sober, practical drawbacks, that don't weigh up against the pure delight of riding such a machine in unison at high speeds and over long distances in perfect cadence. A properly designed and constructed tandem is indeed so reliable that it does not break down more frequently than any other

bike—practically never if properly maintained.

The reason why tandems do present a special challenge to their designers and manufacturers lies in the fact that a higher load has to be carried on a longer structure, at the same time propelled by a greater output applied in two different locations. Combining two bottom brackets, two saddles and two handlebars together so that the whole can be balanced and steered safely and predictably is no mean feat, but it can be done when the machine is properly designed.

Unlike the riders of single bikes, those on a tandem are usually unable to relieve the load when riding over bumps in the road. This often gives the feeling of having lots of dead weight. Actually, the machine itself is not all that heavy: typically 1.6 times the weight of a single bike of

comparable quality—or 0.8 times the weight of the two single machines it replaces. What gives the feeling of dead weight is the fact that the wheels are so far apart that the riders' weight shifts do not affect the overall weight distribution. Consequently, any jolts really give the bike a beating, requiring an even more sturdy construction of bike and components.

TANDEMS AND CHILDREN

Tandeming is a safe and enjoyable way to allow a child to keep up with the parents during even long and strenuous rides. Some tandem manufacturers actually offer custom-built tandems to accommodate a child in the rear without further modification. However, even if you have a series-production tandem meant for

Left: Fig. 23.3. This 10-seater tandem was actually used during the 1890s to pace single riders in record attempts.

Left and right: Figs. 23.4 and 23.5. This Co-Motion tandem with S&S couplings can be disassembled to fit in those three neat cases.

adult riders, there are solutions available to adapt it for use with a child stoker.

The most common conversion is referred to as "Kiddy Cranks." It contains a small crankset that can be bolted to the rear seat tube somewhere above the regular rear crankset. A short chain drives the rear crank spindle and crankset. Before you order such a device, make sure the drive configuration on your tandem can accommodate this type of arrangement.

The child's legs will be spinning at the same speed as the pilot's, but they won't have to put as much force on the pedals. Most children, with their shorter legs, have no difficulty keeping up with a high cadence of around 80 to 100 RPM, but no, they don't have the same strength.

A bigger potential problem is the handlebar location relative to the saddle. Being attached to the stoker's seatpost, the stem may be too short for a child to comfortably reach it. If needed, a different, longer, stem should be

installed when the tandem will be used this way.

It is also possible to convert a single bike for something akin to tandem use. This is done with a single-wheel trailing contraption referred to as trailer-bike. These have their own drivetrain directly driving the extra wheel, and the handlebars are the right distance from the saddle for a child to comfortably reach it.

SOCIABLES

Another type of bicycle for two riders is known as a "sociable." They're rare enough to overlook, but interesting enough to bear mention here. On a sociable, the riders sit side by side instead of behind each other. The two riders sit on either side of the bike's

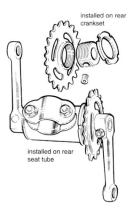

centerline. Surprisingly, perhaps, a sociable can be ridden by a single rider, leaning the bike over far enough to balance his or her mass center over the contact point between the tires and the road.

THE TANDEM FRAMESET

The tandem frame is some 60 cm (24 in.) longer than that of a single bike. Since longer members are basically more flexible than shorter ones, it should be obvious that the tandem frame, which also has to carry double the load, must be specially constructed if it is not to flex excessively, which would lead to unpredictable steering and balancing characteristics. Fig. 23.9 shows how the various static and dynamic forces act upon the tandem frame.

Above and left: Figs. 23.6 and 23.7. Kiddy-Cranks are used to allow a child stoker to reach the cranks.

Right: Fig. 23.8. Antique bicycle collector Donald Adams and partner riding a 1896 sociable—a side-by-side bike for two.

The dynamic, or variable, forces generate a torsional effect along the axis that runs from the rear wheel axle to the bottom of the headset, as shown in the same illustration. In addition to being strong enough to carry the vertically applied static load, the frame has to be constructed so that the resulting torsional deformation is minimized. Ideally, this is achieved with a very large diameter tube that runs along the torsion axis. In practice, several different methods have been tried, as shown in Fig. 23.10.

Of the configurations shown, the ones on the left-hand side tend to be the better solutions, because on these a very rigid member braces the frame close to the torsional axis. The details shown on the right, on the other hand, are obviously designed with at best the static loads in mind (including the recently popular design per detail D). In fact, some of these designs are not even adequate from the static standpoint: none of the designs that provides a low instep, be it in the front, in the rear or for both riders, is statically or dynamically adequate unless extremely heavy walled and large diameter tubing is used. A high top tube has to be used on tandems—even for those women who would prefer a lower instep (fortunately a rapidly receding demand in the U.S., though still very common elsewhere).

A relatively popular solution is the one with two small diameter diagonal bracing tubes, referred to as twin laterals or mixte tubes. This design is inherently inadequate, especially for a lightweight machine used for touring. Some of the problems of tandem design are lessened by using special tandem tubing, made by at several major tubing manufacturers, such as Easton and Reynolds, and by most of the others on special order in some minimum quantity. Obviously, tandem tubing must be of greater diameter and greater wall thickness.

Besides, some special tubes are not found on other bikes, such as the tube connecting the two bottom brackets (referred to as bottom tube or "drainpipe") and the diagonal reinforcing tube. Those two tubes are particularly critical, as are the down tube and the head tube. All these tubes, being both long and heavily loaded, should have greater diameter than what is customarily used even on mountain bikes.

Traditionally, tandems have long been made of slightly oversize steel tubing (manufacturers like Reynolds offered a large variety of oversize Reynolds 531 tubes). These days, the majority of tandems are made of TIG-welded aluminum, although carbon tandem frames are also available, as are titanium frames. Even the Exo-Grid method of combining carbon sleeves with titanium cut-out tubes is also offered, resulting in more riding

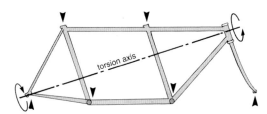

Above: Fig. 23.9. Loading diagram for a tandem frame. Static forces are represented by straight arrows, torsion by an circular arrow.

Right: Fig. 23.10. Overview of some of the various tandem frame configurations in use.

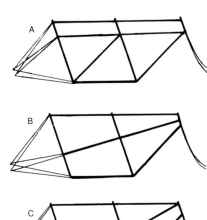

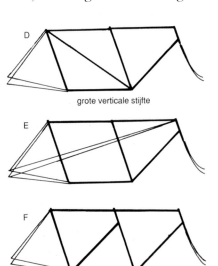

grote verticale stijfte

comfort and reduced weight—at astronomical prices.

TANDEM FRAME GEOMETRY

To be at all comfortable in the long run, the distance between the two seats is quite critical. Racing tandems are kept rigid by minimizing this distance, and they are a royal pain in the neck for the rider in the rear, referred to as the *stoker* in tandem parlance, while the one in front is known as the *captain*. For non-competitive purposes, the length of the rear top tube should be at least 65 cm (26 in.) —preferably up to 75 cm (30 in.).

At the other end of the spectrum are tandem frames built for speed only. Not recommended for anything but tandem track racing, these machines make the stoker rub shoulders with the captain.

TANDEM STEERING

It took a long time for tandem builders to give up on trying to do the impossible: the earliest tandems and other multi-rider bicycles were invariably designed in such a way that both riders could influence the steering. Although that may seem socially responsible, it did make tandem riding extremely dangerous until this idea was given up. For the last hundred years now, tandem riders seem to accept that only the captain can steer the bike, while the stoker just has to trust him.

To achieve a reliable tandem steering system, the fork should be made of thicker tubing than on a regular bike. The oversize headsets with matching steerer tubes recently introduced for mountain bikes are the answer to a maiden's prayer for tandem builders and riders as well. These are so much more rigid that they provide an entirely new sensation of control over the bike's steering, especially on less than perfect road surfaces.

The front handlebars can be normal, like on any single bike of the same kind, although a slightly wider, and perhaps heavier, version may be justified to overcome the greater steering forces. For the rear handlebars, we recommend choosing moderately curved bars installed with the ends pointing forward. This shape allows the rider in the rear to reach forward for a low position or hold the bars near the center to relax. An additional advantage is that these forward pointing bar ends provide excellent locations to mount the gear shifters. The rear handlebars can either be installed with a special stem clamped around the front seat tube, or with a special clamp that is attached directly to the frame.

THE TANDEM DRIVETRAIN

Two bottom brackets, two cranksets, four pedals, and two chains are needed to transfer the riders' effort to the rear wheel. That allows a number of different configurations, the most common of which are shown in Fig. 23.14. Tandems probably need more gears—and a wider range of

Left: Fig. 23.11. Steel-frame track tandem.

Right: Fig. 23.12. This 1894 tandem had synchronized steering. That's not done anymore.

gears—than single bikes. In part, this is due to the more pronounced difference between easy going and hard riding on a tandem: the extremes are more noticeable than on a regular bike: climbing is harder, and cruising is easier.

To maximize the number of available gears, the connecting chain, usually called "timing chain," between the two cranksets should be run on the left-hand side, because no more than two chainrings are effectively available for the derailleur gearing when one of those on the right is sacrificed for this purpose. On the other hand, if you can live with 18- or 20-speed gearing (e.g. in level terrain), the latter solution offers the advantage of simplicity and easily available standard bicycle parts.

Real tandem cranksets, designed for the timing chain on

the left-hand side, are harder to find and quite expensive. For touristic purposes, TA is the only manufacturer whose range is reasonably widely distributed. Campagnolo's excellent tandem cranksets are only intended for racing use and are not available with three chainrings on the right-hand side.

There are other solutions. As can be seen from Fig. 23.14, it is not necessary to connect the rear crankset directly to the rear wheel: when the front one is used, it is easier to shift gears and many experienced touring tandem riders prefer this configuration. Whatever way they are connected, the chainrings over which the timing chain runs should be relatively large,

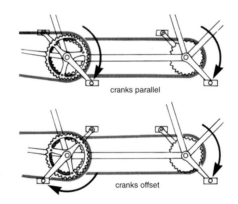

cranks parallel

cranks offset

Above: Fig. 23.13. The cranks can either be run parallel to each other, or they may be offset.

Left: Fig. 23.14. Three possible tandem drivetrain configurations.

Right: Fig. 23.15. Typical tandem drivetrain with triple chainrings on the drive side, and synchronizing chain on the left.

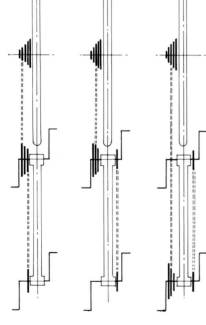

preferably 36 teeth, to minimize wear and get smooth running. That's not to say it can't be done differently: the German frame builder Günter Sattler actually built a tandem on which a small-pitch timing chain ran over tiny chain rings *inside* the very large diameter bottom tube.

The timing chain should be kept adequately tightened, allowing no more than 12 mm (½ in.) vertical movement. Although this can be achieved by means of a sprung chain tensioner, the preferred method is to adjust the crankset locations so that their distance tensions the chain. This is done by means of an eccentrically held bottom bracket bearing for one of the cranksets, allowing about 2 cm of forward adjustment.

It is not necessary to keep the cranks of front and rear crankarms in phase. Many touring tandem riders prefer to offset them relative to one another by 90°, as shown in Fig. 23.13. The advantage of this configuration lies in the fact that both riders' cranks are not in the dead center

position at the same time, resulting in an overall smoother flow of output. Besides, two strong riders may put too much stress on the bike if both are pedaling in synch.

The cranks can be offset relative to each other by undoing the timing chain and installing it again when the cranks are in the desired orientation relative to each other. In fact, you are not even stuck with a 90° offset but can choose almost any angle.

In a pinch, one can use standard components to make a tandem drivetrain with triple derailleur chainrings. To do this, use right-hand cranks on the left as well as on the right. Then the pedal hole of the one installed on the left must be drilled out and a Helicoil insert for a left-hand pedal installed there. Don't do what seems obvious, namely use right-hand pedals on both sides, keeping the threaded pedal hole the way it is, because the right-hand pedal with its right-hand screw thread will

most likely come undone if installed on the left. Besides, pedals are sold in pairs, while cranks can be bought singly and Helicoil inserts are cheap.

TANDEM GEARING

For serious tandem use, only derailleur gearing is suitable, certainly if loaded touring in hilly terrain is involved. Multi-speed hubs have hollow axles, which are just not strong enough for this kind of use, regardless of their relative merits from a gearing standpoint.

Despite the triple cranksets, conventional mountain bike systems may not be suitable for tandem use. Unlike the mountain bike, the tandem also needs very

high gears, with developments of 8.80 m or more (110-inch gear), due to the phenomenal speeds that can be reached on level ground.

However, those restrictions really only apply to the choice of chainrings and sprockets. The derailleurs and shifters developed for the mountain bike, on the other hand, lend themselves very well for tandem use. The modern index shifters, unfortunately, only work well with their pre-cut cables, which may not be available in the right length for tandem use. The one way to get around this is to install the shifters on the front of the stoker's handlebars, where they are accessible to both riders and work with the normal cable lengths.

TANDEM WHEELS

Tandem problem number one is the fact that the wheels are so heavily loaded, especially dynamically. Bent or dented rims and lots of broken spokes are typical headaches on the tandem. With the selection of special

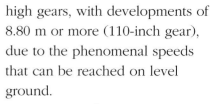

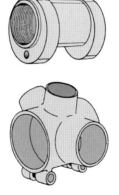

Above: and left: Figs. 23.16 and 23.17. Use of an eccentric bottom bracket insert makes it possible to adjust the chain tension by orienting it differently.

Right: Fig. 23.18. The French TA company offers perhaps the most versatile tandem cranksets, with the widest choice of chainrings.

tandem wheels, with more and heavier-gauge spokes, these problems should have receded, providing those wheels are maintained properly.

More than any other part of the tandem, the wheels suffer any time the bike takes an obstacle in the road surface. High tire pressures and properly tightened spokes are the clues to making tandem wheels last, providing they are sturdy enough in the first place. That means they should not be selected for low weight: considering you only have two wheels for two riders, even the strongest wheels will weigh less than the equivalent on two single bikes, so the effect of the extra rotating mass is not so serious as might seem at first.

The tires should be relatively wide and must withstand a high pressure, because the double weight will tend to push them in more than on a single bike. For touring use on regular roads, we prefer 32 mm wide tires inflated to 6 bar (85 psi) or more, although 28 mm is adequate for continuously smooth road surfaces. Even for a tandem carrying two light riders and no luggage

on smooth roads, 25 mm wide tires are marginal. On rough surfaces on or off road, only mountain bike wheels with matching highly inflated tires should be considered. Aramid (e.g. Kevlar) belted, puncture-resistant designs are of little additional help, because tandems don't puncture in the tread area but by pinching between rim and road, against which no reinforcing helps, high tire pressure being the only answer.

RIMS AND SPOKES

Also the rims should be pretty strong—that means heavy. The introduction of the hybrid bike has been a real boon to the road tandem, because it has popularized wheel components that are superbly suited to tandem use as

Above: Fig. 23.19. White Industries rear cassette hub for tandem use.

Left: Fig. 23.20. Da-Vinci tandem drivetrain with intermediate jack-shaft.

Right: Fig. 23.21. Da-Vinci set of tandem wheels: lots of spokes and no fancy spoking pattern.

well. Installing mountain bike wheels with their smaller diameters, on the other hand, does not work on a tandem designed for 700 C wheels, even if clearances are adequate, because the brakes will not reach the rims.

It has long been customary to install wheels with 40 spokes or more, requiring special rims and hubs with the appropriate number of spoke holes. If you use 40, 44 or even 48 spokes per wheel, these should be spoked in at a 4-cross pattern, while a 3-cross pattern is probably adequate for 36-spoke wheels. Even for tandems, 14-15-14 butted spokes work quite well, as long as they are tensioned adequately. The use of thicker spokes does not seem to lead to reduced wheel problems, but one simple trick does: place a small washer under the head of every spoke at the hub, to fill the distance between it and the hub flange, as described in Chapter 9. This reduces the movement of the spoke bend relative to the flange, thus greatly reducing the likelihood of fatigue-induced spoke breakages.

Wide hubs with solid axles are recommended, rather than

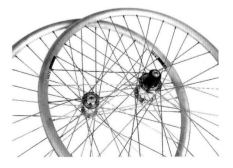

models with quick-release. There are excellent solid axle, "bolt-on" hubs on the market these days. These solid axle hubs should be used with axle nuts with integral washers to reduce the friction resistance against the forkends and dropouts when tightening them.

LIGHTWEIGHT TANDEM WHEELS

Lightweight tandem wheels are available from some reputable wheel specialists. According to those who have tested them for cycling magazines, some of those wheel sets seem to defy every rule we just spelled out. They

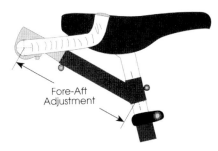

Above and right: Figs. 23.22 and 23.23. The stoker's handlebar stem is clamped around the captain's seat post.

Below: Fig. 23.24. Timing chain on a Rodriguez tandem.

may have something like 16 or 20 spokes instead of 40 or more. They are very light, relying on the use of special hubs, special spoking, and special rims.

They get most of their strength (and unfortunately not enough flex) from very deep-profile rims. These wheels will work if you're in a hurry and find a good road, but for practical tandem touring on varied roads, and perhaps carrying a load, the advice given above still holds good today.

TANDEM BRAKES

Trying to stop or slow down a machine weighing 150 kg (330 lbs) with standard bicycle brakes is a risky affair, especially if one considers the fact that this machine is likely to travel faster in the first place. Downhill, the

Right: Fig. 23.25. Before disk brakes became readily available, tandems often relied on this Araya drum brake, screwed onto a special hub, as an additional brake for downhill use.

problem is an even bigger one. Yet tandem brakes can be quite adequate if a combination of measures are taken to make the most out of their properties.

One advantage from a braking standpoint is that the tandem's weight distribution over the long wheelbase does not lead to the tipping forward effect that limits braking on regular bikes. You can brake in the rear and in the front with about equal effect and with very little risk—assuming the brakes themselves are powerful enough. It also means that the rear brake is much more effective than it is on a regular single bike, because the rear wheel remains loaded during braking.

Probably the most suitable brake arrangement for the tandem is to use cantilever brakes or direct-pull brakes in combination with an additional drum or disk brake on the rear wheel.

Amongst suitable tandem drum brakes, the Maxicar is the finest available. With its large drum, it offers superb brake mantle cooling, and its construction is so superior that it assures light rolling as a hub and reliable stopping power as a brake, combined with a "buttonhole" spoke

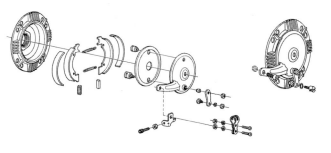

hole design assuring easy spoke replacement. Some tandems are actually used with disk brakes or even hub brakes both front and rear, doing without the usual rim brakes altogether. This solution is not recommended, because it places a very high strain on the front fork when braking.

For the normal configuration with two rim brakes and one disk brake or drum brake, the accepted standard operation is by means of one special lever with double cables that control both rim brakes together and a second lever that controls only the disk or drum brake. Another method is to use the disk or drum brake only as a drag brake, and connect each rim brake to its own lever, installing a little ratchet lever (from a derailleur gearing system) for the drum brake.

TANDEM SEATS

Since most tandems are used as touring bikes, typical touring or mountain bike seats are usually installed. Certainly for the stoker, who usually cannot anticipate road shocks, finishing up fully exposed to them, a sprung leather saddle is recommended. The forward seatpost must be clamped in very firmly, because the rear handlebars are usually attached to it: you don't want panic reactions of the stoker to twist the captain's seat.

Because the stoker cannot usually anticipate road shocks as well as the captain does, the rear seat is often subjected to heavy jolts. An excellent solution for this problem is to install a suspension seatpost, as described in Chapter 17. Indirectly, this will even help protect the rear wheel, because the shocks from the road are somewhat isolated from the wheel by the energy absorbed in the suspension post.

Above: Fig. 23.26. Calfee carbon-fiber composite tandem. Due to the manufacturer's use of reinforcing gussets, this frame is stiffer than it may look. Just the same, it's probably as fragile as it is light.

Top right: Fig. 23.27. A little longer than most: Santana triplet.

Bottom right: Fig. 23.28. A different kind of tandem: Angel Lake Cycling's original Counterpoint design.

24 FOLDING AND PARTING BIKES

HE IDEA OF constructing a bicycle in such a way that it can be easily transported or stowed is almost as old as the pedal-driven bicycle itself. We have found images of 1870s high-wheels that could be broken down to fit in a bag.

Most modern folding bikes, and those that can merely be separated for transport, have small wheels—typically 60 cm, or 20 in. However, quite a number of full-size bikes that fold have also been produced, and an increasing number have been introduced over the last decade. In this chapter, we'll be looking at both small-wheel bikes—folding and parting—and at some of the folding and parting solutions for bikes with "normal" size wheels.

FOLDING HISTORY

Several small-wheeled safety-bike designs were proposed before World War I, but only a few were commercially available until after the World War II. The most significant early example of that period was the Japanese Star folding bike, which was adapted from a bike that had been used during World War II by the Japanese military.

Right: Fig. 24.1. English manufacturers seem to be masters of the quick fold. Here's a Brompton going through the folding process.

In Europe, numerous folding bikes soon followed after several such machines were displayed at the 1958 IFMA bicycle and motorcycle trade show in Cologne, Germany. Unfortunately, most of these were suitable only for short-distance shopping trips, rather than serious cycling.

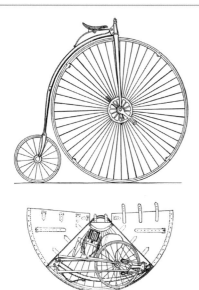

All that changed in 1962, when Alex Moulton introduced his first small-wheel design with front and rear suspension, to compensate for the additional jolts the road surface imparts on the smaller wheels. Smaller wheels do not roll over surface irregularities as easily as larger wheels, making front and rear suspension systems very desirable.

The Moulton's success set off a wave of copy-cat designs from established English and various other European manufacturers.

To keep the cost down, none of these incorporated the suspension concept, and instead relied on fat low-pressure tires to dampen the jolts. In the end, even Moulton's original became a victim of its success, as Moulton was hemmed in by production capacity limitations and eventually sold the design to Raleigh, leading to poor quality control.

What all these small-wheel bicycles did for cycling in Europe can be seen as both good and bad. The bad thing was that these machines took much of the

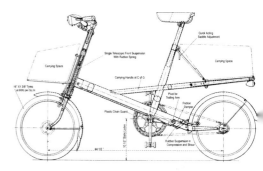

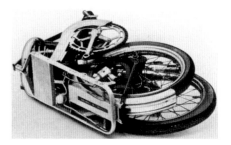

Above: Fig 24.2. English paratrouper with RAF-issue BSA folding bike, 1944.

Left and right: Figs. 24.3–24.9. Folding history: counterclockwise from top left: 1870s English folding high-wheel; 1909 Fongers from Holland; 1938 Petit Bi, from France; 1955 Katakura Silk folder, from Japan; 1955 Graziella Picolo, from Italy (the bike that started the small-wheel craze in Europe during the 1960s); 1962 Trawniczek, from Germany; and the 1962 Moulton, from England (perhaps the first comfortable small-wheeled bike on the market).

joy out of cycling, with a their harsh ride and cramped rider position. But on the other hand, they kept the European bicycle shops in business, the same way mopeds had done throughout the 1950s. In America, we did not see much of this phenomenon, but it kept a number of European manufacturers in business, who would some day be ready to supply bicycles to feed America's ten-speed boom of the early 1970s.

MODERN FOLDING BIKES

The most common way to make a bike that can be folded or parted to form a compact package is by using small wheels and putting a hinge in the middle of the frame. Additionally, the handlebars may be hinged back against the frame, the seatpost telescoped together, and one or both pedals folded out of the way.

Today, there are folding bikes that range from ultra-light speed machines to sturdy

full-suspension mountain bikes, and everything in between. They also vary greatly in ease of folding and their folded size. However, the major market is for relatively simple machines for short-distance commuting and light touring. It is fair to distinguish three main categories:

❏ Short-distance commuter bikes that are above all quick to fold;

❏ More sophisticated folding bikes with better riding qualities, not intended to be folded and transported on a daily basis;

❏ Bikes that ride like full-fledged bicycles, yet can

be disassembled occasionally, when the need arises.

WHEEL SIZE VERSUS SUSPENSION

Obviously, to keep the size of the folded bike down, the wheel size is the main limiting factor. Folding bikes indeed tend to have small wheels, all the way down to 400 mm (14 in. nominal wheel size). Such a small wheel size may be OK for a bike that is used only for short trips, such as urban shopping, but it does not make for either a comfortable or an efficient ride: Larger wheels roll more smoothly over bumps and dips in the road surface, resulting in both more comfort and less mechanical (rolling) resistance.

Even small wheels are available in different tire widths. As explained in Chapter 9, tire width in itself does not significantly effect rolling resistance, but it is tire pressure that does. However, narrower tires tend to be rated for higher pressures, and that in turn is what reduces rolling resistance.

Above, left, and right: Figs. 24.10–24.12. Examples of the three types of folding bikes: super-quick-folding Strida, with belt-drive and disk brakes, from England (above); more comfortable foldable Bike Friday, from the USA (left) and very sophisticated Alex Moulton Esprit "spaceframe" bike, from England (right). It comes apart, but it doesn't fold.

Rolling resistance can be minimized by using high-pressure tires, but those tend to aggravate the lack of comfort. For that reason, Alex Moulton designed his bicycles with a sophisticated suspension system. His bicycles run on light nominally 17 in. wheels (that tire size is unique to those bikes, so you won't find replacement anywhere except at a Moulton dealer). That's smaller than most other folding bikes, but the sophisticated suspension system keeps rider comfortable and the wheels in contact with the ground without bouncing. In fact, long-distance records have been set on some of these bikes.

Several other manufacturers now also provide some form of shock absorption. However, most of today's small-wheel folders use rigid frames and forks. If the bike does not have suspension, 500 mm (20 in.) seems to be the minimum acceptable tire size for a folding bike that is to be ridden over distances beyond a 20-minute trip.

Actually, Alex Moulton's bicycles—including the current generation of "spaceframe"

models—are not folding bikes; they can be separated for reasonably compact stowage. Many riders want to use a folding bike as a traveling companion when they visit places far from home, so they only occasionally need to fold or disassemble it.

Several manufacturers offer folding or parting bikes with more or less regular wheels, typically 650 mm (26-inch nominal) Such bikes may fold in the middle of the frame, or they may come apart by means of sophisticated coupling mechanisms, such as the S&S couplings, which add

Above: Fig. 24.13. Ritchey Breakaway frame with full-size wheels. It fits in a box, but the box is too big to travel free on most airlines.

Left: Fig. 24.14. The Bike Friday Crusoe folding bike (like many of that company's offerings) fits in a box that can be trailed behind the bike, but "some disassembly required."

Right: Fig. 24.15. On the Corrugate travel bike, from Italy, the wheels and other parts would fold in between the frame tubes, and then the whole package fit nicely in a modest-size bag. It's no longer available.

very little to the bike's weight (though a lot to its price) and do not weaken the frame tubes.

PACKAGE SIZE

Unfortunately, airlines have become more and more restrictive when it comes to carrying bicycles, even folding ones. When author Van der Plas arrived at San Francisco airport with a folded bike in a bag (which itself was within the luggage size limits), he was charged a hefty fee for taking a bike along as his (only) checked luggage. The problem was caused when he was asked about the bag, "is that a bicycle?" and, not being a very accomplished liar, he admitted it was.

This problem can be avoided if the bike fits in a hard-shell case (which the author's did not). The airline limit is a combined size of length, width, and height of 1.60 m (63 in.). So, unless your bike fits in that size case (possibly with tires deflated and minor disassembly), it won't travel free on any U.S. airline

(and probably not on most other airlines either).

Bike Friday, of Eugene, Oregon, designs several of its folding bikes to fit in a standard case (which is actually slightly bigger than the permitted maximum, though it usually seems to get the green light at the airport check-in counter). That case can even be converted to a trailer to tow behind the bike, doubling as a baggage trailer. Some bike tourists may find the bounciness of the trailer disconcerting on a long tour, but it is OK for shorter distances. Suspension would eliminate the problem, but that would probably make the package too big and complicated.

FRAME DESIGN

Most typical small-wheel folding bikes use a single large-diameter tube (which may be anything from round, to oval, to rectangular in cross-section). This keeps the frame reasonably stiff and the folding or parting mechanism uncomplicated. Since this solution

tends to be heavy, some high-end models use a regular, or even a triangulated frame construction.

The most intricate frames are those referred to as "spaceframe" and "double-pylon" designs used on Alex Moulton's current generation of small-wheel bikes.

For folding bikes made in series, even the conventional single-large-tube frames can be made reasonably light in weight with the use of hydroformed aluminum tubes. This technique allows the tube to be differentially shaped, so that the areas subjected to the highest torsional

Above: Fig. 24.16. The Bike Friday Tickit is an easy-folding and ultra-portable model with 16-inch wheels..

Left: Fig. 24.17. Brompton makes a simple bike with 20-inch wheels that folds by just lifting up the bike by its seat.

Right: Fig. 24.18. One of the most ingenious folding bikes is the Birdie, a German design made in Taiwan. With its full suspension, it rides well and yet is quite easy to fold into a compact package.

(and other) forces are "beefed up" sufficiently to result in an adequately stiff overall frame design.

The use of carbon-fiber monocoque construction would probably also make it possible to provide a light and stiff frame. It would be expensive, but just because many folding bikes have been made in the low price range does not mean there is not a market for more sophisticated and expensive ones.

The folding and parting mechanisms on a folding bike must be designed and constructed in such a way that they join correctly and reliably. The parts must fit accurately and it must be easy to lock them into place with a secure grip. Several manufacturers have developed proprietary hinges and latches, and in this respect bikes from established manufacturers, such as DaHon, Bike Friday, and Brompton have been significantly improved over the years.

FOLDING SPEED

The fastest bikes to fold tend to come from England and other European countries, where many commuters use them for inter-modal transport (i.e. combining a bike ride with segments by train or bus). They may ride the bike to the station, ride the train into town, finish the trip to work on the bike, and carry the folded bike into the building. Commuters don't want to spend a lot of time folding and unfolding a bike. The Brompton is particularly suitable for this kind of use, since it can be folded in simple stages, starting by just lifting the bike, which then automatically folds onto itself.

At the other end of the spectrum are such bikes as the Alex Moulton, which take about 15 minutes to disassemble on a good day, making them better for touring than for intermodal transport. Most other folding bikes fall somewhere in between, while almost all parting bikes are as slow to deal with as the Moulton.

DRIVETRAIN AND GEARING

On a folding bike, a standard derailleur system can get in the way of the folding operation, and may easily get damaged. For that reason, some manufacturers either have adopted a different design of derailleur that is tucked in closer under the chainstay, or they use internal hub gearing.

Brompton managed to get Sun-Race Sturmey-Archer to design a special wide-range 6-speed hub. It is simpler and probably more durable than most of the other multi-speed hub gears available, using only one set of planet gears, as opposed to three sets for 7- and 8-speed hubs. (And no, I haven't figured out yet how they do it.)

Several manufacturers use a toothed Aramid (e.g. Kevlar)

transmission belt instead of a conventional chain drive on some models without derailleur gearing. Toothed-belt transmission has reached a level of efficiency that makes them quite suitable for anything short of competitive cycling, and of course it cannot be used with derailleurs. Since a toothed belt is endless, the right-hand seatstay must be designed so that it can be removed or opened up for installation or replacement.

ACCESSORIES

It may be hard to find suitable accessories to fit on most small-

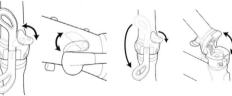

Above, left, and right: Figs. 24.19–24.24. Probably the biggest manufacturer of folding bikes is DaHon, which proudly proclaims to be "designed in California.". Some of their folding patents are used under license by several other manufacturers as well.

wheeled folding bikes. In addition, the installation of some accessories may hinder the folding and stowing. Several of the major manufacturers have developed a range of accessories specifically designed to fit their bikes. Even if you have a bike from another maker, it may be possible to use some of those items on it.

Luggage carriers can be a particular problem on many small-wheel bikes, because anything carried over or beside the rear wheel is more likely to interfere with the rider's pedaling motion. Therefore it is advisable to check for interference before purchase.

Most bicycle computers can be programmed for a wide range of tire sizes, but not all of them work on wheels as small as those used on some folders. Hub dynamos for lighting systems would be turning significantly faster than they do on a bike with regular size wheels, and they may have too many spoke holes in the hub for small

wheels. DaHon sells a special front wheel with a hub dynamo that is specifically designed to work with small wheels (which turn faster than larger wheels, and thus would otherwise generate a voltage that is too high for the bulbs).

Left and above: Figs. 24.30 and 24.31. The Montague full-size folding bikes of today (above) are based on the same idea as Wachtendonk's 1911 design (left).

Below: Fig. 24.32. Foldable recumbent from HP-Velotechnik, of Germany.

Left column: Figs. 24.25–24.29. Some components used on today's folding and parting bikes. From top to bottom: Ritchey Breakaway hinge connectors top at seat cluster and at bottom bracket; Winora seatstay connectors based on hydraulic tubing couplings; S&S frame tube couplings; and folding pedals.

25

RECUMBENT BICYCLES

ALTHOUGH THE VAST majority of bicycles are ridden with the rider in an upright to forward-declining posture, alternate positions should not be ruled out. There are some bicycle designs in which the rider leans back against a fixed support and the legs pointing forward. Such bike designs are referred to as recumbents, or "bents" for short if you're an adherent to this trend.

RECUMBENT FEATURES

The main advantages of the recumbent riding position are:

❏ Increased comfort, with the rider supported on a wider seat with a backrest (especially important for cyclists who suffer from back problems on a regular bike);

❏ Increased force application, not limited by the rider's

weight but by the strength of his or her leg muscles;

❏ Reduced air resistance due to lower profile;

❏ Improved weight distribution, with rider weight low and between the wheels;

❏ Reduced danger of serious head injury in a collision.

Of course, there are some disadvantages as well, which include:

Left and right: Figs. 25.1 and 15.2. Recumbent bicycles, old and new. The 1921 J-Rad, from Germany (left) and the Rans 450 FXP short-wheelbase recumbent from the USA (right).

- Harder to pedal uphill;

- Less visible to others, and limited field of vision for the rider;

- More difficult to balance (yes, being lower to the ground actually makes it harder to stay upright);

- A more cumbersome package, which is harder to store, maneuver, or transport when it is not being ridden.

The greater force that can be applied while pushing back against the backrest is not as important as you might think. What matters in cycling is not how much force can be applied in one pedal stroke, but how much power can be generated continuously. This is not to say recumbents don't have their place—they can make fine touring bikes—but they are not necessarily the holy grail of cycling either.

HISTORY OF RECUMBENTS

As with so many ideas that have (re-)surfaced in recent years, the concept of the recumbent bicycle is not exactly new. Probably the first reference to a commercially available recumbent dates to 1895. It concerns a vehicle called "Normal Bicyclette," referring to what the inventor, a Mr. Challand, of Geneva, Switzerland, called a "normal" riding posture. It had a cumbersome hand-and-foot-drive mechanism, which was replaced by conventional foot-propulsion in 1897.

The Normal Bicyclette did not find many adherents, though several other recumbent patents were taken out before the turn of the century. As early as 1901, at least one batch-built recumbent was available in the U.S. It took until 1914 before any major bicycle maker offered a series-built recumbent. That year, Peugeot took up production of a long-wheelbase recumbent with rear-wheel drive and regular-size

wheels. Soon production had to be discontinued, as French manufacturers were forced to divert their resources to supply the military during World War I.

In 1921, Jarray, a German airship designer, introduced a recumbent bicycle with linear treadle drive. Referred to as the J-Rad, it had a full-size rear wheel, and the rider sat higher up than on most modern recumbents (which had also been the case for the Peugeot's 1914 recumbent). Significant quantities of this machine were sold in Holland, a country with more wind than hills, where reduced air resistance was always welcome.

About 1930, a maker of pedal-driven cars, George Mochet, of France, introduced what may have been the first low-slung recumbent, called Vélocar. It was available in touring and racing versions. Their aerodynamic advantage led several racing cyclists during the 1930s to turn to them for successful record attempts. But in 1933, the governing body of cycle racing, the UCI, stepped in and redefined a bicycle in such

Left: Fig. 25.3. Challand's Normal-Bicyclette was presumably the first recumbent bicycle, complete with chain-drive to the rear wheel, direct steering, and a backrest for the rider. All that in 1897.

Right: Fig. 25.4. Peugeot offered this Vélo-Fauteuil, or armchair bike, in 1914.

terms that recumbents were excluded effective April 1934.

This move greatly hampered real technical innovation in bicycle development. The argument that cycle racing should be a race of human ability, not of technical innovation, may not be fully justified. After all, some argue, many other technical developments have also improved human performance—both in cycling and other sports—and many of these technical developments trickle down from the competitive sector to the benefit of non-competitive participants.

Meanwhile, also during the 1930s, several other manufacturers introduced recumbent bicycles, though none of these was designed for racing, so they all looked a lot less sophisticated than some of Mochet's designs.

By the outbreak of World War II, they had all stopped production.

After the war, an East German engineer, Paul Rinkowski, took up the development of highly efficient recumbent bicycles. Working behind the Iron Curtain, so that much of his work went unnoticed in the West, he refined some of the ideas that only much later found application on commercial recumbents. One idea was specially-designed high-pressure 20-inch tires. These were of radial-ply construction, a design for which Rinkowski was granted a patent in 1954.

It took until 1972 before the idea of the recumbent bicycle was picked up in the United States. David Gordon Wilson and Richard Forrestall essentially re-invented the concept of the recumbent, unaware of any earlier developments in Europe. These

machines were built and ridden by H. Frederick Wilkie II, whose feedback encouraged Wilson to make further refinements, both in long- and short-wheelbase designs. Eventually these machines were made in modest series under the name Avatar. Shortly after, other tinkerers and small-scale builders also started developing their own recumbents. By the mid 1980s, a number of manufacturers in various countries were producing recumbents of various designs, several of which have survived into the 21st century.

Above: Fig. 25.8. Paul Rinkowski, of East Germany, on one of his innovative recumbents, around 1960.

Top left: Fig. 25.5. George Mochet riding an early version of his low-slung Vélocar recumbent.

Bottom left: Fig. 25.6. In 1933 Francis Faure broke world speed records riding one of Mochet's recumbents.

Right: Fig. 25.7. Start of a 1934 race between Faure, on the Mochet Vélocar, and riders on conventional bicycles.

MODERN RECUMBENTS

Since the 1990s, there has been a renewed resurgence of interest in recumbent bicycles. Some of this interest was due to attempts to achieve higher speeds, some for the sake of comfort, and some simply for the (perfectly legitimate) wish to try something different.

TYPES OF RECUMBENTS

Most recumbents on the market today fall into one of the following three categories:

❏ Short wheelbase two-wheelers;

❏ Long wheelbase two-wheelers;

❏ Three-wheelers, usually with a short wheelbase.

The latter will be covered separately in the Chapter 26, while the other types will be discussed in some detail below.

The distinction between short and long wheelbase bikes boils down to whether the center of the front wheel is behind or in front of the crankset. As with any arbitrary distinction, some recumbent bikes fall in between, namely those that have the front wheel close to the crankset (including some with a directly driven, internally-geared, front wheel). However most recumbents clearly fall into one category or the other.

Above and left: Figs. 25.9 and 25.10. David Gordon Wilson, engineering professor at MIT, was instrumental in popularizing the recumbent bicycle in the United States during the late 1970s and 1980s. Here he is seen onboard his early long-wheelbase Avatar 2000 (left). Above is a design sketch for the Avatar 1000 short-wheelbase machine.

Right: Fig. 25.11. One of the major innovators in bicycle design is Mike Burrows, of England, and recumbents are only one of his many varied contributions. Here he is on his Ratcatcher single-sided short-wheelbase recumbent.

Because the rider on any recumbent is unable to lift his or her body weight out of the seat in anticipation of road shocks, some form of suspension is beneficial, at least in the rear. Today's suspension technology offers a wide variety of effective off-the-shelf solutions that are incorporated in several manufacturers' recumbent designs.

A special type of long-wheelbase machine is what may be referred to as the "low-slung" recumbent. On these, the rider sits very close to the ground between the wheels. Though harder to balance, they are the most aerodynamically advantageous, and therefore often combined with fairings for use in human powered speed races and record attempts.

At the other end of the spectrum are recumbents with a full-size rear wheel. Although these bikes often do not allow as much reduction in aerodynamic drag, they tend to be easier to balance. They are also more suitable for carrying luggage, making them most suitable for both urban transport and for touring.

Some consider the conventional steering mechanism, which

places the headset and stem in front of the rider's face, potentially hazardous. To alleviate that problem, Wilson had revised the early designs to offer under-the-seat steering. Some recumbents today also offer this feature, and some are available with a choice of steering configurations.

RECUMBENT FAIRINGS AND HPVs.

Almost as old as the recumbent bicycle itself is the idea of reducing aerodynamic drag using fairings. During the 1920s and 1930s, several world records were broken, both on standard

bicycles with fairings attached to either the bike or the rider, and on partially or wholly faired recumbents.

Although aerodynamic theory was well established at the time, it was not until recently that manufacturing techniques have made it commercially feasible to produce perfectly smooth fairings with adequate strength

and stiffness to be of potential practical use. So why don't we see those faired machines on the

Above: Fig. 25.12. HP-Velotechnik short-wheelbase recumbent, from Germany, with front and rear suspension.

Left: Fig. 25.13. Flevo-Racer, from Holland, also with front and rear suspension.

TABLE 25.1. HUMAN-POWERED VEHICLES: ONE-HOUR WORLD RECORD

Year	Distance (= speed in km/h)	Rider	Designer / Model	Type
1932	49.99	Marcel Berthet	Berthet	Faired conventional bicycle
1938	50.53	François Faure	Mochet	Non-faired recumbent bicycle
1979	51.31	Ron Skarin	Kyle / Teledyne Titan	Faired conventional bicycle
1980	59.45	Eric Edwards	Voigt / Vector	Faired recumbent tricycle
1984	60.35	Fred Markham	Martin / Gold Rush	Faired recumbent bicycle
1985	66.30	Richard Crane	Hendon	Faired recumbent bicycle
1989	67.01	Fred Markham	Martin / Gold Rush	Faired recumbent bicycle
1989	73.00	Fred Markham	Martin / Gold Rush	Faired recumbent bicycle
1990	75.57	Pat Kinch	Kingsbury / Bean	Faired recumbent bicycle
1996	78.04	Lars Teutenberg	Mertens / Tomahawk II	Faired recumbent tricycle
1998	79.136	Sam Whittingham	Georgiev / Varna	Faired recumbent bicycle
1999	81.158	Lars Teutenberg	Vector/IKV / White Hawk	Faired recumbent tricycle
2002	82.60	Lars Teutenberg	Vector/IKV / White Hawk	Faired recumbent tricycle
2003	83.72	Sam Whittingham	Georgiev / Varna	Faired recumbent bicycle
2004	84.22	Sam Whittingham	Georgiev / Varna	Faired recumbent bicycle
2006	85.99	Sam Whittingham	Georgiev / Varna	Faired recumbent bicycle
2007	86.77	Sam Whittingham	Georgiev / Varna	Faired recumbent bicycle
2008	87.123	Damjan Zabovnik	Eivie Team / Eivie II	Faired recumbent tricycle
2009	90.60	Sam Whittinham	Georgiev / Varna Tempest	Faired recumbent bicycle

road very much, you ask? Perhaps it is because they turn the simple bicycle into a more cumbersome device, sacrificing some of the bicycle's inherent advantages—low weight, low cost, easy maintenance, maneuverability, etc.—on the altar of speed and spiffy looks.

Things are different on the racetrack. In fact, every IHPV (International Human Powered

Left-hand column and below: Figs. 25.14–25.17. Some recumbent details. Counterclockwise from top left: Tandem drivetrain on an M5 recumbent tandem; steering detail, crankset detail, and seat adjusting bracket on a Rans recumbent.

Bottom right: Fig. 25.18. Fully faired M5 recumbent, from Holland.

Vehicle) competition presents some new examples of such machines. Most of these are fully enclosed, with the rider either in prone or supine position, and none of them very practical for everyday use.

Almost all who have tried riding this kind of vehicle in "real life" (i.e. not on the racetrack), concluded that they are unbearably noisy. The full fairing shell reverberates and amplifies road and wind noise. Some of the exceptions have been made of more traditional materials, like sail cloth, which serves perhaps more as weather protection than as an aid to improved aerodynamics.

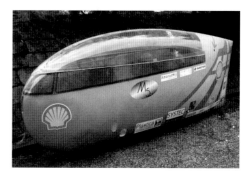

26. NOT JUST TWO WHEELS

Although they are not very common, there are some technically and historically interesting aspects in cycles with 3 and 4 wheels. There are even cycles with just one wheel, and some with two wheels side by side. All such cycle types are the subject of this chapter.

HISTORICAL BACKGROUND

It did not take long after Von Drais developed the first bicycle that he and others followed up with other human-powered vehicles. Most common amongst these were tricycles, or three-wheelers, in various configurations, but some had four wheels, and were referred to as quadra-cycles. Grouped together, they are referred to as multicycles.

Especially during the period preceding the introduction of the safety bicycle, many of the technically advanced solutions were found on such machines. Both chain-drive and multi-speed gearing were first applied to tricycles, before finding use on the bicycle. In addition, the modern automobile can be traced back to tricycle and quadracycle technology. The differential and

Left: Fig. 26.1. Traditionally, tricycles had one wheel in front and two in the rear. They're getting scarce, but in Britain, they're still being raced like this.

Right: Fig. 26.2. You've met him in the previous chapter, Mike Burrows, this time riding another one of his famed contraptions; this is the Windcheetah recumbent tricycle.

rack-and-pinion steering, for example, were originally developed for tricycle use.

Since the balancing act necessary to ride a bicycle was considered awkward in elaborate dress, and at the time considered flat-out impossible for women, these three- and four-wheeled machines appealed particularly to women and older men. But even after the introduction of the safety bicycle, in the 1880s, some riders—both men and women—continued to ride tricycles.

MODERN 3- AND 4-WHEELERS

There are three possible configurations for tricycles:

❏ One wheel in the front and two wheels in the rear, referred to as delta trikes, or endearingly as "barrows" to their British riders;

❏ Two wheels in the front and one in the rear, referred to as "tadpole" trikes, and

currently the most common for e.g. recumbent trikes;

❏ Two wheels in line and one to the side (far and away the least common design these days).

Today, technically interesting cycles with 3 (or more) wheels are made mainly as recumbents and carrier bikes. The advantages of the three-wheel configuration for these two types are summarized below:

Recumbent tricycle advantages:

❏ Allows lower rider position for reduced overall profile;

Above: Fig. 26.3. Before George Mochet introduced his Vélocar recumbent bicycle (see Chapter 25), his family's business built three- and four-wheel pedal cars, such as this one, also called Vélocars.

Left: Figs. 26.4 and 26.5. Historic multicycles: James Starley's Royal Salvo, of 1887 (top), and Carl. Benz's 1888 tricycle with motor, which is considered the world's first automobile.

Right: Figs. 26.6 and 26.7. Different wheels: Richard C. Hemmings' 1869 Monocycle (top) made do with just one wheel; and E. C. F. Otto's 1880 Dicycle had two wheels side-by-side.

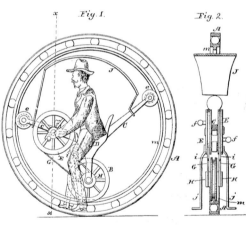

❏ Reduces rolling resistance (compared to two-wheel recumbent) due to reduced friction of tires in steering/balancing;

❏ Offers more possibilities for aerodynamic fairings;

❏ Makes it easier for the rider to balance and steer the vehicle.

Carrier tricycle advantages:

❏ Increased load carrying capacity, in terms of both volume and weight;

❏ Improved balancing and steering.

Although, of course, there are also some disadvantages associated with three-wheelers, such as their greater bulk and weight. However, for tricyclists, any disadvantages are outweighed by the listed advantages for these specific applications.

MONOCYCLES AND DICYCLES

Although today monocycles (now more commonly referred to as unicycles) are generally only

used for trick cycling, they have in the past been taken more seriously. Of course, the biggest problem of the unicycle is balancing—both sideways and back-to-front. Another problem is that the speed is limited by the wheel diameter and the rider's ability to pedal fast, which is not

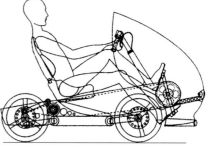

Left: Fig. 26.8. Modern unicycle. Some people actually manage to ride on those machines.

Top right: Fig. 26.9. Delivery tricycle, Vienna, 1888.

Center right: Fig. 26.10. Prototype post office delivery tricycle, Holland, 1997.

Below: Fig. 26.11. Tricycle tandem racing, presumably in England, CA 1885.

Bottom right: Fig. 26.12. Modern four-wheeler design sketch.

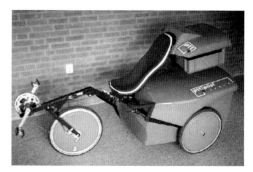

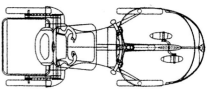

as easy on a unicycle as it is on a bicycle or a multicycle.

Various solutions to these limitations have been introduced. One is the use of a much larger wheel, while placing the rider higher up, which both eases balancing and increases potential speed. In that case, a linkage is attached to the cranks to raise the pedals. The other solution is the use of internal hub gearing, which only increases the potential speed.

Even more ingenious is the use of a very large wheel, with the rider sitting below the wheel

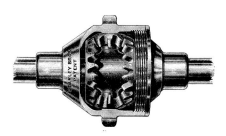

Above: Fig. 26.13. The differential gear, invented by James Starley for the tricycle in 1876, is now a more common application in automobiles. It allows two driven wheels to turn at different speeds when cornering.

Below: Fig. 26.14. Greenspeed Grand Sport recumbent touring tricyle.

axle. Although this solution requires a more complicated, indirect, drive mechanism, it allows not only for greater speed and easier balancing, but also reduced rolling resistance and a more comfortable ride. A bit cumbersome, though…

An offshoot of the unicycle is the dicycle (no, that is not a misspelling), on which the two wheels are not in line but side by side. The idea—first developed as early as 1819—was

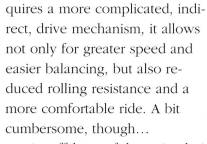

Above: Fig. 26.15. Schlumpf Mountain-Drive 2-speed chainwheel gears used on a Greenspeed tricycle. It is shifted by pushing against the center button with the heel of the foot.

Below: Fig. 26.16. The fully faired Go-One recumbent tricycle.

seriously pursued during the 1870s and 1880s, most notably by E. C. F. Otto, of Germany, whose invention went into production with BSA.

In recent times, the idea of the monocycle has been seriously studied for application in the development of the next generation of the Mars Rover, a vehicle designed for exploration of the surface of the planet Mars. What makes it attractive for such an application is the fact that the monocycle, unlike any other vehicle, is fully maneuverable into any direction with a "zero" turning radius.

Above and below: Figs. 26.17 and 26.18. Two times Flevobike with fairing: a simple flexible cover (above), and a sleek, aerodynamic carbon-fiber composite racing version (below).

27

POWER-ASSISTED BICYCLES

In recent years, bicycle trade shows have witnessed a rapidly increasing offering of machines referred to as "E-bikes," bicycles with electric motor assist.

Of course, power-assisted bicycles are nothing new, but today's digital control technology and lightweight battery developments have made this type of machine more viable than it has been in the past.

HISTORICAL BACKGROUND

The first use of electric-assist bicycles was recorded in 1898, when they were first introduced to pace racers in speed record attempts (previous to that, multi-rider tandems had been used for

the same purpose). And of course, all forms of motorized two-, three-, and four-wheelers were developed from the humble bicycle.

Most motorized vehicle developments, regardless of their auxiliary power source, started out as pedal cycles with motor assistance, meaning the rider was still expected to crank the pedals as well. But soon they developed into motor-driven cycles with "ornamental" pedals, used only to start the motor, or sometimes merely to satisfy a legal requirement so they would not be classified as motor vehicles (thus avoiding taxation, licensing, and insurance requirements).

MODERN E-BIKES

The current wave of E-bikes, or "Pedelecs," as these machines

Fig. 27.1. Electric-assist pacing bikes first showed up on European bicycle race tracks in 1898. This image shows multiple world-record holder Émile Bouhours behind an electric pacing tandem.

are often called, relies heavily on digital controls to provide a balance between rider input and motor assist. A sensor detects the force applied to the rear wheel by the rider, and the digital control unit then apportions the amount of electric power. Until 2008, the Japanese law governing the use of E-bikes allowed only for equal amounts of human and electric input, but since 2009, it is also possible to use twice as much electric input. (This, of course, may be the first step on the road to an all-electric bicycle, just like earlier motor-assists lead to gasoline-powered motorcycles.)

The electric motors come in several different configurations: built in the front wheel, in the rear wheel, or mounted somewhere in between. The advantage of motors contained in the front or rear wheel is that they can be integrated in a standard bicycle design, and can also be made available as aftermarket accessories, allowing cyclists to covert their regular bikes into E-bikes. This works best on mountain bikes and city bikes, but probably also on some recumbents.

RANGE AND SPEED

The range of an electric-assist bike depends on three factors: power output, battery capacity, and efficiency. Obviously, letting the electric motor do only half the work, with the rider pedaling for the other half, results in an expanded range as compared to relying on the motor entirely, or the motor doing two-thirds of the work. Most casual cyclists can deliver no more than about 80 W (watts), or about 0.11 hp. So the electric motor should be able to supply just that much, which is quite modest power for an

ELECTRIC BIKE CATEGORIES

All electric-assist bicycles fall into one of four categories:

1. CEB, or Conventional Electric Bicycle. The electric power turned on or off with a switch, independent of any pedaling effort.

2. SAB, or Simple Assist Bicycle. The motor runs when pedaling effort is detected.

3. EHB, or Electro-Hybrid Bicycle. The motor force is regulated to be proportional to the rider's pedaling effort. Most modern E-bikes fall within this category.

4. SHB, or Synergetic Hybrid Bicycle. In addition to the features of the EHB, energy is recovered when braking or descending, leading to increased efficiency.

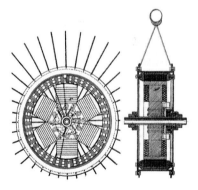

Above: Fig. 27.4. Nothing new: Bolton hub motor, 1895 (that's not a misprint).

Left: Fig. 27.2. Modern E-bike from Gazelle, with motor in the front wheel and battery integrated with the rear luggage rack.

Right: Fig. 27.3. SRAM's Sparc rear hub electric drive, introduced 2001, had two separate motors and integral 5-speed gearing.

electric motor, and allows for a light and compact design that easily fits in an oversize wheel hub. Together, rider and motor will produce about 160 W, or 0.22 hp. On a level surface, an upright cyclist can expect a speed of 30 km/h (19 mph) without great effort, and even going uphill, it is not going to be a big struggle to keep going at a reasonable speed of say 15 km/h (9.5 mph).

To provide a one-hour range under those circumstances requires a battery capacity of 80 W * 1 hr = 80 Wh (watt-hour). Modern battery technology has resulted in quite light and compact rechargeable batteries that can easily produce that kind of energy.

Most promising amongst the various battery types available today is the type referred to as Lithium-Ion-Manganese. They offer a high "energy density" and a high recovery rate (meaning they give off about 95% of the energy used to charge them). In

RECENT E-BIKE DEVELOPMENTS

In recent times, development of the electric-assist bicycle in Britain was encouraged when the 1967 Road Traffic Regulation Act was enacted. It provided that electric-drive bicycles would not be categorized as motor vehicles. Alex Moulton, was granted a patent for a bicycle with a front wheel between two motor-driven rollers. Lucas Industries and several small manufacturers produced some electric bicycles in the early 1970s.

Modern type "pedelecs" were primarily developed in Japan. A Japanese patent filed in 1974, in the aftermath of the first oil crisis, included a feature by which the motor would kick in when the rider's force on the chain exceeded a pre-determined level, and electric-assist

bicycles of that type were first marketed in 1979.

First off the block with a modern E-bike was Yamaha. Their "Vehicle A," a 1990 prototype, demonstrated the practical feasability of proportional electric and human input. The concept was refined in "Vehicle Z" the following year, and the first production model, the Yamaha PAS was introduced in 1994, soon followed by numerous competitors' machines.

In Europe, SRAM introduced its Sparc electric-drive hub in 1999, which included two motors, but discontinued production of this expensive device after a few years. China is now the biggest source for electric motors, which are used by many Asian, European, and American bicycle manufacturers, though at the top end of the market, Japanese E-motor manufacturers still dominate.

Above: Fig. 27.5. 2005 Giant Revive Spirit recumbent E-bike.

Left: Fig. 27.6. Yuba electric cargo bike with front-hub motor..

addition, their ability to take some 3,000 charge cycles sets them apart from the competition. The greater life expectancy of lithium-ion-manganese batteries may make them cheaper in the long run than other types of rechargeable batteries.

E-bike manufacturers tend to emphasize the range of their machines—how far they can go on a charge. However, for most

potential users, the range question is not really so critical, because the vast majority of urban and suburban trips does not exceed 8 km (5 miles), even in a car. Thus even a 10-mile range (16 km) is adequate and allows for the battery to be recharged at home before the bike is needed again. Besides, these bikes really do ride much like regular bicycles when the motor is not activated. Yes, without motor assist, the rider will be going slower, or will have to exert more effort, but won't be stranded when the juice runs out.

Left: Fig. 27.7. Panasonic Sugardrop small-wheel E-bike with bottom-bracket-mounted motor. With its front rack, modest price, and 59 km range, it is popular with Japanese housewives.

Right: Fig. 27.8. BionX electric-assist conversion kit, from Canada.

As for efficiency, the modern brushless electric motors used are quite efficient compared to internal combustion engines. There is some difference in efficiency between the various voltage ratings of 12, 24, and 36 V. The higher-voltage motors tend to be both more powerful and slightly more efficient.

The overall efficiency of the entire system can be enhanced slightly by recovering braking and descending energy, switching the motor to be used as an electric generator.

BRUSHLESS MOTORS

Most suitable for E-bikes is a motor type referred to as BDC, or Brushless Direct Current, motor. They work according to the same principle as the generators, or dynamos, used for bicycle lighting on most city bikes. Like any other electric motor, there is a fixed part, called stator, and a rotating part, called rotor. With the brushless motor, one of these parts contains one or more permanent magnets, and the other part contains electric wire

coils wound around a laminated metal structure.

When the rotor turns relative to the stator, the polarity of the stator coils rapidly changes, generating electricity: the device becomes a generator. When electricity is fed to the stator coils, the rotor will rotate: the device becomes a motor. Although in most electric motors, the rotor is inside the stator, in many E-bikes the rotor rotates around the stator. The latter configuration makes it easy to design the motor as a wheel hub:

the stator is connected to the wheel axle and the rotor to the hub flange, driving the wheel when electricity is supplied.

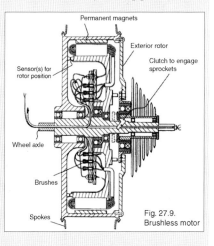

Fig. 27.9. Brushless motor

28 THE FUTURE OF THE BICYCLE?

This last chapter of the book is author Van der Plas's personal interpretation of the bicycle and its role in the future, presenting his own expectations for the future, comparing them, as well as the premises on which they are based, with those of some of colleagues.

WHAT'S NEW?

Over half a century of following developments in the world of cycling, I don't think fundamentally very much has changed. True, top-end bikes have become lighter (and very much more expensive), but the vast majority of bicycles sold in the world still looks much like they did 20, 40, and even 100 years ago.

And as for usage, the only significant development is that two billion inhabitants of China and India are in the process of abandoning the bicycle in favor of the motor car. Meanwhile, back in America, the bicycle is still seen as a toy. This is a society where "serious" cyclists are considered those who would not dream of using their expensive high-tech toys for practical transportation. What makes anyone think those trends are going to reverse any time soon?

Of course, I may be mistaken in these predictions—and indeed

Right and left: Figs. 28.1 and 28.2. Futuristic ideas for the development of cycling and the bicycle itself are a dime a dozen. Here two examples: an entry for the 1972 Honda Idea Competition (right) and a proposal for a bicycle-assist moving beltway (left).

it would make life more interesting if that were the case. But most of what is being projected had as fair a chance in the past as it ever will in the future; if they didn't make it then, why should they make it now?

BICYCLE DREAMS

Most of what I call the *Bicycle Fiction* images that are conjured up by those who see a golden future for two-wheeled human-powered transportation are unrealistic. They present visions of a world with roads dominated by sleek pedal-driven cars, with overhead monorails in which the passengers sit merrily pedaling

away, while fully enclosed recumbents dart by on separate bicycle freeways. From the air, the whole pedal-driven landscape is being controlled by police in human-powered helicopters.

The underlying assumptions are so unrealistic as to make this vision a sure loser. In fact, nowhere today are we any closer to realizing any of this in practice

ALTERNATE DRIVES

One of the recurring themes in presumable improvement to the bicycle is the idea of different methods of driving the bike. To some, the bicycle chain appears to be inappropriate technology for their idea of a future bicycle revolution. The idea is usually to "tidy up" the bike's drivetrain.

The three most frequently suggested alternates are shaft-drive, lever drive, and belt drive. All three have been proposed and tried in the past, and all have lost out to the chain drive and conventional gearing on account of efficiency differences.

The shaft drive, universally used on motor cars and some

high-powered motorcycles, is heavier, noisier, and less efficient than the chain drive.

The lever drive principle is almost as old as the bicycle itself, and was used on tricycles before the pedal-drive was introduced on the first boneshakers in the 1860. MacMillan's machine (regardless whether it was a 2-wheeler or a multi-wheeler) was presumably propelled by means of a treadle drive, as were several other machines of the period.

Figs. 28.3–28.5. 1889 Shaft drive, from FN, Belgium (left); also from 1889, lever-drive, from Sweden (above); and a modern belt-drive system, from Germany (right).

An interesting two-wheeled lever drive bike was the Svea, first introduced in Sweden, later licensed to the French Terrot company. It had 10-speed gearing, achieved by moving the engagement point of the lever in or out relative to the wheel axle, and controlled by means of a twistgrip.

As for the belt drive, yes, it has found a niche market in the area of quick-folding bicycles. Modern toothed belts with aramid carcasses are flexible and stretch-resistant enough to become practical—as long as slight efficiency penalty is accepted. These drives are clean and silent-running, and lend themselves to be fully encapsulated for protection.

than we were when such concepts were first drawn up in the 1950s.

Such visions are all based on unrealistic assumptions. One of these assumptions is the total collapse of external energy sources, combined with a sudden desire on the part of the populace to maintain their mobility, while accepting the need to provide the requisite propulsive power themselves. The alternative, and more popular vision, is the one by which bicycles and other human powered vehicles become so much more attractive that those who now drive around in cars will be converted to the cause of self-propulsion. The one scenario is as unlikely as the other.

PRACTICAL HPVS?

Let us first take a closer look at the presumed prototype of tomorrow's vehicle, the HPV, or human

powered vehicle. Although most interest in these sleek machines was generated since the 1970s, similar concepts have been around since record attempts were first made on streamlined bicycles by renowned bicycle racers before the outbreak of the First World War. (See Chapter 27 for a more detailed discussion of this phenomenon.)

In addition to the things said in the preceding chapters about the concepts on which these machines are based, we should take a look at their actual form and use as developed until now. Whether another 10, or even 100 years of development will lead to such improvement that they will lend themselves to mass use can perhaps best be judged by extrapolating their development to date.

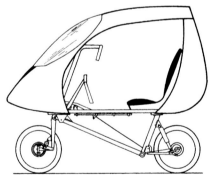

Above: Fig. 28.6. Garbien semi-enclosed recumbent proposal, 1974.

Left: Fig. 28.7. Vector HPV against road bike, Germany, 1984.

Right: Figs. 28.8 and 28.9. Ferrari and Colnago's 1989 proposal for flywheel energy storage (near right), and the 19th century prototype (far right).

In the HPV races that are held regularly under the auspices of the IHPVA (International Human Powered Vehicle Association), some impressive speeds have been reached with such machines—at the time of this writing the record stands at about 105 km/h (65 mph). That's in an all-out sprint with a flying start over a distance of 200 m (650 ft)—quite impressive when you realize that regular bicycles in competition reach speeds of "only" 70 km/h (44 mph) over similar distances.

Although the speed reached over such a short sprint obviously says something about the vehicle's aerodynamic properties, a more practical measure is the speed reached continuously over a longer distance. Even under such conditions, as established in the one-hour time trial, the HPV's performance is quite impressive. So far they have improved on the records established on regular machines by about 25%, and these higher speeds were achieved by riders who were not necessarily world-class racing cyclists.

Even so, that is after nearly a hundred years of development, of which the last forty were quite intensive, with international cooperation and commercial

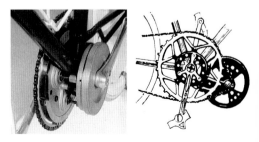

sponsorships. Percentage-wise, the hour record on regular bicycles (presently more than 52 km) has been improved about as much during the last 90 years as that on HPVs.

IN PURSUIT OF COMFORT

Most of the concepts for tomorrow's dream bike include the wish to sit back the way you do in a Ferrari. If you've ever driven any distance in that kind of car, you may know that it is not as comfortable in the long run as it is exhilarating at first. On a bicycle, it makes even less sense than in a car, because you have to move your legs around and around at about 100 RPM.

Whatever else one tries to achieve, three goals remain essential:

❏ minimizing rolling resistance;

❏ minimizing wind resistance;

❏ keeping the whole structure as light as possible.

A rider who is leaning back needs a suspension in order to remain comfortable Adding any kind of suspension negatively affects at least one, of these criteria. Fatter tires add weight, and if inflated less to increase their cushioning effect, the rolling resistance increases. For road use, all other kinds of suspension have the same effect of increased weight.

Of course, futurists also expect their utopian regular

bicycles to have more, rather than less, comfort compared to the conventional bike of yesterday. In the low-slung design that is taken for granted in many of these concepts, small wheels and a low body position are required. Both increase the need for an effective suspension, even to get the same comfort—much more so if a higher degree of comfort is required. All this not only adds weight, it also complicates the machine.

The point I am trying to make with this example is that, to be practically suitable, any bike design that differs drastically from that of the conventional model requires so much in the way of other tricks as to become hopelessly complicated and often harder to handle.

ALTERNATE MATERIALS

Another thing bicycle "futurists" often suggest is the use of alternate materials. This too is not a new idea either. Wood, bamboo, plastic, and fiberglass have all been tried in the past. To date, carbon-fiber composites are the first and only materials to pass the test of time—at least for limited

applications where weight is critical, and price is no object.

The accompanying illustrations show some of the early uses of some of the alternate materials

that have not stood the test of time. An exception should perhaps be made for bamboo, which has been used in combination with carbon-fiber composite by Calfee, but only as an interesting gag, rather than as a serious mass-production technique.

Figs. 28.10–28.12. Bikes made of cast magnesium, the Kirk Precision of the 1980s; fiber-reinforced plastic, the Swedish Itera, of 1980; and lugged bamboo, from Austria, 1897.

CYCLING UNDER COVER

Very similar to the arguments for the other aspects of the HPV and similar special designs are those in favor of enclosures. Since people drive around in cars that are covered, it is assumed they will be more easily converted to riding bikes if they are covered too. But cycling can be hard work, generating enough heat to make any enclosure unbearable. Air conditioning cannot be the answer: to remove the heat generated by the cyclist, approximately ten times the cyclist's output has to be made available to the air conditioner that would be needed.

There are other problems with this idea. Whereas a conventional bicycle is relatively insensitive to cross winds, the enclosed model is easily swept aside by a strong wind, even by the air stream generated by a passing truck. Handling an enclosed HPV can be much more difficult than one might expect.

The materials used must be very light, and are quite prone to damage caused either accidentally or by vandalism. And while today's bike can be transported or parked relatively easily, their enclosed counterparts resist most attempts in that direction.

WHAT ABOUT THAT FAMOUS DEMONSTRATION?

At least one experiment with the presumably practical use of a roadworthy versions of an HPV for commuting was carried out in 1981 during the otherwise laudable though short reign of Adriana Gianturco as head of the California state transportation agency. An early version of the 3-wheeled 2-rider Vector was ridden between Stockton and Sacramento in California on a closed-off freeway lane.

The route did not really represent your typical commute run, which is usually characterized by plenty of cross traffic, sharp curves, and other obstacles. An entire infrastructure was provided, with (motorized) escort vehicles, changing facilities, and transport into the city center. And, of course, there were reporters and press photographers, medics, traffic police, and others standing guard. The result was proclaimed a great success and promptly buried in the files: the HPV had managed to complete the trip in 70% of the time required on a regular bicycle, at times reaching speeds of 80 km/h (50 mph) on level ground.

A success after all? Not really. Unless the state can be counted on to provide all commuters with enough training to bring up their speed to the point where an HPV is of any speed advantage. Unless whole freeway lanes (with their merging on- and off-ramps) are permanently blocked to other traffic to allow HPVs to do their thing. Unless enclosed storage and changing facilities, shuttle service, and police escorts are provided for every trip. Unless California

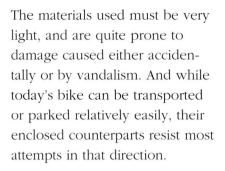

Above: Fig. 28.13. Yes, bikes have flown, but your bike won't ever take to the air.

Left: Fig. 28.14. Bicycle "conveyor belt."

Right: Fig. 28.15. Covered overhead bikeway proposal, 1994.

summer weather can be guaranteed everywhere year-round.

Don't take our skeptical approach too seriously, though. There may be sound reasons for some people to believe in, or at least dream of, a golden age for self-propelled transportation. There are understandable, if not substantiated, reasons to have faith in man's perfectability, which should also increase his appreciation of the bicycle as a means of transport (a hard one to sell in an age when cycling is equated with fitness).

Even if most of tomorrow's bikes will look just like today's machines, even if most people riding them will do so because they are a little different from the rest, there is nothing wrong with hoping some will choose different machines, and that some who prefer to drive their cars today may someday voluntarily choose to cycle. Just don't expect either a social or a technical bicycle revolution—whether now or in the future.

MORE QUESTIONS THAN ANSWERS?

Coauthor Baird did some relevant musings of his own, and noted that there are many unanswered questions that affect the future of cycling and the bicycle industry. Here is but a sampling of the some of the issues that seem to deserve further investigation:

❑ The great majority of goods available in the U.S. today are made in China. So far that's not the case in a typical bike shop (though it already is in the bicycle sections of big-box stores), but isn't that likely to change? What will that mean to shops, cyclists, and traditional manufacturers?

❑ Almost all cars, and many motorcycles, these days have anti-lock braking. Bikes need it much more than autos ever did. When are we going to see a practical ABS on a bicycle? What technical hurdles must be overcome?

❑ Likewise most autos have automatic transmissions. What are the shortcomings of current bike transmissions? Can automatics be practical for all kinds of riders? Will improved transmissions be entirely mechanical or have a significant electronic component?

❑ Materials continue to get stronger and lighter. Where are improved materials most needed on the bicycle?

❑ Cyclists keep getting less capable of performing maintenance and making simple repairs, while bicycles keep getting more difficult to repair in the field (and in some respects, possibly less in need of repairs). This trend parallels one with drivers and automobiles. How about a few years from now? Will it be possible to make any repair or adjustment outside a bike shop with highly specialized equipment? Is it possible to make a practical bike which never even gets a flat tire?

❑ Some aspects of bicycle design and riding continue to be guesswork, e.g. what makes a saddle comfortable for different types of riders and riding, how can riders detect and prevent the onset of fatigue, how does a rider know when a bike fits, how well are the tires rolling and how close are they to failure from puncture or pinch flats, how does a rider know when doing the extra mile will make him stronger or merely more tired? What kind of research or sensor apparatus can help answer these questions?

❑ A significant recent trend has been in electronic communications—Internet search engines, smart phones, social networks via sites such as Facebook and Twitter. How can bicycles get in on this trend, or should they be havens away from this trend?

ELECTRIC FUTURE?

Covered extensively in Chapter 27, this development offers at least one ray of hope for the survival of cycling as a mode of transport. Since electric assist makes cycling less work at a modest cost, I believe that it may help slow down the flight to cars. Whether it will help increase the appeal of the (quasi) bicycle amongst those who do not now ride a bike remains to be seen.

So far, most sales successes for E-bikes have been booked in countries where cycling is already a common means of transport: Japan, Taiwan, Holland, Germany, and Denmark. Lots of them are also available in the U.S., but so far there has been no evidence of any mass conversions to the cause of (E-)cycling.

MORE QUESTIONS THAN ANSWERS? (CONTINUED)

❑ Media such as television, radio and Internet tend to shape public opinion. What will it take to have cycling presented in a more favorable and attractive way in the U.S.? Another Greg LeMond or Lance Armstrong? Is the country ready for completely different, non-competitive approaches?

❑ The world's oil production is nearing its peak. Although ways to extract more oil from existing resources continue to be developed, in a few years the oil supply will begin to decrease. In addition, countries such as India and China are not only getting more populous, but wealthier, adding thousands of new automobile drivers every day. These trends will cause increased demand, cause the price of oil to increase greatly, may lead to further conflicts between oil-producing and oil-consuming nations, and will give additional push to alternative forms of energy. What role will the bicycle play? What features of the bicycle or the bicycling infrastructure will need to change if bicycles are to play a more prominent role?

❑ Akin to the above, what needs are not being met well by existing modes of transportation, and how might bicycles and the cycling infrastructure do better (with some changes)? For example, if the major deterrents to urban cycling are traffic and weather, under what conditions would separate paths topped by a roof or enclosed be practical and useful? How could coordination between bicycles and buses, trains and airplanes (and automobiles) be improved?

❑ The last couple of decades have seen a huge increase in the construction of both long-distance and short-distance bike paths and trails. While many cyclists see this trend as a blessing, some serious cyclists are more skeptical, feeling that trails have been shown to be relatively unsafe compared to roads, that they encourage novice cyclists to think that only cyclist-specific facilities are safe, and further encourage drivers and transportation engineers to think that bikes don't belong on the road. Similar comments apply to mountain biking. Meanwhile, the population continues to increase, motor traffic along with it, and suburban sprawl decreases the quantity of decent cycling roads. Are dedicated trails the future of cycling? What can cyclists, organizations, and industry do to ensure a safe, enjoyable, and livable future for bicycling?

❑ Many organizations state that one of their goals is to get more people onto bikes. Is that realistic, or even desirable? Is cycling for everyone?

Appendix

1. Gear Tables

Gear-inch table (gear in inches)

Chainring Sprocket	30	32	34	36	38	39	40	42	44	46	48	50	52	53	54	56
11	74	79	83	88	93	96	98	103	108	113	118	123	128	130	133	137
12	68	72	77	81	86	88	90	95	99	104	108	113	117	119	122	126
13	62	66	71	75	79	81	83	87	91	96	100	104	108	110	112	116
14	58	62	66	69	73	75	77	81	85	89	93	96	100	102	104	108
15	54	58	61	65	68	70	72	76	79	83	86	90	94	95	97	101
16	51	54	57	61	64	66	68	71	74	78	81	84	88	89	91	95
17	48	51	54	57	60	62	64	67	70	73	76	79	83	84	86	89
18	45	48	51	54	57	59	60	63	66	69	72	75	78	80	81	84
19	43	45	48	51	54	55	57	60	63	65	68	71	74	75	77	80
20	41	43	46	49	51	53	54	57	59	62	65	68	70	72	73	76
21	39	41	44	46	49	50	51	54	57	59	62	64	67	68	69	72
22	37	39	42	44	47	48	49	52	54	56	59	61	64	65	66	69
23	35	38	40	42	45	46	47	49	52	54	56	59	61	62	63	66
24	34	36	38	41	43	44	45	47	50	52	54	56	59	60	61	63
25	32	35	37	39	41	42	43	45	48	50	52	54	56	57	58	60
26	31	33	35	37	39	41	42	44	46	48	50	52	54	55	56	58
27	30	32	34	36	38	39	40	42	44	46	48	50	52	53	54	56
28	29	31	33	35	37	38	39	41	42	44	46	48	50	51	52	54
29	28	30	32	34	35	36	37	39	41	43	45	47	48	49	50	52
30	27	29	31	32	34	35	36	38	40	41	43	45	47	48	49	50
32	25	27	29	30	32	33	34	35	37	39	41	42	44	45	46	47
34	24	25	27	29	30	31	32	33	35	37	38	40	41	42	43	44

Development table (development in meters)

Chainring Sprocket	30	32	34	36	38	39	40	42	44	46	48	50	52	53	54	56
11	5.9	6.3	6.7	7.1	7.5	7.7	7.9	8.3	8.7	9.1	9.5	9.9	10.3	10.5	10.7	11.1
12	5.4	5.8	6.2	6.5	6.9	7.1	7.3	7.6	8.0	8.3	8.7	9.1	9.4	9.6	9.8	10.2
13	5.0	5.4	5.7	6.0	6.4	6.5	6.7	7.0	7.4	7.7	8.0	8.4	8.7	8.9	9.0	9.4
14	4.7	5.0	5.3	5.6	5.9	6.1	6.2	6.5	6.8	7.2	7.5	7.8	8.1	8.2	8.4	8.7
15	4.4	4.6	4.9	5.2	5.5	5.7	5.8	6.1	6.4	6.7	7.0	7.3	7.5	7.7	7.8	8.1
16	4.1	4.4	4.6	4.9	5.2	5.3	5.4	5.7	6.0	6.3	6.5	6.8	7.1	7.2	7.3	7.6
17	3.8	4.1	4.4	4.6	4.9	5.0	5.1	5.4	5.6	5.9	6.1	6.4	6.7	6.8	6.9	7.2
18	3.6	3.9	4.1	4.4	4.6	4.7	4.8	5.1	5.3	5.6	5.8	6.0	6.3	6.4	6.5	6.8
19	3.4	3.7	3.9	4.1	4.4	4.5	4.6	4.8	5.0	5.3	5.5	5.7	6.0	6.1	6.2	6.4
20	3.3	3.5	3.7	3.9	4.1	4.2	4.4	4.6	4.8	5.0	5.2	5.4	5.7	5.8	5.9	6.1
21	3.1	3.3	3.5	3.7	3.9	4.0	4.1	4.4	4.6	4.8	5.0	5.2	5.4	5.5	5.6	5.8
22	3.0	3.2	3.4	3.6	3.8	3.9	4.0	4.2	4.4	4.6	4.8	4.9	5.1	5.2	5.3	5.5
23	2.8	3.0	3.2	3.4	3.6	3.7	3.8	4.0	4.2	4.4	4.5	4.7	4.9	5.0	5.1	5.3
24	2.7	2.9	3.1	3.3	3.4	3.5	3.6	3.8	4.0	4.2	4.4	4.5	4.7	4.8	4.9	5.1
25	2.6	2.8	3.0	3.1	3.3	3.4	3.5	3.7	3.8	4.0	4.2	4.4	4.5	4.6	4.7	4.9
26	2.5	2.7	2.8	3.0	3.2	3.3	3.3	3.5	3.7	3.9	4.0	4.2	4.4	4.4	4.5	4.7
27	2.4	2.6	2.7	2.9	3.1	3.1	3.2	3.4	3.5	3.7	3.9	4.0	4.2	4.3	4.4	4.5
28	2.3	2.5	2.6	2.8	3.0	3.0	3.1	3.3	3.4	3.6	3.7	3.9	4.0	4.1	4.2	4.4
29	2.3	2.4	2.6	2.7	2.9	2.9	3.0	3.2	3.3	3.5	3.6	3.8	3.9	4.0	4.1	4.2
30	2.2	2.3	2.5	2.6	2.8	2.8	2.9	3.0	3.2	3.3	3.5	3.6	3.8	3.8	3.9	4.1
32	2.0	2.2	2.3	2.4	2.6	2.7	2.7	2.9	3.0	3.1	3.3	3.4	3.5	3.6	3.7	3.8
34	1.9	2.0	2.2	2.3	2.4	2.5	2.6	2.7	2.8	2.9	3.1	3.2	3.3	3.4	3.5	3.6

2. GEAR SELECTION MONOGRAPH

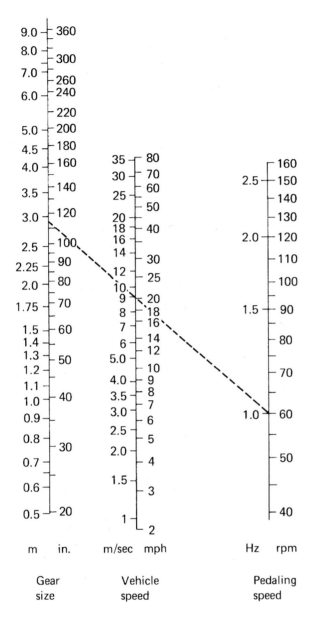

m in.	m/sec mph
Gear size	Vehicle speed

Hz rpm

Pedaling speed

3. TYPICAL SPOKE THICKNESSES

Thickness mm	British gauge no.	French gauge no.	Application
1.4	17	10	time trial records
1.6	16	11	light road racing
1.8	15	12	racing and fitness
2.0	14	13	touring and mountain bike
2.3	13	14	heavy duty and tandem
2.6	12	15	expeditions

4. CONVERSION FACTORS

Mass:	x lbm = 0.4536x kg (kilograms)
Force:	x lbf = 4.448x N (newtons)
Length:	x in. = 25.4x mm (millimeters)
	x ft = 0.3048x m (meters)
	x miles = 1.609x km (kilometers)
Area:	x ft² = 0.0929x m²
Volume:	x ft³ = 0.02832x m³
Pressure, stress, modulus of elasticity:	x lbf/in.² = 6,895 Pa (pascals) (1 Pa = 1 N/m²) = 6.895x kPa (kilopascals) (100 kPa = 1 bar = 14.503 lbf/in.²)
Density:	x lbm/ft³ = 16.017x kg/m³
Velocity:	x mph = 0.447x m/sec (meters/second) = 1.609x km/h (kilometers/hour)
Torque:	x lbf-ft = 1.356x N-m (newton-meters)
Energy:	x ft-lbf = 1.356x J (joules)
	x Btu = 1,054.9x J
	x kcal = 4,186.8x J
	x kWh = (3.6 × 10⁶)x J = 3.6 MJ (megajoules)
Power:	x hp = 746x J/sec = 746x W (watts)
	x kcal/min = 69.78x W
	x ft-lbf/sec = 1.356 W
Specific heat:	x Btu/lbm-°R = 4,187x J/kg-°K
Heat flux:	x Btu/ft²-h = 3.154x W/m²
	x kcal/m²-h = 1.163 W/m²

5. DERIVATIONS OF UNITS

Force (newtons) = Mass (kilograms) × Acceleration (m/sec²)

Energy or Work (joules) = Force (newtons) × Distance (m)

Power (watts) = Work (joules) per Unit time (seconds)

When we refer to the weight of (for instance) a bicycle or its rider, we are, strictly, giving the gravitational force. The correct units would therefore be newtons or pounds force (lbf). If we were to take a bicycle to the moon, its weight would be about one-sixth of its weight on the earth. The mass would remain unchanged. Therefore, we have usually given the mass (in kilograms or in pounds mass, lbm) when we have by common usage referred to the "weight." Weight is given by the relation

$$\frac{\text{Mass} \times \text{Gravitational acceleration}}{g_c}$$

where g_c is a constant that in the S.I. system equals unity and in English units equals 32.17 lbm-ft/lbf-sec².

6. TIRE AND RIM SIZE DESIGNATIONS

Nominal wheel dia inch (mm)	Rim shoulder circumference (mm)	ETRTO designation (mm)	British/Dutch designation (inch)	French designation (mm)	US designation (inch)
14 (350)	939	32–299	14 x 1⅜		
	911	37–290		350A	
16 (400)	1096	32–349	16 x 1⅜		
	1068	37–340'		400A	
	996				16 x 1¾
18 (450)	1253	32–399	18 x 1⅜	450 x 32A	
	1225	37–390		450A	
20 (500)	1417	32–450	20 x 1⅜	500 x 32A	20 x 1⅜
	1382	37–440		500A	
	1327	47–406			20 x 1.75
22 (550)	1574	32–501	22 x 1⅜	550 x 32A	
	1539	37–490		550A	
24 (600)	1728	32–550	24 x 1⅜	600 x 32A	
	1700	37–541		600A	
	1646				24 x 1.75
					24 x 2.125
26 (650)	1876	32–597	26 x 1⅜	650 x 32A	
	1854	37–590		650A	
	1835	40–584		650B	
	1805	47–559			26 x 1.750
		54–559			26 x 2.125
	1794	47–571	26 x 1¾		
27 (675)	1979	32–630	27 x 1¼		27 x 1¼
		28–630	27 x 1⅛		27 x 1⅛
		25–630	27 x 1		27 x 1
28 (700)	1954	32–622	28 x 1⅝ x 1⅜	700C	
		28–622	28 x1⅝ x 1⅛	700 x 28C	
		25–622		700 x 25C	
	2017	37–642	28 x 1⅜	700A	28 x 1⅜
	1995	40–635	28 x 1½	700B Std	

7. SCREW-THREAD STANDARDS

Location	BCI standard (British)	ISO standard (French)	Italian standard	Swiss standard
bottom bracket fixed (RH) side	1.370 x 24tpi (L)	35 x 1mm (R)	1.370 x 24tpi 55˚(R)	35 x 24 tpi (R)
bottom bracket adj. (LH) side	1.370 x 24tpi (R)	35 x 1mm (R)	1.370 x 24tpi 55˚(R)	35 x 24 tpi (R)
pedal LH side	9/16 x 20tpi (L)	14 x 1.25mm (L)	(BCI)	(BCI)
pedal RH side	9/16 x 20tpi (R)	14 x 1.25mm (R)	(BCI)	(BCI)
headset (standard)	1.000 x 24 tpi	25 x 1mm	1.000 x 24 tpi 55˚	(BCI)
headset (oversize)	not standardized in any system			
freewheel	1.370 x 24 tpi	34.7 x 1 mm	35 x 1mm	(BCI)
derailleur eye	(ISO)	10 x 1mm	10 mm x 26 tpi	(ISO)

8. TYPICAL BALL BEARING SIZES (FOR ADJUSTABLE BEARINGS)

Bearing location	ball size inch	ball size mm (approx)	to measure 8 balls (mm)
bottom bracket	¼	6.4	51
rear hub	¼	6.4	51
front hub	3/16	4.8	37
	7/32	5.0	40
headset	5/32	4.0	32
	3/16	4.8	37
pedals	5/32	4.0	32
freewheel	⅛	3.2	25

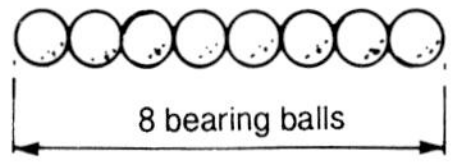

8 bearing balls

BIBLIOGRAPHY

Abbott, Allan V., and David Gordon Wilson (Eds.). *Human-Powered Vehicles*. Champaign, IL: Human Kinetics, 1995.

Adeyefa, B. A. *Determination of the Loads, Deflections and Stresses in Bicycle Frames* (Dissertation). Manchester, England: University of Manchester Institute of Science and Technology, 1978.

Allen, James T. *Cycles Patented in the U.S. from 1789 to 1892*. Washington DC (publisher unknown), 1892.

Ambrosini, Giuseppe. *Ciclismo: prendi la bicicletta e vai* [5th Edn.]. Milan: Sperling & Kupfer Editori, 1981.

Baird, Stuart. *Performance Cycling: A Scientific Way to Get the Most Out Of Your Bike*. San Francisco: Cycle Publishing, 2000.

Ball, Bryan. "Getting Down." *Adventure Cyclist*, July / August 2007.

Ballantine, Richard, and Richard Grant. *Richard's Ultimate Bicycle Book*. New York: Dorling Kindersley Inc., 1992.

Barlo, R. J. *Statistics, a Guide to the Use of Statistical Methods in the Physical Sciences*. Chichester (UK): John Wiley & Sons, 1989.

Bartleet, H. W. *Bartleet's Bicycle Book*. London: Ed. J. Burrow & Co / Dunlop Rubber Co., 1931.

Barzel, Peter, Michael Bollschweiler, and Christian Smolik. *Die Neue Fahrradtechnik: Material, Konstruktion, Fertigung*. Bielefeld (Germany): BVA Bielefelder Verlag, 2008.

Baudry de Saunier, *l'Histoire Générale de la Vélocipédie*. Paris: Paul Ollendorf Editeur, 1892.

—. *Histoire de la Locomotion Terrestre*. Paris: l'Illustration, 1935.

Beiser, Arthur. *Physics*. Reading, MA: Addison-Wesley, 1991.

Berto, Frank. *Bicycling Magazine's Complete Guide to Upgrading Your Bike*. Emmaus, PA: Rodale Press, 1987.

—. *The Birth of Dirt: History and Development of the Mountain Bike* [2nd Edn.]. San Francisco: Cycle Publishing, 2008.

—. *The Dancing Chain: History and development of the derailleur bicycle* [3rd Edn.]. San Francisco: Cycle Publishing, 2009.

Bowden, Gregory Houston. *The Story of the Raleigh Cycle*. London: W. H. Allen, 1975.

Brady, George S., and Henry R. Clauser, editors. *Materials Handbook*. New York: McGraw-Hill Inc, 1991.

Brandt, Jobst. *The Bicycle Wheel*. Menlo Park, CA: Avocet Inc, 1981, 1983.

Bueche, F. *Technical Physics*. New York: Harper & Row, 1977.

Frederick J. Bueche. *Schaum's Outline of Theory and Problems of College Physics*. New York: McGraw-Hill Inc., 1989.

Burrows, Mike. *Bicycle Design: Towards the Perfect Machine*. York (UK): Open Road Publishers, 2000.

Cycling. Rome: FIAC / CONI Central Sports School, 1968.

Daily, James W., and Donald Harleman. *Fluid Dynamics*. Reading, MA: Addison-Wesley, 1966.

The Data Book: 100 Years of Bicycle Component and Accessory Design. Original edition published in Japan, 1983. Reprint edition San Francisco: Van der Plas Publications, 1998

De Long, Fred. *DeLong's Guide to Bicycles and Bicycling*. Radnor, PA: Chilton Book Company, 1974.

Dodd, Alastair. *Scottish Bicycles & Tricycles*. Edinburgh: NMS Publishing, 1999.

Dodge, Pryor. *The Bicycle*. Paris and New York: Flammarion, 1996.

Evens, David E. *The Ingenious Mr. Pedersen*. Gloucester (UK): Alan Sutton, 1979.

Facchinetti, Paolo, and Guido P. Rubino. *Campagnolo: 75 Years of Cycling Passion*. Boulder, CO: Velo Press, 2009.

Fahrrad – von der Draisine zur Hightech-Maschine. Vienna: Technisches Museum Wien, 2003.

Fehlau, Gunnar. *Recumbent Bicycles* [4th Edn.]. Out Your Backdoor Publishing, 2006.

—. *Das Modul Bike: faltbare Fahrraeder.* Kiel (Germany): Moby Dick Verlag, 1997.

— and P. Barzel. *Das E-Bike: Die neuen Fahrräder mit elektrischer Antriebsunterstützung* [2nd Edn.]. Kiel: Moby Dick Verlag, 2010.

Forester, John. *Effective Cycling* [6th Edn.]. Cambridge, MA: MIT-Press, 1992.

—. Bicycle Transportation. [3rd Edn.] Cambridge, MA: MIT-Press.

Gordon, J. E. *The New Science of Strong Materials.* Princeton, NJ: Princeton University Press, 1968.

Greene, James, et al. *Bicycle Accident Reconstruction and Litigation* (4th Ed.) Tucson, AZ: Lawyers & Judges Publishing, 1995.

Gronen, Wolfgang, and W. Lemke. *Geschichte des Radsports und des Fahrrades.* Eupen (Belgium): Doepgen Verlag, 1978.

Gross, Albert C., Chester R. Kyle, and Douglas J. Malewicki. "The Aerodynamics of Human-powered Land Vehicles." *Scientific American,* December 1983.

Hayduk, Douglas. *Bicycle Metallurgy for Cyclists.* Grand Junction, CO, 1987. [An updated version of this text is included in Greene et al listed above.]

Heine, Jan, and Jean-Pierre Pradères: *The Golden Age of the Handbuilt Bicycle.* Seattle: Vintage Bicycle Press, 2005.

—.*The Golden Age of Handbuilt Bicycles: Craftsmanship, Elegance, and Function.* Seattle: Vintage Bicycle Press, 2009.

Hadland, Tony. *The Moulton Bicycle: The Story from 1957 to 1981.* Coventry (UK): Hadland, 2000)

—. *The Spaceframe Moultons.* Coventry (UK): Hadland, 1994.

—. *The Sturmey-Archer Story.* Coventry (UK): Hadland, 1988.

Henry, Raymond. *Du vélocipède au dérailleur moderne.* St. Etienne (France): Association des amis du musée d'art et d'industrie, 1998.

—. *Paul de Vivie, dit Vélocio: l'evolution du cycle et le cyclotourisme.* St. Etienne (France): Association des amis du musée d'art et d'industrie, 1998.

Herlihy, David V. *Bicycle: The History.* New Haven, CT: Yale University Press, 2004.

Hodgman, Charles D. [editor-in-chief]. *Handbook of Chemistry and Physics.* 44th edition Cleveland, OH: Chemical Rubber Publishing Company, 1962.

Kolin, Michael J., and Denise M. de la Rosa. *The Custom Bicycle.* Emmaus, PA: Rodale Press, 1979.

Krausz, John, and Vera van der Reis-Krausz. *The Bicycling Book.* New York: The Dial Press, 1982.

Langley, Russell. *Practical Statistics Simply Explained.* New York: Dover Publications, 1970.

Lessing, Hans-Erhard. *Automobilitaet: Karl Drais und die unglaubichen Anfaenge.* Leipzig (Germany): Maxime Verlag, 2003

—. *Fahrradkultur: Der Hoehepunkt um 1900.* Reinbek bei Hamburg (Germany): Rowohlt Taschenbuch Verlag, 1982.

Lide, David R. [editor-in-chief]. *CRC Handbook of Chemistry and Physics.* 72nd edition. Boca Raton, FL: CRC Press, 1991.

Lloyd-Jones, Roger, and M. J. Lewis. *Raleigh and the British Bicycle Industry: An Economic and Business History, 1870–1960.* Aldershot (England): Ashgate, 2000.

Marr, Dick. *Bicycle Gearing: A Practical Guide.* Seattle, OR: The Mountaineers, 1989.

Matthew, Peter [editor]. *The Guinness Book of Records 1993.* New York: Facts on File, 1992.

McGurn, James. *On Your Bicycle: An Illustrated History of Cycling.* New York: Facts on File, 1987.

Milne-Thomson, L. A. *Theoretical Aerodynamics.* New York: Dover Publications, 1958.

Morchin, William C., and Henry Oman. *Electric Bicycles: A Guide to Design and Use.* Hoboken, NJ: Wiley-Interscience, 2006.

Navarro, Ricardo A., Urs Heierli and Victor Beck. *La Bicicleta Y Los Tridiclos: Alternativas de Transporte en America Latina.* St. Gallen (Switzerland): SKAT, 1985.

Oliver, Tony. *Touring Bikes: A practical guide.* Ramsbury (UK): The Crowood Press, 1990.

Perry, David B. *Bike Cult: The ultimate guide to human-powered vehicles.* New York: Four Walls Eight Windows, 1995.

Pinkerton, John, and Derek Roberts. *A History of Rover Cycles.* Birmingham (UK): Pinkerton, 1998.

Rauck, Max J. B., Gerd Volke, and Felix Paturi. Mit dem Rad durch zwei Jahrhunderte. Aarau (Switzerland): AT Verlag, 1979.

Rebour, Daniel. *Cycles de competition et randonneuses.* Paris: Technique et Vulgarisation, 1976.

Reimann, Arnold L. *Physics.* New York: Barnes & Noble, 1971.

Ritchie, Andrew. *King of the Road: An Illustrated History of Cycling.* London: Wildwood House, 1975.

Rosen, Paul. *Framing Production: Technology, Culture, and Change in the British Bicycle Industry.* Cambridge, MS: MIT-Press, 2002.

Ross, Marc, and John DeCicco. "Measuring the Energy Drain on Your Car." *Scientific American,* December 1994.

Rodriguez, Angel, and Carla Black. *The Tandem Book: The Complete Guide to Buying, Riding and Enjoying Bicycles Built for Two.* San Clemente, CA: Info Net Publishing, 1997.

Schmitz, Arnfried. *Human Power: The forgotten energy.* Coventry: Hadland, 1999.

Schubert, John. *The Tandem Scoop: An Insider's Guide to Tandem Cycling.* Eugene, OR: Burley Design Cooperative, 1993.

Schubert, Karl. *Das Tandem.* Kiel (Germany): Moby Dick Verlag, 1994.

Sharp, Archibald. *Bicycles and Tricycles: An elementary treatise on their design and construction.* First published London, New York: Longmans, Green, 1896. Reprint edition Cambridge, MA: MIT-Press, 1979.

Shortley, George, and Dudley Williams. *Principles of College Physics.* Englewood Cliffs, NJ: Prentice-Hall, Inc., 1959.

Smith, Robert A. *A Social History of the Bicycle.* New York: American Heritage Press, 1972.

Smolik, Hans-Christian. *Fahrrad Rahmenbau: Material, Geometrie, Fertigung.* Kiel: Moby Dick Verlag, 1994.

— and Stefan Etzel. *Das grosse Fahrradlexikon* [2nd Ed.]. Bielefeld (Germany): BVA Bielefelder Verlag, 2002.

Synge, John L., and Byron A. Griffith. *Principles of Mechanics.* New York: McGraw-Hill, 1959.

Tyler, Paul A. *College Physics.* New York: Worth Publishers, 1987.

Van der Plas, Rob. *Bicycle Repair: Maintenance and Repair of the Modern Bicycle.* San Francisco: Cycle Publishing, 2007.

—. *The Mountain Bike Book.* San Francisco: Bicycle Books, 1983.

—. The *Penguin Bicycle Handbook.* Harmondsworth (UK): Penguin Books: 1983.

— and Charles Kelly. *The Original Mountain Bike Book.* Osceola (WI): Motorbooks International, 1998.

Vötter, Manfred, et al. "Betriebslasten an Fahrrädern" (Operating Loads Placed on Bicycles. German with English Summary). *Fahrzeugtechnik,* No. 27. Bergisch Gladbach, Germany: Bundesanstalt für Straßenwesen, 1999.

Watson, Roderick, and Martin Gray. *The Penguin Book of the Bicycle.* Harmondsworth (UK): Penguin Books, 1978.

Weast, Robert C. [editor]. *CRC Handbook of Chemistry and Physics,* 65th edition. Boca Raton, FL: CRC Press, Inc, 1984.

Whitt, Frank Rowland, and David Gordon Wilson. *Bicycling Science.* Ergonomics and Mechanics. Cambridge, MA: MIT Press, First published 1976; current, 3rd edition by David Gordon Wilson, 2004.

Wolf, Wilhelm. *Fahrrad und Radfahrer.* Leipzig (Germany): Otto Spamer, 1890; reprint: Dortmund (Germany): Harenberg Kommunikation, 1979.

Zinn, Lennard. *Zinn and the Art of Mountain Bike Maintenance* [3rd Edn.]. Boulder, CO: Velo Press, 2005.

—. *Zinn and the Art of Road Bike Maintenance* [3rd Edn.]. Boulder, CO: Velo Press, 2009.

—. *Zinn and the Art of Triathlon Bike Maintenance. Boulder, CO: Velo Press, 2007.*

ADDITIONAL REFERENCES

The catalogs of the major bicycle mail-order companies are also a valuable source of information regarding the availability and weights of components.

Articles consulted include the following periodicals, several of which are no longer published; whereas some others no longer include significant technical information (those that are still published with significant technical content are marked with an asterisk):

* *Adventure Cyclist*, USA

Bicycle Guide, USA

Bicycle Science, USA

Bicycling, USA

Bike-Tech, USA

Bike World, USA

* *The Boneshaker*, UK

CTC Gazette, UK (also see *Cycling*, below)

Le Cycle, France

* *Cycling*, UK

Cyclisme, France

* *Dirt Rag*, USA

Fat Tire Flyer, USA

* *Fiets*, Netherlands

The Low Gear Bulletin, Australia

* *Mountain Bike Action*, USA

* *Road Bike Action*, USA

Radmarkt, Germany

* *Tour*, Germany

Rivendell Reader, USA

* Velo-News, USA

* *(Vintage) Bicycle Quarterly*, USA

* *The Wheelman*, USA

Finally, a rich source of historical and technical information are the Proceedings of the International Cycling History Conferences, which have been held annually since 1990. Volumes 1 through 13 and 15 through 18 are available from Cycle Publishing, USA; volume 14 was published by the Canberra Bicycle Museum, Australia; and volumes 19 and 20 are published by John Pinkerton Memorial Publishing Fund, England.

Index

A

acceleration, 39

accessories, 23, 29, 254–261, 270, 286–287
  for folding bike, 286–287
  for small riders, 270
  mounting, 254–255
  selection criteria, 254

acetylene lamp, 243

adjustable bearing (*see also* cup-and-cone bearing), 85–86

adjustable stems, 150

aerodynamics, 32–33, 71, 111, 252, 261, 293

aero wheels, 111

aerobic metabolism, 42

aerodynamic drag, 32–33

aerodynamic drag, of luggage, 252

aerodynamic fairing, 261

aerodynamics, as a factor in bicycle design, 71

aerodynamics, of recumbents and hpvs, 293

aerodynamics, of wheel, 111

air friction, 32

air pressure, of tire, 116–119
  of suspension element, 237

air reaction force, 32

air travel size limitations, 284

air turbulence, 32

airfoil shape, and effect on aerodynamic drag, 71

airfoil shape, for seatpost, 225

Alex Moulton bicycles (*see also* Moulton, Alex), 283

Allan-head bolts or screws, 79

alloying, of metals, 51

aluminum, and its alloys, 50–60, 80, 93
  alloy designations, 55
  for threaded components, 80
  early use of, for bike frames, 57
  strength of, 51
  welding of, 93

anaerobic metabolism, 42

annular gear, 187

aramid, used instead of spokes, 131

ATP-CP cycle, 41

auxiliary brake, on tandem, 27

axle nuts, 26

B

backpedaling brake (*see* coaster brake)

bag attachments, 250

bake pads, 208,

balancing, 11, 28,

ball bearings, 84–86, 311
  sizes, 311
  adjusting, 85
  loading specifics, 86

bamboo, used for bicycle frames, 61, 307

band brake, 219

bar-con (handlebar-end shifter), 183

battery capacity, and E-bike range and speed, 300

battery lights, 239–242
  schematic, 241

battery types, 241

Baudry de Saunier, Louis, 12

bearings, 84–87
  adjustment, 86
  inspection, 87
  lubrication, 87
  types, 84, 87, 191
  used on hub gears, 191

belt-drive, 106, 286, 303
  for folding bike, 286

bichain gearing, 170–171

bicycle computer, 257–258

bicycle handling, 133-135
  test, 134

bicycle size, 263–264

bicycle stability, 135

bicycle types, 18–22

Bike Friday, folding bike, 283–285

binder bolt, for seat, 226

Biopace, and elliptical chainrings, 159

Birdie, folding bike, 285

bladder-forming, of carbon-fiber frames, 97

Blake, Vernon, 171

bleeding, of hydraulic brake system, 213

body lean, 134–135

bolt-on hub, or nutted-axle hub, 112

bonding, of aluminum, 93

Boston, Bill, 266

bottom bracket, 25–26, 102, 105, 151–154, 277
  adjustment, 154
  bearing check, 154
  height, 102
  types, 152
  for tandem, 277

bottom-bracket gear, 191–192

bottom-bracket generator, 244–145

bottom bracket shell, 105

brake adjustments, 208

brake blocks (*see* brake pads)

brake bosses, 25

brake bosses, 106

brake cable, 27

brake design and construction, 195

brake lever, 27, 206–208, 269–270
  for fixed-gear bike, 206
  mounting detail, 206
  types, 206
  for small riders, 269–270

brake maintenance, 208

brake pad, 27, 207–210

brake shoes, 207–208
  adjustment, 207
  mounting, 208

brake size versus effectiveness, 215

brakes, 23, 27, 194–208, 209–213, 214–219, 269–270, 279
  for small riders, 269–270
  for tandem, 279

brake-shift levers, 184, 205

braking theory, 198–204

braze-ons, 107

brazing, 92–93

breaking in, of leather saddle, 221

bridge pieces, 106

Brinell hardness, 55

Brompton, folding bike, 281, 285

Brown, Sheldon, 221

Browning swinging gate front shifting system, 181

BSA bottom bracket bearing adjustment detail, 154

Burrows, Mike, and bicycle design, 71
  and recumbent design, 291
  and three-wheeler design, 294

butted tubes, 91

C

cables, and cable controls, 82–85, 205
  adjusting, 83
  friction, 84, 205
  operation options, for derailleurs, 181
  routing, 82, 84
  maintenance, 83

cadence (*see also* pedaling rate), 46

cam-operated brake, also, 197, 202

cam-operated brake, 197

cam-operated brake (also roller-cam brake, Parapull brake), 202

cantilever brake, 197, 199–200

captain, of tandem, 275

carbon-fiber, 17, 47, 50, 61–63, 88, 97

carbon-fiber, 50, 96–97
  and fiber orientation , 59, 97
  and failure, 62, 96, 132, 145
  repairing, 58

"carbon-look," 59

cargo bicycle, also carrier bike, 21, 247, 253
  and chain width, 253

carrier bicycle (*see* cargo bicycle)

cartridge bearing, 85–86, 113, 152–153

cartridge bearing, also sealed bearing, Conrad bearing, 85–86
  crankset, 152
  hub, 113

"Célérifère," 12

centerpull brake, 196–197

central battery, 239–240

ceramic, rim surface, 124

chain, 26, 160–163, 176, 178–179
  deflection, 176
  details, 161
  gap, 178–179
  line, 162
  lubrication, 162
  maintenance, 161
  pitch sizes, 163
  skip, 163

chain guard, 260

chain stays, 25, 103–105
  length, 103
  wear check, 163
  width, and number of sprockets, 161; and carrier bike, 253
  clearance, 104

chainrings, also chainwheel, 26, 156–160, 176
  attachment, 158–159
  bolt circle diameter, 158
  maintenance, 160
  size selection, 176
  wear, 159

chainwheels (*see* chainrings)

changer (*see* front derailleur)

child seat, 262

child, on tandem, 272

Cinelli clipless pedal, 166

climbing and gear selection, 173

clincher tires (*see also* wired-on tires), 120

clipless pedals , 164–166

coaster brake, 27, 215
  operation, 215

"coffee bike," 21

cogs (*see* sprockets)

cold-weather gear, 262

comfort, as a factor in bicycle design, 72

component nomenclature, 23

components for small riders, 269

Conrad bearing (*see* cartridge bearing)

constant-trail suspension fork, 233

contraction-expansion brake, 219

conversion kit, for E-bike, 301